MARY PAGLIA

LA
POPESSA

La Popessa

PAUL I. MURPHY
with R. René Arlington

WARNER BOOKS

A Warner Communications Company

Permission is gratefully acknowledged to quote material from the following previously published sources:

Pope John XXIII by Paul Johnson (Boston: Little, Brown and Company, 1974)

Eleanor and Franklin by Joseph P. Lash (New York: W. W. Norton and Company, Inc., 1971)

The Cardinal Spellman Story by Robert I. Gannon, S.J. (Garden City, New York: Doubleday and Company, Inc., 1962)

The New York Times ("Papal Secretary of State Coming Here; Rome Speculates on Subject of Mission" by Arnaldo Cortesi, October 1, 1936, and "Pacelli Reported Seeking Aid of U.S. in Anti-Red Drive" by Arnaldo Cortesi, October 2, 1936)

A Reporter Looks at the Vatican by Barrett McGurn (New York: Coward-McCann, Inc., 1962)

The Papacy in the Modern World by J. Derek Holmes (New York: The Crossroad Publishing Company, 1981)

Inside the Vatican by Corrado Pallenberg (New York: Hawthorn Books, Inc., 1960)

Crown of Glory by Alden Hatch and Seamus Walshe (New York: Hawthorn Books, Inc., 1958)

Ciano's Hidden Diary, 1937–1938 by Count Galeazzo Ciano (New York: E. P. Dutton and Company, Inc., 1953)

The Ciano Diaries, 1939–1943 by Count Galeazzo Ciano (Garden City, New York: Doubleday and Company, Inc., 1946)

Wartime Correspondence Between President Roosevelt and Pope Pius XII (New York: Macmillan Publishing Company, Inc., 1947)

Adolf Hitler by John Toland (Garden City, New York: Doubleday and Company, Inc., 1976)

The Honored Society by Norman Lewis (New York: G. P. Putnam's Sons, 1964)

Every effort has been made to ensure that permission for all material was obtained. Those sources not formally acknowledged will be included in all editions of this book issued subsequent to notification by such sources.

Warner Books, Inc., 666 Fifth Avenue, New York, NY 10103
A Warner Communications Company

Printed in the United States of America

First printing: May 1983
10 9 8 7 6 5 4 3 2 1

Designed by Giorgetta Bell McRee

Library of Congress Cataloging in Publication Data

Murphy, Paul I.
La popessa.

Includes index.
1. Pascalina, Sister, 1894–   .   2. Nuns—Biography.
3. Pius XII, Pope, 1876–1958—Friends and associates.
I. Arlington, R. René.   II. Title.
BX4705.P37687M87 1983   282'.092'4   [B]   82-61880
ISBN 0-446-51258-3

For Pascalina
  And all women of strength
  tempered with gentleness and love
  who shape men into greatness.

Acknowledgments

To Helen Barrett, formerly of the William Morris Agency, whose inspiration and guidance helped greatly to turn a simple idea into a magnificent experience.

To Ross Claiborne and Reid Boates, of Warner Books, Inc., whose guidance and unflagging devotion to every detail gave shape to the book and heart to the authors.

To Julie F. Murphy, who, with superb professionalism, expertise, wit, grace, and charm, shared the heavy burden of virtually every aspect of the book through fourteen-hour days of research, counsel, comments, and criticisms.

To each, we extend our profound gratitude.

Paul I. Murphy

R. René Arlington

LA
POPESSA

Foreword

At eighty-seven, she is as I first saw her at middle age—disarmingly petite and angelic, yet startlingly alive and exciting. Now, as then, she appears a full generation younger than her years, a woman with luminous blue-gray eyes and a fresh, rosy blush about her face.

"For heaven's sakes, stop staring and have a seat," she says, trying to maintain her Mother Superior image. But this pretense of severity thinly coats her vanity and is lost in a tender smile. She knows that you've made the long journey to Rome for a purpose, and she is enough of the old school—disciplined and direct—to waste neither your time nor her own.

"You would like to talk, maybe?" Mother Pascalina asks, after a quick exchange of pleasantries. The nun speaks in a low, soft blend of her Bavarian accent and your own native tongue, and for the moment you alone have the mind and heart of the woman who captivated a pope.

We move onto the terrace of her Casa Angelicus, a sprawling retreat set on a hill of stately trees and romantic pathways overlooking the Tyrrhenian Sea. She had the secluded and serene haven built years before for lost and lonely women and has remained there herself to give them courage and hope. Off in the distance the lights of Rome glow faintly against the darkening sky. The air is lush with the scent of flowers; the silence is complete.

"The weather is delightful for December," she remarks, casting her head backward as she takes in a full breath of the glorious night.

Then, quite abruptly, she turns and says, "Holiness has been dead nearly a quarter of a century and they still haven't canonized him!"

I could not help but recall my first meeting with Pascalina thirty years before, in 1951, when I was Archbishop Richard J. Cushing's co-author and confidant. I had heard beforehand of the woman's inexorable devotion to and hold upon the lonely Pontiff, Pope Pius XII. Her immense impact on his controversial papacy had so aroused the Sacred College of Cardinals that many of the Vatican's purple-robed prelates had repeatedly demanded her ouster. She had fought back—rallying to her own defense and Pius's, too—by leveling pitiless and unrelenting humiliations upon the cardinals. Though her disdain was real, no one could say truthfully that Pascalina acted out of revenge, rather than for what she considered rightful purpose.

It wasn't until my own arrival in the Vatican those three decades ago—until I was allowed within her then self-imposed, almost complete isolation inside the Papal Palace—that I came to realize that whatever I had heard of the secretive Sister Pascalina explained little of her formidable character.

Listening to her then, as I have recently, reflect for days on end of the best and worst of the Vatican's world, I had to marvel at this woman's special force. It became clear how the nun had filled such a void in the Pope's life, despite the considerable disparities in their ages and social backgrounds. In that a middle-aged prelate of Eugenio Pacelli's Roman aristocratic background placed a peasant girl at his side by the papal throne, one senses Pius's intense need for her.

"Some within the hierarchy tried their best to read so much into our relationship," she says, her mouth tense as she slips back through time. There is a trace in her eyes of the old hurt, of the "challenge to her dedication," as she once characterized the cardinals' irreverence. She pauses and suddenly she forces a smile, and her eyes begin to beam again at some inner secret. "It wasn't that Holiness had no needs of the heart," she bursts forth, blushing slightly as if feeling sinful for letting so much be known. "If Lucia had said yes, he would never have become Pope." After some coaxing, she says that Lucia—a beautiful young girl from Italy's mountain hamlet of Onano, where Eugenio Pacelli spent his summers—had been proposed to by the young seminarian just before he became a priest.

She grows pensive once more. To one who has known her over the years, there are faint signs, suggested by her changing moods, of another, quite different side to the nun, a darker nature that the old hierarchy of Pius XII's reign had broached so often at their own peril. She awaits your next question, her eyes fixed upon you like a fawn alerted to danger, and yet no question is ever too probing. So profoundly confident is she that one wonders if the shy and reclusive Pacelli would ever have moved beyond his simple nunciature in Munich without her.

From the beginning of their relationship, whenever Pacelli was ill, it was Pascalina who gave him succor. When he was prey to private melancholy and had nightmares, she sat by his bedside through the long, dark hours. When in 1919 the atheist enemy stormed their nunciature with guns blazing, she came rushing protectively to his side. She was his buffer against another kind of enemy, the Sacred College of Cardinals. She was his impassioned sense of conviction in the writing of encyclicals and speeches, his decency and conscience at the center of personal dilemmas and a torn life.

The Pope's vulnerability had been countered time and again by the nun's stoicism; his pathos and frustrations by her inspiration and remarkable fortitude; his inner turmoil, his neuroses, by her insight and objectivity and candor.

Through intellect—through honesty, subtlety, and sensitivity—she helped transform an insecure mother's boy into the most powerful pope of modern times. Out of her fanatical passion and commitment, out of her ambition and self-sacrifice, she helped shape Pius into a symbol of holiness for a worldwide following that would approach one-half billion Catholics by the end of his reign. And though she toughened Pacelli's mind and body for their journey to the throne of Saint Peter, she tempered the way with tolerance and unquestioning love.

Many who admire Pascalina—even those who have detested her—agree that were she a man, the nun probably would have been elected as Pius XII's successor. Even some of her die-hard enemies within the Vatican concede that had she a male's Roman collar, she might well have become the most influential pope of any century. The most despotic, too, it's been said.

There are those within the Vatican who have maintained that Pascalina, were she of a later era, would set her own eye and heart upon the papacy. But if such lofty visions were ever dreamed by her in the past, they were dreamed for Pacelli alone. Certainly she had been obsessed enough in her drive to make of Pius a spotless Vicar of Christ. Viewing him from the start as a priest of storybook realm, Pascalina's romanticism fired the self-discipline and the boundless, brassy courage that became so evident in Pius's climb to the throne. It was tragic, indeed, that her tough intolerance would polarize Pope and hierarchy. But far more crushing to her were the occasions—and there were many—when nothing she did could prevent Pacelli's succumbing to his own great weaknesses.

In an era of double standards and hypocritical ethics, when morals and beliefs and actions are so often faked, Pascalina stands as a welcome disciple of the traditional Mother Church. With the passion to do good always at the center of her life, her fundamental commitment is doctrinaire and complete. Her example of integrity is merciful balm for the minds and hearts of those who might have felt let down by organized religion.

If today's nations and humanity itself are darkened morally and spiritually, the nun sees the shadows lifting only by kinder human ways—everywhere the turning away from selfishness and decadence.

"Is it too farfetched to look to principle for answer?" she asks.

The temperature about the Casa Angelicus has dropped, and a stiff breeze blows in from the Tyrrhenian. "Well, is it?" Pascalina repeats, a bit impatiently, as she gathers her nun's robes more tightly about her. Before one can answer, she herself says it all. "I suppose such thoughts are but idle dreams these days," she murmurs, shaking her head as we go inside.

PAUL I. MURPHY

I

The administrators of the Church were more worried by the Pope's housekeeper [Sister Pascalina] . . . than the social disasters which threatened mankind.

—*J. H. Plumb*

Shortly after midday on July 24, 1958, Sister Pascalina came in carefully guarded secrecy through the rear of the Vatican's Papal Palace to a secluded courtyard, the Holy Father, Pope Pius XII, at her side. They went directly to a waiting limousine as the Swiss Guard, loyal protectors of Vatican security since 1505, stood by in silence.

Settling back inside the immense custom-built vehicle, shades drawn to shield them from onlookers, the nun took the Pope's hand and placed it gently in hers. Neither said much at the moment, both too depressed for talk. Pius's health had been a constant source of worry to Pascalina. Though the Pope tried his best now to perk her spirits, the nun was too painfully aware of his pallor to respond. She had a sudden premonition that despite all his pretense of vigor he would never again see the Eternal City. In fact this drive, from their home of nearly thirty years to the Vatican's luxurious summer retreat villa at Castel Gandolfo, was to be their final journey together.

Pius admitted he was feeling far from his usual self, yet he wanted no slow drive. Instead he goaded the chauffeur into as fast a trip as possible. Pascalina, too, was most anxious to reach the summer villa.

Like the Pope, she loved the beauty and seclusion of the papal residence at Castel Gandolfo, the vacation paradise atop a tiny mountain
town 17.4 miles from the Papal Palace. The locale always brought
her back to her youth in Bavaria, a land where so little had changed
in two thousand years.

The black Cadillac sped through the gates of Rome's Aurelian
Wall to the Via Appia. Pascalina smiled as the Pope held out his stop
watch. Like most Romans, Pascalina and Pius loved speed. "He
would be a heartless man who opposed speedways," Pius had once
openly declared.

The trip always prompted a private little game for the nun and the
Pontiff, a practical joke aimed at Angelo Stoppa, their chauffeur of
more than twenty years. Whenever Stoppa made the trip of 17.4
miles from Rome to Castel Gandolfo in the specified time of eighteen
minutes, Pascalina and Pius laughed and applauded. But if the drive
took even nineteen minutes, both would put on their worst possible
frowns, completely unnerving the ever serious Stoppa. The chauffeur
so feared displeasing the Pontiff and his lady that he would burn up
the roadways, thrilling the nun and the Pope as the papal limousine
outdistanced all other vehicles on the roadway.

The spirit of wild challenge was very much a part of Pascalina's
dual character, a marked contrast to her staid and conventional
authoritarian side. Like Pius, road racing brought her to a pitch of
excitement, often causing her to stomp her feet and shout, *"Più
presto! Più presto!"* ("Faster! Faster!") Pascalina had been twenty-
seven and Pius in his mid-forties when she first introduced him to
speed, in the form of a motorcycle. It had all seemed somewhat
bizarre, as she reflected now on the long-gone past. She had been at
the handlebars and he, the aloof intellectual, his dark eyes protruding
with fear and excitement, had been seated in a side carriage, holding
on for dear life.

Suddenly, on this last trip to Castel Gandolfo, she suggested that
they challenge a contingent of motorcyclists cruising alongside the
papal car. Anticipating his reactions, she felt the race would give him
life and spirit. The Pope agreed. Motioning the riders to give chase,
Pius gleefully ordered his driver into full power. "Those who complain of the noise you make," the Pope shouted to the motorcyclists,
"be patient with them!" The wild riders were astounded by the Pontiff's affinity with their life-style, never dreaming that he was an old
hand at such sport. With the roar of motors and the Pope's shrill

racing instructions, they sped past car after car, whose drivers were left gawking at the sight of the triumphant Holy Father peering from the rear window, laughing and waving victoriously at the motorcyclists he far outdistanced.

As their limousine ascended the long, winding hill leading to the little town of Castel Gandolfo with its distant view of Rome and the dome of Saint Peter's, Pius ordered their pace slowed to five kilometers. The usual large crowd anticipating the papal visit lined the roadway to herald his arrival. As Pius blessed the people they fell to their knees to receive the papal benediction. The shades remained drawn on Pascalina's side of the car, and they entered the summer residence in the same guarded secrecy in which they had left the Papal Palace.

The nun and the Pope settled into Castel Gandolfo, anticipating the luxury of a holiday of two and a half months. The papal residence, set peacefully amid a framework of trees by a tranquil lake, was where the rich and famous came year after year upon the Pope's invitation to frolic in the "best of two worlds, the ecclesiastical and the temporal."

Despite her careful vigilance and warnings that he guard his health, Pius maintained a heavy work schedule. From his second-story balcony he delivered a speech almost every day to visiting pilgrims from all parts of the world who filled the courtyard below. These audiences were much less formal than the ones held at the Vatican, and Pius loved them. He'd speak to each delegation in its native tongue, then spread his arms and raise them on high in characteristic homage to God. As he finished, the enthusiastic and cheering voices of the people echoed through the surrounding hills, while Pascalina watched discreetly with pride and love from the papal apartment high up in the villa.

Pius had agreed to reduce by an hour his morning schedule of work in order to sit alone with Pascalina in the seclusion and shade of a cluster of trees in the villa's rear gardens. There were times during the golden days of that September, as they sat and talked together or read from their missals, that they never seemed happier. Soon they found additional rare hours of leisure to stroll the beautiful terraced gardens that Pius himself had designed a quarter of a century before when he was Vatican secretary of state. Often as they meditated they lifted their eyes to the rolling hills that spread multicolored splendor all about them.

"It was such a romantic, nostalgic time for Holiness and myself," she recalled many years later. "And yet such a sad time, too."

As summer drew to a close Pius was stricken. He suffered a severe attack of hiccups, his first since the attack in 1954 that had almost claimed his life. Though Pascalina had been expecting the worst for some time, it was still quite a shock to her. She was more alarmed than ever and insisted that he take to his bed at once. His physician advised that the Pope rest and remain in seclusion. But despite all the strong advice, and though he was unable to speak, Pius spent ten minutes on the balcony on the day he was stricken, waving to some ten thousand pilgrims.

Day after day, despite his worsening condition, the Pope struggled on, granting audiences, addressing small and large groups, even braving violent changes in the weather that brought sharp winds blowing off the surrounding hilltops.

On the morning of October 6, Pius appeared to rally. After saying early Mass in the villa's chapel, the Pope seemed to Pascalina to be in surprisingly good humor for one in such precarious health.

"Mother Pascalina, let's listen to some music to further enhance this beautiful day," he said with unusual merriment in his voice. His words and high spirits startled her, because only two days before he had received Extreme Unction, the sacrament given to Catholics in severe danger of death. Yet for his sake she showed no surprise.

"Holiness, shall I have the Gramophone brought to the dining room from your study?" she asked casually.

"Good idea!" the Pope responded. "We'll enjoy some Bach and Beethoven's First Symphony while we breakfast together."

As they awaited the Gramophone and their favorite recordings, she sensed that he was disguising his true state of health in order to lull her into a false sense of hope. She prepared a simple breakfast for them of coffee, fruit, and rolls. It was a daily ritual for him to eat breakfast alone while she stood by to serve him and exchange comments about the weather and the address he expected to write that day.

Suddenly, after a few minutes of Bach, he lapsed into silent prayer and deep meditation.

After long silence the Pontiff spoke. "Mother Pascalina, I'm so anxious to be busy," he said. "There is still so much to be done." His words were scarcely spoken when she noticed a slight dizziness come over him.

In deepening fear she rushed to his side, but he arose suddenly, though with much effort, as she came toward him. Pius managed a smile as he bent and gently kissed the small nun's cheek. She was trembling with fear as he turned to go to his study. She stood watching while he closed the door after him, but this time there was no turn of the latch.

Filled with apprehension, she sensed the Pope's end was near. Though she knew Pius had no fear of death, she also realized that he could not bear to have her watch him die.

For almost an hour she remained in prayer, all the while listening to his little typewriter clicking away in its customary stop-and-go rhythm. Then suddenly, about half past eight, it was silent.

Anticipating the worst, she rushed in to find him collapsed over his desk. "I feel so dizzy," he whispered faintly. Pascalina raised him, then half carried his emaciated body to a couch nearby. As he lay down the Holy Father lapsed into unconsciousness.

For a long moment the small figure of the nun in the black robes of ascetic life stood looking down in anguish at the still face of Eugenio Pacelli, one of the ablest of all popes to command the throne of Saint Peter. "Holiness!" she called out helplessly to the man she had so dearly loved and respected for all their forty-one years together. Her gentle lips brushed the startlingly white brow of the great aristocrat. She felt as if her heart were tolling the tragedy of the moment and, with it, the emptying of her own life.

Pascalina's long and carefully guarded relationship with Pope Pius XII had forced her into a life of secrecy and mystery not of her own doing. Even after she had shared the Pope's quarters in the Papal Palace for nearly twenty years, few in the world outside the papacy knew Pascalina even existed. Within the Vatican, though, Pascalina was irreverently called "La Popessa," a woman both feared and hated by the Church hierarchy. Though her name and presence always remained anonymous, it was the marvel of Pascalina that often she held as much—even more—influence over the Pope than anyone in the Vatican. It was more the marvel that at no time did she forget her rightful place, second always to Pacelli.

To Pascalina and millions of others who thought of him as next to God, Pius was what a pope should be and should appear. His emaciated features seemed always fixed in tension and concentration, radiating profound spirituality. She knew him intimately and had come to accept his many trying faults and eccentricities, which she had lived with day after day. Sometimes she had found him overly humble; other times he had been the absolute monarch over everyone and everything, including the Church, which he ruled as his own kingdom.

His male chauvinism had often manifested itself in the irritating, petty ways to which men of his nature and breeding could be so oblivious. She had detested his habit of expecting women to bow and scrape and do all the picking up. Pius had servants to do that, Pascalina reminded him, yet he had still expected everything of her, even at her advanced age. He had taken for granted all of her delicate catering to his every whim. The caring and pampering, too, when things didn't go just right, or when he didn't feel quite up to par. There had seemed no end to it all, nor to the thankless, even cold and hard, moments when he would abruptly shut her out of everything.

Still, she stood by him unflinchingly, largely because of his other side, the old-fashioned man in him. Pius had believed with all his heart that women should be held in a protected realm, to be cosseted and revered, even patronized, by men. Most of all she knew that he had cared for her, and cared greatly. He could be very tender and sympathetic, understanding, too, of so many of her own trying deficiencies. And he had always stood up for her—and by her—even within the Vatican and against its Sacred College of Cardinals.*

Startled to reality by the Pope's fading vital signs, Pascalina moved swiftly across the room, phoned his physician, then closed the door of the study. She wanted to shut out the world until the doctor arrived. Now that all hope seemed to be gone, she needed one final time alone with Pius.

Gently sponging his ashen face, Pascalina braced herself for a completely new life, the ignominy of which, she felt certain, would be complete.

She was sure that once Pius was gone, the Sacred College of Cardinals, the Church's ruling body, would no longer bow to her. The cardinals had long been jealous of her formidable power and position with the Pope, having been forced for years to go through her to reach the Holy Father.

---

*The Sacred College of Cardinals is the papal senate, officially the pope's closest advisers.

With Pius XII gone those reputedly holy men—one in particular—might well retaliate with some form of revenge. A feud between Pascalina and Eugene Cardinal Tisserant, the bearded dean of the Sacred College of Cardinals, had been simmering for years. Knowing Tisserant to be especially envious of her, she viewed the cardinal with disdain, sometimes referring to him as "the gruff and grisly bear from France." For his part Tisserant was unwilling to accept Pascalina as the classic, motherly nun, claiming much of her surface behavior was a facade.

"It is a disgrace for a woman to be given authority within the Church!" she once heard Tisserant tell Pius. Pascalina knew full well the slap was intended for her, although she held no official position within the Vatican's high command. When she complained to the Pope about the insinuations by this dean of cardinals, Pius tried calming her with his promise not to take Tisserant seriously.

Now, after all the years of suppressed resentments, she was more convinced than ever that no sooner would Pius be buried than Tisserant would have her out of the Vatican. The Papal Palace, one of fifty official Vatican residences with a combined total of some ten thousand rooms and two hundred staircases, would cease at once to be hers to run. Gone, too, would be her long-guarded image as a kindly and devout nun possessed, in the words of Robert I. Gannon, S.J., of "bright, sparkling eyes whose presence lighted . . . lives with humor and human understanding."

This silent masquerade had kept her constantly battling conflicts within herself. What to Pascalina was a beautiful and loving relationship with the Holy Father had often been soiled and besmirched over the years by eyebrow-raising gossip whispered among certain cardinals. She blamed her troubles on the Vatican's hierarchy, whose red hats brought them into the "know" of the papacy's guarded inner circle. "It is most unfortunate that Pascalina's cooking does not equal her physical beauty," it was rumored among cardinals. "If it did, His Holiness would be doubly blessed."

It was common for many of the Vatican's high command—cardinals, archbishops, and bishops—to delight among themselves in the Latin trait of reading everything into any man-woman alliance. They sat in prejudiced judgment of anyone's morals, no matter how innocent the relationship might be, even in Pascalina's instance, when the man involved was the Pope himself.

No one, not even the most powerful and trusted within the Vatican, dared breathe a word of suspicion to the Holy Father. Nor did anyone speak directly with Pascalina about the gossip. As far as she knew, Pius was kept blissfully above all knowledge of talk. Mystic and dreamer that he was, the Pope never suspected for a moment that anyone would think anything but the kindest of his devout, ascetic life.

Though grateful for the Pope's ignorance of the rumors, she deeply resented the hostility the hierarchy aroused within her by their malicious gossip. In the early years, when she first met Pacelli, Pascalina was characteristically reserved, hoping to remain inscrutable. Though richly invested with love, she was blessed as well with unusual perception, and as the years passed the easily detectable jealousies of those she was forced to shunt from the impressionable Pius seared her tolerance and compassion. Though she was increasingly alienated and threatened, nevertheless her austerity and self-command flowered with the resentments she faced.

The cardinals, in their opinion, had reason to oppose the nun and to want her ousted. Over the years her native German authority, which so often came across as bold arrogance when her sensitivities were pricked, remained a thorn in their dignity. Several of the hierarchy complained that Pascalina's presence in the papacy decidedly eroded their influence with the Pope. In truth, her rapid mood swings often caused her to blow up at any cardinal who in her eyes was taking advantage of her or the Pope.

One in particular, Angelo Cardinal Roncalli, whom she thought to be intellectually inferior to Pius, became a target for her outbursts. Roncalli had the annoying habit of dropping by the Pope's office whenever he pleased and without an appointment. In Pascalina's estimation Roncalli played upon his own "overly humble manner to convince me to slip him past the usual line of callers for a private audience with His Holiness." Pascalina was embarrassingly curt toward Roncalli. She took a cue from her close friend, Francis Cardinal Spellman of New York, who scorned the aged and squat Roncalli, likening him to a "simple banana peddler."

"Stop making a bother of yourself!" she shouted at Roncalli, never dreaming that one day the old cardinal would become Pius's successor as Pope John XXIII.

In turn, the cardinals intensified their scrunity of her, magnifying her indulgences in the hope of entrapping their victim and bringing about her ouster. "The woman is evil and not wanted in the Vatican!" she heard whispered among the clergy. There was hardly a letup, even when it became widely known that the Pope's days were numbered.

Pius's spirit remained strong, even to the hour of his death. The authoritarian, iron-willed Pope had never yielded easily to any of life's challenges and was not about to slip away without some fight, despite his rapidly sinking vital signs. Helped by her comforting hand in his, he began to rally slightly, his sunken, emaciated features radiating concentration and tension.

"The doctor is on the way, Holiness," she reassured. "He will be here any moment."

Pascalina saw no real hope in the person of the Pope's physician, Professor Riccardo Galeazzi-Lisi. In her estimation the doctor had not accomplished much, if anything, in alleviating the Pontiff's condition. To her, Galeazzi-Lisi was merely an eye specialist and nothing more. Pascalina had been furious over the years with the way the Pope had gone about seeking a doctor. It had seemed inconceivable to her that a person with Pius's intelligence and high position would be naive enough to be so taken in. He had been out walking and saw a gaudy sign with a huge painted eye dangling from a building, advertising Galeazzi-Lisi's services. Pius was reminded that he needed new glasses and marched up the stairs to the doctor's offices.

Dr. Galeazzi-Lisi was overwhelmed by his important new patient; and when his medical training and experience failed, his flattery and fast talk succeeded. From the first visit on, whenever Pius's health needed attention, be it routine care or serious treatment, he would always send for the eye specialist. "I know only one doctor in Rome," he insisted despite Pascalina's outspoken objections. "Send for Galeazzi!"

The eye doctor had been careful enough, though, when Pius was believed to be dying, to introduce into the case two specialists in internal medicine, Dr. Antonio Gasbarrini and Dr. Ermanno Mingazzini. By the time the team of doctors arrived, the Pope was again motionless. He had suffered a second massive heart attack; his lungs were collapsing and his temperature had risen to 106 degrees.

Several hours later, at 3:52 A.M., on Thursday, October 9, 1958, two and a half months after arriving at Castel Gandolfo, Pius XII died.

The ascetic face, the piercing eyes, the slim figure robed in immaculate white, the hands that had moved like doves as Pius gave his blessing to the cheering throngs—all were still.

The hill town of Castel Gandolfo heard the bells of San Sebastiano toll at 4:00 A.M. to announce the passing of the two hundred and sixtieth successor to Saint Peter and the spiritual leader of the world's five hundred million Roman Catholics.

To the north the bells of Rome filled the silence of the still sleeping city with solemn music as they rang out the sad tidings. Later that morning the Reverend Francesco Pellegrino, S.J., the Vatican's radio announcer, spoke the official words: "The Supreme Pontiff, Pope Pius XII, is dead. Pius XII, the most esteemed and venerated man in the world, one of the greatest pontiffs of the century, with sanctity passed away."

In the Pope's final hours those closest to the Pontiff had gathered by his simple and narrow brass bedstead, covered with the traditional crimson silk, upon which he lay comatose, a painting of Christ above his head. His aged sister, Elisabetta, the last of Pius's childhood playmates, collapsed upon seeing him unconscious and had to be carried from the white-walled bedroom. His three nephews, Carlo, Marcantonio, and Giulio Pacelli, upon each of whom the Italian government, at Pius's prodding, had bestowed the title of prince, were in low voice, sharing their grief with numbers of cardinals and bishops attached to the Curia, the Vatican's bureaucracy.

If Pascalina had had her way, none of these, except Elisabetta, would have been present during the last moments. To her, Pius had personified nobility, and she wanted to keep her Pope's passing crowned with the dignity that enshrined his life. She could not stomach the idle chatter and pretense of those she thought of as intruders at a time so sacred and important to her, nor could they understand why she continued to be coldly efficient and shed no tears.

Her great agony came when she was made to stand helplessly by and watch Cardinal Tisserant, a stickler for protocol, take full charge. Dutifully, at the final moment, Tisserant gathered Pius to his breast and kissed the lifeless form. With much flourish he loudly proclaimed, "The Pope is dead!" It was Tisserant's official responsibility to attest to the Pope's death, to sign the certificate and approve the formal announcement.

Pascalina remained too emotionally involved to relinquish her coveted place entirely to Tisserant. She insisted that great, towering candles burn at the foot of the Pope's bed, as Pius had wanted, and ordered the Noble Guard, wearing golden helmets, to stand alongside at attention, their swords drawn.

With a sudden resurgence of authority Pascalina decided to take it upon herself to perform the last ceremonial ritual at the bedside, the removal of the Fisherman's Ring from the hand of the deceased Pope. But Tisserant sensed her intention once again to defy Church tradition, and before the nun could act, he brushed her aside and fell to his knees. Grasping Pius's bony hand, he slipped the ring from the long, clawlike finger and began chanting the *De Profundis*.

Tisserant was now clearly in charge. Pascalina was no longer any match against the Sacred College of Cardinals, the red-capped and purple-draped men who had grudgingly paid her court for so many years. Dr. Galeazzi-Lisi, observing the transition of power, caught the fracturing of the nun's authority. He no longer feared her objections to his planned method of embalming the Pope's body, an untried procedure that she had fiercely fought from the moment the idea was first proposed. Disregarding her entirely, Galeazzi-Lisi insisted on official Vatican permission, through Cardinal Tisserant, to proceed immediately with the embalming. He explained that no time should be lost in order to prevent rapid decomposition and discoloration of the Pope's body.

The eye specialist described how he had once shown the Pope a human hand, severed in an accident, that had been embalmed by his method and had remained perfectly intact long afterward. He further claimed that Pius was astounded by the hand's flexibility and the preservation of human tissue. The Pope was said to be convinced that the method would preserve his remains "for at least one hundred years." It was Pius's explicit wish, Galeazzi-Lisi argued, that his body after death be preserved as he, the Pope's doctor of thirty years, recommended.

Pascalina interceded, claiming that no authorization had ever been made by Pius for what she described as "such an outlandish procedure." Galeazzi-Lisi insisted that the Pope's diary and other personal papers be investigated for proof of what had been decided.

At ten the same morning, slightly more than six hours after Pius's death, Pascalina was ordered by Tisserant to accompany him in a dash to the Vatican's papal apartment, which she had shared with Pius. Tisserant demanded that she make available to him, as dean of cardinals, all of the Pope's personal effects, including Pius's diary.

Though they found no proof that the Pope had ever authorized any such embalming as proposed by Galeazzi-Lisi, Tisserant nevertheless gave official Vatican approval for the experiment. Some said Tisserant deliberately sided with the doctor because of the nun's emotional opposition.

The embalming would prove humiliating to the Church and degrading to Pius XII, the Pope regarded upon his election in 1939 as one of the ablest churchmen ever to take command of the throne of Saint Peter, for so offensive was the stench arising from the Pontiff's rapidly decomposing remains that a shield of thick cellophane was erected about the casket.

In the midst of her heartbreak and Pius's humiliation, Pascalina was told that Galeazzi-Lisi had kept a diary of her private life with the Pope. The physician was threatening to write a mortifying article, complete with photographs, for the French weekly *Paris-Match*. When news spread of the potentially explosive scandal, wild bidding erupted among the European press and wire services for the sensational copy and pictures. The press was most anxious for Pascalina's deathbed scenes with Pius, which the doctor had secretly photographed. The Vatican's powerful connections were rushed into action. Galeazzi-Lisi was later expelled from the Italian medical profession and censured by the Church.

Throngs of mourners lined the ancient Appian Way on the day of the solemn procession from Castel Gandolfo to Saint Peter's Square to pay final tribute to Pius, the first pope in more than one hundred years to be borne in death through the streets of the Eternal City. The purple-clad body was set for all to view in a horse-drawn, glass-enclosed golden hearse. An escort of one hundred police on motorcycles cleared passage as the cortege moved slowly on to Rome for great ceremonial Masses and burial. A million people were paying their last respects, countless numbers on their knees, along the roadways, in fields and ditches, and on rooftops. Whole flocks hovered together, weeping at the loss of so great a spiritual leader.

Cardinal Tisserant allowed no official place for Pascalina in the procession and ordered her to remain as inconspicuous as possible throughout the burial ceremonies. Everyone knew that the nun was too uncompromising and unrelenting to permit Tisserant, or any churchman, to bar her from these final hours with the man she had served and loved for so many years. There was serious consternation over how she was going to react to the cardinal's directive.

The great bells of Saint Peter's Basilica were tolling the grief of all Rome and of Catholics everywhere when Pascalina arrived at dusk, looking utterly exhausted. It had been the first time in her nearly thirty years in Rome when no limousine had awaited her. She had been lucky even to find a ride with Vatican domestics in a small, crowded car. That didn't bother her nearly as much as when the car was rerouted out of the procession.

Pascalina was in her sixty-fifth year and feeling cranky and frustrated and played out. The debilitating stress that came from watching Pius die all those many weeks seemed doubly hard now that Tisserant and Galeazzi-Lisi were acting against her. She attempted to make her way through Saint Peter's Square to her quarters in the Papal Palace, only to become all the more frustrated by the dense crowd. There was such a throng kneeling and praying for the repose of the soul of the Holy Father that no room could be found for her to join them.

In spite of her sorrow and the overall ache of her body, Pascalina showed little concern for her own well-being. Her uppermost thought at the moment was to reach Cardinal Spellman, who, she had learned, had flown on to Rome immediately upon hearing of Pius's death. Spellman had long been one of Pius's closest friends—hers, too—the only prelate throughout the Catholic world trusted enough by the Pope and herself to share their private hours. In the early days of her relationship with Pacelli, Spellman had proven his fidelity. He had risked his reputation with the Sacred College of Cardinals by spiriting her out of a nun's retreat house in Switzerland and into the Papal Palace, where she could live with Pacelli, who had recently been appointed the new Vatican secretary of state.

As the mourners continued to chant their grief late into the night in Saint Peter's Square below her window, Pascalina sent message after message to Spellman asking that they meet at once. None of her appeals was acknowledged, even into the next day.

Fearing that her notes were being intercepted and not trusting the telephone, she rushed off to Spellman's private suite in the palace, a move she knew to be outside Vatican protocol. Understanding how much Pius had meant to Spellman, she brought along a few of the Pope's prized possessions, including his favorite cassock and the zucchetto she had placed upon His Holiness's head after death.

Spellman was visibly startled by her sudden, unannounced presence but turned pleased at the sight of the gifts she bore.

"It's not wise for you to be here, Sister," the cardinal gently admonished after tucking away the choice belongings. He appeared noticeably concerned that she might have been detected entering his quarters. Exhausted, hungry, wracked as she was with the emotion of Pius's passing, Pascalina appeared altogether unlike herself as she spoke.

"Tisserant will have me out within the week," she said. "Already he has denied me a place at the funeral. I need your help!"

Spellman was patently sympathetic, but, like hers, his own great power within the Church had died with Pius. This he made clear to Pascalina. Spellman, whose enormous authority had earned him the unofficial title of "The American Pope," was himself suddenly in an embarrassing and adversary position. The majority of cardinals within the Roman hierarchy had long been as jealous of Spellman's pet status with Pius as they were of Pascalina. The best Spellman could now offer her were his prayers.

So they went off to chapel to pray. Then suddenly they both started to cry together. Twenty minutes later he was leaving her side, touching her arm gently as a parting gesture. He was to light a candle, to bless himself, to genuflect one last time and leave, closing the chapel door behind him.

More than two million solemn mourners filed in slow procession through Saint Peter's Basilica in the two and a half days that the rigid body of Pius XII, Christ's Vicar on Earth, lay in state upon the high altar under Michelangelo's great dome. Some wept as they paid their last respects; most were moving their lips in silent prayer. Tens of millions of others honored Eugenio Maria Giuseppe Giovanni Pacelli in services throughout the world. Pius was a pope to remember, for he had set a record achieved by no other pontiff in Church history. During his nearly twenty-year reign the Roman Catholic Church added more than one hundred and twenty million members to its ranks.

The Pope's body was clad in a white silk cassock covered by a brilliant red and gold chasuble. Draped about his neck was a pallium of lamb's wool, symbol of his exalted office, and upon his head was a tall white and gold miter. Swiss Guards in splendid costumes designed by Michelangelo nearly four centuries before surrounded the red catafalque on which lay the eighty-two-year-old deceased Pontiff.

On the day of the burial the basilica, amid all the pomp, pageantry, and devotion, was barred to everyone except the chosen, and they were mostly of celebrity, power, and wealth. The Requiem Mass began in ancient Gregorian chant as hundreds of archbishops, patriarchs, and bishops filed in for seating in sections of honor. Forty cardinals in purple robes were already on the high altar, seated upon thrones forming a crescent about the deceased.

As flags of fifty-three nations descended to half-mast, delegates from each of the represented countries were escorted to places of honor within the basilica by colorfully garbed Knights of Malta in plumed headdress. Rays of golden sunshine streamed through the high stained-glass windows and shone upon the rows upon rows of royalty, nobility, foreign ministers, and other high-ranking diplomats. Among the first to be assembled were those representing the United States: Secretary of State John Foster Dulles, former U.S. Ambassador to Italy Clare Boothe Luce, and Atomic Energy Commissioner John A. McCone.

Pius's nephews, their wives and children, and his sister, Elisabetta, were assigned special places of honor on a tribune close to the main altar.

To the rear of the edifice, and off to one side, Pius's servants were hidden away, Pascalina among them. Her treatment could not have been more ignominious. Yet she showed no sign of bitterness or emotion. Her glance remained fixed upon the ceremony; her lips moved in quiet prayer as she knelt throughout the grueling two-hour Solemn High Mass. Only when the choir sang *In Paradisium,* as the magnificent bronze casket was slowly lowered beneath the basilica to a white marble tomb close to Saint Peter's, did tears fill her eyes.

With the ceremonies ended, her emptiness was complete. She returned alone to the papal apartment on the third floor of the palace overlooking Saint Peter's Square, the home she had shared with the Pope for so many years. The simple arrangement of their quarters (dining room, bedrooms, bathroom, study, and small chapel) was not of her design but rather of Pius's frugal taste and in keeping with his monastic style. The bedrooms were little more than monk's cells with simple walnut beds. There was also a small dressing table and mirror in each room, and hand-hooked rugs were at the center. Pius's desk had always been piled high with papers.

The dining room, though hardly impressive, seemed rich by comparison. Near the center was a round mahogany table with a lace runner upon which stood a crystal vase that nuns filled each day with freshly cut flowers. Against the wall a side table held brass candelabra, and between the door and the room's only window (which Pascalina had draped with lace) there was a china closet. Off to one corner a radio had been placed on a mahogany table. She listened to it rarely, but he had kept an ear at night to the news and classical music. The only touch of magnificence was the highly polished, beautifully veined marble floor.

The Pope had loved the simplicity of it all. "Beauty is everywhere!" he would exclaim, sometimes pointedly so when she would suggest change.

There was also the chirping and twittering of Pius's beloved birds to contend with. The Pope allowed them to fly about the apartment from the numbers of cages he himself had hung in various rooms. Pius had always insisted to Pascalina that she keep the cages open, particularly for Gretel, his pet goldfinch. The nun had deplored the idea, often shaking her head impatiently when Gretel flittered after him, twittering away. The bird frequently was his wake-up alarm and often perched herself on the Pope's shoulder while he shaved. "Cardinal Spellman gave me this electric shaver," he repeated time after time, talking to the bird as if she understood everything he said.

The ritual had been the same every day. She would hear Pius pedaling away on his stationary bicycle for ten minutes; hear him grunt while working out with dumbbells and tension cables. At times he would look embarrassed and explain to her his reasons for the daily exercise routine. "God has given us a body to perform those duties which he has assigned to each of us," Pius said. "It is, therefore, the obligation of everyone to maintain his body in good condition to permit the best performance of those duties." She had heard the same story over and over; ever since his sickly youth, when the boys would taunt him for being weak and scrawny, he had put aside a half hour almost every day for keeping muscular and trim.

Pascalina usually walked out; she had no time to listen to old conversation, or for exercise, a practice she considered "a waste-of-time nonsense." The nun got all the exercise she considered necessary, she'd say, taking care of their quarters and catering to his every whim.

By seven fifteen the Pope would be off to his private chapel to celebrate Mass. She would join him soon afterward along with the congregation of other nuns from the German order of the Holy Cross who would always assemble for Pius's prayers and blessing. Afterward, while he bathed, Pascalina would prepare his simple choice of breakfast: fruit, a slice of bread, coffee and milk. She ate as sparingly.

Now all that was over. Pius was gone, and a directive from the Sacred College of Cardinals was on its way—on the day of the funeral—ordering Pascalina to depart. And at once!

"I was shocked by the order telling me to leave immediately," she said. Pascalina was to pack her bags and be gone by nightfall. After a lifetime in the service of the Church and devotion to Pius, the nun was to be on her own. She had only her personal belongings and a stipend in Italian currency amounting to about $110. The gratuity was to be picked up at the Curia's treasury office as she was leaving. Her banishment was the doing of a majority of the Roman hierarchy. But the cold, merciless words were Tisserant's, the document's signatory.

The nun felt defeated. An old-fashioned woman of class, she was tragically humiliated at having her life with Pius relentlessly scrutinized and denigrated. For her, it was crushing beyond anything she could have imagined to be relegated to the status of an unwanted, disgraced nun. Then, too, she was in pitiful financial plight and drained of her mental and physical strength. For the moment she could not function—but only for the moment.

At this, her darkest hour, little remained but for her to draw upon her unfailing self-mastery, which she had refined and strengthened during years of struggle with rigid orthodoxy. She decided to face down Tisserant, as she had done with so many of the hierarchy over the years. It mattered little to her, at this time, that the cardinal was in full charge of the Vatican, including the upcoming election of a new pope. Pascalina's private life with Pius had taught her not to believe that anyone was inviolable.

En route to her confrontation she decided she would not resort to loud demonstration. She was too old and shrewd for such behavior, yet she knew her volatile nature was not always as under control as she would like it to be. It was this unbridled emotion that she feared most during her meeting with the dean of cardinals.

They met in the palace's most opulent office, done in the elegance of rich crimson damask, its great windows hung with heavy velvet drapes. Cardinal Tisserant, behind an immense mahogany desk, a gold and white telephone at his elbow, studied her with passive indifference.

"You appear quite resigned, Mother Pascalina," Tisserant said abruptly without greeting. "Undoubtedly, you realize that you are no longer needed or wanted in the Vatican."

"I shall leave the palace," Pascalina responded in a quiet, cold tone. Any attempt at compromise now appeared fruitless. She was too strong and efficient to beg for mercy, and she despised sentimentality in such circumstances. Yet it remained that there was no place for her to go and nobody to turn to.

"I ask Your Eminence that I be given a few days to make proper plans," she continued. "I ask as well that I be permitted to take a few of His Holiness's personal effects, those which I most treasure."

"You will leave by nightfall, as the Sacred College has decreed," Tisserant replied, his words cold yet calm, his face expressionless. "You may take one thing of Pius's, his birds. We will be well rid of them, and of you."

Pascalina rose, blessed herself, genuflected, and left.

At 7:56 P.M., October 14, 1958, the day of Pius's funeral and five days after his death, Mother Pascalina left the Vatican. There were tears in her eyes as she took one final glance at the Papal Palace, her gaze lingering upon the pontifical apartment she had shared with Pius for so many years.

Finally an old taxi arrived, and she struggled in without help for the ride to the train station and a journey that would take her far from Rome. With her were two small packed bags and a pair of cages filled with frightened, twittering birds.

II

Pascalina was born to George and Maria Lehnert on August 25, 1894, on a small farm in Ebersberg, Bavaria, a rural village of fewer than two thousand, situated some twenty-five miles southeast of Munich. She was christened Josefine.

From the moment the midwife delivered her on the farm, Josefine was the family's darling, an irrepressibly gay addition to the Lehnerts' otherwise drab peasant household. She was as fair, golden, and blue-eyed as the other children were dark. Her older brothers and sisters, six in all, remembered her as always in motion until the age of seven: running with a dog, flying back and forth on a swing from some tree in the yard, sliding down a hill on a makeshift sled, diving headlong into a tributary that flowed past their farm, then swimming fearlessly to midstream and back.

Her mother remembered Josefine from the age of seven on as mostly serious, the only one of her brood, which finally numbered six daughters and six sons, who deliberately skipped her childhood. "Josefine was a lady at seven, the year that she received her First Holy Communion," her mother once said of her favorite child. "From the time she took her first step—determined and unafraid—we saw how mature she was; how independent and courageous, too."

"No!" was Josefine's first word, and it became the theme of her entire life. She said no to everyone and everything she considered silly or wrong. From an early age she took such complete charge that the family started calling her "Mother Superior."

Those who knew her from the time she reached "the use of reason" have memories of Josefine seldom doing any of the delightful or mischievous things that possessed little girls of her age. There was no playing with dolls, no asking to sleep over at friends' houses, no giggling, no shy blushes when boys were around, no making a nuisance of herself with older brothers and sisters or teasing the younger ones, no refusing to go to bed on time. To the contrary, it was tiny Josefine (who never quite reached five feet two) who made sure the others in the family obeyed. She wanted her sisters and brothers to be good Catholic ladies and gentlemen, and even at the tenderest age she pressed her skill and determination for this dream.

Bavaria during her youth was still a monarchy, a backward land held in chains for more than seven centuries by a line of dukes and kings of the house of Wittelsbach, many of them devious and oppressive. From earliest childhood Josefine loved the beauty of the Bavarian countryside, an almost imaginary wonderland, to her, of fantastic castles, blue lakes, snow-capped mountains, and dense pine forests. Even into her old age her most cherished memories are of Sunday mornings in Ebersberg, where the hills and valleys echoed and reechoed with the deep sounds of church bells. They were melodious reminders, Josefine would say, for everyone in the town to come and pray to God at Saint Sebastian's, their parish church.

Like their neighbors for miles around, whose ancestry reached back hundreds of years, the Lehnerts were peasants and lived a difficult, dull life. Up without fail before every dawn, they worked their fields and in their barns for twelve to fifteen hours every day, never quitting until everything was done. Only the bitterest blasts of the severe Alpine winters could force them indoors. Almost everyone in Ebersberg was Catholic, and nearly all owned their own small farms, living off the livestock and fruit and vegetables they raised "with God's help."

Her father had been an only child and as a boy had dreamt of going to sea. But tuberculosis, then death, struck the family early, claiming both his parents while they were still in their late thirties. All they had to leave a heartbroken and frightened seventeen-year-old son was their run-down and debt-ridden farm.

The neighbors, as poor as the Lehnerts, could offer nothing but prayers to young George. They brought him warm chicken soup and shed tears as the young man grew pitifully thin working himself to the bone to save the dilapidated old place. His years of hard work paid off the debts, but George was never able to put anything aside for repairs or for the future.

He and Maria, Josefine's mother, had known each other since starting the first grade together at Saint Sebastian's parochial school. From then on, they were classmates—taught by the same nuns— almost every year. They married a few weeks after graduating from the Catholic high school; he was barely eighteen and she was seventeen. Neither had been off the farm since, except to go to Munich and a few nearby towns on rare occasions.

Time and constant struggle had turned George sour, but Maria's sad eyes and sallow skin could still brighten a bit during those rare trips away from the farm. She enjoyed shopping, even though it meant only bringing some small necessity back to the children, usually shoes for the boys and perhaps warm underwear for the girls. Josefine would be joyful for weeks when they brought her a holy medal or one more new picture of Jesus.

When they were in Munich, George always insisted that they spend an hour or two in a beer hall. Maria didn't mind because she loved to dance, and the only time he cared to whirl about with her anymore was after he drank a few beers.

Their gothic home, with its unusual red tin roof and set by a dirt road, was built two hundred years earlier and had been in his father's family for generations. Still badly in need of repairs both inside and out when Josefine arrived, the house had six small bedrooms on the second floor, not nearly enough as the family grew larger. When the children were small, some of her brothers and sisters slept together in the same rooms, but as they grew her mother—a model of respectability and conservatism—insisted that the boys and girls remain apart at night.

As devout Catholics the Lehnerts always began the day with prayer. The whole family assembled on their knees in the sparse kitchen with its potbelly stove and flooring of wide planks. Even after more than eighty years Pascalina remembers the cracks between the boards that showed the earth beneath.

"It was indeed a spartan room," she recalled with a warm smile, "but the only one in the house large enough to hold all fourteen of us at one time." Papa George Lehnert—a squat, heavyset, severe German of middle years—knelt at the center of the wide circle of kneeling supplicants, leading them in the saying of the rosary. By the time she was four Josefine had come to kneel beside her father. With rosary beads dangling from her tiny hands, she led the prayers along with him as the others responded.

At age five, Josefine's love for Jesus so overflowed that the spirited and persistent child was easily able to persuade her family to increase their religious devotions. "Can we please make our own novena to the Blessed Mother?" she asked one morning just as they finished their prayers. "May we say the Memorare and other prayers for ten minutes every day after the noon Angelus?"* Her parents and the older children were delighted to see how grown-up and devoted the child was. But it seemed that no sooner had they gone along with her pleadings than she began campaigning for a half hour of gospel readings every night.

At seven, Josefine suggested that she be allowed to help out in the fields. It was an unorthodox idea for a child in those days to express, and still more jolting when spoken by a girl.

"It will be such fun for me!" she exclaimed one night to the family. They were all seated at the long dining table, their evening meal of sauerkraut and sausage almost finished. Josefine had never seen her father put down his huge mug of beer with such swift force, the foam on his thick black mustache even less apparent than the shock upon his face. Her brothers and sisters looked as astonished. The boys had always loathed the idea of getting up at four thirty every morning to work the fields, and his sisters had never even considered such a thought. It was women's work to help out in the home—cooking and sewing and cleaning and washing—but never in the fields.

Her mother was the most horrified. "No, Josefine! Absolutely not!" Maria shouted. The child had seldom seen her pathetically passive mother with the sad, sunken eyes react with such an outburst. Her father and the others were as stunned as she, and remained speechless. The woman had spoken with fierce determination, leaving no doubt that the subject was to end at once.

Several nights later Josefine found her mother alone in her room, preparing herself for bed. "May I please speak with you, Mama?" the child asked in a quiet tone. Maria nodded pleasantly, and Josefine came to her in smiles. Taking the woman's hand and drawing it to her lips, she kissed the hard lines and rough spots that were more from hard work than of age.

---

*The Angelus is a devotional prayer to commemorate the Incarnation, the embodiment of Almighty God in the form of Jesus. In Ebersberg, as in other Catholic areas, church bells would peal at high noon, and the farmers would stop whatever they were doing to commence the prayer: "The Angel of the Lord announced unto Mary . . . and she conceived of the Holy Spirit."

"Mama, why is it wrong for a girl to work in the fields?" she asked in soft voice. Before Maria could answer, Josefine spoke again, "When did Jesus say that women and girls should not be in the fields?"

Maria was too exhausted from a day of scrubbing and cleaning to find words. A look of complete hopelessness crossed her face, for how was she to handle a child who at times seemed wiser than herself? At last, throwing her hands into the air, she ran from the room in tears.

It was several weeks before Josefine found heart and courage to broach the subject again. Once more her mother was alone in her bedroom, seated before a mirror and removing pins that held her hair in a tight bun at the back of her head. Josefine poked a timid face inside the room, and when Maria smiled at her, she rushed forward, her face brightening instantly as her arms reached out and encircled her mother.

"I love you so much, Mama!" she said tenderly. Seating herself close, she began to finger Maria's long, flowing curls. "You have such beautiful golden locks," she continued. "Why don't you let all of us see more of them?" Her words were so filled with warmth that Maria couldn't resist pulling her favorite child tightly into her arms. She kissed Josefine again and again. "You are so nice, Mama," the little girl responded. "But I wish that you were not so old-fashioned."

Maria did not answer. Josefine saw the familiar sadness creep back into her mother's eyes. But the child, even then, saw no victory for anyone in self-pity. "Papa would not be so hard on you, Mama, if you stood up for yourself," she continued in a low whisper, her finger gently brushing the woman's lips.

"Do you believe that I'm depriving you, Josefine, when I ask you not to work in the fields?" Maria asked quietly.

"Yes, Mama," she replied in a sincere tone. "Please. I don't want to be sad." She paused before speaking again. "Is it wrong for me to want to do different things?"

Maria saw the wisdom in her daughter's words. There was a long silence, and Josefine understood how deep her mother's thoughts went in moments like that. Finally, Maria turned from her faraway look and glanced back at her daughter. Her face seemed to show a new understanding.

"My dear little girl," she began, "if working in the fields means that much to you, then I say may dear Jesus speed your happiness. I will speak to your father and get his permission." A broad grin covered Maria's lips. "But I warn you!" she added knowingly. "You'll get tired of your foolishness soon enough!"

"Oh, Mama, I love you!" Josefine retorted. "Even though you're such a tease!" They clung close and kissed again.

At four thirty the next morning Josefine was dressed and already out in the fields, scattering feed to the chickens. When she finished, she found fascination in watching one of her older brothers milk a cow. Within a few minutes the child was sure that she could do a better job, even though she was only half his age.

"John, you're hurting that cow!" she exclaimed. "Besides, you're putting too much milk in that bucket. It'll spill!"

It was part of Josefine's character from an early age to see better and easier ways of doing almost everything. This ability, the nun would one day admit, wasn't too difficult to come by "since my beginnings were rather primitive and very routine."

Her second day in the fields she was in the barn before anyone, milking away like an experienced hand. When Papa Lehnert and her brothers strode by, they saw tiny Josefine sitting squat on an upside-down bucket beneath a huge cow, humming merrily to herself as she drew milk from the beast. She startled them even more by her dress than by her talent as a cowhand. She was in a starched white blouse and pleated checkered skirt that she herself had pressed the night before, using her mother's solid metal iron that she had heated over hot coals. Though she had kept carrying buckets of milk from the dirty barn to the house, there wasn't a spot on her.

"There's no reason why people working at hard labor cannot dress cleanly and neatly," she remarked years later. "Discipline is the answer. If one learns discipline during childhood, all things are possible. I wanted to look neat and attractive, so I taught myself to be cautious, and the discipline worked."

Despite the hard labor for which she showed such love, Josefine gave her brothers and sisters no reason to call her a tomboy; she had too many female traits for any such derision to stick. Her talents were as spirited and skillful in the kitchen as in the fields and barn. The girl loved to spend hours sewing, and her older brothers, who went out on the town on Saturday nights, took advantage by seeing to it that she had plenty of their clothing to mend. "Every time one of you boys starts taking out a new girl, I know about it, just by your asking me to mend and press something special for you to wear," she'd say.

To everyone's delight, her attraction to the stove turned her into a superb cook with a special knack for making blueberry pies. She alone in the family could bake a crisp, lip-smacking crust that kept her father and brothers pestering her regularly to make several more every week.

Yet, despite all she did for the family, there were times when her brothers wished that Josefine would disappear into thin air and stay away for a long time. It was her scrupulous way, her perfectionist attitude and punctilious nature, that they complained about.

"I hate clutter!" she once said, her eyes ablaze at the frustration caused by seeing the older boys' clothes scattered about everywhere. Their parents had gone to Munich in the family's horse-drawn wagon, leaving Josefine to take over, as she customarily did when George and Maria were away.

"I'm tired of picking up after you boys!" she shouted, pretending to be angry. "Now you come here, John, and put away everything of yours, or you'll never hear the end of my nagging!" John was sixteen, more than twice her age, but from then on he knew enough not to tangle with Josefine.

"Mama and Papa are easier to handle than this Mother Superior we have standing over us," he complained to his brothers. "What a pain in the ass she can be!"

At nine, she was even more of an authority in the home. "Mama, I don't like the idea of the boys taking baths in the kitchen in front of everybody!" Josefine insisted. "It's not right!" Her mother agreed, but what were they to do? There were only large wooden barrels for them to bathe in, and everyone—their neighbors as well—had always washed themselves that way on Saturday nights. "But I bathe in private out in the barn," she protested. "And they're going to as well!"

She brought the whole family out to the barn, to a stall that had been left vacant at the very end. "See!" she said, excitedly pointing to the place she had set up for everyone to bathe in. It was a simple enough bath, with only a barrel, but she had erected racks along the walls to hold towels and had made the place immaculately clean. At the entranceway she had tacked up a burlap curtain for their privacy.

"What nonsense!" her father said in disgust as he turned to leave for the house. "I've bathed in the kitchen all my fifty years. And I ain't changing now! No young of mine is going to tell me what to do!"

"Mama, make him wash here!" Josefine insisted, her hands on her hips to show determination. Maria Lehnert had never spoken up to her husband, and could not find the words now. The young girl understood the embarrassing predicament she had placed her mother in, and was sorry. Yet she wasn't about to let her father continue doing what she knew was wrong. Running in front of the man, she then whirled about and grabbed both of his arms, stopping him in his tracks.

"Papa, how much do you like my blueberry pies?" she asked, almost out of breath.

"Love 'em!" he replied.

"I'll make you a deal," she continued. "I'll bake as many as you want if you wash in the barn. But no more pies for you or anyone else if everyone doesn't bathe there!" She walked off then, on her own, into the fields, leaving the rest of the family stunned.

None in the Lehnert household had ever before taken a defiant stand against Papa Lehnert, and everyone wondered how the proud and authoritarian family head was going to react. For days her father smoldered with repressed anger, his anticipated outburst against Josefine expected to flare at any moment. But by Saturday night he had somewhat cooled, and he smiled after Josefine cut him an extra large piece of blueberry pie and brought it to him herself.

After dinner she took him by the arm and said, "Papa, let's take a walk together."

He said nothing at first, but puffed away on his cigar as he thought deeply, his wounded pride weighing what action to take. Finally he spoke. "All right, daughter," he said matter-of-factly. She led him to the barn, a clean towel over her arm.

"Did you like the pie, Papa?" the girl asked, looking coyly upward at him as she held his hand.

"Loved it!" he replied enthusiastically.

"I'm so pleased," she said. "Now it's your turn to make me happy." She handed him the towel. "Papa, please start taking your baths in the barn. I built the place especially for you."

"Daughter," he said, looking down at her with a widening grin, "I wonder if there's more devil in you than good." He went inside and closed the canvas curtain after him. She heard the man mutter, "God made her for certain, but it took a bit of the devil, too, for her to be what she is."

Her teachers had the same idea of the brilliant, no-nonsense young German girl with enormous confidence in herself. Even in grammar school she showed her proud and fiercely determined nature that was the key, they said, to making herself important.

In one way she was thought of as a loner, for she usually trudged the several miles alone to and from school. Even in winter she'd make her way by herself through the heavy Alpine snows, often filling her time practicing French or Italian aloud. She felt the need to get away from the giddiness of many of her own age. "If there was no one about to captivate her mind, she'd rather remain with her own thoughts than be bored," a childhood friend who knew her well said of her.

Yet Josefine was far from withdrawn in the classroom. She was as much a leader in the Catholic school she attended as she was at home. None of the nuns had to chastise her for not doing her homework, for she found as much pleasure in study as she did working the farm or knitting a quilt for her parents' bed. She took to history and languages as easily and with as much interest as girls her own age took to the polka and boyfriends. Yet even more she loved to read; biographies and other nonfiction were her favorites. Writing was another great diversion; little hand-scrawled memories of her early life. She had a straight-A average throughout grammar and high school and was absent only eleven days in all her years of schooling. Still, few of the nuns who taught Josefine felt any close tie with her.

Once when her eighth-grade class was dismissed early because of the threat of heavy snow, she raised her hand to remind the teacher she'd forgotten to assign homework. The nun was infuriated at what she believed to be the child's deliberate attempt to show up her laxity.

"You are such an insolent little girl," the sister shouted. "Don't ever again tell me how to run this class!"

Josefine's face flushed with embarrassment at being so misinterpreted. "But, sister," she innocently protested, "you said yesterday that you were going to give us the catechism to study tonight. Was it wrong for me to want to read the teachings of Christ? I am sorry if I have been offensive."

"You are impossible!" the nun retorted. "You're always implying how right you are and how wrong the world is. I'll be thankful to God when you're promoted."

As she grew into her teens the childhood differences between her brother John and herself began to lift. He was nearly twenty-one, old enough by then to appreciate fully the girl's unusual devotion and dedication to the family. But it took an extraordinarily thrilling moment in the Lehnerts' colorless world to bring Josefine and John closer. The happy event occurred when the young man returned home early one evening from his second job as a mechanic in Munich.

"He came roaring onto the front lawn on a motorcycle, his proud face all lit up in smiles," she said with a laugh many decades later. The nun raised her clasped hands above her head and shook them in glee as she happily remembered the exciting occasion. "None of us had ever seen a motorcycle before, and we all stood gaping on the porch with our mouths wide open," she continued. "Everyone was scared to death to ride on such a strange and dangerous-looking vehicle. But I was jumping up and down in excitement, pleading with John to take me for a spin. He did, even though Mama was screaming at him not to. I had the time of my life as we sped through the Alpine hills, my insides coming apart as we struck the many deep ruts in those terrible winding dirt roads."

From that day on, the thrill of fast wind against her face and body was in her veins, and though she remained the archconservative in most of life's ways, she could hardly ever set foot in any vehicle without ordering the driver to press down hard on the accelerator. "Faster! Faster!"

At fourteen, boys her own age and some older were at wide variance with Josefine's ideas and ideals. Spirited males saw in the turbulence of her deep blue eyes a lust for life and a challenge to their smoldering passions. Her flawless, peach-colored skin, her full, expressive lips, the excitement and vitality of her youth, all were contradictions to her decorous manner.

Boy after boy followed her lonely trail home from school, each certain that he'd be the first to capture her love. A young man from her class brought his horse-drawn wagon one golden October afternoon and asked her to climb aboard. She did without hesitation, and they had driven scarcely a mile before he suddenly pulled tight on the reins and stopped the horses. Putting his arm about her waist, the boy exclaimed, "Someday, Josefine, I'm going to marry you!"

She looked at him quite calmly, feeling more sad than surprised. The boy, scarcely her own size and with such a baby face, had always appeared to be a child to her. She almost burst into laughter but successfully managed to hold her composure.

"Neil," she replied. "That's so cute of you." For a moment the thought crossed her mind that this boy could easily be the doll her family could never afford to give her.

Another young man, attracted by the beauty of the slender blond girl, was handled quite differently by her. She had gone to Munich with her parents—the only one in the family her father could afford to take along—and was approached by a stranger who came up to her in a beer hall and asked her to dance the polka. It was her first time in such a place, her father having decided that the family's "best little helper" was old enough at fifteen to see "another side of life."

During the first dance the man's hands began to roam over her body. "I remember striking him with almost the same force that I struck Cardinal Tisserant many years later," the nun recalled. "Papa was so pleased, especially when he saw the man scurry off, holding a handkerchief to his nose. From then on, Papa said he never had to worry about how able I was in taking care of myself."

As Josefine grew to womanhood she had far less patience with the difficulties and privations of farm life. She loathed the embarrassment of having to make her toilette in a field outhouse. The days of tending livestock and digging in the fields before going to school, and upon returning in the late afternoon, no longer held her fascination. Often she found herself resenting her militant father for their regimented and boring existence, and she pitied her timid mother for enduring it all for so long. She anguished at the thought of how old her parents had become before their time.

She tried to hide her deepening resentment of her destiny, being forced to come to womanhood amid the Bavarian peasantry. These people she now saw as wasted. Subjugated throughout so much of history by misery and bitter defeat, her family and friends and neighbors had succumbed to abject poverty, and there appeared no escape.

Excitement for fifteen-year-old Josefine Lehnert in the Bavaria of 1909 amounted to a single yearly event, the Mozart summer festival at Augsburg, some fifty miles away. Though she herself played no instrument, her love of music was so great that somehow her father always seemed to manage to scrape together the means to take the young girl to the festival.

Every year Josefine threatened not to go. "It would be selfish of me," she insisted, reminding them that there were fourteen mouths to feed. Her father had been forced to take a second job, eking out meager earnings as the village postman. He worked relentlessly, completely exhausting himself between his chores on his own farm and carrying mail to neighboring farms over a route of some fifty kilometers a day in his horse-drawn wagon. Yet the man never failed to insist that she attend the festival. He'd pound the table and shout in his robust German way that his special daughter deserved her day away once a year for all the hard work she was always doing about the house and farm.

Earlier, when she was a small child, he had expressed the same determination about taking her to the children's pageant at Dinkelsbühl, a fairy-tale place that filled her young romantic mind so much of the time. Then, as she grew, her favorite pastime became the Oktoberfest at Munich, Bavaria's beloved ancient capital. Her reason, she said, was that her mother, who usually looked so sad, loved life there and danced and laughed so easily at the once-a-year event. Munich during the Oktoberfest saw the flow of Bavarian wine and lager beer and the crisp smell of native sausage. To laughing, excited Josefine there were few pleasures that seemed more wonderful.

Now, at fifteen, she was turning away from such concerns, and these excursions to far-off places were only fleeting desires, purposefully kept by her at the recesses of her mind. Too much play, and she quickly became bored. She was most alive when dealing with the real world on a high mental plateau.

On the surface there was nothing about Josefine during her midteens to suggest that she would ever become a nun. No one, not even her mother, with whom she was close, could imagine the willful, headstrong teen-ager living a life of humility in a strict religious order; obeying vows of poverty, chastity, and obedience; giving herself forever to an existence even harsher than the world of privation into which she had been born.

Yet deep within, far deeper than her rebellious nature, there was building a determination to succeed in a world of her own choosing. Had the family been wiser in understanding her psychology, they might have seen much earlier the track she was taking. She dwelt much of the time meditating and praying in her own room, a tiny, immaculate place of Spartan simplicity, which she had built herself in the attic. She had covered the bare boards with pieced-together burlap and had hung there every picture she came across of Jesus and the Blessed Mother and all the saints.

Her bed was a mattress of straw that she had collected from the barn. The only sunlight that ever entered the room came through slim cracks in the wood where the boards were separated, shrunken by the weather. Her few clothes were neatly piled in the corner, and her choicest possession, her rosary beads, hung draped during the day upon a long nail by the entranceway. At night she clutched the beads close to her heart. She'd have loved to have vigil lights burning at all times, but as she knew the danger of fire, the small candles remained unlit.

From the time Josefine was nine, she had had thoughts of serving Jesus in some meaningful way. But not until she had turned fifteen were there any real beckonings from Almighty God for her to devote a lifetime of service to humanity. In 1910 she attended the Passion play at Oberammergau, and seeing all that Christ gave up for mankind, seeing His pain and suffering, and hearing His cry for servants, finally pushed her into her decision, a move that she knew would prove more drastic than impulsive.

She was afraid to face her family with her plans, especially fearful of her father's rage; frightened too of the strength of older brothers who might stop at nothing to keep her from leaving home. Even more troubling, she couldn't bear to see the panic she knew would cover her mother's face.

Then, too, her devotion to Christ had become so great that she couldn't bear to turn away from Him, either. Fear was telling her to run off to the convent, to say nothing to anyone. But the anguish that her sneaking away would cause her family, her mother most especially, made her hesitate.

Finally courage came and she spoke alone with her mother, pouring out her heart for the woman's understanding of her great need to leave home and serve Christ. Though the Lehnerts, like two thirds of Bavaria's nine million people, were devout Catholics, Maria Lehnert still refused to understand her daughter's pleadings.

"No, you cannot leave!" the woman shouted, tears and rage upon her face. "I'm going to tell your father, and he'll never let you go!" At that, Maria ran from the room.

Papa Lehnert was even more enraged. Appearing suddenly in the doorway, with jaw locked in wild anger and his fists clenched, the man looked far more menacing than Josefine could have imagined.

The young girl knew then how completely unwise would be any challenge to his male authority. She mustered all her composure.

"Father, this is your moment," Josefine said in cool voice. "As your daughter, I bow to your will. When you have calmed down, I would like to talk to you." She slid past him and went directly to her room in the attic.

But there was no opportunity for her to talk with Papa Lehnert. At no time would he listen to her. After days of frustrating attempts on the girl's part, she felt ready to burst, yet, quite remarkably, she held her temper out of the love she bore her parents and family.

And so it was, with practically nothing to her name, Josefine left home at fifteen, without a single good-bye, knowing what the tears would do to her own will, knowing too that once she left, she would never be allowed to return.

Convent life at the early part of the twentieth century, a time when women's rights were unheard of, was to prove more stifling than anything Josefine could have imagined. Sponsored by her pastor, whom she had known since childhood, she was accepted into the order of the Teaching Sisters of the Holy Cross at Altötting, outside Munich. There the Mother Superior, an enormous, angry woman of middle years, ruled with unquestioned authority over numbers of timid and cowering young postulants. Strict adherence to obedience and privation were the ancient traditions of the repressive religious order.

Arriving at the Mother House, a convent and training center for nuns that always seemed in need of more hands, Josefine was assigned at once to a small, boxlike cell, somewhat resembling a horse's stall, strewn with straw on which to sleep. Scores of these cells lined the corridors for every member of the community from Mother Superior on down.

Just as promptly Josefine was summoned to her first meeting with the Mistress of Postulants, in whose custody she was to remain for the next six months. The severe, demanding nun in bulky black robes, wooden rosary beads dangling from a leather belt at her waist, took immediate command and allowed for no change in Josefine's decision. The old woman's approach was to dominate, declaring that Josefine now belonged to the convent for all time. The nun's recitation, more than the actual vows of poverty, chastity, and obedience, completely terrified the young girl.

Yet, despite her fears and all of the unyielding pressures placed upon her, Josefine was no fool; she was too clearheaded and strong-willed to be railroaded into a life she did not want, or could not bear. She was well aware of the rigid rules and regulations of the religious life she had chosen, the privations and hardships of which people in the outside world might consider shocking and unbearable. Her decision to enter the convent and make an almost complete break with the past was entirely her own, an attitude she would always maintain.

She was shut off at first from everyone except the Mistress of Postulants, a test of strength that she would later liken to quarantine before her crossing into a nation of silence. Rarely allowed to speak, she was given only one chance to learn whatever she was told.

"We walk with our eyes lowered and our hands out of sight," the old nun ordered, and from then on, Josefine always looked straight downward, never to the side.

A snap of the nun's fingers stood her up; two snaps turned her around. The tricky sign language used by nuns during periods of silence was hardest of all for her to follow. An upraised hand with waggling index finger meant she wanted water; a cutting motion with the back of one hand against the palm of the other hand was a request for a serving of bread; two taps on the breast meant "Excuse me"; hooked middle finger and index finger said "Fork, please."

To most of the postulants the loud clanging of handbells at four thirty each morning, an unmerciful wake-up alarm, was the worst of the rules; but the sound didn't bother Josefine in the least. Coming from farm life, she was an old hand at getting up early and all too used to the thunderous noise of her brothers knocking about, getting ready for the day.

What did offend her senses was the piercing sound of Mother Superior's whistle and what it commanded: having to stop in a split second whatever she was doing or saying whenever the old nun wanted attention. It meant cutting a syllable in half if she was speaking, leaving a word unfinished while writing, or swallowing a mouthful of food in one gulp. If Josefine could not achieve command over the simplest acts of obedience, the Superior warned, she would never attain her ultimate goal, total obedience to the will of God.

It was all terribly trying for her at times, this constant testing of one's memory, obedience, and will; worrying and staying awake all night, fearing that she would never make the grade.

But soon enough she was given a short black cape, which hooked at the neck and dropped without flare to the center of the forearms, and a black veil to pin over her hair; her temporary habit, at last! She still had six grueling months to wait, however, before she would receive the more formal robes of a novice, an intermediary role in a society of humility before becoming a fully professed nun.

Each day, it seemed, brought harder, more painful sacrifices. No sooner was one test of strength over than something worse would strike. First, it was the horror of seeing herself shorn to the bone. Her glorious golden curls, worn shoulder-length since early childhood, were her favorite feature. She took tender care of her hair, keeping her head well protected from the sun's drying rays. Having to remain nearly bald throughout her life as a nun left its psychological scar for years. "All for Jesus," she kept telling herself until the trauma faded away.

Then came her trial at fasting, having to go without food as a holy sacrifice, being given only bread and water for days on end until Mother Superior decided she had the devotion and strength of will to prevail in the service of the religious order.

There was the humiliation of having to keep a daily record of everything she did wrong, as would a small child made to report the slightest mistake to teacher. "Let the door slam after me," she had to jot down. "Ran down the corridor instead of walked. . . . Spoke to one of the sisters after the bell. . . . Forgot to use sign language. . . . Desired a glass of beer." The little misdoings ran on. It seemed the harder she tried, the easier it was to fail.

Her humiliations were severe for any offense Mother Superior said "tested the patience of the order." Once Josefine was late for chapel, and it meant that she had to lie stretched out at the foot of the altar before everyone, and remain there, prostrate, throughout Mass. Another time she had to bend and kiss the bare feet of each of the old nuns for burning a sister's coif while ironing.

On still another occasion she failed to blow out the candles in her stall when the nine o'clock lights-out bell sounded. The next day she was forced to go to the dining hall, carrying an empty cup, there to beg on her knees from nun to nun for a spoonful of soup from each. In most instances the women had already sipped some of the nourishment from their bowls. It was so nauseating to her, she nearly threw up.

As with all postulants and novices, Josefine was not allowed to leave the Mother House throughout the four years of her training, nor could she make contact with her family or friends. Yet, in spite of all the privations and pressures, there were many more happy moments for her than bad during the grueling fifty months leading to her perpetual vows. She loved daily meditation, the hours of silent prayer, the choir singing, and especially Holy Mass.

Her spirits were generally high. "All for Jesus!" she told herself again and again. Thus, with God always on her mind, her devotion and dedication to her faith grew with each passing month.

By the age of nineteen Josefine had been molded into the Mother

Superior's idea of a holy nun. She had been taught everything a nurse must know, retaught as well everything she had learned at home—to cook, serve table, wash, iron, mend clothes, and to perform with grace whatever additional domestic chores a servant might be called upon to do.

"It was so much easier now for me to understand Mother Superior," she said. "During my early days in the convent, I felt all the pressures and thought she was so lacking in understanding and compassion. But by the time I took my final vows, I could easily see the wisdom of her words and actions. Her insistence on what was right, her firmness and determination that each of us acquire a full measure of patience and endurance—for those reasons and more, I wanted to become so much like her. I also hoped that I could show the same example to others that she had shown me."

Josefine remained serene when she took her final, lifelong vows of poverty, chastity, and obedience and donned the full black robes of a professed nun, a shiny new crucifix hanging over her chest. Certainly she felt the stab in her heart—the terrible black cloud that hung over her during the ceremony—caused by the rift that persisted between those she loved most, her parents and brothers and sisters, none of whom was present.

Otherwise she had never been at such peace within herself, or with the world. "It is impossible to describe the serenity and courage one receives when in constant communion with Almighty God. I was taught the ways to make Jesus my constant companion. With the taking of my vows, I gave myself to Jesus for all eternity, and he was my Lord and Savior for all time as well."

Her garb was symbolic of the yoke of Christ: a bulky black woolen robe, made of the two wide panels that draped from her shoulders to her feet and trailed whatever surface she walked. A cape with folds, made of the same material, fell to her waist, and she was held at her middle with a wide leather belt looped through a large metal buckle. An impressive, firmly starched black headpiece, with heavy white inner lining, covered her head and scooped wide about her face, shutting off her sideways view, its drape falling to her shoulders. Across her forehead and eyebrows she wore a stiff coif that gripped the sides of her face. Her wide white guimpe, as heavily starched as the coif, encircled her neck and tucked at the shoulders. For the first few days Josefine felt strangely bound and uneasy. Her head, held stately high by such a stiff saddle, showed a certain dignity, as she was forced to turn it from side to side simply to see. With her beautiful black scapular and shiny new Cross of Christ strung over her breast, the proud young nun looked quite elegant in her full habit.

During the ceremony she assumed the name of Pascalina, taken from Paschal, synonymous with Easter, the Christian feast that celebrates the Resurrection of Christ and symbolizes a new life. Within days she was assigned to the Stella Maris retreat house at Rorschach in the Swiss Alps, where the Roman Catholic clergy came to recuperate from bouts of ill health.

Her life seemed to speed by during the next four years, her time constantly filled by nursing priest after priest back to health. Up every morning at five o'clock, weekends included, she was forever seen racing about the retreat house, taking temperatures and pulse-rate readings, carrying meals on trays and emptying bedpans. As if she hadn't enough to keep her busy, many of the old clerics made her sit by their beds and read to them or, worse still in her view, do their letter writing.

There never seemed to be a moment for herself between when she arose and when she finally fell limp into bed long after midnight. At times she was so exhausted, she felt unable to wash her own face, so tired that she could not go to sleep.

Into this Swiss retreat house there came one day in 1917, when Pascalina was not yet twenty-three, a prelate in seriously ailing health, a cold and rather uncommunicative Italian named Eugenio Pacelli, a mystic with piercing black eyes and emaciated yet arresting features. All the nuns held Pacelli in great awe, as he was a great power within the Vatican's highest inner circle and a close friend to the Pope himself. This clergyman was so well respected in Rome that, at forty-one, he was already an archbishop, and though not yet secretary of state, he was the official in charge of the Vatican's foreign office.

Although young, Pascalina was the best qualified and the most confident of the nuns at the abbey to care for this particular patient. She saw at once that this new charge of hers, this famous Vatican diplomat, was broken in health and spirit. He had been in the thick of international negotiations since the eruption of World War I three years before, and the constant day-by-day political pressures had been too much for his frail body and intense mind.

Pope Benedict XV had handpicked Pacelli for the trying job for a number of political reasons. The prelate came from a long line of Church aristocracy, his ancestors stretching back to the early nineteenth century as members of the Black Nobility, who owed their fealty to the papacy.* A prominent member of the Black Nobility was his grandfather, Marcantonio Pacelli, who had been Vatican under secretary of interior and founder of *L'Osservatore Romano*, the official Vatican newspaper, of which he had remained editor until his death in 1902. Eugenio Pacelli's father, Filippo Pacelli, was equally active in high papal affairs and eventually was named dean of Vatican lawyers. His mother, Virginia Graziosi Pacelli, was marchioness of the papacy's old aristocracy.

To his credit, Pacelli fully merited his family's heritage of brilliance and dignity, traits that enabled him to move with ease into the papal inner circle. Almost overnight, while still in his thirties, he had become the Pope's choice emissary to the Court of St. James's, where even Britain's royalty paid him honor for his grace and manner.

To the young Pascalina, Pacelli was nothing like the usual easygoing Italian priests who arrived in the Swiss Alps in anticipation of good food, amusing table talk, and gleeful tidbits of gossip.

Like her, his manner was mostly serious and his graces impeccable. And though she was slightly more than half his age, she shared Pacelli's perfectionist nature and devotion to hard work.

Though he was coldly aloof toward her at first, she set out to break down what she perceived was a deliberate facade. Pacelli was occasionally contrary and short of patience, but this she attributed to his having worked so hard for many years. His main endeavor had been the writing of a peace plan with Pope Benedict XV, and he had worn himself out trying to sell it to "selfish and impossible" leaders of the Allied nations and the opposing Central Powers.† Then, at the very point in time when all his great efforts seemed ready to fall apart, his

---

*When the Papal States were seized by the Italian government in 1870 and the Pope shut himself away in the Vatican for the next fifty-nine years, members of Italy's rich aristocracy who had received titles from the Holy See kept their own doors closed in mourning for the Holy Father. As a consequence they became known as the "Black Nobility."

†The peace plan Eugenio Pacelli proposed was to foreshadow President Woodrow Wilson's Fourteen Points, which were accepted as the basis of peace by all of the belligerents at war's end. The Wilson pact became the cornerstone of the League of Nations, but more than one million casualties were to occur between the time the papal peace plan was proposed and the one written by Wilson was finally accepted.

father, whom Pacelli adored, had died suddenly while the prelate was off in Munich on diplomatic assignment. It was too heavy a blow.

Now, Pascalina, with her German will and motherly resolve, had every intention of bringing health and spirit back to this great man. From the moment of his arrival at the Stella Maris retreat house, she was almost constantly at his side with medicine and food, and would not budge until he had completely downed everything. She insisted that he go to bed on time, and she tired herself out with all his washing and ironing, seeing that his clothes were always hung up neatly and doing all the cleaning up after him. Even while Pacelli slept, the nun was there, checking in on him at all hours, making sure that he was in complete comfort and never in need. Though she had other ailing clergy to care for, Pascalina always made Pacelli feel that he was her only patient.

Within two months her caring and dedication yielded wonders. Pacelli was fully recovered; his thin frame had filled out, and he was healthier in body and spirit than ever before. For the first time she saw a smile on his stone-like face, and heard him laugh.

Pascalina knew Pacelli all too well by then. Her great fear was that he might take his newfound health too much for granted. Knowing that he had suffered from tuberculosis several times throughout his youth and had nearly died during severe attacks, she was set to reprimand him the moment he broke any of her rules.

Her first outburst came a few days before his planned departure from the retreat house. To her astonishment she suddenly came upon him standing alone by the stove in the kitchen, making himself a cup of cappuccino.

"Your Excellency!" she said in amazement, her eyes flashing. "You are hardly back on your feet and already you are up to your old habit!" Her short frame was trembling with anger as she reached for his mug of coffee and dumped the contents into the sink.

Pacelli flushed with shock and anger, for no one had ever so challenged him, Church power that he was. But she wagged her finger at his naughtiness and smiled, hoping to break the tension. Pacelli cooled quickly, and his face lit up in a broad smile. They both laughed heartily, and that was the end of Pacelli's coffee habit for a long time.

By week's end he was gone, departing with all his belongings early one morning without as much as a thank you or good-bye to her, or to any of the other nuns except to the Mother Superior and the Prioress. Pacelli had been educated in the caste system by the Vatican, expecting everyone of humble station, especially lowly nuns, to bow and scrape to the noble hierarchy and be ever grateful to God for the opportunity. Despite her training in humility and obedience, Pascalina was deeply resentful.

Yet, Pacelli wasn't the ungrateful snob he had suddenly appeared. Were she to know at the time how struck he had been by her, struck by her warm care and consideration and untiring help, struck too by her beauty and manner, she would have been shocked beyond belief.

Pascalina was passing the Prioress's office just three months later when she heard his unmistakable voice. She could not see him and took care that she herself remained unseen.

"Have you a sister who is capable of keeping house for me at the nuncio's office in Munich?" she heard Pacelli ask the Prioress.

"I could give you Sister Pascalina," came the reply. "She has been trained as a nurse and teacher and is very competent. Perhaps you would give her a trial, Your Excellency?"

"If you so recommend the good sister, I shall be delighted," the prelate replied.

Pacelli and the Prioress spoke of Pascalina as if he had never heard of her, yet the prelate and the old nun understood each other perfectly. Both were playing the little game of those well trained in the ways of the Vatican. It appeared that a message had come from the Pope to the retreat house earlier that week, authorizing Pascalina's transfer to Pacelli's residence in Munich, where she would work and reside as mistress of his household. It dawned on her later that Pacelli had used his close friendship with Benedict XV and his own important role as head of the Vatican foreign office to gain for her this special privilege.

Later, after Pacelli's departure, Pascalina was called to the Prioress's office for word of her transfer. The young nun showed no emotion as she nodded her willingness to join Pacelli. Her convent training in the use of few words placed her in good stead. The transfer had been arranged, she was overjoyed, and that was all that counted.

By nightfall Pascalina was packed and on her way, happier than at any previous time in her life.

Munich, the Bavarian capital Pascalina so loved, a city of priceless masterpieces and more museums than any place else in the world, was a city under siege by the devastating effects of war when she arrived at Pacelli's nunciature in December 1917. The tides of battle had already turned against the Central Powers, and Munich, once Europe's liveliest cultural center next to Paris, was in deep mourning for its countless thousands of young military who would never return from the battlefields. With Bavarian currency almost valueless, poverty and starvation were already at hand.

Until her arrival in Munich the war had seemed strangely remote to Pascalina, hidden away as she had been in the retreat house. As mistress of Pacelli's residence, she tried to shut her mind from the horror of battle, believing her first responsibility was to take firm charge of his household. Hard convent training and her own strong will gave her all the strength she needed for the job and courage to face whatever the war could send her way.

The residence was a dignified three-story brick embassy, with seventeen high-ceilinged rooms tastefully decorated, but, to her critical eye, in need of more dusting and polishing and picking up. It was no simple matter for a girl, still twenty-three, to take command of a house full of seasoned domestics, none of whom was anxious to overwork himself. Most were as strong-willed as she, and all were considerably older and set in their ways of doing things.

Pacelli, like so many pampered prelates, had increased the staff far beyond what Pascalina considered necessary. He had surrounded himself with an aide, a valet, a cook, a butler, a chauffeur, and two elderly nuns to do the cleaning. Especially when Pacelli was off traveling, there was so little to do that Pascalina couldn't understand why he needed anyone besides herself.

Until her arrival there had been too much time for idleness and quarreling, in her view, and she was determined, as mistress of the household, to set everybody straight, including even those known to be close to Pacelli.

Nobody paid much attention. In everyone's eyes Pascalina was too young and new to take seriously. All of them, including the old nuns, simply continued on as they always had, doing as they pleased, ignoring her and haughtily defying whatever rule she set down. As for herself, Pascalina felt cold resentment rising inside her against what she considered "their shameful, callous manner," but she never showed anger, patiently biding her time for the right moment.

With the war causing increasing devastation, she realized that Pacelli had too much on his mind, juggling peace plans between the warring nations, to be burdened with problems of a household under the increasing threat of rebellion. Having tried to ignore her, the staff now took a different stand. Pacelli had just returned from a trip to Berlin when he was surrounded by the entire household staff.

"Your Excellency, she leaves or we leave!" one of the old nuns said, her voice trembling with emotion as she spoke for all of them.

The prelate was too preoccupied to prolong such trouble. "I will talk with Sister Pascalina and all will be well," he promised, trying to placate everyone. He blessed each with the sign of the cross. "Go in peace to your posts," he said, implying a promise that everything would be set straight if they returned to their work.

But Pascalina, having overheard the conversation, had no intention of making peace with the strikers, even though they had done what Pacelli asked and were back on the job. The staff had taken things to the extreme, in her judgment, and now she was going to show everybody who was mistress of the household. Facing the prelate afterward, she told him that she herself would leave the residence for good rather than allow them to continue lying down on the job.

"Your Excellency, I was trained to be efficient," she began, her distress quite obvious. "Either I must live up to my training to do things right, or else I must return to the Mother House."

He was shocked and hurt, and she appreciated his dilemma, so she offered a compromise.

"I beg Your Excellency to let me do all their work. Let them sit idly by until they are shamed enough," Pascalina said.

Pacelli shook his head, a determined no; but finally, unable to listen longer to her pleadings, he reluctantly gave in.

For the next several weeks Pascalina made a slave of herself, cooking all the meals, washing glassware and hundreds of dishes, scrubbing floors throughout the nunciature on her hands and knees, polishing the furniture, using the scrubbing board to hand-wash his personal linen, cleaning and ironing scores of his vestments, surplices, all of his holy garb that filled closet after closet. She worked around the clock, almost to the point of exhaustion, turning the entire household inside out, transforming it throughout into the gracious mansion it was intended to be.

Pacelli had been away most of the time, getting permission from the Pope and the Vatican hierarchy to negotiate with the battling nations for an exchange of prisoners of war. He had succeeded— nearly 65,000 prisoners on both sides of the war, many of them seriously wounded and near death, would return to their homes; but he had also worn himself out in the marathon round-the-clock effort.

When he returned to the Munich nunciature, he was stunned by its transformation; everything was spotless and in proper place. Pacelli's aristocratic breeding called for his surroundings to be immaculate and in perfect order—something Pascalina knew from the start—and now they were so.

He never thanked her, never even acknowledged his awareness that she alone was responsible for everything. But his coldness toward the staff, freezing them out completely even after they returned to work and outdid themselves with renewed effort, told her all she had to know. She was doubly certain of his feeling toward her when he nodded and smiled knowingly at her as they passed on the staircase, a signal of how pleased he was. Coming from a man of the hierarchy, a man of few words, his silent message was enough to make all she had done for him so worthwhile. No question now remained as to who was mistress of Pacelli's household.

By the summer of 1918 the war had become all the more terrible to Pascalina, mostly because of what it was doing to Pacelli, sapping his mental health and robbing strength from his frail body. He was again as emaciated as when she had first laid eyes on him at the retreat house. More on edge than ever, he snapped at everyone at the least provocation. He was having nightmares, often raving on for long periods, calling out in a loud voice his pain over the inhumanities of warfare.

Once, while passing his private quarters, she could no longer bear hearing him scream and came hurrying in, shaking him from a terrible dream. He was shocked by her presence, and embarrassed. Though he appeared relieved to have been awakened, he said nothing to her and made no attempt to show gratitude, but indicated by his irritated manner that he wanted her to leave at once. Without either of them exchanging a word, she backed out immediately.

Things on the home front seemed to go from bad to worse in the months ahead. Despite a collapsing economy, Germany continued fighting a desperate battle against overwhelming odds. The Allies, looking for a quick end to the war, imposed a merciless blockade of food and medical supplies. Starvation and death were at every doorstep in Munich, and those still remaining alive were drained of hope and strength.

Pacelli was off for days at a time, pleading with the Vatican, the Red Cross, and the neutral Swiss to hurry up with relief campaigns of food and medical supplies. He attacked the Allied blockade as genocide, claiming that the civilian populations of Bavaria and Germany were being wiped out; that thousands of women and children and old men were dropping in the streets by the week, dying of mass starvation.

Pascalina throughout was Pacelli's only real support in his seemingly hopeless campaign. While the prelate argued with the authorities in Rome and Geneva, the nun was on her own, feeding and caring for the wretched who came begging at the rear of the nunciature. She handed out parcel after parcel of food and other scarce supplies, even as her arms ached with pain and her back seemed to break from exhaustion. But she kept a smile on, trying to inspire hope and courage to each among the endless stream of people who came to her, drained of confidence and their belief in God.

"Jesus will not let you down!" she insisted, pleading that they pray to God for intercession.

But despite her deep concern for the starving, it was Pacelli for whom she feared the most. He looked worse than ever. She finally had to insist that he take a few days off for complete rest, but the prelate wouldn't think of it, complaining that she was trying to mother him to death. She kept up her drumbeat, in spite of all that he said, until he grudgingly gave in when there seemed no other way out.

She ordered Pacelli to bed for three days and fed him only the most nutritious dishes, which she herself cooked. Knowing what a finicky eater he was, she sat alongside until he finished the last morsel. Pacelli complained constantly, but she knew that within that obstinate mind of his, he appreciated all she was doing to keep him alive.

Germany's Kaiser Wilhelm II fled to safety in Holland during the fall of 1918, and at last the guns of war fell silent on November 11. But the worst was still ahead for Germany, particularly Munich, where Pascalina and Pacelli continued to live. Millions of German soldiers, still with rifles and ammunition, slogged their way back home through heavy rains, their spirit embittered by the Kaiser's betrayal and their own defeat in the field. As the cold deepened, privation and misery intensified, heightened by the chaotic economy and the Allies' refusal to relax the blockade on the starving nation. The bitter, hopeless setting was perfect for revolution.

Pascalina, taking a cue from Pacelli, had become an avid reader of the press soon after joining the Munich nunciature, and, like all frightened Bavarians, she kept an anxious eye on a phenomenon known as the Free Corps, bands of idealistic young activists bent upon taking power in the wake of Germany's abdicated authority. For the most part they were from the once well-to-do middle class. They had come together as part of the prewar movement of 1914 and now were heard in Munich and throughout Bavaria. They despised the liberal bourgeois society from which they sprang, and their goal was to establish a youth culture for fighting the bourgeois trinity of school, home, and church.

The war had bound them even closer; four years of killing and seeing their own killed on battlefields and in trenches had forged a ruthless brotherhood of hatred and violence. They had come home from the front lines to chaos and hunger and no jobs, and were agonizing in the shame of Germany's total defeat. Yet these Germans were stauncher than ever in the righteousness of their own beliefs. The Free Corps were aching for action.

To add to their frustrations, a Berlin journalist named Kurt Eisner, a revolutionary and self-styled liberator, came to power after toppling the seven-hundred-year-old Wittelsbach dynasty. Though Eisner formed the first parliamentarian republic in Bavaria's history, he was a bitter disappointment to the growing numbers of young anti-Semitic militants within the Free Corps. In their view Eisner, who took over on November 8, 1918, three days before the armistice, was not a socialist, as he professed, but an ambitious Jew offering a radical form of democracy that did nothing to feed their own ambitions.

In less than four months after gaining office, Eisner's revolutionary regime was voted out and he himself was assassinated, on February 21, 1919.

The Bolsheviks, in the meanwhile, having overthrown czarist Russia, were exploiting Europe's misery in their drive to communize everyone. By late February 1919, Munich was a sea of death as communist mobs, with Red flags flying, stormed the city. After six weeks of heavy street fighting the Reds seized control and the new Communist Soviet Republic of Bavaria was proclaimed.

Munich's diplomats promptly fled their posts, most to Berlin's comparative safety, others back to their native countries. All except Pacelli, who was in no mood to budge. The prelate ordered his household to leave, but Pascalina refused, along with Pacelli's secretary, valet, and chauffeur.*

Despite communist threats upon his life, despite Pascalina's pleadings for his safety, Pacelli continued his errands of mercy to the desperate and the despondent. He went throughout the city, often on foot, a pectoral cross upon his cloak, overseeing the distribution of relief packages. The Reds feared Pacelli's presence, a symbol to them of defiant opposition to atheistic communism. They were especially concerned about the hold he was taking upon the increasingly grateful Munich population. To counter Pacelli's work, the Bolsheviks instigated a campaign of hate against him in April 1919, to such an extent that a mob of armed terrorists was ordered to seize his nunciature.

Pascalina was alone on the ground floor of the holy residence when the mob, yelling for blood, stormed the building with guns blazing. Windows shattered throughout the nunciature with the hail of bullet fire. The nun instinctively took cover. But when Pacelli came rushing down the staircase to face the violent mob, now beating at the doorway and jumping through the windows, she raced to his side. Despite the butcher knives and Luger automatics leveled at them, the prelate and the nun held their ground.

"You must leave here at once!" Pacelli ordered in a calm voice. He was standing tall and defiant, his thin figure in black, a violet sash about his waist and a Cross of Christ dangling from his neck. "This house does not belong to the Bavarian government, but to the Holy See. It is inviolable under international law."

The unruly mob roared in bitter mock laughter. "What do we care for the Holy See?" their leader shouted. "We'll leave when you show us your secret store of money and food."

"I have neither money nor food," Pacelli replied. "For, as you know, I have given all I had to the poor of the city."

"That's a lie!" the communist shouted.

"It is true!" Pascalina replied defiantly.

The leader glared at the nun, then hurled his heavy automatic at

---

*The Reverend Robert Leiber, S.J., a German Jesuit, historian, and professor, remained Pacelli's secretary and, later, an assistant speech writer until Pius's death in 1958.

Pacelli, striking the prelate on the chest, denting his pectoral cross. Pacelli instinctively placed a hand upon his breast, his eyes showing pity and sorrow. But his stand remained defiant.

Shocked and outraged, Pascalina shouted, "Get out!" Her contempt was obvious, yet she was in full control. "Get out at once! All of you!"

There was embarrassing silence. Then, after a long, uncertain moment, the leader, with a strange look of shame and bitterness, called to his mob, "Let's go!" The band of terrorists turned and began shuffling out the door. When they were gone, Pascalina felt Pacelli's arm about her shoulder for the first time.

The ruling Bolshevik government, known as the Central Soviet of Munich, angered by the show of Pacelli's defiance against the mob, grew increasingly ruthless in its determination to expel the prelate and close down the nunciature. Anti-Church propaganda was intensified, and threats of violence against Pacelli and Pascalina became still more terrifying.

Within days Pacelli and Pascalina were again attacked by a raging mob. They were returning home together in a touring car, after delivering food and vital medical supplies to a center for children dying of starvation, when a crowd gone wild, shouting threats and blasphemies, rushed their car to overturn them.

Pacelli ordered the chauffeur to stop the vehicle and put down the top.

"Nein! Nein!" the horror-stricken driver cried.

"Do as I say!" the prelate insisted. "Put it down!"

Pascalina blessed herself and prayed to Jesus for help. With no show of fear Pacelli came to his feet in the open car, his great purple robe an easy target for the heavily armed mob. He raised the Cross of Christ high above his head for all to see, an inspiring gesture, and bestowed upon the crowd his blessing: "In the name of the Father, and of the Son, and of the Holy Ghost."

The mob was silenced. The prelate began to speak in loud, clear voice. "My mission is peace," he said. "The only weapon we carry is this holy cross. We do no harm to you, but only good things. Why should you harm us?"

He stood above them in silence, looking deeply into the eyes of each who dared to join his glance. The crowd began slowly to make a pathway for their car. The prelate returned to his seat, and they moved on. Pascalina joined him in silent prayer until the mob was lost from view.

Within days after the communist attack on Pacelli and Pascalina, bloody revolution erupted. The Free Corps and their allies ranged wildly through Munich's streets, armed with bayonets, guns, and ammunition brought home from the war, slaughtering everyone thought to be a communist. By May 3 the short-lived Red government had been destroyed, its followers killed, driven out of Bavaria or gone underground, and the streets of Munich secured by the anti-Semitic rebels.

A new socialist-democrat interim government was immediately formed, with the aid of the Free Corps; General Erich Ludendorff, Germany's chief of staff during the war, was named its head. One of Ludendorff's first acts in office was to walk in on Pacelli unannounced and demand the prelate's aid in smoking out all Reds hiding underground. Pacelli refused, despite all the terror the communists had hurled against Pascalina and himself. He told Ludendorff that he believed in strict Church neutrality in political matters.

Ludendorff was furious. "This isn't Christian behavior!" the general retorted. "It's just a dirty trick!"* And he stormed out.

Meanwhile, an ambitious man of vision was waiting in the wings throughout the epidemic of revolution, shrewdly evaluating the purpose and strength of the rising nationalist movement. With the signing of the Treaty of Versailles on June 28, 1919, Germany's humiliation was complete: the Allies had forced Germany to accept sole responsibility for the war; great chunks of territory were wrested from the Reich, its colonies taken away; German naval and military power were reduced to practically nothing.

With Bavaria and all of Germany in disgrace, a defeated people on their knees politically and economically, Adolf Hitler saw the Free Corps and other Bavarians as ready instruments to advance his cause. Even those morally and spiritually opposed to violence and warfare and not involved in any political movement were ripe for slogans that promised national rebirth. Grasping at straws, they would be the easiest of victims, Hitler concluded.

It was there in Munich in 1919, amid the war's resulting impoverishment and unrest, that Hitler's nationalism was born. From then

---

*Ludendorff, who backed Adolf Hitler in the Führer's unsuccessful Munich putsch of November 8, 1923, was later to retract his words when Pacelli intervened in his behalf with an Allied court, saving the general from trial for alleged war crimes.

on Bavaria was destined, in the years ahead, to become a nest and breeding ground for the Führer and his growing legion of malcontents.

And so, in this state of ferment and desperation, nowhere more erosive than in Munich, Hitler came one night to the holy residence of Archbishop Eugenio Pacelli. All others in the household were asleep by then, except Pascalina. The nun proceeded to let Hitler in and escorted him to the sitting room to await the archbishop. She had never seen Hitler before or even heard about him. Neither had Pacelli. The caller bore a letter of introduction from General Ludendorff, extolling him for acts of bravery while serving as a corporal under Ludendorff's command.

Years would pass before Pascalina would begin to understand a certain naiveté of the prelate's character, a peculiar trait she could not combat any more than she could combat the occasional and exasperating shortsightedness of this highly opinionated Church power who sat down with the revolutionary.

Hitler told Pacelli that he was out to check the spread of atheistic communism in Munich and elsewhere. Through the door, which had been left ajar, Pascalina overheard the prelate say, "Munich has been good to me, so has Germany. I pray Almighty God that this land remain a holy land, in the hands of Our Lord, and free of communism."

Pascalina knew that Pacelli lived in fear of atheistic communism because of its professed aim to annihilate Catholicism. For that reason, and despite the Church's historical claim of strict neutrality, the prelate had made his goal the complete destruction of this "insidious new threat to world freedom and brotherly love."

It did not come as a surprise to her, therefore, in light of Pacelli's hatred of the Reds, to see the prelate present Hitler with a large cache of Church money to aid the rising revolutionary and his small, struggling band of anticommunists.

"Go, quell the devil's works," Pacelli told Hitler. "Help spread the love of Almighty God!"

"For the love of Almighty God!" she heard the young man reply.

III

Pascalina was on skis, trembling a little; so was Pacelli as they stood crouched in freezing cold and deep snow at the top of a terrifyingly steep slope of the Swiss Alps.

The year was 1921, the war was long over, and they were not to miss this great new craze of downhill skiing which had hit the snow areas of Europe. With ski poles in hand, she in nun's robes and he in clerical garb, they blessed themselves and whispered a little prayer together—"In the name of the Father, and of the Son, and of the Holy Ghost"—and shoved off with shrieks of fear and delight.

In the past weeks she had put every pressure on him so that they could get away for a month to the Stella Maris retreat house at Rorschach, where they had met four years before. Pascalina and Pacelli had worked themselves relentlessly in the years since, helping the war's starving and broken back to life and hope, and now they, too, needed reviving. They needed time and place for meditation and silent prayer. And, as Pascalina insisted, they needed to get in some skiing.

Others seemed to agree with her idea of putting sparkle into Pacelli's life. A group of skiers broke into spontaneous applause and cheering when the nun and the archbishop came to a breathtaking stop at the foot of the slope, safe at last after the most daring chance either had ever taken. Though Pacelli at first appeared embarrassed and awkward, the unexpected, enthusiastic response was just what his confidence needed, and they both glowed with satisfaction.

She was making the best of their stay in the Alps for Pacelli's sake, believing strongly that it was time for him to think of himself, away from constant work and what she called "the horrible habit of burying himself in dictionaries during the little free time he had for himself," a hobby she would never understand.

Pascalina had spent weeks trying to convince him that they should take skiing lessons, a radical departure from their strictly ascetic lives of total dedication to the Church. He had grave reservations and misgivings at first, conscious, as ever, of his public image. The idea of a priest, let alone an archbishop, being seen vacationing with a nun was even more troubling to him. People love to stir gossip, he kept reminding her, adding that he was not at all convinced of the wisdom of fanning such flames.

Apparently the prelate thought the public would never believe the spirit of their relationship, were it ever to become known openly. Nor would they understand that there was a lifelong need in him for her kind of mothering, just as she had her own need to mother him.

Though the prelate was the most opinionated and obstinate of men, Pascalina usually won out in the end, for it remained in her province, at that point in their lives, that he surrender to her whenever the rules of maternal instinct were at stake. In that sense she could become downright despotic.

"Excellency, it's almost one o'clock in the morning and you'll be up again at five thirty!" she would shout. "Now go to bed at once!" If he failed to leave his desk, she would keep turning the light switch off and on until he retreated.

Pacelli needed Pascalina for comfort, for humor and survival, but also, more and more, he needed her sense of practicality and judgment. With her clear headed intellect, she handled everyone and everything he chose to thrust her way. She arranged his life, his materials and men, with military precision and bore the brunt of all the inevitable criticism. Some believed her strength came of farm breeding, others credited her convent training. But whatever the source of her strength, Pascalina had become Pacelli's ideal chief of staff, never attempting to issue orders of her own, yet always insisting that his interests and demands be served.

Little doubt remained at this point in their lives that Pascalina was having a profound effect on Pacelli, particularly on his behavior as a man and to an increasing degree on his career in the Church. He was coming out of his shell, thanks to the nun, and seemed to be shedding the "mother's boy" image that had been so apparent all his life.

Though Pascalina was the kind of woman who understood and appreciated male force, it was the quality of profound intellectualism that she most admired in a man, a quality that Pacelli had in abundance. She understood his display of rather delicate mannerisms, which some considered effeminate, as his way of expressing holiness. Having grown up in a family of tough farmhands, she could see how some among the clergy and certain of the laity might not take the frail and pious-looking Pacelli for the man she knew he was.

Yet, she still blamed his mother for smothering him too much. "Father Pacelli's mother was too inclined to baby him," Pascalina said many years later. "As a result, he became a deep introvert, and overly concerned with his health. There were times, when we were both young, that I wished I had the courage to tell him, 'Excellency, you're not made of glass, you know! Don't be so worried about your physical being!'"

She also blamed the papacy for his odd ways because it had allowed him to live at home with his mother until he was thirty-eight. Pope Leo XIII was particularly at fault, in her view. The Pope had made the unusual situation possible by yielding to pressure because of Father Pacelli's frail health. It was unheard of for a Catholic cleric to sleep and work in his family's home, and it caused prattling and jealousies among the Vatican clergy. Yet, Pacelli's influential grandfather, Marcantonio Pacelli, founder and editor of *L'Osservatore Romano,* the Vatican's official newspaper, kept insisting to the Pontiff that only the young priest's mother could provide the necessary proper and loving care his grandson's health required. Pope Leo was aware of the editor's pen and power but was more moved by the family's aristocracy and wealth, and he grudgingly granted Father Pacelli the precedent-setting dispensation of living at home with his mother.

"If Father Pacelli had left his home as a young man, instead of remaining with the family to be pampered by his mother, he would have adjusted much more easily to the ways of the world," Pascalina said. Having left home herself at fifteen to join the convent, she always maintained the move had done her "worlds of good."

A noticeable change occurred in Pacelli during their brief vacation together in the Alps and became even more evident to Pascalina after they returned to the nunciature in Munich. She did not have to keep after him nearly so often when it came to trying his hand at sports. Motorcycling was coming alive in postwar Europe, and several factors explained his sudden affinity for "speed bikes," as he called them. He had grown to love the challenge of skiing during the time they had spent in the Alps, and he couldn't get enough of the slopes. To him there was a link between skiing and motorcycling that appealed to his spirit of challenge. His health and state of mind were so dramatically improved by then that he was beginning to look and act like a new man. Pacelli's practical mind also saw advantages in the motorcycle beyond its use for speed and thrills. The military had used the vehicle for many practical purposes during the war, and this appealed to his utilitarian mind. He was already thinking that priests stationed under him could use motorcycles to visit the sick and dying, or for any number of other dispatching purposes.

Perhaps it was that he was well into middle age and wanted one final fling in the hope of recapturing a youth he never had. Or perhaps he was serious about the motorcycle and looked upon it as a faster and cheaper means of getting around. But for whatever reason, Pacelli once again gave in to Pascalina's wishes and ordered a motorcycle that came equipped with a side carriage. She insisted even before it was delivered that it would be his toy. She claimed that he had never gotten over the thrill of skiing with the fast wind at his face and that he was looking to the motorcycle for the same wild challenge.

When Pacelli asked the nun to find someone to teach him to drive, she stunned him by claiming she knew more about motorcycles than any instructor. Her older brother John had taught her to drive a motorcycle when she was only fourteen, she said, and there was hardly anything about the mechanics and operation of these vehicles she did not know.

Even so, it was days before Pacelli found courage to take Pascalina at her word. When he did decide to let her try her hand, it was late one night when the people of Munich were fast asleep. Though there was no one standing around to embarrass him, his heart was thumping and his hands sweating as he cautiously lowered himself into the sidecar. The nun, in flowing robes, was already behind the handlebars and showed all the confidence in the world.

There was a roar of the motor, a sudden jerking backward, then a blast-off. Pascalina, in ecstasy, screamed with delight. "See, I told you so! I know how to drive these things!"

Amid the flow of happy times there were the dark, sad hours when his aged mother, Virginia, died. Long before the old woman's passing in 1921, Pascalina had prepared herself for the severe toll his mother's death would exact from him, even though Pacelli was well into middle life. The news of her death plunged him into deep melancholia. He despaired for days, unable to eat or sleep. The nun exhausted herself nursing him back to health, substituting throughout for the mother he had just lost, and keeping as well to all of her other household chores and responsibilities.

A second tragedy, the death of Pacelli's beloved mentor, Pope Benedict XV, in January 1922, further turned him to Pascalina for comfort and help. Not having fully recovered from the death of his mother, he suffered a relapse. Again he took to his bed for several days, his depression so immobilizing him that it was impossible for the prelate to eat or sleep, or tend to his daily schedule. Fortunately another friend, Achille Cardinal Ratti, formerly the Vatican's librarian, was elected Pope. Ratti's first unofficial act after becoming Pius XI was to send a sympathetic get-well message to the nuncio in Munich.

Pascalina came rushing into Pacelli's chamber, excitedly waving the Pope's letter above her head. It was her way of jarring him out of his dark mood. "Excellency, the Holy Father loves you!" she shouted. "We all do! Now show your love by helping to brighten the world for us. In plain talk, Excellency, get out of bed and be yourself again!"

A decade of growth was at hand for both Pascalina and Pacelli, she would recall almost sixty years later. The 1920s were years when the nun expanded her already major role in converting Pacelli, the once classic stick-in-the-mud, into the most influential religious leader of modern times. It was she, in the dual role of nurse and substitute mother, who helped rid Pacelli of his bouts of melancholia, who encouraged his role in political affairs and high society, who nurtured his very climb to the papacy.

In 1925 the Vatican moved them to Berlin, to a large, palace-like nunciature surrounded by magnificent grounds at the center of the

German capital's official and social life. As mistress of the awesome stately mansion where chiefs of state and the social set presented their calling cards to be wined and dined and to dance into the wee hours, the nun from the farm, at age thirty-one, was in a world of splendor far beyond her imagination.

The Vatican had picked Pacelli, one of its cleverest minds, to win Germany's diplomatic favor. Pacelli, who had done so much to feed the starving Germans after the war, two years later was made the first Apostolic Nuncio to the German Reich, a title that gave the new republic important status in the Catholic world. Germany, essentially a Protestant nation, was expected to reciprocate by granting the Church important concessions. The Holy See sought the right to operate parochial schools without state interference and permission for its clergy to perform their duties with no interference by the German state. It also wanted authority to establish new dioceses and to be able to freely elect bishops. Earlier, Pacelli had concluded a concordat with Bavaria that granted the Church important rights and privileges denied for centuries under the old monarchy. The Vatican's hope at the moment was to have its shining diplomat accomplish as much with the postwar German government.

In the belief that more diplomatic battles are won by impression than by substance, Pacelli himself had picked out the splendid mansion at Rauchstrasse 21 for his center of operations.

Pascalina was soon moving in three worlds within that magical residence. As a nun, there was first her life of silent prayer and meditation. As Pacelli's mistress of the household, she anticipated his needs, relieving him of all routine details. As chief cook, she personally prepared every one of his meals, with never a day off. As housekeeper, she took painstaking care of his clothes, making absolutely certain that his holy vestments were always immaculate. She was almost fanatical in insisting that his detachable sleeve cuffs, which became so easily soiled by ink during his extensive periods of writing, were changed several times a day. His papers were always kept in perfect order by her, and never did he have to complain that she had allowed any one of his many fountain pens to run dry.

Pascalina was so meticulous in her care of Pacelli that others in the household were known to whisper that she was treating him more like a god than a priest. She'd rush in after every audience he held to disinfect his much-kissed hand and bishop's ring. It didn't bother

her that he took her devotion so much for granted. Nor was she troubled that he was totally unaware of her presence much of the time. Indeed, she prided herself that she could enter and leave his office so quietly and swiftly he wouldn't be distracted for an instant from his pressing work.

"We had grown so accustomed to each other's habits and thinking," she said, "that during work hours few words had to be exchanged between us. We shared that kind of silent communication."

Pacelli's stream of open-house parties added a new dimension, a mesmerizing pleasure cycle that kept her hopping and breathless until the small hours and almost until it was time for her to start the dizzying pace all over again.

Pacelli's parties were auspicious, tastefully sprinkling glitter with the strictest of European etiquette, delighting the whims of diplomatic snobbishness. The nunciature was soon a major center of Germany's social and official worlds. Streams of aristocrats including President Paul von Hindenburg, Germany's field marshal during World War I, were frequent callers, blending with students and workers, anyone whom Pacelli, the shrewdest of diplomats, chose to smile upon.

Pascalina was Pacelli's ideal steward, standing watch like a mother hen over everything, making every use of her exacting convent training, personally overseeing every meal, making certain that each serving was a gourmet's delight. The nun was so precise and insistent upon perfection, it became almost impossible to hold on to a staff. No matter how great the number of guests, she saw that dinner started exactly on time and finished by ten for the start of dancing on schedule. As if she hadn't enough responsibilities, Pascalina took it upon herself to direct the selection of all musicians, insisting that only Germany's best string players be permitted to perform at Pacelli's affairs.

As to her own propriety, Pascalina was always garbed in the full robes of a nun, keeping rigidly to the role of a well-trained servant, darting among the mingling guests to make certain everything was moving along just right, then retiring from sight immediately after her official duties were successfully concluded.

The hardest part of all her responsibilities, Pascalina recalled many years later, was handling Pacelli himself, whom she found to be such a contradictory, dualistic man. When guests were around, he was filled with life and humor; the diplomat in him always served Vatican interests to the tee. But when everyone was gone, except herself and the staff, when he no longer had to guard his image, Pacelli often receded into a cold, hard shell, saying little or nothing to anyone. He gave the unmistakable impression of wanting to be left strictly alone and not to be bothered by anyone or anything. It was Pascalina's responsibility, her most trying, she often claimed, to make certain that he had his cherished privacy and was not vexed in any way.

"Archbishop Pacelli had the mind of a mystic, who drew strength from prayer and meditation," she explained. "It was essential for him to have a certain amount of solitude each day. He was happiest when in solitary communion with Jesus. If he had his way, he would have withdrawn into a world of asceticism, largely away from people."

Pacelli retreated into his inner self so frequently that Pascalina insisted he make his private quarters on the third floor, far removed from the household staff and the small council of priests living and working in the nunciature. He was so sensitive to noise that she asked everyone, priests included, to keep their voices down and wear felt slippers around the house. The nun was tactful in giving orders, but anyone forgetting, or taking advantage, was struck by her awful silence and a coldness that made them think twice the next time.

Life had become so hectic, her responsibilities wearing her to the point of sheer exhaustion, that she had to have two more nuns from her own order brought in to help out. The nuns from the Sisters of the Holy Cross were given all the menial work that she had been exhausting herself with all those years, cooking and cleaning and dusting, doing the washing by hand and scrubbing floors.

She alone continued to care for Pacelli's personal affairs. Stickler that she was for his wants and needs, she at last had all the time she desired to devote to the preparation of his meals, hoping to stimulate his birdlike appetite for his health's sake. She made a full-time job of the work and care she put into his private quarters.

Pascalina had been at his side now for eight years and knew with increasing certainty how to keep his moods in balance and Pacelli himself content. There was always some surprise, a little treat from her to him, to bring up Pacelli's fluctuating spirits; often it was a tray with some of his favorite fruit, a cookie, and a glass of milk. Simple things, because they both loved simple things.

Pascalina's ascetic life extended to her plain but immaculately kept room on the second floor with its small adjoining bath, both overlooking the rear of the courtyard. The simplicity suited her perfectly. There was a small but comfortable bed, an inexpensive bureau for her clothes and linens, a simple table for writing reports and notes, and the rocking chair she loved. Pictures of Jesus and the Blessed Virgin hung above her bed and table, and snapshots of her family stood framed on the bureau. Sworn to a life of poverty, everything the nun owned was there in her room.

When she couldn't sleep, a bad habit from early childhood, she sat in her rocker, sometimes for hours, and knitted socks, or stitched a quilt for his bed to keep him protected from a susceptibility to colds. She would have loved to spend some free time with her family, but all visiting, apart from caring for the sick and dying, was strictly forbidden by her religious order. Then, too, her father was exceptionally strict and possessive with all of his children, making it abundantly clear to them that if they were to leave his shelter at an early age, they would be on their own forever. It would not be until she was well ensconced in the Papal Palace, years later, that Pascalina would finally be reunited with her parents.

Like Pacelli, she was a very private person in many ways, although he carried it to the extreme at times. He was noticeably uncomfortable with anyone in his quarters except Pascalina, and, like her, he wanted everything about him kept immaculate and untouched. Both shared certain other fanaticisms, particularly for frugality. Everyone in the house, from priests to nuns to servants, learned quickly enough that no light was to be left on when not in use.

Though they kept to the ascetic life in their private world, she could see major changes in the way Pacelli projected himself in public. He was being heralded everywhere with much enthusiasm and was called one of the most influential members of Europe's diplomatic corps. Even Dorothy Thompson referred to him as "the best informed diplomat in Germany" in her widely syndicated column. Though he would never admit it, Pascalina knew Pacelli loved it all.

Pascalina, by contrast, lived for their quiet moments together. Pacelli understood this need in her and made it a rule to call her to his study on nights when the residence was silent of parties, first to say the rosary with him, then for discussion. Usually their talks followed dinner, when they found it delightful to sit alone, he by the fireplace if it was cold, both praying and speaking in German, his favorite language. The discussions were usually serious, mostly Church matters close to their hearts. On occasion he would divulge little secrets that she was inclined to believe he would later regret, not because he mistrusted her, but because it was his nature to shrink entirely from the world when it came to private thoughts. To him, confidential matters belonged strictly locked within one's mind and soul.

On one such occasion, Pacelli staggered Pascalina when for the first time he broke his own code of silence on a subject of utter secrecy.

Speaking in the strictest confidence, Pacelli revealed to her that the Vatican was in dire financial trouble and was facing bankruptcy.

For generations the Holy Roman Catholic Church had been at the "most awful mercy," in his view, of certain anti-Catholic factions within states and territories that now constituted the nation of Italy. "These enemies of Almighty God were inspired by the devil and took to warring against Mother Church, depleting much of the strength and reserve which dear Jesus had placed in the hands of each Holy Father."

The five Holy Fathers, who lived through all "the pain and suffering, had decided in their great wisdom to retreat from the evil of war" and close themselves in exile within the Vatican, a state of affairs that had existed since 1870 and would continue to exist until the "once good Catholic people of Italy and their sadly misguided leaders came to their senses and returned to the Church."

In the meanwhile "this terrible man, Benito Mussolini," Italy's new dictator, who had been "born a good Catholic," had turned away from the Church to become an atheist. He and the "fascist sinners who followed him" had been attacking Mother Church over the years, saying "all sorts of lies and accusing the good cardinals and bishops and priests of every sort of sin." All this hate and violence had been going on for so many generations, striking away at "the dear Holy Father and the poor hierarchy," that little remained of the Vatican's temporal strength. Its treasury, as a result, was nearly empty.

Pascalina could scarcely believe what she was hearing and would have cast everything aside as being utterly ridiculous were it not being said by Pacelli himself. It seemed unthinkable to her that the most powerful religion in the world, with nearly two thousand years of history and more than three hundred million followers, could be in such dire trouble. She did not realize at the time that the Vatican was using every means within its power to keep its shocking state of affairs secret from the world. Only a few of the Pope's most trusted aides, Pacelli among them, had any knowledge whatsoever that the Church of Rome was crumbling.

The Vatican desperately needed tens of millions of dollars to save itself from bankruptcy, and had ordered certain cardinals to put pressure on their banking connections. George Cardinal Mundelein, archbishop of Chicago, had been successful in floating a loan of $1.5 million but had been forced to pledge valuable Church property in his diocese as collateral. Despite all its worldwide influence, the total raised by the Holy See from all other sources had fallen far short of averting potential disaster.

Pacelli, like the Holy See itself, shared prejudiced views of the cause of the Vatican's plight, but history's interpretation was another matter. At the time of Pascalina's arrival in Berlin in 1925, the ancient city of Rome, to which she and Pacelli were tied by their fealty to the Vatican, had been long divided by bitter factions of Church and state. Since 1849 violence against the papacy had erupted almost continuously, instigated in instance after instance by one ruling Italian government after another. Centuries of revolutions, foreign occupations, and bloody wars had repeatedly torn Rome apart and had seriously weakened the Vatican. Then, too, papal corruption had given rise to an antipapal populace, which had long been impoverished and was stirred by emotions of hatred and revenge toward the Vatican, an elitist Church that remained smugly indifferent toward Rome's widespread poverty.

Since September 1870, when King Victor Emmanuel II seized the Papal States, each pontiff (Pius IX, Leo XIII, Pius X, Benedict XV, and Pius XI) had chosen to remain a prisoner within Vatican City. Pius IX had set the example, and neither he as Holy Father nor any of his successors, at any time in more than half a century, had ventured outside the limits of the religious state.

Victor Emmanuel had proposed that the Vatican come under the protective control of his kingdom. But the Pope totally rejected the "scheme," claiming that to do so would be "tantamount to surrendering Vatican sovereignty." The papacy's dramatic stand had been instituted to demonstrate to the world how much the Holy See anguished, with increasing alarm, over each changing Italian government.

By 1925 a new, even more terrible menace was threatening the very foundations of the Church. An absolute dictatorship had gripped all of Italy. Benito Mussolini, a crusading journalist and the nation's dominant fascist leader, was officially declared dictator by King Emmanuel III. The Vatican hierarchy was outraged.

The present pope, Pius XI, despised the forceful new ruler and feared his legions of Black Shirt followers. The papacy's alarm was not unwarranted.

Il Duce, as the dictator's loyalist army preferred to call Mussolini, was anticlerical from an early age. Though born a Catholic, he was forever heaping criticism on the "do-nothing," "subversive" Church. To peasants and beggars he pointed sarcastically at the Vatican's flagrant display of great wealth. To the voters he charged Catholic Action groups with subversive political activities. The clergy, he said, had an illicit stranglehold on the politics of Italy. And to Catholics everywhere his claim was that the Church and the Mafia were bedfellows. He had gone to Sicily as a journalist, Mussolini said, and had seen for himself Catholic priests and monks committing all sorts of crimes. Even as a young revolutionary in 1909, Mussolini had rocked Rome with his scathing novel, *The Cardinal's Mistress,* which depicted immorality among the Vatican hierarchy.

With millions of disillusioned Italian Catholics turned away from the Church and backing the fascist regime to the hilt, the Vatican's plight grew more menacing by the day.

It was at this time, with the Church increasingly humiliated by Mussolini, that Pacelli came to think of himself as a prelate of destiny. He was convinced that he had the intelligence and vision to lift the Vatican above its peril. But it remained for Pascalina, the doer who was afraid of nothing and no one, to embolden his spirit. She urged Pacelli to rise to Il Duce's challenge by seeking the office of Vatican secretary of state, "to save the Church!" she rallied.

Pascalina realized that Pacelli had shortcomings, but they seemed minor to her, mostly emotional quirks. He was too silent and withdrawn, for one thing, when he didn't have an important mission to accomplish; these traits tended to aggravate, she thought. Yet he didn't seem to care. People of little import stood no chance with the churchman, but the high and the mighty, anyone who could well serve him and his Church, were handled by Pacelli with consummate skill and grace. This was the gift that made great diplomats, in her view. He had a great responsibility to the Church in its darkest hour, Pascalina insisted, and she never let up thereafter until one day Pacelli said: "I will become secretary of state."

In the not too distant future the nun, feeling deserted by the rising diplomat, would have grave misgivings about her decision.

Personal glory was not what Pacelli was seeking, for it meant nothing to him, he went to great lengths to explain to her. If he was to gain the high office, second to the Pope, Pacelli would do more than secure the Vatican's coffers. His ultimate goal remained the same: stop atheistic communism, even if it meant trading with another avowed enemy, Mussolini. As a diplomat, he felt the Holy See could somewhat contain the fascists, but the Reds, with their professed intent to destroy Catholicism completely, offered no hope of compromise. Pacelli emphasized Mussolini's staunch anticommunist stand. He reminded Pascalina that one of the dictator's first acts upon coming to power had been to suppress communism throughout Italy. "Fire is best fought by fire!" the prelate told the nun.

The present secretary of state, Pietro Cardinal Gasparri, in his mid-seventies and anxiously praying for retirement, thought of Pacelli as his right arm and favorite heir. Pope Pius XI called Pacelli indispensable. But with the ways of the Vatican being what they were, where nothing was certain but the will of God, Pacelli's ambitions remained far from secure.

It was understandable, in light of such uncertainty, that Pacelli looked to Germany's new leaders, who carried great weight in the Vatican, for lobbying support. Germany loved Pacelli for all he had done to aid its starving people after the war. The feeling was mutual, for he saw in Germans the best in human ingenuity and enterprise. Pacelli's love for Germany's temporal capabilities made him sound to Pascalina more like a business executive or politician than a churchman.

By the spring of 1926, Pascalina was well placed at Pacelli's elbow as mini brain trust in his challenging new role of arbiter between the Vatican and its archenemy, dictator Mussolini. Though her participation remained unofficial and without recognition, this still was an unusual, exciting move upward for Pascalina, since the Church and its clergy have never been inclined to acknowledge need of female mind and authority. The knowledge that she, a simple nun, was worthy of even minor consultation on such an important Church matter suited her sufficiently. "I was thrilled, I felt that honored," she recalled years later.

The papacy and the Italian fascist government had decided by then that it was in their own best interests to call a halt to their widening feud and begin peace talks. Mussolini had been publicly hurling so much anti-Church propaganda, much of it true, that the Pope and the Vatican hierarchy lived in fear that it all would stick. Yet the fascist leader was as much a realist as Pius XI, and now that he had come to power as Italy's first dictator, he saw more to gain for himself and his regime with the Church on his side.

Subtle maneuverings by both sides for a peace treaty had begun in mid-January with Mussolini casting feelers and the Pope taking the bait. The Pontiff forthwith appointed Pacelli's brother Francesco, in the Vatican's view as clever and devoted a lawyer as Eugenio Pacelli was a churchman, to spearhead the responsibility. Francesco was commissioned first to meet with Mussolini, then to head up a team to play the Church's best hand.

Francesco, in selecting his choice players, thought first of his extraordinarily capable brother, Eugenio, who was delighted to serve. Eugenio, in turn, long convinced that Pascalina was his able and most trusted aide, quite naturally looked to the loyal nun as his right arm in this, the very sort of mission Pacelli knew could one day make him secretary of state.

Always out of the limelight, Pascalina sat with Pacelli for hours, day after day, listening to ideas he would try out on her, contributing her own thoughts, passing much information along on long-distance phone to his brother Francesco during those times when Pacelli himself was off on other affairs of the Church.

"It was one of the most exciting times of my life," she said more than half a century later, her eyes glittering, as if it all were yesterday.

The Church's demands upon Mussolini were great. The Vatican wanted no more attacks by the dictator or by anyone in his government. It wanted Catholicism to be recognized as Italy's official religion. It wanted all marriages to be performed by the Church and divorce outlawed. It wanted tax exemptions on all Church property and certain added privileges for its palaces, basilicas, and apostolic institutes. It wanted mandatory religious instruction, taught by Church-appointed teachers, in all of Italy's public schools. Most of all the Vatican wanted to be recognized as a sovereign state, with recognition of the Pope as its sovereign head. And the Vatican wanted money, the equivalent of almost $100 million in American currency, ostensibly as compensation for Church properties seized by the Italian state in 1870. The Church had been extremely careful not to let on to Mussolini, or to any outsider, that its very survival now depended upon the fascist funds.

All Mussolini appeared to want in return for his signature was the Pope's goodwill and to live in peace with the Vatican. The dictator tied his sudden about-face to a philanthropic dream, a plan he had that supposedly would draw millions of travelers to Rome each year by promoting the Eternal City as the center of the Catholic world, a mecca of peace and love and holiness. In Mussolini's view the Vatican and Rome would flourish in untold wealth with such a cooperative arrangement.

Pacelli and others of the hierarchy were not prepared to accept Mussolini's altruism at face value, though the dictator swore he had turned his back on atheism, had returned to God, and wanted to do the right thing.

Pascalina, young as she was, showed more skepticism than anyone. "A man like Mussolini can never be trusted!" she insisted to Pacelli. "Why should an enemy like he has been to the Church give up so much and ask so little in return?"

"Mussolini has begged God's mercy and forgiveness," Pacelli responded. "Jesus has said that none among us must turn a deaf ear to even the most evil of mankind. We shall give Mussolini his chance, but always with our eyes close upon him."

In the final analysis, like men who run government and business, perhaps like people as a whole, the clergymen of the Vatican were prepared to hear only what sounded most appealing to their ears and to themselves. And so the day came when the Church of Rome created a spectacular extravaganza of pomp and circumstance to herald to the world its triumphant victory, its pact with Mussolini and the Italian state. For the first time in history the Holy Roman Catholic Church was now an independent and sovereign state, to be known as the State of Vatican City, with the Pope recognized as its undisputed ruler. Catholicism was now Italy's official religion, and the fascist state would underwrite parochial schools. Italian Jewry loudly protested the deliberate exclusion of funds for Jewish education, one spokesman calling the Church-fascist deal "a moral pogrom." Incredibly, every important demand put by the Church to Mussolini and the fascists apparently had been accepted.

To celebrate the signing, a great ceremony of color and pageantry was held in the Vatican's historic Lateran Palace on February 11, 1929, three years from the start of negotiations. The Lateran Treaty, named for the palace where it was signed, was heralded by the Vatican as the most important event in modern Church history. Cardinal Secretary of State Gasparri, in the Church's most impressive robes, placed hand and seal to the treaty in behalf of His Holiness. Benito Mussolini, heels clicking, bedecked with medals and dressed in the full military style and splendor of his fascist dictatorship, then signed with a flourish and a smile on behalf of the Kingdom of Italy.

The Vatican would now have its own currency, police force, citizenship, a small armed force, and its own flag of yellow and white.

The Pope and the Catholic world were euphoric.

Back in Berlin, Pascalina was too emotionally distraught to be pleased with the outcome. After listening for three years to little else but Vatican negotiations with Mussolini, she had been jaded by the goings on behind the scenes, the wheeling and dealing of religious leaders and politicians, and could not be that jubilant. She had all that time to look into the Vatican's conscience, the most secret of closets, and was turned to tears.

Trained to be humble and obedient, the nun had hesitated for days before finding courage to face Pacelli with her fearful and ugly questions. By then she was certain the Vatican had sold out to Mussolini and the fascists. Considering it a matter of routine, she had read highly confidential notes and papers that he had asked her to file upon his return from Rome. What she saw made her more sad than bitter.

"I want to cry," she told Pacelli when they were alone in his study. He was seated behind his desk, looking startled and curious at the piqued nun, her sincerity and devotion obvious.

Not for an instant did she doubt her belief in God, but she was older now, and tougher, and she wanted tough, honest answers. She also needed her Cross of Christ to clutch and a rosary said to restore her. She desperately hoped he would not see how upset she was as she handed him the incriminating documents that revealed so much.

In its desperation to stave off bankruptcy, the Vatican had surrendered its honor to Mussolini for what amounted to $92.1 million in American currency. The Church had told the world the money was payment for lands seized long ago by the state. In one view the Church's position was true enough, but in taking the money the Vatican had granted Mussolini's fascist government sweeping authority over the Church. The Catholic clergy were now required by law to swear oaths of loyalty to Italy's fascist government. Any priest refusing to obey Mussolini would be fined and imprisoned. Equally mortifying, the Vatican could no longer appoint priests, bishops, and cardinals for service in Italy without Mussolini's approval. And these were but the most venal of many more concessions by the Church to the state.

"Is there some explanation?" Pascalina asked, her hands gripping his desk for control.

Pacelli looked away for the moment, apparently too sad himself to answer. Finally he spoke, not as a priest but as the diplomat he had become.

"Concordats generally result in surrender of certain Church privileges," Pacelli responded. "In return, Holy Mother Church is granted permission to carry out its evangelical missions and to educate the young in Christian principles. For this, no sacrifice is too great. The Holy Father himself has said that he would negotiate with the devil if the good of souls required it."

More muddled than ever before, Pascalina left, retreating behind a cold wall she found building within herself.

It was inevitable that Pascalina, if only by her presence, would eventually pose a threat to Pacelli's career. In their rigid Catholic world, celibacy was a time bomb, ready to explode at the slightest hint of impropriety. Even in Berlin, one of the most sophisticated and cosmopolitan cities of Europe, it was regarded as somewhat daring for a young nun to be mistress of a religious nunciature. But it was quite another matter to challenge the sensitivities of an intransigent Vatican with a nun as beautiful as Pascalina.

They never spoke of their future together, though both must surely have realized that a prelate of Pacelli's capacity and soaring stature would one day be called to Rome. Now, with the way the Vatican was proudly portraying the Lateran Treaty, the accord that the Pacelli brothers had played such a hand in putting together, Pascalina expected word to come any day.

It was nearly ten o'clock one night in 1929, a late hour for a call from the Vatican, when the news came in that the Pope was sending great tidings of joy for Pacelli. Pascalina took the call from Cardinal Secretary of State Gasparri and rushed to the study to have Pacelli pick up.

A strange look of awe and exhilaration came over Pacelli as Gasparri spoke, a look she had never seen before, as if a saint were suddenly told to take seat at the right hand of God.

"I am being transferred to Rome. The Holy Father needs me," Pacelli exclaimed as he hung up. His excitement changed him entirely from the silent, sedate prelate she had known these past twelve years.

She could not tell at the moment how he felt about leaving their way of life in Berlin, a life that both had come to love so greatly. Quite naturally Pascalina expected to be going along as his housekeeper. But he stunned her with his abrupt, "No, not for the present!" He would be living at his family's home in Rome for the time being, he said, and no place could be made for her there. Instead, his sister, Elisabetta, would be taking care of his needs.

Pascalina felt a faint twinge of rage toward the callous attitude he assumed about leaving her behind. Later, when she cooled, she realized this was his way. Most of his life he had been taught to jump whenever the Vatican ordered, taught to follow protocol to the letter, and he did not know how to react differently.

"When will a place be found for me?" she implored. "You need the many things I do for you!"

"I do not know!" he said grimly. "It cannot be now. The Vatican is not Munich, nor Berlin. Say no more!" He was coming to his feet, coldness written all over him. "The entire staff is to remain here!"

There was no need of her arguing more. Nobody, not even she with all her influence, could win out when he was in such a fierce mood.

But Pascalina was in just as angry a state by then, and simply had to have the last word.

"You will need me yet! You will see!" Her words came over her shoulder as she rushed out, visibly crushed.

Pascalina wanted to continue to believe in Pacelli. She tried to convince herself after he left that he would return for her once he was set up in the Vatican and at ease there. Like many brilliant, successful men, he was a child in many ways, always requiring attention and some sort of help that only she had the patience to give. Then, too, he being a sickly person, she was more concerned about his wants and needs than her own desires. She hoped he realized that.

With Pacelli gone, Berlin no longer held anything for Pascalina. The great residence was dead, empty of people and spirit. For someone so active, her engines were running without fuel. She was driving herself mad, the servants too, saying rosary after rosary, trying to make work, washing and cleaning and polishing everything so many times over that they were beginning to wear out.

Pacelli wrote occasionally, but never what she wanted to hear. A place would be made for him to live in the Papal Palace, close to the Pope, he told her. Wonderful for Pacelli, but what about her? No woman had ever shared a prelate's quarters in the Papal Palace as mistress of his household. It was all beginning to sound so hopeless.

Then came a total about-face. In late fall 1929, Pacelli called unexpectedly, saying he was exhausted from all his new responsibilities and wanted to spend some time with her at their old vacation retreat in Switzerland. He was going there to enjoy complete solitude for prayer and meditation, and he hoped that afterward they could ski together for several days. Pascalina was so thrilled, she was at the retreat house before him.

It was almost December, and the Alps, deep in snow, were perfect for skiing. Then, the last straw. They had just arrived on the slopes, as excited together as they had ever been, when someone came rushing up with a message from the Vatican. Pacelli was to return to Rome at once.

She wanted to scream: "No, I don't want you to leave! It's been so long, and now you're here at last. I won't let you go!" But she was a nun and had taken the vow of obedience. Since the order had come from the Pope himself, all she was able to manage was one meekly asked question: "Do you think the Holy Father would let you stay a few days, if you said it would do your health a great deal of good?"

But Pacelli wasn't even listening, for the message said further that he was to be made a cardinal, the greatest of all rewards from the Pope.* The Vatican's treasury had been restored with the $92.1 mil-

---

*Cardinals are nominated only by the Pope and are named at secret consistories of other cardinals to serve as members of the papal senate. Their function is to elect popes and serve as papal counselors in the worldwide operation of the Roman Catholic Church. Their symbol, the red hat, dates back to 1244 or 1245, to the rule of Pope Innocent IV, when the Pontiff granted Church approval for the red hat to be worn officially. Their title of "Eminence" was made official by Urban VIII in 1630.

lion from Mussolini, and a most grateful Pontiff was moved to bless his brilliant, productive disciple with this title and position of great honor. For Pacelli's sake Pascalina could not have been more pleased and thankful to God. As to her own future, she was convinced then, without him needing to say a word, that he had grown worlds above her. Soon he would be so close to the Pope, Pacelli would not have time even to remember her.

Germany was as saddened as Pascalina at the loss of Pacelli. During his final trip to Berlin before becoming a prince of the Church, tens of thousands of Germans, both Protestants and Catholics, turned out for a tremendous ovation and send-off, an emotional outburst of love for Pacelli for all he had done for them since the war.

Pacelli's years of wheeling and dealing in Berlin, his hundreds of open-house parties in the great nunciature, his crisscrossing the nation, making personal appearances and delivering speeches, were paying off on a grand scale for the Church and himself. In a Lutheran-dominated Prussian nation, where anti-Catholicism and atheism were on a rapid rise, it took Pacelli's amazing diplomatic skills to have so successfully maneuvered the "Solemn Agreement," a treaty between the Vatican and the German government that both sides were pleased and comfortable with. This agreement was no Vatican sellout, as with Mussolini and Italy's fascist government. In the Vatican accord with Germany the Church was completely free to establish new dioceses and entirely unhampered in appointing bishops. Although the delicate question of education was left out of the treaty for political reasons, a gentlemen's agreement between Pacelli and his friends running the German government assured the Vatican that its parochial schools would function without interference.

On Pacelli's last night in Berlin before leaving for Rome to receive his red hat and become a member of the Sacred College of Cardinals, General Paul von Hindenburg, Germany's president, toasted the prelate at a state dinner and told the world of Germany's devotion to Pacelli. "I can assure you that we shall not forget you and your work here," the elder statesman promised, a prophecy of both the good and evil effects that Pacelli's German connection would have upon his name in the years ahead.

Pascalina was at one of the front windows of the nunciature that night, trying desperately to hold back the tears as she waved her final good-byes to Pacelli. The prelate was standing tall and proud in an open limousine, the streets of Berlin lined as far as she could see with thousands upon thousands of cheering people, many of whom held flaming torches high above their heads.

She watched until she could no longer see him as he turned from right to left, giving his blessing to the great masses of people, many kneeling in the winter's slush. How different was this scene, she thought, from the one in Munich many years before when the communists had taken to the streets to kill them both.

At Christmas he sent her a photograph of himself in his new robes as prince of the Holy Roman Catholic Church. It was all she saw of the great and colorful Vatican consistory that brought cardinals from throughout the Catholic world to Rome's historic Sistine Chapel to take part on December 19, 1929, in the honoring of Eugenio Pacelli with a red hat. It was obvious from the way the Pope beamed upon Pacelli and the way the press played him up that the nuncio from Berlin was being prepared for more and even greater blessings from Rome.

Less than two months later, on February 10, 1930, Eugenio Cardinal Pacelli was appointed Vatican secretary of state, a post second only to the Pope himself.*

Back in Berlin, alone and apparently deserted, Pascalina remembered how strongly Pacelli had fought against the idea of holding the high Church office when she first suggested it to him, a time that now seemed so long ago.

---

*The cardinal secretary of state is the Pope's prime minister. As head of the secretariat, he is chief of the Curia Romano, or "Curia," as the Vatican bureaucracy is popularly known. The secretariat, with its numbers of dedicated traveling diplomats (all priests of the Church), is similar in makeup and policy to the departments of state and ministry of other governments. It designs and oversees Church diplomacy throughout the world. Constituted largely of well-educated, carefully trained Italians, the bureaucracy handpicks all the prelates (cardinals, archbishops, and bishops) whom it commissions to represent the Holy See as apostolic delegates. Each day, before dealing with other Church matters, the Pope meets with the cardinal secretary of state, or with his deputy when the cardinal is off on assignment.

IV

By the early 1930s, economic and social convulsions were occurring on every continent, turning governments and peoples inside out. The worldwide Depression was paralyzing the United States, Great Britain, Italy, and Germany. At the nadir of crisis, thirteen million were unemployed in the United States, more than one fourth of the nation's total labor force, and in Britain some two million people hopelessly roamed the streets, unable to find work. Italy's fortunes were worse still.

In Germany, a defeated nation seething with resentments and hostility toward the Versailles Treaty with its heavy reparations imposed by the victorious Allies after World War I, the crisis was even more acute. With one third of its workers unemployed, Germany's industries were grinding ever more slowly. The federal treasury was bottoming out, and the government reneged on its war payments to the Allies. With France and England hit by their own economic disasters, they, too, defaulted on their war debts to the United States.

The jolt could not have come at a worse time for the United States, a nation of 122 million recoiling from the recklessness and intemperance of the Flapper era of the 1920s. The stock market crash of October 1929 had sent severe financial shock waves across the country and throughout the world. The press reported a rash of suicides in the United States, but the U.S. Bureau of Census released no official figures. Newspapers in New York and elsewhere carried accounts almost daily of people losing everything in the crash, then committing suicide by jumping out windows or by other bizarre means. Soup kitchens by the thousands were opening, and banks by the hundreds were closing. In Washington and elsewhere hunger marches were stark realities of humanity falling apart.

As conditions everywhere grew increasingly bleak, Agnes Meyer, wife of Eugene Meyer, the head of the U.S. Federal Reserve Board, put into simple perspective man's universal plight in the early 1930s. "The world is literally rocking beneath our feet," she declared.

Eleanor Roosevelt recognized the world crisis as a depression more of mind than of economic disaster. Fear, the future first lady said, "was the worst thing that had happened" and mirrored the mood of the world: ". . . fear of an uncertain future, fear of not being able to meet our problems . . . fear of not being able to cope with life as we live it today."

For its part the Holy See claimed that the universal "sad state of affairs" was indeed *more* ominous than a blind temporal world wanted to see or admit.

"The human spirit throughout the world is in chains," Pacelli told an audience of religious pilgrims visiting the Vatican. "The world is imprisoned financially, politically, and spiritually," he added.

Europe's social and economic upheavals had become fodder for the rising totalitarianisms of Hitler and Mussolini. Nationalism flourished, and anti-Semitism spread as Germany and Italy languished in the watershed years of poverty and the humiliations of World War I. The smoldering fires of a second, greater, war were being cleverly fanned by Hitler.

Within a cheerless, dull-gray nation of self-pity and hatred, Pascalina took to her own brooding. Her emptiness, as she paced the Berlin nunciature while saying her rosary, was of another sort, a melancholia for the absence of Pacelli, not for just the man himself but largely for what he stood against, social attitudes and behavior that imprisoned the human spirit.

She saw Eugenio Cardinal Pacelli, the Vatican secretary of state, as the colossal instrument to address and resolve the world's ills.

"Religion and belief and trust in Jesus are the only means of bringing mankind out of the depths of despair into which so many have fallen," he had so often reminded her and others.

"The love of God is humanly good and humanly necessary," he would add, underscoring rudiments of their faith that they shared and she had come to believe in long before she knew Pacelli. Now, as when she was a child, she adored Jesus; there was no question of that. What remained to be seen was how much of that belief and adoration she felt for Pacelli, the priest she had likened to Jesus in her own mind. Further, she had discovered qualities in Pacelli she had never before known in a man, which stirred her mind and imagination. She boasted about his intellect at every opportunity. She saw him as a prelate of size and dimension, and if some of his traits were exasperating—picayune human faults, such as his abrupt temper— still he had propriety, serenity, and a trust in God that gave him boundless courage. His was a gift that seemed to sweep away all fear, from himself and from those around him.

Perhaps as much as at any time in the history of the Holy See, the Vatican—in Pascalina's opinion—needed a prelate of Pacelli's unique character to protect its integrity. The nun had been enraged upon hearing whispers of what she considered the "loose handling" of the $92.1 million the Church had received from the Lateran Treaty. She had learned that a so-called "man of mystery," an Italian banker by the name of Bernardino Nogara, had been granted sole control by the papacy over the entire fortune.

It mattered little to her that Nogara was considered by experts to be one of Europe's shrewdest financiers. A priest in the Berlin nunciature had told her that the investment banker was manipulating the Church's money as he saw fit, investing the funds in certain ventures that, she claimed, were totally against Catholic teachings and principles.

She had heard that no Vatican official, not even the Pope himself, was allowed veto power over Nogara's decisions. Nor would the banker permit any religious or doctrinal policies of the Church to stand in his way. Her priest friend had told her over coffee of the papacy's intense desire to pyramid the money and keep its treasury from ever sinking again.

Some of Nogara's investments seemed appalling to the nun, specifically, the Vatican's purchase of controlling stock in a drug company, Istituto Farmacologico Serono di Roma, Italy's largest manufacturer of birth control products. Throughout its history the Holy Roman Catholic Church had vehemently denounced artificial birth control as a mortal sin. Now the Vatican, to fatten its coffers, was playing double standard behind the scenes by making money through sin.

It was equally dreadful to her that the Vatican was allowing the Church to be used by Nogara in so many other ways: manipulating the currencies of nations; juggling the value of gold; buying into other immoral corporations—specifically those making war materials and ammunition. Never before in modern Church history had anyone been granted such sweeping authority by the Church, not even popes themselves with all their supposed infallibility, let alone a layman and non-Catholic, as in Nogara's case.

Pascalina knew everything there was to know about Pacelli. She felt sure that the prelate was as opposed as she to Nogara's power, but that he needed her support to speak up. She trusted him as much as she could any man and loved him for what he was. Pacelli loved her in return. On both sides it was a comfortable trust and a good love, as Jesus had taught humans to live, but it was inevitable that their separation would take its toll.

Pacelli had been in her mind and heart and soul for so many years, and now the awful loneliness—the need of him—kept her sleeping fitfully and able only to pick away at her meals.

With little to do after the day's chores were finished, with her state of mind rapidly deteriorating, with her inability to take hold of herself, she was pushed by her own desperation into writing Pacelli.

"I miss you and I truly hope that you need me," she scrawled in desperation. She realized that her letter was terribly daring, especially since he was now the secretary of state. But after four months of not seeing him, she was left with no alternative. She pleaded for a place at Pacelli's side; a room for her in the Vatican could be anywhere, she suggested. "I'll even be content in the basement," Pascalina added. "I don't mind, just so long as I can be at your side and care for you. May I please be of help again with your decisions and ease the burdens?"

Pacelli replied sooner than she expected, but his harsh words weren't what she had prayed to hear. Writing by hand on beautiful parchment stationery richly embossed with his red and gold coat of arms, he turned her down. Pacelli sounded cold and aloof at the start, in every way the cardinal secretary of state the Vatican had just appointed with such pride and flourish. She had expected as much from him, despite her prayers; his outward manner was always more severe than his heart and mind.

What the nun hadn't dared to pray for, Pacelli put in a warm postscript. He missed her, he admitted in his p.s., missed her companionship and needed her brilliance. But being cardinal secretary of state, being in the international limelight with heads of state throughout the world, his very success was their nemesis. Any suggestion of impropriety on his part would scandalize the Church.

To her, Pacelli was sounding like a pope; and for a flash it crossed her mind—as it had occasionally since she had first met the impressive prelate—that perhaps God, or Pacelli, or both, had already decided that one day he would become Holy Father.

Indeed, Cardinal Pacelli was busy building a heaven on earth for the papacy and himself, a world of glamour and excitement quite apart from anything Pascalina or he had ever known. It had been Pacelli's idea that Italy return Castel Gandolfo to the Vatican as part of the Lateran Treaty, and Mussolini agreed to the proposal, as a further demonstration of fascist good faith. Since 1623 the cherished vacation paradise at Rome's outskirts had been the pope's escape from the Eternal City's oppressive summer heat. In 1870 it had been seized, along with other papal territory, by King Victor Emmanuel's government and held in its protective custody since then.

Pacelli was hardly in office and seated at the right hand of the Pope when the Italian government handed over the spectacular expanse to the Vatican. The papal summer compound included a luxurious palace and chapel and a complement of plush villas set on seventy splendorous acres at Castel Gandolfo, a tiny, romantic town atop the famed Alban Hills overlooking beautiful Lake Albano.

Pacelli was elated by the fascist cooperation, but Pius XI remained coldly aloof, thanking neither Mussolini nor the king. Italy should have turned over Castel Gandolfo long before, the Pope maintained. Pacelli took an opposite view. Unlike the Pontiff, the secretary of state was much too opportunistic to dwell on the unfortunate past. Nor did he want to strike sensitive nerves; he charmed Mussolini even as the Pope deliberately froze out the dictator.

With his brilliant successes at the Berlin nunciature still vivid, the new secretary of state saw even greater horizons for the Church and himself at Castel Gandolfo. He looked to the papal summer residence as a place of prayer and play, a mecca for the best of two worlds—the ecclesiastical and the temporal. With the Pope present to grace and bless the evening scene, the influential and wealthy from throughout the world would be there at Pacelli's whim, toasting his diplomatic dreams and filling his temporal needs.

Finally, the Vatican's annexation of the pontifical villa of Castel Gandolfo, as the entire zone became officially known, was formalized by Prime Minister Mussolini. He knelt at the feet of Cardinal Secretary of State Pacelli and kissed the prelate's ring for all the world to see.

Pacelli lost no time in advancing his first major project as secretary of state. He talked the papacy into making sweeping renovations at Castel Gandolfo. The landscaping alone cost millions, but the result was breathtaking. The prelate's dream of a classic sylvan world of cultivated hills and gardens, set with holly oaks, cypresses, laurels, olive trees, and vines, and manicured lawns stretching beyond view, took four years of artistic, painstaking labor. In the end, as observed by the magazine *Architectural Digest,* Castel Gandolfo would become known as "one of the major reconstruction operations of this century."

The golden day of Catholicism was at its dawn. Eugenio Pacelli, a prelate of clever vision and colossal enterprise, was already diligently preparing the Church's destiny; a future of enormous worldwide power and wealth, which one day would stagger the imagination. In less than four decades the Holy See would have assets estimated to be greater than the gold reserves of Great Britain and France. In 1952 *United Nations World Magazine* would report the Vatican's gold alone amounted to several billion dollars and was stored in the U.S. Federal Reserve Bank, as well as in banks in Great Britain and Switzerland. *The Wall Street Journal* would say the Vatican often bought or sold gold in lots of a million dollars or more at a single time. Though the Church maintained strict secrecy in its financial matters, reliable sources would place its assets by 1972 in the United States and Canada alone at $82 billion.

In 1930, Pascalina was so out of touch with Pacelli's life that she had no inkling of the great new threat to her peace of mind and future—one greater than the Vatican, with all its prejudices, and the splendors of Castel Gandolfo. Her rival in far-off Rome for the attentions of the secretary of state was Monsignor Francis J. Spellman, a clever and enterprising priest from the United States, who was mesmerized by Pacelli's soaring star and had grabbed immediate hold upon the prelate.

The first American cleric assigned to the solidly Italian Curia, the Vatican's bureaucracy, Spellman had been in the Eternal City for five years, having arrived in 1925 with three strikes against him. From the first, Spellman saw Rome's native-born clergy as pointedly aloof toward all but their own kind, and especially hostile when any outside priest invaded their special world. Their prejudice went even deeper in Spellman's case, since he had been assigned to the lowly rank of clerk and, literally, playground director. Worst of all, in their eyes, were the American priest's overt wheeling and dealing. That he forever unabashedly practiced it, and with such success, drew their fullest ire.

Spellman could not have cared less, for his years of skillful patronage in behalf of the papacy's high inner circle brought him the prayers and blessings of those who mattered. The "hot shot from Boston" (a term of contempt for the short, roly-poly priest wielded by jealous clerics of the Curia's lower rank) had captured the mind of Pope Pius XI and the heart of Cardinal Secretary of State Pacelli. Spellman was already an old hand at manipulating the papal high command. He had won friends and favor with lavish gifts—such as Pius XI's luxurious custom-built limousine—that Spellman's sharp wit and Kewpie-doll grin had plucked for free from U.S. contacts.

Suggesting to Pacelli that he, too, should ride in splendor, Spellman boasted of the ease and grace with which he had obtained limousines for both the Pope and Pacelli's own predecessor, Cardinal Secretary of State Gasparri.

"I suggested to Mr. Brady to give Cardinal Gasparri a new Chrysler Limousine '82 and he said 'Sure,'" Spellman proudly told Pacelli.* "Both Mr. Brady and the cardinal are delighted."

But Pacelli was not yet that secure in his new post and wanted no part of ruffling the Pope's better nature. Pius XI's many complexities were impossible to fathom. His behavior often turned in a flash from good-natured humor to tyrannical outbursts when the wrong nerve was struck. The possibility of heating up the old man at the sight of his new secretary of state riding about in equal splendor was not Pacelli's way of taking hold.

"Later," Pacelli told Spellman emphatically. Pacelli, at the moment, had other, more important plans for Spellman.

It was well known in those days that no Vatican secretary of state had traveled outside the papacy in more than half a century, yet, for personal reasons, Pacelli had every intention of breaking that long-

*Nicholas Brady was son and heir to Anthony N. Brady, a pioneer in U.S. public utilities. A staunch convert to Catholicism, Nicholas and his wife, Genevieve Garvan Brady, vacationed yearly in Rome and were "dedicating their lives and everything they owned to the service of God."

standing tradition. Summer was at hand, a time when he had vacationed year after year with Pascalina in the Swiss Alps. This year,
with the nun feeling so deserted, Pacelli had no thought of failing a
tradition that had come to mean so much to them both. To keep eyebrows from raising, he would take Spellman along as escort.

"It is a wonderful thing to be the traveling companion of the cardinal secretary of state, the person who most people believe is to be
the next Holy Father," Spellman wrote home as soon as Pacelli gave
him the good word.

Pascalina's reunion with Pacelli was one more of shock for her
than of joy. His red hat and flowing crimson robes made him appear
regal, though stiffer and more unreachable than ever. Worse still, she
was offended by the figure of Spellman, always at Pacelli's side, per-
petually looking up with adoration at the prelate, and forever grin-
ning in his coy manner.

They were reunited in the Swiss Alps at the Stella Maris retreat
house, run by her religious order of the Sisters of the Holy Cross,
where she and Pacelli had met thirteen years before. Perhaps it was
her womanly possessiveness and jealousy; perhaps it was Spellman's
unfortunate appearance and sugary manner that turned off so many
people when they first met him in the years before he grew in stature;
but whatever the reason, Pascalina took an instant dislike toward
him. She had felt the same negative reaction when the American
priest came to Berlin earlier that year, bearing official Vatican papers
confirming Pacelli's nomination as secretary of state. She hadn't
liked Spellman then, and she liked him less now. It would have
seemed inconceivable to her, at the time, that Spellman would one
day befriend her as few others ever would in her lifetime, and that
she and the American priest would share the closest of friendships
thereafter.

Pascalina's unsettling chill when they arrived at the retreat house
left no question in anyone's mind that Spellman was to be sent off at
once and kept away until it was time for Pacelli to be escorted back
over the border to Italy. Spellman himself could not be happier. The
first night at the retreat house he wrote his family a light, sardonic
appraisal of the strange place, suggesting that he was most anxious
to be off elsewhere.

"I am lodged in a Young Ladies' Academy. . . ." Spellman began,
tongue in cheek. "It is a funny place to pick out for a vacation. . . .
[It is like] sleeping in Grand Army Hall in Whitman [his hometown

in Massachusetts]. There are ten or twelve windows [in his bedroom], a blackboard, chairs and tables, the teacher's desk and a bed and a wash stand. Everything is here except a piano."

Early the following day Pascalina pointedly suggested to Pacelli that the priest, who was within hearing distance, be allowed to enjoy the Passion play at Oberammergau. She had loved the play, she said, and asked that Spellman be granted permission to leave immediately for Bavaria to see it. Pacelli grudgingly consented. "He could hardly say no," Spellman noted with delight in a letter home before he spun off on his own. He made no mention to the family that the nun's severe look and pointed words left the secretary of state with no alternative.

Pascalina was nearing her thirty-sixth birthday that summer, yet the marvel of the nun was that no one, nothing in life, not even her own human needs and desires, had ever come before her faith and loyalty to God. To serve Jesus Christ in what she called "the sincere, old-fashioned way," she had turned her back completely on the family she loved and everything the world had to offer. Yet not then, nor throughout her later lifetime, did she feel pain or regret for her decision.

Pascalina's complete surrender to God, her utter devotion and dedication, was part of her rare complexity. As a nun, bound by the sacred vows of humility and obedience, she was compassionate and self-sacrificing, and worked herself to the bone. But she was also a peasant and, born of the earth, she was a tough-minded woman of principle. Men of the clergy whose conscience needed watching, Pacelli in particular, sensed the cat poised just beneath her surface manner, ready to spring at provocation. When Pascalina attacked, everyone, whether mighty or weak, backed away, not in fear but in shame. It was well known that the nun pounced only for good reason—when she perceived a threat to the teachings of Christ.

From the moment Cardinal Secretary of State Pacelli arrived at the retreat house that July of 1930, he sensed in Pascalina a smoldering rage that went far beyond Spellman's unexpected presence. Her real anger, which had been smoldering for months, was aimed at the banker Bernardino Nogara and his manner of handling the Vatican's treasury.

The explosion came soon enough. "Eminence, what sort of secretary of state are you becoming?" the nun demanded when they were alone in his quarters. Her eyes flashed and her voice was trembling with emotion as she faced Pacelli. Sensing her imminent tirade, the prelate stood aghast, so completely stunned by her fierce, threatening mood that he was unable to speak. "Have you and the Holy Father lost your senses?" she continued; her biting words sounded more accusing than questioning. "Imagine allowing one person, a near stranger—worse still, a close friend of Mussolini's—to do as he alone pleases with the entire treasury of Holy Mother Church! I have heard that Nogara alone has full say—on a no-strings-attached basis—how the money is to be handled," she added. "Is this so?"

Pacelli failed to reply but instead went to the window to gaze out upon the Alps—his way of regaining composure. The awful truth was finally confirmed in her mind. Until that moment Pascalina had prayed that the full extent of Nogara's grip upon the Church was more rumor than fact.

His silence caused her to press harder. "Is it true that Pius and the Vatican hierarchy have agreed to all of Nogara's extreme terms?" she asked. "Does the papacy feel it knows so little about finance and that the banker knows everything?"

By now the prelate had regained his composure. Her words, as cutting as she could make them, seemed wasted. By no means had she moved him as she might have in the past. After all, he was now Vatican secretary of state and next to the Pope in power. Pacelli's controlled, almost detached response to all her charges shocked her; hurt her, too. Suddenly he appeared in her eyes more like a corporate executive than a priest. His reaction was more upsetting to her than all she had learned about the goings-on at the Vatican.

Pacelli, in an easy, matter-of-fact way, pointed out to her that Nogara was making great sums of money for the Church. He quoted a fellow cardinal's feelings toward the banker, a sentiment that apparently was quite widely shared in the papacy: "[He is] the best thing that has happened to the Vatican since Our Lord Jesus Christ."

This was the saddest part, she thought, hearing Pacelli admit that he had allowed himself to be used as a front, with absolutely no voice, on a three-cardinal committee set up by Pius XI. Called Amministrazióne Speciàle (Special Administration), its purpose was to make everything the Vatican was doing look good and perfectly legitimate.

"Where is your loyalty to Jesus Christ, Cardinal Pacelli, eminent secretary of state?" she demanded.

There were many, both within the Church and outside its faith, who agreed with the Vatican's temporal policies for making money, policies completely denounced by Pascalina and those of her mind and belief. In the nearly thirty years that Nogara was to remain lord and master of the Vatican treasury, the Church's near bankruptcy was turned into a mighty surplus, with billions of dollars invested in large numbers of major corporations and banks in the United States, Italy, Germany, France, and other European countries. The seemingly endless list includes the Chase Manhattan Bank, Morgan Guaranty, Bankers Trust, General Motors, Bethlehem Steel, General Electric, TWA, IBM, Shell Oil, Goodyear, Anaconda Copper, Celanese, Firestone, Paramount Pictures, Con Edison, and the Bank of America, which the Holy See helped found.

In time, after Pacelli became pope, he would take a leaf from Nogara's book; as Pius XII, he appointed his nephew, Giulio Pacelli, chairman of the board of the drug company making birth-control pills.

Pascalina knew now that she was in danger of losing all grip upon Pacelli. It was a terribly frightening thought, especially following the anticipation of seeing him again after nearly eight months of hollowness. There was no one else close enough for her to turn to; no one to confide in, or feel for. Her family, friends, everyone, neglected for him. Her predicament seemed hopeless.

"If I hadn't my faith in Jesus, there would have been nothing to keep me going," she later confessed.

But the nun's resiliency was too strong for her to fall apart; her friendship too stalwart for any turning of the back and walking out. What kept her at Pacelli's side was an overriding fear that he might lose more and more of the great qualities she respected in him. His present manner taught her how carefully she must now tread in protecting him. Were she to keep up her criticisms and condemnations, there was no question in her mind that he would turn completely away from her, perhaps forever.

She could see that he was impatient for Spellman's return, after only three days. Though she was hurt by such knowledge, it didn't surprise her when, on the fourth day, Pacelli was on the phone, ordering the priest back to the retreat house.

"I was amazed and moved on my return from Oberammergau to see His Eminence standing alone on the dock in Rorschach awaiting the finish of my transit of Lake Constance," Spellman wrote in his diary.

To Pascalina's surprise, it wasn't long before she saw Spellman in a better light. He had become to her "such a jolly little fellow, with a perfect knack for knowing just how to strike the right chord" with Pacelli, especially when the prelate was down and acting grouchy. In spite of herself she was starting genuinely to like the priest. Her months away from Pacelli had dampened her own spirits so considerably, it was a welcome relief to have Spellman, so often the perfect comic, at their side.

Spellman's happy suggestion that they all get away from the dreary retreat house, his adventurous idea that they do some traveling about Europe and perhaps some mountain climbing along the way, was exactly what Pascalina and Pacelli needed to hear. Both jumped at the plan.

"Spelly, you're so much like our dear Sister Pascalina when it comes to abounding with daring ideas," Pacelli said, his mood improving almost instantly. The cardinal wrapped his arms about his two dearest friends and pulled them close to his sides. "Sister encouraged me to ski and to motorcycle. Now it's to be mountain climbing," he continued, looking from side to side as he smiled their way. "Are you hoping to make a sportsman out of me, Spelly, with this mountain climbing of yours?" Pacelli asked, breaking into laughter. The nun and the priest beamed with delight at the secretary of state's rare show of light humor.

He seemed to have no qualms about taking off as much time to unwind as he thought necessary. "Tell you what!" he exclaimed, his enthusiasm gathering momentum with his every word. "In the weeks ahead, let's do all the foolish things we'd do if we were children again!"

Pascalina was astounded, especially after the cold and calculating way he had acted earlier. Yet she hoped her shock wasn't as obvious as Spellman's. But Pacelli glimpsed the priest's wide eyes and open mouth, and quickly took teasing advantage.

"Wipe that silly look of amazement off your face, Monsignor Spellman!" he ordered in a good-natured tone. "Don't act like we're still back in the Vatican with the Holy Father watching every move."

The rebel in Pacelli was hardly ever seen. Everyone thought of the reserved prelate as fanatically dedicated to the papacy and a stickler for responsibility and perfection. They knew his gift of packing into a few hours all the wisdom and strategy for the day. Any desire for relaxation was something Pascalina had taught him over the years. She prayed now that the weeks ahead—their future moments of lighthearted gaiety together—would restore the mind and heart of the prelate she had originally come to love and respect.

Though he might not have shown it on the surface, Spellman couldn't have been happier with Pacelli's self-indulgence. Privately the priest reveled in the company of so stern a prelate, who was now at least temporarily inclined toward the lighter side of life: " . . . he [Pacelli] was in no hurry to get back because he said here we can breathe all we want to and back in Rome with the visits and the letters we shall be massacred," Spellman wrote.

Climbing the Alps was treacherous enough for Pacelli and Spellman, since neither had ever scaled jagged peaks, but the risk was that much greater for Pascalina, with no experience either and dressed in bulky nun's robes that constantly got in her way.

Pacelli, now fifty-four, was by far the oldest of the group. (Pascalina was almost thirty-six and Spellman had recently turned forty-one.) Yet it was he who did most of the urging, reminding the nun and the priest that Pius XI was an agile mountain climber before becoming pope, and therefore they should follow in the Holy Father's footsteps, with nothing to fear. Prayer and courage and faith in Almighty God was all that was needed, Pacelli said, handing each of them a rope and ax.

Pascalina's suggestion that guides accompany them was totally out of the question to the prelate, and he immediately vetoed the idea. It was eyebrow-raising enough for him, as secretary of state, to be away from the Vatican, he insisted, the first "Vice-Pope"—as some referred to his post next to the Holy Father—to leave the Eternal City in more than half a century. But for a member of the hierarchy of his stature to be seen by outsiders mountain climbing with a nun and a priest certainly could stir press coverage around the world and keep gossipers talking forever.

After three days of joking and loud laughter and backslapping encouragement, but with so little of the rugged climb covered, they gave up. They were out of supplies and exhausted. But despite their turning back, all three were in the highest of spirits, Pascalina not having felt so good in years. "The Cardinal is in fine humor and delighted with everything," Spellman wrote in his diary one night before turning in.

Their future plans were more realistic and rewarding. With Spellman along as chauffeur and traveling companion, Pacelli and Pascalina spent a month driving leisurely through thousands of miles of the beautiful summertime countrysides of Switzerland, Austria, and Germany. At night they stopped along the way at monasteries and convents and church rectories for the new cardinal secretary of state to give his blessing and for them to stay at a religious house in keeping with the covenants of their faith.

Though the trip was by no means an official pilgrimage, it was for all three a thoroughly enjoyable religious experience during which they met numbers of priests and nuns and monks. It was particularly gratifying and eye-opening for Pascalina, who was so used to the ascetic life and had seen so little of the world.

For Pacelli the trip was one of his greatest ego-boosters, with nuns and the clergy falling all over themselves to make everything perfect for the new cardinal secretary of state. A priest visiting from New York remarked that Spellman looked completely enraptured at being Pacelli's aide, and likened the priest to a pet poodle being walked by his master on Fifth Avenue. "He is very kind and pleasant and confidential with me," Spellman wrote to his mother.

Though Pascalina, Pacelli, and Spellman were exceptional linguists, fluently speaking German, French, Latin, and Italian, they conversed mostly in German, Pascalina's native tongue and Pacelli's favorite language. To fill in the gaps while traveling, Pacelli suggested that Spellman teach them English. Pascalina found the language difficult at times, but Spellman was amazed by Pacelli's progress. "He is learning English very well," the priest noted.

Often when they stopped at some holy place for a day or two of rest, a religious holiday was declared by the cardinal secretary of state to show his love for the people of the area and to give them a chance to demonstrate devotion to God and love for him. High Mass was always said and often afterward there followed a colorful ceremony in the streets with flags flying, bands playing, and the schools closed for the day.

While Catholics in droves swarmed about Pacelli for his blessing, Pascalina kept discreetly out of sight in some nearby convent, praying silently or meditating. She asked God not to let the public display of adulation affect Pacelli adversely. The prelate was beginning to believe all the pomp and ceremony was his rightful due, she felt, and Jesus should put a stop to such foolish thoughts.

As for Spellman, the priest could not have been more pleased by all the religious holidays Pacelli was declaring for the Swiss and Germans and Austrians. "Every time [we visit] a convent there is a holiday," he wrote his mother.

> If we stay around here [Switzerland] much longer, this will become the most ignorant country in the world. The way the holidays are distributed makes me wish I was a child again. . . . Some days we go to Austria and Germany which are very near and give them a few holidays over there too. There is nothing narrow about the Cardinal when it comes to distributing holidays. All the nations are the same to His Eminence.

By late summer the pace and pomp of those many weeks of travel together had given Pascalina and Pacelli new life. The pageantry, the laughter, the sharing, the nights of praying together, the fulfilling conversations afterward, for these reasons and many others nun and prelate were swept into an understanding and need for each other that transcended everything they had ever felt before. He was a man of such changing moods; of this she had years of convincing evidence. Perhaps for that reason she had finally let go of her anger when he had turned so silent and sullen during her accusations against the banker Nogara. Now, with Pacelli in a more relaxed mood, he was explaining, in an almost apologetic tone, his hopeless position with the Pope. Even though Pacelli was secretary of state and second in command at the Vatican, the Pope's order was that no tribunal—no one—was to question Nogara's activities or decisions. "I, too, am obligated to a vow of obedience," he reminded her. If even he, Pacelli, were to disobey Pius, the punishment, he said, would be as severe as if he were merely a lowly penitent.

"You're not the only one," the prelate confessed. "There have been mutterings and rumors about Nogara and his privileged position with the Holy Father. Some among the hierarchy are feeling very uneasy about this layman, who has been granted such unlimited authority."

Pacelli's admissions to Pascalina and his present mood of hopelessness underscored how lost he felt inside.

"All along, I've needed you and wanted you at my side. But my hands have been tied," he said, speaking in a whisper. His far-off gaze as he uttered mumbled words gave the impression that he was trying to explain his past behavior more to himself than to her. There was no doubt then in her mind that he sincerely wanted her with him in the Vatican, but she would simply have to wait until Pacelli's mind joined his heart. It must remain his decision, she now knew; he alone must choose the time to beckon to her. And call he would. Of that, at last, she was now certain.

Spellman, not Pacelli, was first to write her from Rome after she returned to the Berlin nunciature. His letter was the only knowledge she had of the extremes the secretary of state had to undertake in order to sneak back to the Vatican. She instinctively knew that Pacelli was too embarrassed to tell her of the charade he and the American priest had engaged in so that they could return home unnoticed. According to Spellman, Pacelli had received word the morning of their departure for Rome that two-dozen reporters and photographers were already camped out in the Stazione Termini, the city's main train station, awaiting their arrival.

So anxious was Pacelli to avoid coverage of his unprecedented leave from the Vatican, a risk that no previous secretary of state had dared in more than fifty years, that he decided to slip incognito into the Eternal City. Hoping to pass himself off as a simple priest, Pacelli put on ordinary clerical garb, packed away his cardinal's robes and red hat, donned sunglasses, and had Spellman disguise himself in civilian clothes. "Even though the tickets were in my name," Spellman wrote Pascalina, "the Cardinal was at once recognized and in five minutes we were again surrounded . . . after having ducked them [reporters] for more than a month. We had [tried to keep] our arrival in Rome [so] secret."

But it all ended well, he assured her, adding that Pacelli was in such a happy state after their vacation, it would take more than a little newspaper publicity to jar him now. As for their vacation together, "The Cardinal was immensely pleased with everything and so was I. We shall probably take another trip together next year."

What greatly impressed Pascalina was the quality of sympathy and consideration that Spellman showed for her. She now had a strong ally working on her side in the Vatican, of this she was certain. Still, the nun suspected that the priest might have very human motives of his own in wanting to help her, fearing her possible jealous reprisals were he to build his own bridges with Pacelli while she remained so far away and left out. But no matter what Spellman's reasons might be, she loved him dearly now, especially for writing her so often, saying how steadily and tactfully he was prodding the cardinal secretary of state to have a place made for her in the Vatican.

Finally the call came—from Pacelli himself, saying she was to come to the Vatican, to live and work in the Papal Palace. Spellman had accomplished it all, Pacelli said. The lowly priest had won Pope Pius XI's undying gratitude for all the wonderful blessings he had delivered: a private train for His Holiness that was arranged through wealthy Americans, three new Graham Paige cars, and a gift of $45,000 from philanthropist John J. Raskob.

In a letter home Spellman described how pleased the papacy was with him. These gifts, he wrote, have "certainly caused quite a sensation, and just at present I am in very strong even if there were any efforts made by anyone to hurt me." For all he had done, the priest added, the Holy Father had rechristened him "Monsignor Precious."

With the Pope so indebted to Spellman, it was an easy matter for the priest to request the transfer of a simple nun from Berlin to work as a housekeeper in the Vatican. Of course, it was all accomplished with Pacelli's knowledge and permission.

Shortly before Christmas in 1930, Sister Pascalina arrived with all of her belongings at the Stella Maris retreat house in Rorschach, Switzerland. In her simple canvas bag she carried a second complete habit, small statues of Jesus and the Blessed Mother, an extra pair of rosary beads, her missal, two medals, one of Saint Theresa and the other of Saint Francis, a crucifix of Christ given to her many years before by her mother, and an envelope of family photographs.

Two hours later Monsignor Francis J. Spellman, dressed in civilian clothes, drove up in an old, somewhat battered car.

They drove all night and arrived at the Vatican before noon the next day.

Spellman took the nun directly to the Papal Palace, to the servants' quarters at the rear of the ground floor.

Pascalina was to cook and wash and clean, chores as menial as when she had first gone to work for Pacelli in the Munich nunciature more than thirteen years before. But none of that mattered, for once again Pacelli was close by, and this was a new beginning, however humble.

V

The Vatican of the twentieth century rises majestically alongside Rome's Tiber River, at whose banks thousands of Christ's followers were martyred nearly two thousand years ago.

There, at the present sight of the Holy City, Nero had his palace and gardens and watched Rome burn. It was there as well that the early Christians, bands of devout and impoverished men who defied the world and stood ready to die for Christ, buried Peter's remains around A.D. 67. Upon Peter's grave they built a small, modest house of prayer, site of modern-day Saint Peter's Basilica, the largest and most resplendent church in the world.

Though the origins of the Holy See were humble and tragic, by the fourth century the wave of Christianity had grown so greatly as to engulf the Roman Emperor Constantine the Great himself. So thoroughly taken was he by the Christian faith that in A.D. 326 he ordered the building of an impressive basilica on the site of the nearly 260-year-old oratory that had remained the rude seat of Christianity.

As the centuries passed, Constantine's edifice grew increasingly lavish in order to please the popes. In the middle of the fifteenth century Pope Nicholas V said time and ruin threatened God's main house of worship and ordered the structure replaced by a basilica of artistic splendor and colossal size, such as never before seen on earth.

Starting in 1452 and for the next 174 years, many of the great masters of the Renaissance, Raphael and Michelangelo among them, spent much of their lives embellishing the basilica and its magnificent dome. Finally, on November 18, 1626, Pope Urban VIII officially dedicated the present Saint Peter's Basilica.

To this day Vatican temporal glory continues in its worldwide course. Though geographically the smallest autonomous state on earth, covering an area of only about one square mile, its present membership of nearly three quarters of a billion Catholics throughout the world is greater than the combined populations of the United States and Soviet Russia.

Like all independent governments, the State of Vatican City, as it is officially known, flies its own flag, a banner of yellow and white bearing the papal coat of arms. The Vatican coins its own currency, maintains a police force, a court system, two jails, and a fire department. It operates its own communications systems—telephone, telegraph, and mail services—and publishes an official newspaper, *L'Osservatore Romano,* with daily and Sunday editions. Vatican interests are served by these publications and its radio and television stations. The Church's first radio station was the gift of Guglielmo Marconi in 1932, and Eugenio Pacelli, during his reign as Pius XII, built the Holy See's first TV station.

The Vatican also runs a railway system that provides connecting service throughout Europe. The entire railroad and its station of pink, yellow, and green marble were built by funds from the Lateran Treaty.

The Vatican maintains no army, but its colorful Swiss Guards are kept armed and continuously patrol the papal grounds.

Pascalina arrived in Vatican City during the Christmas season of 1930, staggered by the papacy's magnificence; from childhood the Vatican had been the romantic fantasy of her life. She came filled with Christ's teachings, yet she knew little about the Vatican's past and less of how this world center of the Holy Roman Catholic Church functioned. Like all Catholics of her time, Pascalina had never been allowed to read anything scandalous about the Vatican, simply because the Church said to do so was heresy, and further, that the Pope, as Christ's Vicar on Earth, is infallible and must not be challenged. Her years with Pacelli had opened her eyes to some extent, making her less naive than most Catholics, but still it was her more romantic view of the Vatican that prevailed that Christmas.

Soon she would learn a good deal of harsh truth that would overwhelm her early rapturous enjoyment.

* * *

Like the Church's own origins, Pascalina's start at the Vatican was anything but auspicious.

Though for years she had been mistress of Pacelli's plush households in Munich and Berlin, an exalted position for a nun, she was realist enough to know that no such place of authority would be made for her in the Vatican. Indeed, she considered herself fortunate to be but a simple, lowly servant in the Papal Palace. The nun was also well aware that if she was to remain in the Vatican without causing embarrassment to Pacelli, she would have to be quartered with the servants at the rear of the palace, floors away from her beloved prelate, "to prevent any wrong impression being whispered," she later said.

As the high and mighty of the Church came and went, she remained at the stove, standing for hours, cooking, mixing, chopping. When she wasn't busy in the kitchen, Pascalina shut herself away in her tiny room, praying or meditating. Pius XI was as lavish a host as Pacelli had been at the Berlin nunciature, but in the Papal Palace the nun was not allowed to serve the guests or play any part in the hospitality, as she had done in the German residence.

As weeks passed the papacy came to be increasingly disappointing to the nun, for whom religion meant compassion and love. She found it a strange world of men with temporal values, strutting about in robes of splendor. The Holy See and its hierarchy seemed so alien to her life of poverty, chastity, and obedience.

For one whose memory of hard farm life was still vivid, the Vatican appeared more of solid gold than of Christ. Little wonder, she thought after the first few days, that Mussolini had allied himself with such a partner.

The prelates residing in the palace were pointedly aloof, making it obvious that she was to keep her distance. It was a painful stand-off for Pascalina, but, as a well-trained nun, she valiantly toed the line. There was no little smile, no friendly greeting, no giving whatsoever of human warmth—on either side, theirs or hers.

Hardly a moment passed when she didn't have grave misgivings. The Vatican was a world solidly of male supremacy and prejudice, and she wondered if she would ever be tolerated. Then, too, could she herself cope in a society of priests and prelates where she was so obviously out of place?

Her fears, it seemed, were well founded. One day only a few weeks after her arrival, she slipped out of the palace kitchen for a moment or two to examine a Raphael masterpiece hanging in a quiet corridor nearby. A group of cardinals happened along, and the enormity of their outrage at seeing a nun roaming about freely in the palace sent Pascalina running for cover.

Pacelli was of little comfort to her at the time. As secretary of state, the prelate was exceedingly conscious of his pure and lofty image, and intentionally kept a wide distance from her. It was left for Spellman, their dependable Yankee friend, to see that she was comfortable.

Spellman appeared to be the right medicine for Pascalina at this difficult time. The priest from Boston was infusing a new and typically American note into the Curia's routine activities. According to Spellman's biographer, Father Robert I. Gannon, S.J., "Men within the age-old walls of the Vatican were not too used to the unusual electric qualities of the young priest from the New World. But they were becoming increasingly intrigued with what they were seeing. His zeal and care and competence, his social graces, had won him regard from the higher-ups."

Spellman's ecclesiastical world was constantly brightening. More and more he was being privately appreciated, particularly by the Pope and Pacelli. But he wisely did not take advantage of his rising image. "He was not aggressive or forward; he waited to be asked," Gannon also noted. "But when he was asked, he gave his opinion with common sense directness. He opened his mouth at the right time."

Though Spellman kept Pascalina amused during their brief talk-sessions several times a week, it was Pacelli whom she yearned to be with. Occasionally she would catch a glimpse of the secretary of state, his red sash flying as he sped past for conference with the Holy Father. With upraised hand he would flash a blessing her way. That was enough greeting from the great prelate to encourage Pascalina and to let her know that he still remembered and prayed for her; enough for her to bide her time.

"Pacelli was a wise man who did not let small matters stand in the way of what was important," Pascalina commented years later, her eyes gazing off into the distance. "It was my responsibility to be important to him; to help him to achieve his goals, no matter what the sacrifice might have been on my part."

Spellman from the start perceived the nun's brilliance and common sense. He suggested to Pacelli that she spend less time peeling potatoes and more at the typewriter and mimeograph machines. Pascalina's abilities could easily be put to greater use in the Curia's offices, Spellman advised Pacelli.

The American, at the time, was in charge of Vatican press relations, and he instinctively realized the asset she'd be in his department. From the moment he had first set foot in the Church's public relations office six years before, Spellman knew how entirely outdated the whole setup was. "There were no professionals," he told Pascalina, "just a few grumpy old priests who lectured newsmen against writing anything but good about the Church. And even the good, the clergy wanted to censor."

Historically the Vatican had always kept a safe distance from the working press. Only a trusted handful of journalists, well within the control of the Vatican bureaucracy, had been privileged to Church news. The strictest guidelines were enforced; everything of interest to the press, before Spellman's arrival, was subject to censorship by the Curia.

Foreign correspondents had been obliged to get their material secondhand by digging through *L'Osservatore Romano,* "the anything-but-revealing, nor interesting" Vatican newspaper. Spellman had felt that a great deal of information that probably could be helpful to the Vatican was being overlooked. To the young priest, newly arrived for service in the Vatican, a professional press relations office was essential to the Vatican. What was more, he intended to run it. And he did.

When opportunity arose, Spellman had proposed a number of changes in the system through which Vatican news was disseminated. None was drastic, since the priest was too politically minded to shock his superiors. Drawing upon his years as a reporter and editor at *The Pilot,* the Catholic newspaper in Boston, and earlier experience as a high school stringer for the *Brockton Enterprise* and the *Whitman Times,* Spellman had successfully sold his superiors on the idea of allowing him to write press releases. Once into his new job he translated tidbits of Curia information—news that he carefully screened—into a number of foreign languages, and ran off copies on an antiquated mimeograph machine. Though Vatican news still remained largely bland, foreign correspondents covering the Holy City in the mid-1920s were astonished at the sight of a priest writing releases and passing them out himself.

Spellman assured Pascalina that by no means would she, as a nun, be out of place in his office at the Curia, which was the headquarters for the three branches of the Church government: the executive, the legislative, and the judiciary. The Curia Romano, official title for the vast Church bureaucracy, was but a stone's throw from the Papal Palace, where the Pope sat in supreme authority and where the Sacred College of Cardinals convened as a so-called papal senate, more for show than for power.

The Curia's bureaucrats—priests, nuns, and lay people—functioned the way executives and workers in any large American corporation did, carrying out the boss's orders. In her case, Pascalina could be especially blessed since the superboss, in full charge of the Curia, was Cardinal Secretary of State Pacelli.

Nobody knew better than Pacelli himself the nun's great genius for getting things skillfully done, so he needed little convincing.

In this instance it was Pascalina who required prodding.

"But I can't type, and I've never worked in an office," she told Spellman.

"I will teach you," he replied. They knew each other well enough by then to laugh together and banter with ease. Though entirely convinced that he would never lead her into any embarrassment, she still maintained grave doubts.

It was widely known that she was Pacelli's former household mistress. As such, she wondered how the bureaucratic priests and nuns were going to accept her favored status. She finally agreed to the challenge, but with great reservations, fearing that she might be deprecated and disgraced, and cause the secretary of state much embarrassment as a result.

By late spring, Pascalina felt the pressures slacken, and her apprehensions eased considerably. She was Spellman's assistant in the growing press relations office, remote from the forefront of gossip and doing work she thoroughly enjoyed.

Between her palace chores of cooking and cleaning, she'd rush back and forth to her desk in the Curia. Often with hands scented by onion peelings, she typed news releases and cut stencils. She would roll off clean, sharp copies on the mimeograph for *L'Osservatore Romano* and the flocks of foreign correspondents who clustered about each day waiting for tidbits of Vatican news.

"I was shocked when His Eminence [Pacelli] dropped by unexpectedly one day and said 'Bravo!' as I was passing out press releases and coffee to the reporters," Pascalina told Spellman.

Though she felt quite at home in Spellman's office, the attitude toward her in the adjoining departments remained cold and aloof. The nun was more frozen out by the clergy at the smug Curia than even in the Papal Palace, with all its pomp and rich crimson damask. The kitchen hands in the palace tried their best to make her feel appreciated, but the cynical and reserved Italian clerics at the bureaucracy kept her at distance. From the start most of the priests barely acknowledged her existence. A slight nod by the closely knit, class-conscious prelates and clerics was all the greeting she could expect.

Spellman told her to say as little as possible to everyone. "Silence concerning matters within the Holy Office [Curia] is the first requirement," the priest warned. He pointed to a large stuffed fish hanging on the wall above his desk, with a label that read: "If I had shut my mouth, I wouldn't be here."

Spellman's pink benign face began to twinkle at his own pointed humor, but the nun failed to appreciate his sarcasm and became a bit perturbed that he'd think her so naive. "If the clergy were as careful with their tongues as the good sisters are, it would be an easier world," she retorted, a hint of huff in her tone. One of the primary unwritten rules of her religious order, she said, was to observe everything and repeat nothing.

Despite all the peculiarities of the Vatican, despite her years of religious training and dedication to a holy life of humility and poverty, the nun was becoming fascinated with her new world, the world of Church politics and power plays conceived in the Curia, to be carried out in the nations of the world.

Her clever understanding of human nature and her excellent command of Italian soon helped considerably to break down the cold barriers of the Curia. Difficult as the Roman clergy were in the self-serving bureaucracy, Pascalina soon was calming personal jealousies and artfully soothing jangled nerves. Often she'd volunteer to finish up a priest's work if he was too tired or felt lazy at the moment. Her shrewd, skillful ways were working wonders in no time.

Spellman appreciated the nun's cleverness and tact, qualities he himself exercised to great advantage throughout his life. "Who can dislike someone who helps you with the copying of dull orders, the typing of trivial instructions, the editing of pointless speeches, the translating of endless encyclicals and other documents," he once said.

While many of the clerics began softening their hard line, even coming to Pascalina for a helping hand, others stiffened all the more at her presence. She felt the jealous sting of those who napped at midday, as most Romans did, while she labored on, pouring her energies into kitchen chores and what was so often merely trivial desk work at the Curia.

A few showed their dislike simply because it was rumored Pascalina was Pacelli's pet. She felt the particular scorn of Monsignor Giovanni Montini, a lowly typist and filing clerk, who made it pointedly clear from the start he wanted no part of her. Montini, whose desk was in an office close by, was often the disappointed and angry recipient of trivial work, while she received increasingly choice responsibilities.

The nun responded to Montini's freeze with a chill of her own, grudgingly acknowledging his terse "Good morning" with a stiff nod.

As time passed and the serious-minded, hard-working Montini came to appreciate Pascalina's skills, even to the point of praising her to Spellman, she still did not fully unbend in his direction.

Montini, like most of her adversaries among the clergy, could not understand or come to grips with Pascalina's deeply divided personality. She could be the charming, elegant, convent-trained "perfect lady" whose warm smile and poise held everyone fascinated. Then there was her second side, her "Mother Superior" complex, a ruthless resolve that showed itself in a fierce, cold stare. Worse, the nun's anger flared at even the slightest taunt.

In at least one case—Montini's—the nun would greatly regret her harsh attitude when, some three decades later, he became Pope Paul VI.

The first opportunity that Pascalina and Pacelli had to be alone since her arrival in the Vatican did not come about until the late spring of 1931. They came together in the papal gardens, well hidden at the rear of the palace and already abloom in myriad beautiful colors.

Pacelli was so distraught that he began unraveling his anxieties the instant they sat down. He was finding the Pope very difficult, he confided. Despite the Vatican's peace treaty with the fascists, and despite the return of Castel Gandolfo to the papacy, Pius XI, a man of extreme moods and obstinate mind, was about to lock horns with Mussolini.

As Pacelli explained his concern to Pascalina, the ink was scarcely two years dry on the Lateran Treaty, and Mussolini was already demanding his own payoff from the papacy. The dictator wanted his fascist friends appointed to high positions within the Church, and any priest or prelate whom Mussolini did not approve of was to be thrown out at once.

Pacelli was particularly unnerved because of what he at last perceived as the mistakes made in the Lateran Treaty, errors of judgment that Pascalina had denounced at the Berlin nunciature.

The papacy had placed itself in the uniquely embarrassing position of allowing Il Duce to have equal say with the Holy See in the selection and appointment of bishops and archbishops to rule all Catholic dioceses in Italy. Now, just as the nun had forewarned, Mussolini was insisting that he be given opportunity at once to exercise this unprecedented privilege.

"The Holy Father, and you, too, Eminence, were so concerned about the financial plight of the Holy See, you closed your minds to the eventual consequences," she said, taking his hand in hers to soften her accusation. "I realize that extreme measures usually have to be taken to ward off bankruptcy. But, as I said before and repeat again, when one bargains with a ruthless dictator, one must be prepared to face a bitter fate. To have given Mussolini the right to say who may or may not become a bishop of Holy Mother Church was a grave mistake! You, as one of the chief architects of the Lateran Treaty, as well as Cardinal Gasparri and the Holy Father himself, must share blame."

Pacelli sadly nodded his head. "How can I disagree with you?" he asked, his anguish increasing the more they pondered the Vatican's desperate situation.

There were many large issues, besides the appointment of bishops, that again divided Church and state. According to Pacelli, Mussolini was refusing to budge on his long-held opposition to religious teaching in the schools. Even though the concordat gave the Church the right to educate Italy's youth in Catholicism, the dictator had reverted to his old way of thinking. He now insisted that public education remain solely the prerogative of the fascist state and must be kept entirely outside the province of the Holy See.

For his part Il Duce saw the papacy as the treaty's repudiator, Pacelli went on to say. The fascist dictator claimed that many among the clergy and segments of Catholic youth were not abiding by the terms of the concordat. Numbers of priests were still active in politics, speaking out against the fascists, and Catholic Action groups were shouting denunciations of Mussolini in the streets. Even more serious, in Mussolini's estimation, was his belief that the papacy was doing nothing to quell the renewed uprisings.

The pope had vehemently denied Il Duce's charges, Pacelli said. Pius insisted that his Church in no way sanctioned any unrest in its clerical or lay ranks toward the fascist government. The secretary of state described the Holy Father to have been in such a state of utter exasperation with the dictator that he shook his hands wildly above his head as he spoke. "Holiness could not have more dramatically demonstrated how frustrated he was in his belief that Mussolini was deliberately trying to sabotage everything," Pacelli told Pascalina. Pius was certain, he said, that the dictator was using "every sort of political trick" to reinforce his power among those fascists who thought the treaty was too one-sided toward the Church.

The Pontiff was not going to buckle to fascist pressure, Pacelli went on to say. Even more alarming, as Pascalina saw events developing, the papacy was bent upon politically embarrassing Mussolini.

At his cabinet meetings in Rome the dictator was complaining that he had been completely taken in by the Holy See. Mussolini recalled that he had pressured his government to come up with the $92.1 million to save the Vatican from bankruptcy, and had arranged numerous other expensive gifts and concessions to help the Holy See. It was frustrating to him now to think that he, an atheist most of his life, had taken the extreme step (he had returned to the Church and was regularly receiving the Holy Sacraments), yet the Pope had not been willing at any time to meet with him, even as a public gesture of goodwill and gratitude.

Pascalina herself had heard whispers in the Curia that numbers of antifascist priests were grumbling among themselves at being politically muzzled. One or two had spoken out in public, calling upon Catholics to overthrow Il Duce's government. Though they were soon silenced by the Holy See, Mussolini blamed the papacy for having allowed unrest to surface. The dictator was said to be on the verge of sending fascist troops to beat down any further challenge to his rule.

"It appears that there may be open warfare between the fascists and Holy Mother Church," Pacelli said sorrowfully, looking to the nun for advice and hope.

Pascalina was impressed that this great man of the Vatican, the cardinal secretary of state of the Holy Roman Catholic Church, a man much older and wiser than she, not only thought of her as a woman to mother him but respected her as a thinking person capable of momentous decisions. The challenge, she was to admit in her old age, gave her a magnificent sense of individuality and authority. Her unique situation seemed ironic to the nun. Church tradition kept her hidden in the Vatican's dark recesses, yet she was being sought out in secrecy for consolation and advice on the papacy's most immediate and serious problem.

Pascalina anguished for days over the tremendous responsibility Pacelli had thrust her way. She realized that it was his style to draw ideas from many he respected and trusted, usually cardinals and others of the hierarchy, and then to act on the consensus. But in the final analysis it was her own great influence on him that she felt would sway his judgment. Pascalina had been with Pacelli more than thirteen years, and as a lonely man with no intimate friends other than herself, he had come to rely heavily on her advice.

In one respect it was grating to Pacelli to seek such extraordinary advice from a nun. Here he was, the Vatican secretary of state, long imbued with the prejudice of male supremacy and certain of his conviction that the hierarchy is all-knowing, having to bow to a woman's intellect.

Yet if he was to find solution to seemingly impossible conditions, who was wiser and more adept than Pascalina? He had pondered the question many times. Finally he concluded that no one, at any level within the Church or among his important diplomatic friends, could compete with this ever faithful woman. Through the years, in test after test, he had come to trust her wisdom at times more than he trusted his own. Had she alone not been right about so many of the conditions in the Lateran Treaty, and he and others so wrong? She had never given him reason to doubt her ability, or her honesty, or her sincerity.

"At times, it is most difficult, even embarrassing to me, to hear your harsh words," Pacelli once shyly admitted to Pascalina. "But after my boiling blood has cooled down, I always know how right you are."

Could Pacelli have come to realize fully, at last, how truly important she was to him and the Church? Could this have been their turning point?

Though the nun had a natural aggressiveness and confidence in accepting any challenge, still she spent hours in meditation, praying for the right answers. She asked herself over and over the same question: What if she advised him incorrectly? Pacelli had such a strong influence on the Pope that any ill-conceived advice from her passed along to Pius XI could subvert the Lateran Treaty, perhaps even intensify the already explosive crisis between the Vatican and the fascists.

On her knees at an altar to Jesus, Pascalina sought desperately to know what she herself would do were she the Pontiff.

Her inspiration came swift and clear. A voice within cried for a strong stand against Mussolini and any enemy of the Church.

"Holy Mother Church must never yield to any evil," her conscience demanded. "The Holy See must remain free! Free to name its own bishops. Free to spread the teachings of Christ. The clergy, everyone, must be free politically. It is better for Holy Mother Church to return to Mussolini all the funds received through the Lateran Treaty than to surrender its freedoms."

At thirty-six, Pascalina was far more toughminded than when she had run away from home at fifteen to join the convent, too afraid, in those days, to face her family. Struggle and age had given her a harder view of life. She had come to believe that principle must be defended with full commitment.

In all conscience the Holy Father must not yield to the threats of any enemy of the Church, no matter what the consequences may be," Pascalina said in speaking her mind to Pacelli when they met again several days later. "Return the dirty money and see that the Vatican stands tall against this scheming dictator!" she added, her stare as defiant as her words.

Pacelli was horrified; he was too much the diplomat to think so militantly. Without as much as a word in reply he turned abruptly and stalked off, leaving her in stunned silence.

When the secretary of state met with the Pope, he made no mention of Pascalina's all-out position against the fascists. As he so often did, Pacelli held to the traditional safe line of the Vatican's conservative secretariat. "Holiness, perhaps we should meet with Mussolini and seek to tone him down?" he suggested.

But Pius was in one of his frequent heated moods and flatly refused to agree. With blistering tongue and table-pounding fist, the Pope was even more upset than Pascalina had been. Vowing to take the offensive and disgrace Il Duce in the eyes of the world, Pius said, "We will not yield to that devil Mussolini! We'll show the world what he is!"

In the months ahead upward of one million Italians from among the Federation of Catholic Men, the Union of Catholic Women, Boy Scouts and Girl Scouts, stood in open defiance of Mussolini. Apparently these Italian Catholics were as antifascist as Pascalina and the Pope. Calling themselves the Catholic Action Group, tens of thousands of them took to the streets to shout, "Down with Mussolini!"

Il Duce ordered his fascist militia to attack the insurgents with clubs, then to use whatever other force was necessary to quell any further uprisings.

To Pascalina it seemed like the bloodshed of Munich was starting all over again. Yet all her sympathies remained with the rebel action.

When the Pope's portrait was burned in the streets by fascists and photos of the Holy Father were hung with crude obscenities in Rome's public toilets, Pacelli was convinced that Pascalina had been right all along. In a total about-face the secretary of state switched to the nun's hard line. Now he encouraged the Pope's rage toward Mussolini rather than attempting to quell the Pontiff, as he had in the past.

Emotions were running so high in the Vatican against Mussolini that many were praying for his downfall. Pascalina and Pacelli said rosaries that God and the Blessed Mother would see need for Il Duce's overthrow. If the time was not yet right for the dictator's downfall, Pascalina told Pacelli, certainly his political wings needed quick clipping by the papacy.

In a desperate attempt to salvage the Church's honor and pride, she suggested the writing of a papal encyclical denouncing Mussolini's actions. She believed the denunciation should be released outside of Italy, since Il Duce was in full control of the Italian press and radio.

No one knew better than the secretary of state the extent of Pascalina's superior intelligence and gift of great common sense. Yet to spare his personal pride and to avoid the embarrassment of admitting he conferred with a nun, Pacelli, at her suggestion, presented the bold plan to the Pope as his own. Pius XI jumped at the idea.

The papal encyclical *Non Abbiamo Bisogno* (We Have No Need), written in part by the Pope but mostly by Pacelli, was as tough on Mussolini as Pascalina suggested. Monsignor Spellman was the Holy See's ideal choice to release the encyclical.

"You are to smuggle this to Paris and give it to the world press," Pacelli told Spellman. "Don't waste a moment, and don't get caught!"

The Pope's sizzling attack on fascism headlined front pages around the world, but its unprecedented release in France, rather than in the Vatican, both surprised and troubled the media. The Rome bureau of the Associated Press was disturbed enough to send this dispatch to its member papers:

> A great deal of Fascist criticism was being leveled at the Pontiff's method of publishing the encyclical. The fact that the document was published abroad, with no hint given here or at Vatican City until it had almost reached the newspapers, was being construed as a reflection on the good name of Fascism. It was interpreted as meaning that Pope Pius believed Premier Mussolini might have prevented the transmission of the document.

The papacy couldn't have cared less whose feelings were hurt, press included. Pius XI had accused the fascist government of "acts of oppression" and "terrorism" against the Church and members of the Catholic Action Group. And the world now knew the Pope's position, the Lateran Treaty notwithstanding. And that was all that mattered to the papacy.

Pascalina was more realistic than the Pope or Pacelli. Pius's blast at Mussolini had caused a far greater uproar around the world than anyone had expected. She feared the fascists would seek revenge against Pacelli, who was widely known to be the clever brain and power behind the papal throne. Her womanly instinct convinced her that Il Duce would use any means to discredit the cardinal secretary of state and cause his downfall. She told the prelate that their own relationship had to be kept all the more discreet and tightly hidden because of Mussolini's mind and vicious tongue.

Fortunately for Pascalina and Pacelli, her fears at the time were overblown. Neither the prelate nor she herself came under any fascist attack. Mussolini's harassment was aimed solely at Spellman, the papacy's obedient messenger who was simply carrying out orders.

The Vatican feared for a time that Spellman would not be allowed back into fascist Italy; some even believed that were the priest to return, he'd be immediately slapped in jail.

The priest thrived on all the excitement and the attention he was getting. The scurrilous cartoons about him that appeared in the Italian press triggered his jolly sense of humor. Said he jovially,

One had me in an airplane scattering encyclicals, tearing down from the heavens the motto, "Peace On Earth To Men Of Good Will," and putting up another slogan in its place, "Death On Earth To Men Of Good Will." The second [cartoon] had a *blind* man coming to me and asking help. And I say to him, "For you— read this!" and I hand him an encyclical. Then the funniest of all was a man running up to me while I was passing out encyclicals like handbills on the street and the man says to me, "Hurry up— come quick, there is a man dying!" And I answer, "Tell him to wait a few hours because I have a few hundred more encyclicals to distribute!"

Upon his return to Rome, Spellman did face minor harassment, but nothing more severe. He thought so little of the incident that he said nothing of it to his superiors, nor to Pascalina.

The nun, whose favorite pastime was reading the foreign press, saw a report in her native Munich paper commenting on Spellman's ordeal at the hands of the fascists. The paper said that the priest's troubles had begun immediately upon his return from Paris. Pascalina read that

He [Spellman] was watched by the Fascists and followed by a couple of them as he went about his daily schedule. He knew it, but ignored it for some time. Then one day he swung around on them and said:

"Well, here I am. What do you want?"

There was no answer.

"I'll be here again tomorrow," he challenged, and stepped toward them. They backed up. "I am ready any time you want to start something. I can take care of myself. Now go."

They did and were never put on his beat again.

The report surprised Pascalina, but she couldn't imagine why Spellman had kept his harassment from Pacelli and herself. It greatly pleased her, though, that the priest was so courageous.

"You are such a little man," she said, a light attempt at teasing her boss. "I never thought you had it in you to be so daring."

Spellman enjoyed playing the buffoon and tried flexing his arm muscle in roguish response. "My dear Sister Pascalina, I am quite a boxer!" he boasted with a show of mock pride. Indeed he was, having worked out faithfully in the Vatican's gym several times a week for many years.

The papacy's public lash at fascism set the stage for much give-and-take on both sides. The fascists had felt the sting of the papacy and His Holiness's influence on world opinion. Now it was time, in Pascalina's view, to show Christian charity.

The nun suggested a new tactic, a total about-face to cool hatreds and prevent further violence. Her advice to Pacelli was to offer Mussolini an olive branch. "The Pope should stop all overt political activity by the clergy," she said, branding priests in politics as "Church interference in matters of the state." Equally important, in Pascalina's opinion, was for Pius to invite Mussolini to a private audience at the Papal Palace "to soothe the dictator's blistering wounds."

Cardinal Secretary of State Pacelli was his own man and by no means a pushover for another point of view, Pascalina's brilliance notwithstanding. But he was no longer a skeptic when it came to her judgment. She saw the prelate's stern face smile, and he patted her on the shoulder, his way of indicating how right she was once more.

Pacelli again took Pascalina's ideas to the Pope, again claiming the plan as his own. Pius, in turn, was delighted.

In due time Mussolini was extended an invitation to come to the Papal Palace to meet His Holiness in private audience. Apparently the dictator was as happy as everyone else with the idea. Pius's encyclical had so greatly blackened Mussolini's image in the eyes of the world that the Pope's timely signal for reconciliation was more than pleasing to the fascist's political mind. On February 11, 1932, the third anniversary of the signing of the Lateran Treaty, Il Duce came rushing to the Holy Father and bent to kiss the Fisherman's Ring.

Pius's own political instincts, buttressed by Pascalina's suggestions, which the Pope assumed to be those of his secretary of state, made him easily the master of the moment. The Pontiff presented the dictator with the Vatican's high honor, the papal Order of the Golden Spur. From then on it was all smiles and warm embraces on both sides. The Pope promised to call a firm halt to all antifascist actions by his priests and flock, and Mussolini guaranteed that everything agreed upon in the Lateran Treaty would be upheld by his government.

With few exceptions, peace reigned relatively supreme between the Holy See and the fascist government until Mussolini's ouster on July 25, 1943. Relations did deteriorate for a time when the dictator concluded the Axis pact with Germany prior to World War II. Pius XI was again on the verge of a denunciation of Il Duce, but he died early in 1939, only days before his scheduled attack.

Whenever Pacelli balked at her ideas, even after he himself became pope, Pascalina never failed to remind him that the taming of the fascists was mostly her own brainchild.

In the summer of 1932 the Pope appointed Spellman auxiliary bishop of Boston, a fitting reward for the priest's fealty to the papacy. The bishop left Rome shortly thereafter to assume the new duties in his native diocese.

With Spellman gone, Pascalina knew that were she a man, the path would have been wide open for her to become Pacelli's assistant in the secretariat, with an official title. But it wasn't a title that she sought. As a nun, vowed to a life of humility, she had no interest in temporal trappings. She simply wanted to be closer to the man she had loved and mothered all those years. And so she remained hidden from sight, stirring away at the stove and proofreading behind a rolltop desk.

It was Pope Pius XI himself who finally acknowledged her superior talents, after she saved the papacy from potential embarrassment. As part of the nun's routine job at the Curia, she had come across glaring errors of ancient dogma in one of the Pope's planned speeches. She made notes of the mistakes in a memo to Pacelli, suggesting that he be the one to call Pius's attention to the errors.

Pascalina didn't realize at the time that Pacelli had been suddenly called away on a diplomatic mission. As a result her memo and the Pope's corrected manuscript wound up on the Pontiff's desk.

Pius, himself a stickler for perfection, was exceedingly impressed, and sent for the nun.

"So you are Sister Pascalina," the Pope said as the nun bent to kiss his ring. They were alone in what she considered "God's holy throne on earth." She was shaking all over, entirely overcome by awe and fright at being in the presence of the Holy Father. Though she had lived in the Papal Palace for more than a year and a half, she had only caught fleeting glances of the Pontiff from her servant's quarters. Never before had she come face-to-face with Pius XI.

"I am pleased that you know so much about the dogma of Holy Mother Church," the Pope said, making reference to her corrections. "I shall chastise His Eminence, Cardinal Pacelli, for having you work in the kitchen. Better use should be made of your mind."

Pascalina's great day had finally arrived. She was to be moved immediately from the Curia's lower floor to the upstairs grandeur of the secretary of state's suite. Only hours after her audience with the Holy Father, Pacelli himself—upon returning from his trip— brought her the stunning news of the Pope's decision.

The secretariat, as it is known, was similar in makeup to the departments of state and ministry of many nations. A contingent of about fifty well-educated, carefully trained Italian clerics constituted the headquarters staff, carrying out routine desk assignments. Its diplomats, chosen from the ranks of the hierarchy (cardinals, archbishops, and bishops), were called nuncios or apostolic delegates, and traveled abroad, representing the Vatican in its dealings with foreign governments.

But Pascalina had mixed feelings about being assigned to the secretariat. The cherished opportunity of again being close to Pacelli, the excitement of sharing the high drama of his ascendency, were wonderments all too desirable to the emotionally inhibited nun. Yet she was torn by troubles that lay deep within her conscience.

Her hesitancy was not because long-standing Vatican tradition would be broken by a nun serving as confidante to the secretary of state. Nor was she overly troubled that her presence in the papacy's high inner circle would shock everyone, particularly the staid and pompous hierarchy. Even the humiliation of wagging tongues and snide remarks, as prevalent in the Vatican as elsewhere, wasn't the nun's great worry. She brooded mainly because her confessor, an old and gruff monsignor, told her it was the wrong thing to do.

"It would be scandalous!" he roared at her in the confessional. "And I don't care if the idea is the Holy Father's! Pius is seventy-five. He must be getting senile. As for the secretary of state, he should be ashamed of himself! Now forget the whole idea!" He slammed shut the small sliding door that separated them, leaving her trembling in the cubicle.

Since coming to the Vatican, Pascalina had been seeing her confessor at least twice a week. He was her cherished means of cleansing herself of all sin, her judge and conduit for receiving the Blessed Sacrament at daily Mass. Pouring out her mind and heart to the wise monsignor gave her firmer hold on right and wrong and bolstered her adherence to Christ's teachings.

But when the priest took his harsh stand, sternly reproaching her for even considering the idea of moving close to Pacelli, the nun's nerves frayed and she almost fell apart.

It was to be Pascalina's most fateful decision. In the weeks ahead, as she searched deep into the mirror of her soul for God's answer to her dilemma, Pacelli pressed her several times. With his exhausting round-the-clock schedule he looked weary and haggard and could not comprehend her reluctance to join him. His abrupt impatience showed that his want and need of her was greater than ever.

The responsibilities of the secretary of state's office kept his mind throbbing, he confided. With Spellman gone, all the pressures and forces seemed to converge on him. He was using desperate excuses to wean her to his side.

There were many able clergy on Pacelli's staff, processing mountains of details. He didn't need her as one more hand in the ranks. Rather, he was instinctively reaching out for that special understanding and reassurance that only a kind and loving person of perception and intellect can give to one of his complexity.

In the past he had responded splendidly to her presence and care. Now his health, failing seriously once again, was in greater need than ever, as was Pacelli's peace of mind and his future within the Holy See.

He had always been frail-looking, but now he seemed barely a wisp of himself. His large dark eyes appeared bigger and more haunting. He had lost almost fifteen pounds, a tenth of his normal weight. She cried inside that he looked and felt so beaten.

"You women are all alike!" he shouted at her. "For months you pleaded to come to the Vatican. Now that you are here, and have the Holy Father's blessing to do as you please, you hesitate." Pacelli was terribly hurt, and he shook his head in utter disgust.

The prelate's burst of anger cut Pascalina deeply, seeing that he could not comprehend her hesitation, now that they had the Pope's enthusiastic blessing. She felt acutely sympathetic, as well, and yearned to embrace him. Yet she was stunned at how pathetically like an ordinary man the prelate appeared at the moment. Despite her sorrow for him she couldn't help but burst into laughter, for it appeared Pacelli was about to stamp his feet in utter frustration.

Her totally unexpected response, her ability to turn the awful anxiety of the moment into light humor, broke all tension. Pacelli saw the humor too, and he laughed along with her. Turning then to be on his way, he shook a finger in her direction. "I am going to have His Holiness get after you!" he said.

The next morning when Pius XI sent for her to come to the papal throne, the nun instinctively knew that she no longer had any say in her own future.

"Sister, you are going to have a new desk outside His Eminence's office," the Pope said, his wry smile starting to show. "We expect you to take good care of His Eminence. Now be on your way and do as the Holy Father says."

From the moment Pascalina took her post behind the imposing oversized desk outside the secretary of state's office, she was in for a far greater storm than she had anticipated, particularly from the more blustery members of the Sacred College of Cardinals. Her sense of perception, though exceptionally keen most of the time, had underestimated the bitterness and intense resentments of the stiff and unyielding men she would encounter.

Largely it was the nun's own no-nonsense and perfectionist mind, her insistence on doing her job efficiently, that provoked the criticisms and hatreds of the august red-robed hierarchy. She would not allow anyone, regardless of position, to see His Eminence without an appointment. In her view Pacelli's time had to be respected, if he was to keep to a successful schedule. It had to be her way, she explained, if his health was to be spared and he was to remain effective.

Old prelates, accustomed for years to running in and out of the secretary of state's office, were appalled that they had to go through a nun to make an appointment with Pacelli. A few of them at first thought Pascalina was teasing. But when she stood defiantly at Pacelli's closed door and shouted "No! No! No!" the old men were enraged.

At one point a group of cardinals, seething with resentment, confronted Pacelli as he was coming out of the Holy Father's office. The prelates demanded an explanation for this "effrontery of an ordinary nun."

Their outrage struck Pacelli as somewhat ridiculous, and, unable to control himself, he broke into spontaneous laughter. He mistakenly thought his reaction might soften the tension; whether it did so or not, he was not about to back down. He had made that mistake years before when confronted by his rebellious staff at the Berlin nunciature, but never again, he vowed.

"Remember the golden rule the good sisters taught us all in school," Pacelli, with tongue in cheek, told the cardinals. "When we conduct ourselves properly, there's no problem. Good Sister Pascalina may even reward us for good behavior with remembrance in her prayers." Turning, Pacelli raised his hand in the sign of the cross.

Pascalina considered herself a fortunate woman, she told her confessor in 1936. The nun was forty-two and into middle age. She still looked remarkably young and felt her spirits couldn't be brighter. She worked side by side with Pacelli, "the most fascinating, brilliant man in the world," of whom she still stood in immense awe. Her room, down the hall from his, gave her peace and escape from the real world. Pacelli had thoughtfully erected a small altar at one corner, upon which she kept vigil lights burning at all times. Under her cherished crucifix she prayed and meditated in unbroken solitude.

Like Pacelli, she continued to be a very private person, but they had each other as companions. Each afternoon, weather permitting, they strolled the protected, well-hidden papal gardens at the rear of the palace. They prayed together, and they enjoyed talking about simple things.

Pacelli was then but a breath away from becoming Pope. He had been named camerlengo, tantamount to executive director of the Vatican, and was assuming ever-increasing authority for the physically and mentally deteriorating Pius XI. The Pope was almost eighty, and had less than three years to live. As secretary of state and camerlengo, Pacelli would be in charge of the next conclave to name the new Pontiff.

"It is a good relationship," she told her confessor, with whom she also walked the papal gardens. "Ours is the respectable love Jesus Himself would bless."

She was still trying her best, through the years, to convince her confessor to be less harsh on her for joining Pacelli in the secretary of state's office. The old monsignor had not refused her absolution, because he had no reason to deny her, but throughout he had relentlessly kept up his drumbeat upon her conscience.

But was her life enough for a woman, the monsignor asked? She felt his deep concern as he studied her carefully. Wrinkled and bent over by his advanced age, her confessor carried a lifetime of wisdom and common sense.

His question, so surprisingly personal, startled her for the moment, and caused her to pause and take stock of her life. Since early childhood all she had ever done was work. It had been more than a quarter of a century since she had seen her parents, or any member of her family, or a single friend from back home. And she had no worldly goods of her own.

As both a woman and nun, close to a man of enormous, worldwide power, she had remained the center of gossip and attack within the Vatican. She lived every day of her life frozen out by resentments of the bitter hierarchy and the frigid priests of the Curia's lower ranks, with whom she had worked side by side when she first arrived in Rome.

Pascalina believed she had tried with all her heart to be pleasant when she first took over as protectress of the secretary of state's office. But because her role demanded a firm, unrelenting stand, any blend of cordiality was compromising. The few times she relaxed her stand, she found that the clergy took instant advantage. And so, to protect Pacelli, her manner soon turned brusque, very often impatient, and always authoritarian.

If Pascalina had lived for life's pleasures alone, perhaps she would have felt poverty-stricken. But the nun was that kind of remarkable woman who lived entirely to please Jesus. Destiny had singled her out to serve Pacelli, she said softly, since he was still God's best steward on earth. Pascalina felt tears of pleasure in her eyes as she told the confessor her strong convictions, her tender words spoken without a breath of hesitation.

Not long thereafter Pascalina was driven to real tears. Pacelli told her that members of the Sacred College of Cardinals had met with the Pope to demand her immediate banishment from the Vatican. The prelates had complained bitterly to Pius that they had gotten absolutely nowhere with Pacelli. They accused the secretary of state of siding with the nun over them because of his personal feelings toward her.

One prelate had stingingly referred to Pascalina as "Pacelli's female valet," pointedly implying impropriety because she took personal care of his private quarters.

"I am terribly upset," Pascalina said, overwhelmed by her sense of frustration and lost hope. "Perhaps I should leave the Vatican and return to the retreat house in Switzerland," she blurted out, then quickly added, "For your sake." Pascalina had never looked more depressed.

Pacelli appeared as upset by her threat to leave as she was by the charges made against her.

"His Holiness would not allow you to go," he said, his words sounding more determined than she had ever heard from this autocratic man.

"His Holiness was outraged by these baseless charges and ordered Their Eminences never to discuss you again," Pacelli said reassuringly. "Dear Pius then sent them from his presence. I agree with His Holiness, and I, too, will not let you leave." He seemed as resolute as the words he spoke.

Pascalina had always felt in complete control of herself. As a nun, she had built walls within, always hoping for more, but expecting less, from everyone. Certainly she had hoped for greater fealty to Christ's teachings from these princes of the Church than their petty jealousies and acrimony. For perhaps the first time in her life, she found herself almost breaking apart.

Pacelli had never seen her cry, nor known her even to come close to it, but he realized that at the moment she desperately needed encouragement.

He chose this occasion to tell her his great surprise: he was planning to make his first trip to America, he said, the first by any Vatican secretary of state in the history of the Holy See. With the Pope's approval and blessing Pacelli was going to take the nun along with him to the United States.

He promised Pascalina an excitement transcending her greatest expectations. Spellman had long ago inspired her with the wonders of the new world, but traveling overseas had always seemed far beyond the nun's reach.

Pascalina felt an immediate surge of self-confidence, a renewed strength of purpose, and now, with the Pope's blessing, an eagerness for the journey.

She also knew, after nearly twenty years, how truly important she was to Eugenio Pacelli.

VI

"We sail for the United States under a cloud of suspicion," Pascalina wrote in her diary their first night at sea aboard the Italian liner *Conte di Savoia* on its maiden voyage from Naples to New York.

Many serious reasons—political and personal—compelled Pacelli publicly to minimize the significance of the trip. "I am going to America simply on a vacation," he told the Associated Press in an interview before they sailed. "I have a great longing to see the United States." In response to reporters' questions the secretary of state added, "There is no political aspect to my trip whatever."

But *The New York Times* and other papers around the world were not convinced that the Vatican secretary of state would make a historic journey at so crucial a time in Church history merely for enjoyment. Pacelli was too responsible, in the press's view, to leave Rome and travel to a foreign land for an extended period with the Pope in his late seventies and not in the best health.

Punching holes in the papal announcement that the trip was purely for pleasure, the *Times* said that Pacelli was forced to come to America because of a serious rift that had been developing between the Holy See and the Roosevelt administration. "He will most certainly visit President Roosevelt," the paper reported of Pacelli's visit, "and is also expected to investigate the situation brought about by the Reverend Charles E. Coughlin's radio attacks against President Roosevelt." The *Times* further claimed that their undercurrent of difficulties had finally reached crisis proportions.

The trouble between Church and state had started a few years earlier when a priest from Canada, bent upon destroying Franklin D. Roosevelt and the New Deal, took to a radio microphone in Detroit, Michigan, and began attacking the new President, calling him "a liar," "a double-crosser," and "an upstart dictator in the White House." Though decidedly out of line with the Holy See's hands-off policies in politics, the rebel priest—Father Charles E. Coughlin—so inflamed emotions among Catholics throughout the United States that he began to politicize the nation and the Church itself in America.

As mail poured in to the priest—sometimes as many as 350,000 letters in a single week and almost all supportive—the radio priest, as Coughlin became known, kept up his tirade against FDR. Every Sunday afternoon from his Shrine of the Little Flower in Royal Oak, Michigan, the cleric addressed the nation for a full hour over a growing network of stations. His followers increased rapidly into the millions, and by the time Roosevelt sought reelection in 1936, the priest's influence on the Catholic vote was considerable.

Though FDR's New Deal policies had the blessing of the nation's vast army of liberals, millions of conservatives saw their personal freedoms threatened and were in a crusading mood. For a President whose strategy was to rule through his hold upon the country's combined minorities, the Catholic vote was essential. It was this crucial vote, which Coughlin claimed as his, that posed such a serious threat to Roosevelt. A poll published by the *Literary Digest,* the leading news magazine at the time, not only had the Democratic President's reelection in doubt but predicted his Republican opponent, Governor Alfred M. Landon of Kansas, as the winner by a landslide.

The Vatican anguished in silence, torn by its strong affinity toward Roosevelt and by fear of Father Coughlin, who—though merely a priest in the Holy See's lowliest ranks—had taken extreme hold upon much of the Catholic mind in America. At the time that Coughlin first came upon the scene in the early 1930s, the Vatican and the White House were seen as having never been closer. Anxious to continue to build his bridges with American Catholics, FDR had proposed a plan with Catholic leaders for formal recognition by Washington of the Vatican as an independent state. The President himself had been quietly conferring with Joseph P. Kennedy, later to become ambassador to the Court of St. James, and with Bishop Francis J.

Spellman, FDR's favorite Catholic churchman at the time,* since he was the Vatican secretary of state's intimate friend and choice confidant in the United States. It was important to the Church that Roosevelt be reelected, for it appeared that only a short time remained before an exchange of diplomats between the White House and the papacy would become official.

Not only had the radio priest driven a wedge into the Church-state diplomatic discussions, but the Holy See itself started to suffer serious financial reverses because of Coughlin. Catholics by the millions began pouring dollars by the tens of millions into support of Coughlin, diverting to the priest funds they would ordinarily have given to the Church. A serious rift within the Holy See's membership appeared when American Catholics in ever-increasing numbers became convinced that Father Coughlin expressed far more interest in their welfare than their local clergy, whose passive, neutral sermons were condemned as being more boring than inspiring.

The Catholic hierarchy in the United States for the most part was incensed by Coughlin's rise to power, but few of the clergy dared to speak out publicly. The only prelate to have had the nerve to denounce Coughlin from the altar was William Cardinal O'Connell, archbishop of Boston and dean of the American hierarchy. The old cardinal was so enraged at seeing collections in his own diocese drop drastically that he called the radio priest a "demagogue" from the pulpit of the Cathedral of the Holy Cross in Boston and ordered his flock to stop listening to the rabble-rousing cleric and send him no more money. But O'Connell's emotional attack backfired considerably, as droves of Catholics were infuriated that a prelate would publicly denounce one of his own kind, and they openly sided with Coughlin. The crusading priest's rectory quickly overflowed with mailbags loaded with contributions as gifts to the Holy See dropped even more drastically.

Not surprisingly, *The New York Times* theorized that Pacelli would "convey to President Roosevelt formal assurances that the attacks made against him by Coughlin have received no encouragement from the Vatican," going on to say that Pacelli's planned visit

---

*During World War I, when FDR was assistant secretary of the Navy and Spellman was a priest in Boston, Roosevelt had thought so little of Spellman that he refused the cleric's request for a simple chaplaincy. After Spellman later appealed, FDR, aggravated by Spellman's persistent brashness, went out of his way to block the priest's appointment.

with the President was expected to "separate the Vatican's responsibilities from Father Coughlin and prove to the world that the Catholic Church as a body is in no way hostile to the policies with which President Roosevelt is identified."

In the *Times*'s view the Church, though walking a tightrope with its traditional neutral stand, was implying endorsement of Roosevelt's reelection to the presidency. In return the Holy See expected Washington officially to recognize the Vatican as an independent state.

On the day Pacelli sailed, Bishop Spellman met secretly with the President in the White House to arrange a meeting between the two leaders. Since it was only a few weeks to the November presidential election, Pacelli, as secretary of state of a neutral religious state, had to exercise extreme diplomacy and not imply any leaning toward Roosevelt by the Holy See. For the Church to side with any candidate in any election was to open itself to charges of impropriety. But now—in the heat of emotions stirred by Coughlin against the Democratic administration—even the slightest show of goodwill by the Vatican toward FDR would prove all the more explosive. Pacelli thought of his dilemma as "the sword of Damocles," for if he were to say anything either way—in favor of Roosevelt or against the radio priest—during his trip to America, the Holy See would be in for serious, far-reaching consequences.

Spellman appeared out of breath when he finally contacted the secretary of state aboard ship; the American bishop's words were infused with ominous overtones. He reported that the President was in a rage over Father Coughlin. FDR was convinced, he said, that the priest's increasing attacks against him were making their mark and had already turned millions of Catholics against his New Deal. Roosevelt was certain that he'd suffer great losses, as a result, at the polls in November.

Prior to Pacelli's leaving Rome, Spellman had told him how important it was to appease the President. He had expressed the opinion that though the Holy See could not endorse Roosevelt, Pacelli had at least to meet with him. Pacelli had agreed, but had insisted that everything be kept entirely undercover with absolutely no leaks; that meant even Spellman's own talk with Roosevelt must be off the record.

"The President arranged the visit so that no journalists or anyone outside of the President's immediate household knows of my visit," the bishop reassured Pacelli in their shore-to-ship conversation. But as they hung up matters still remained unresolved. Never before had the Church in the new world been in such great internal turmoil, and the Holy Father expected Pacelli, as secretary of state, to cool down this boiling pot of political emotions. Rome's problem was now Pacelli's predicament.

To add to their concern and frustrations, Pacelli and Pascalina had their own personal worries. Both wondered how impulsive they had been in having her along with him on a trip that drew so much attention from the press. They had been together for nearly twenty years and often had quietly vacationed with each other without drawing public criticism. Always she had traveled with him in utmost secrecy and had remained a mystery, as unheard-of to the outside world as if she had never existed. But only they alone knew the full extent of the care and cleverness that were required to protect their reputations.

It has always been grounds for gossip when a nun vacations with an ordinary cleric. But for a prelate of Pacelli's stature to defy convention and travel with a nun on a historic mission—this rash act was a glaring invitation to scandal. The implications were all the greater because of Edward VIII's present embarrassing entanglement with Wallis Warfield Simpson. At that very time the king was being besieged in headlines because of his anticipated abdication to marry the woman he loved. The public was so emotionally intrigued by the royal scandal that Pascalina began to envision the possibilities of the press speculating about Pacelli and herself in the very same light.

She was confident that officials of the Holy See, were they to find out about her going along, would never breathe a word to the press or to any outsider. But had anyone of authority within the papacy learned the truth before they sailed, he would have tried mightily to dissuade Pacelli, for the Vatican was inordinately sensitive to Pascalina's potentially explosive role.

Neither had expected the rush of reporters who turned out for their sailing, and the nun and the prelate concluded, with much despair, that they had become overly confident in themselves. It was only after anxiety, prayer, and cold fear that Pascalina believed no one among the press was about to ask any hard questions about her. In fact, the journalists seemed oblivious to her traveling at Pacelli's side.

Pacelli had chosen the *Conte di Savoia* with the understanding that the owners would protect his privacy. But when an official of the line leaked the news and allowed the press aboard ship to interview him, the prelate had become so piqued that he threatened to cancel their reservations and sail aboard the *Queen Mary,* the huge new Cunard liner that had recently made its own maiden voyage to the United States.

In hopes of easing the touchy situation, Pascalina had jokingly suggested that they fly to America by dirigible. The famous German zeppelin, the *Hindenburg,* was making regular transatlantic flights between Berlin and New York at the time, and Pacelli had leaped at the idea with unexpected exuberance. *"Fantástico! Fantástico!"* the prelate shouted. The nun had been aghast at his response. She had never flown and was terrified at the idea, and now believed that once again she had foolishly allowed things to go too far, as she had by jumping at the chance of traveling to America.

"Wouldn't a routine sailing, Eminence, be the wisest, quietest way?" she had nervously interjected, moving to quell his runaway enthusiasm. He reconsidered. If the *Conte di Savoia* had them in the spotlight, what would a transatlantic flight aboard a dirigible do to their reputations?

"All right, we'll remain aboard the vessel," Pacelli said reluctantly.

"Since we were still at the dock, I again suggested that it might be wise for me to return to the palace and for Eminence to travel to America without me," Pascalina reflected many years later. "But he wouldn't hear of it. 'I've always been able to handle the press, and I'll continue doing so,' he told me. Apparently, Eminence felt that he had promised me the trip and that it would be unfair to disappoint me at that late date. He was that kind of man. At times, he could be most difficult, but on other occasions—such as then—most considerate and kindhearted."

Apparently, Pacelli had noticed how much of a little girl's enthusiasm she had shown coming aboard ship for the first time. "I am like a child with excitement," she wrote in German during their first day out. "Feel heart pounding. . . . It is my first time at sea. . . . Weather warm, sunny. . . . Everybody in vacation spirit."

It wasn't surprising to Pascalina that Pacelli and the Vatican colored the truth by way of obscuring the real purpose of this trip to the United States. The Holy See was traditionally oblique in its ambitions and operations, often using simple subterfuge as diversion. Nor did it jar her senses, after all the years in his service, that political intrigue was at the root of Pacelli's plan to take her to America. He was primarily a diplomat, and she had not believed for a moment that he was being deliberately deceptive when he told her at the palace that they were going abroad to cheer her spirits.

Their special world, the joint arena of religion and high diplomacy, had a particular communication that only they could interpret and understand. It was expected, even appreciated, by the nun that the prelate would embroider little sentimentalities, such as telling her a white lie about the trip being planned all for her. It was their private, intimate way of coping with the denial of human desires that both were under lifelong obligation to sacrifice. Pacelli's tender form of deception she took as a sensitive show of his love for her. She was perceptive enough to realize that he was sugarcoating news of a mission with the most delicate political implications.

Though Pacelli held great respect for her, Pascalina always accepted the idea that nuns in the minds of the clergy were women of tough mold. She had no regrets about the subservience that was required of her. She had vowed to be a servant of the Church, one from whom everything was expected with nothing given in return, except remembrance in the prayers of those she served.

She wasn't sensitive to being stored away aboard ship like secret contraband. As a nun, she expected privations and was used to stepping quietly through the shadows. She was sensibly conscious of her delicate place and appreciated the problems that would greet any nun foolish enough to flaunt her own presence. Then, too, there seemed to be too much aimlessness and frivolity in shipboard travel for one whose mind was so accustomed to running at full power and purpose, and so she found escape and comfort in meditation and prayer during the long hours she had to herself.

For the other passengers, including the clergy, there was table tennis, or swimming, or card playing, even dancing, or any one of numerous attractions. But for someone in her sensitive position public pleasures and pastimes were entirely out of the question. Nuns were supposed to set Divine example and shatter no illusions. Fortunately she loved to read, so she spent hours in her cabin, poring through newspapers and magazines, often clipping out items for Pacelli's own perusal.

Part of her responsibility was keeping Pacelli, as diplomat, informed about current goings-on. Since his immediate interest was the United States, he should know what was happening in America, even have knowledge of subjects that a prelate of his stature would ordinarily consider trite or of no interest. She kept herself as well-versed as he on most subjects, including topics that bored or even disgusted her.

Having often heard that Americans were "sports crazy," Pascalina saw to it that Pacelli was especially familiarized with baseball. The New York Yankees and the Giants were to play in the 1936 World Series while she and Pacelli would be in New York, and she felt the prelate should show his knowledge of the great American pastime.

Pascalina's briefings for Pacelli portrayed her keen insight of current events. Her writing pad, scrawled during the seven-day voyage, contained notes of events few suspected a nun or future pope would give second thoughts to:

Crooner Bing Crosby outselling all singers on phonograph records.

Publisher Henry Luce of Time and Fortune to publish new magazine called Life.

Important Broadway play: "The Women" by Clare Boothe. At Ethel Barrymore Theatre. Play features Ilka Chase, Jane Seymour, Arlene Francis . . .

Important musical films: "Gold Diggers" and "Broadway Melody of 1936." Stars: Eleanor Powell, Jack Benny, Robert Taylor.

Big bands: Benny Goodman, Louis Armstrong, Duke Ellington.

"Monopoly" game of day.

American humor: "Knock-Knock, Who's There?"

American public divided over controversial execution of Bruno Richard Hauptmann for kidnapping and murder of Charles A. Lindbergh, Jr.'s baby.

Charles Lucky Luciano sentenced to 30 to 50 years in New York State prison for compulsory prostitution of women.

It was a habit of Pascalina's to study Pacelli as he scanned her daily briefing list. Sometimes she'd look at him knowingly, often quizzically. When he finished, they frequently exchanged understanding glances, or smiled, or shook their heads in a silent, condescending language all their own.

"Americans are most peculiar people," he once remarked to her with a wry wink.

Though the nun and the secretary of state had become the closest of friends in many ways, Pascalina was beginning to feel increasing concern toward Pacelli's flippant handling of the truth with those he sought to influence. He had never tried to be maliciously deceptive with her, for it was not in his nature to behave that way toward her— and furthermore she was far too clever and too much his match at any game of wits.

Reality had taught her that some fudging of the truth by a world diplomat might be necessary at times in the thick of international gamesmanship. Perhaps under certain pressing circumstances it was even vital for Pacelli to create disguises for real intentions, if the end result seemed honorable.

Pacelli had convinced her that Father Coughlin had to be sacrificed. He had taken pains to explain that the priest's silencing by the Holy See must be done with the utmost tact and without the slightest knowledge of the press and the public. Otherwise, Holy Mother Church had far too much to lose, Pacelli had said.

Still, Pascalina had grave misgivings about the prelate's decision to deceive the world press, a deception she felt sure would catch up with him. While she usually agreed with Pacelli's handling of most matters, her years in the Curia's press relations office had shown her that American journalists, in particular, were quite different from their counterparts among the run-of-the-mill foreign correspondents stationed in Rome, whom the Holy See silenced routinely. Indeed, they could be "dangerous," she would remark many years later.

As the *Conte di Savoia* moved into the Narrows of New York Harbor, Pascalina stood alone on the top deck by the rail, the brisk October breeze rippling her black robes. She could see Pacelli in the distance, holding audience on the captain's bridge, beckoning the gathering crowd for benediction.

The fading sunlight blended with the purple of the prelate's

Roman mantle as he raised on high the consecrated Host. The bridge for the moment had become the throne from which the cardinal secretary of state would bestow his blessing upon New York City.

The sea beneath her churned from green to blue to purple, with streaks of gold cast by the sun's lowering rays. Overhead, Pascalina saw clusters of planes defying reason and sudden death as they dipped and rolled in the exciting pageantry of an American-style greeting.

Their ship churned past the Statue of Liberty and headed up the Hudson. The river was jammed with craft of various sorts, each out to welcome the Pope's emissary. As far as the nun could see, there were sailboats, excursion steamers, yachts, barges, rowboats, nearly all showing the papal colors of yellow and white.

Suddenly there was the ear-shattering explosion of official salute. Warships of the United States were firing volley after volley high into the sky, and fireboats were spraying the harbor with multicolored streams. America's magnificent adoration had been let loose upon their ship. Though ordinarily Pascalina disliked gaudiness, the jumping, shouting, flag-waving people on the docks meant much to her at that moment; not for her sake, or for Pacelli's. She glowed with warmth because Americans were showing they were good people and worshiped God. Tears of joy came to her eyes at this tremendous display of love and respect for a symbol of Christ. To Pascalina it was clear that Americans wanted Almighty God in their lives.

"I tremble with joy," Pascalina wrote hurriedly, so overwhelmed that she had to capture on paper "every blessed expression of exhilaration." . . . "I feel very happy and excited. Like I am 15 again, back in Munich during glorious days of Oktoberfest, with Mama and Papa. Someone points finger at skyline. Says, 'There is Radio City and Waldorf Astoria.' I see Empire State Building, too. It is tall and straight, like Eminence. A great sight!"

The Holy See's view of how the press had supposedly been easily thwarted by the Vatican's confident cardinal secretary of state was later described by the Reverend Gannon, Spellman's authorized biographer. According to Father Gannon the liner had no sooner docked in New York Harbor than the "distinguished visitor [Pacelli] put the reporters at their ease and charmed them with his affability and wit, without, at the same time, saying a single thing."

Choosing the right moment, Pacelli read from a carefully prepared statement:

> Despite the private character of my visit I know well that I am expected to make my little contribution to the representatives of the Press as a sort of "journalistic tax of entry" into the United States. Accordingly, I am happy to be able to say that the Holy Father in the midst of the heavy burdens of his apostolic office, with youthful energy and untiring devotion, ever labors by every means in his power to extend to all peoples and all nations in their present difficulties the incomparable aid and encouragement found only in the teachings of Christ.

The press's quite different view of Pacelli's arrival was expressed by Barrett McGurn, a news reporter who subsequently covered the Vatican throughout Pacelli's reign as Pius XII.

"One of my first assignments as a reporter on a New York newspaper had been to join the crew of ships' news photographers and writers on a chill morning in 1936, sailing down New York Harbor to interview the Cardinal Secretary of State," McGurn wrote.

> We scrambled up the gangplank as the ocean liner docked . . . ducked through narrow hallways and up stairwells. The Cardinal awaited us in one of the broader corridors. The Vatican dignitary . . . smiled cordially but a shade coolly, inviting none of the rough camaraderie which the ultra democratic ships' reporters and cameramen considered their privilege. There was a continental air of courtesy and dignity which impressed and somewhat repressed all of us.
>
> Pacelli was withdrawn throughout his interview. Aides said he was not the person the world thought him to be. Some of his most intimate collaborators said that he was bafflingly difficult for even them to penetrate to the depths of his soul.
>
> There was reason to suspect that the Vatican prelate, the main assistant of Pope Pius XI, had come to silence the Michigan priest [Father Coughlin] and to take the Catholic Church out of the American [presidential] campaign.
>
> The interview was over in minutes. The Cardinal handed out a prepared statement. It told us that he was on vacation and that he was excited at the thought of seeing such a dynamic and important

new part of the world as the United States had become. There was no word about the Michigan radio orator.

The deans of our press group tried a few questions about the Detroit priest, but a distant, inscrutable and determined smile was the only reply. The round-cheeked young American Monsignor [Spellman] at the Cardinal's side found it unneccessary to do any coaching. It was evident that in helping with the cautiously non-political statement, the American priest had already given ample and shrewd advice.

Dealing with us in that unsatisfactory interview had been two of the most dominant figures of American and world Catholicism of the generation then rising.

Despite all the front-page coverage and the explicit detail with which the cardinal secretary of state's arrival was noted in the press, no mention was made of Pascalina.

At the precise moment when all attention was upon Governor Herbert Lehman and Mayor Fiorello La Guardia as they emerged through the gathering of Church dignitaries to kiss Pacelli's ring, Pascalina stepped unnoticed from the ship, going alone, swiftly and quietly, down the gangplank. Not once during all the fanfare of welcome had she emerged into the spotlight, and never for a moment was she missed. No one had needed to conceal her presence, for she was fully intent upon remaining inconspicuous. Everyone, even roving, suspicious reporters who caught a glimpse of her, thought of the nun as merely a lowly servant, perhaps present to serve Pacelli a cup of coffee.

As the cardinal secretary of state and his imposing entourage later sped off in a trail of sleek limousines, amid the blaring sirens of motorcycle police, Pascalina was driven away in a small black Ford. Bishop Spellman had thoughtfully reserved the car for her. She was ever grateful for all Spellman's little courtesies, a delightful quality of the man. She understood too why he had ignored her presence on the liner, a wise move that her cautious German mind fully appreciated.

While Pacelli paid an official visit to the Madison Avenue residence of New York's Archbishop Cardinal Patrick Hayes, the nun went directly to the Long Island residence of wealthy Duchess Genevieve Brady.

Pascalina had never seen anything quite like Inisfada, the Brady estate in fashionable Manhasset, New York, except among the palaces of the Vatican itself. It was well after sundown when she arrived, and the long, winding driveway leading to the imposing mansion was lined with hundreds of towering candles flickering in the breeze of the calm fall night.

As she entered the castle-like residence there was a welcoming backdrop of flowers, and the soft, pleasant scent of roses. Scores of guests had already assembled, among them politicians, philanthropists, and business tycoons, surrounded by adoring women dressed lavishly in feathers and furs. Interspersed among this noisily chattering assemblage of the elite were cardinals and archbishops and bishops in brilliant cinctures and silk ferraiolone.

A poised lady of wealth and class, obviously Duchess Brady, was receiving her guests in the great hall beneath a masterpiece depicting Christ and the Blessed Virgin.

To Pascalina's critical, no-nonsense mind, everyone seemed too giddy and too well taken care of. The sipping of drinks, the mindless chatter, the too easy laughter, the blast of organ music, all grated the nun. This was going to be a trying night of frivolity.

At first glance Pascalina knew that she wasn't going to like Duchess Brady, nor did she expect to get along with the high-powered socialite. For years the nun had been hearing stories from members of the Vatican hierarchy of "how wonderful and kind" the wealthy, middle-aged American heiress was. It seemed so false, even disgusting, to Pascalina that Genevieve Garvan Brady was idolized by the higher-ups of the clergy. She never had doubts about the churchmen's motives. The Duchess was fawned over with such extreme attention by the hierarchy simply because she had inherited more than $50 million from her late husband, Nicholas Brady.

The socially fast-moving Bradys had summered year after year in Rome and had become the darlings of the Vatican's cardinals and archbishops. For years they had wined and dined the richly robed prelates at their splendid Casa del Sole estate atop the Janiculum hill. Even in the early days, during the 1920s, Genevieve and Nicholas Brady, he a convert to Catholicism, were whispered to be extremely generous to the Church. Genevieve in particular was especially flush with expensive gifts to her favorites among the cardinals and archbishops.

Pascalina wondered what it was about Duchess Brady that instinctively brought out all the false attention by the Vatican hierarchy. At first sight the nun thought the woman seemed too intelligent to delude herself by basking in such foolishness. But what bothered Pascalina even more was the hierarchy's way of bowing to the Duchess, instead of it being the other way around, as it always was with those without wealth or influence.

Spellman, a pet of Mrs. Brady's since his early days in Rome, had been at the root of influencing Pacelli and Pius XI to find some means of conferring honor upon the woman. The papacy had then proceeded to order the Knights of Malta, the Church's highest laymen's organization, to make Mrs. Brady a Dame of Malta; later she was given the papal title of duchess.

At a time when Pacelli seemed most vulnerable to criticism, Pascalina confronted him squarely about the appellation. "What significance in the eyes of God does the title of duchess have?" she asked forthrightly. Pacelli was caught entirely off guard and replied rather sheepishly, "It's merely to please a whim of Genevieve's."

Pascalina was repulsed. As a nun, and like so many others in religious life, she had always worked herself to the bone. But not for a moment did she expect temporal trappings, or empty rewards.

"Ridiculous!" Pascalina muttered to herself as she turned away. She was speaking of people who she thought were too much into themselves, as well as of those who contributed to their pamperings.

The nun was barely inside the spacious marbled entranceway of the grand estate when Duchess Brady came rushing to her side.

"My dear Mother Pascalina!" the woman of title exclaimed, her exuberance too effervescent for the nun. "What an unexpected pleasure! I hadn't thought you were allowed to travel with His Eminence."

The Duchess was saying all the wrong things. If there was one word that irked Pascalina, it was being called "Mother." Though a nun was not supposed to dwell upon age and beauty, Pascalina's pride in her appearance remained as intense as any woman's. She knew she was beautiful, and to show herself off, she carried her person with grace and great poise. Now that she was at the menopause, she didn't need Duchess Brady to label her "Mother," a term reserved for old nuns.

Pascalina nodded in greeting and presented a half smile, but her manner could easily be taken as aloof and her words, though pleasant, were coolly reserved. The nun was the most attractive woman present, certainly younger-looking and far more fetching than the Duchess. She was as human as anyone, and it pleased her ego that men still noticed her radiance. How much nicer, she thought, to be admired as a person than to be sought out for money or influence.

But those were sinful thoughts for a nun to indulge in, she realized, and for the moment she felt ashamed. In a flash Pascalina shook all vanity from her mind. She was there to do her job as Pacelli's protectress, and was hard on herself for forgetting.

After engaging in the necessary amenities and brief exchange of pleasantries, she was impatient to get on with her responsibilities.

"I would like to see Eminence's quarters," Pascalina told the Duchess, her air of authority quite apparent. "I travel with Eminence for he has been straining himself too much with work. His health is frail. As you know, I am Eminence's housekeeper, and my one great responsibility is to see that no one imposes upon his holy spirit. He must get his rest, and not be bothered with frivolity."

Pascalina's tone was deliberately biting, even though she knew it would have been wiser to be less difficult under the circumstances. Certainly it would have been easier for all, she realized, if she had been more extroverted and pleasant. But the nun was so filled with nervous energy, so anxious to get everything done in exact order for the arrival of the cardinal secretary of state, she found it almost impossible to behave otherwise. Then, too, there was something about Duchess Brady that made it impossible for Pascalina to relax and smile.

Like a stately queen, Pascalina moved quickly through the flatteringly attentive circle of guests, with barely a nod and a smile. All heads turned to follow the haughty nun with the gorgeous ivory skin as she went directly upstairs.

Pascalina's deliberately scrupulous examination of Pacelli's quarters proved deflating to her pride. It was abundantly evident that the Duchess had gone to great lengths in making certain that everything was in perfect order. The arrangements of red and white roses, Pacelli's favorites, and the burning vigil lights upon the small altar specially constructed at the far end of the spacious room could not have been more cleverly inspired. There was absolutely nothing Pascalina could find fault with, or that needed her own painstaking touch. It seemed the Duchess was as much a mother figure as Pascalina herself.

The nun's most crushing blow came later that night when the Duchess personally escorted the cardinal secretary of state to his quarters. If they had been back in the Papal Palace, Pacelli, who was so often withdrawn and unappreciative when they were alone, would have overlooked all the effort Pascalina had put into enlivening his quarters. But his whole attitude with Duchess Brady was just the opposite.

"Oh, Duchess, everything is so beautiful!" the cardinal secretary of state exuded. For the moment Pascalina wished that she weren't a nun and Pacelli a great prelate.

"I would have gone in there and given His Eminence a piece of my mind," she recalled years later, a reflective smile lighting her face.

For nearly twenty years her life with Pacelli had been constantly motivated by Church tradition and principle. As a devoted nun, she fully understood that it would have shocked all sensibilities for her to be prominently seen in public with the prelate. It was not unexpected or unusual, therefore, for Pacelli to tell Pascalina to remain at the Duchess's estate and keep out of sight as much as possible during this period in the center of the international spotlight.

In the immediate days ahead the nun remained mostly by herself, praying and meditating, away from the people with whom she felt so uneasy. Pacelli was off, in the meanwhile, seeing New York City with Spellman and visiting members of the American hierarchy in the tri-state area of New York, New Jersey, and Connecticut.

"Eminence went to the top of Empire State Building today," Pascalina wrote. "When he returned tonight, he looked like a small boy, so excited, telling me how far off he could see through telescope. . . . Eminence plans many sight-seeing trips: Liberty Bell, Washington, D.C., where he will address National Press Club; Notre Dame to receive honorary degree, Boulder Dam, Grand Canyon, Hollywood (to watch movies being made), Niagara Falls. I am most happy because Eminence is so happy."

But the cardinal secretary of state's mission was not all pleasure. In the three weeks that followed, Pascalina saw little of Pacelli as he crisscrossed the United States by chartered plane. The busy, anxious prelate covered sixteen thousand miles, met in serious confidential session with seventy-nine bishops, and was afterward dubbed by the world press as "the flying cardinal."

She had her suspicions of the political wheeling and dealing that Pacelli was up to. But it wasn't until he said he was taking her by limousine to Boston for a special hush-hush meeting with William Cardinal O'Connell that Pascalina knew for certain their visit to the United States had far graver implications than even she had guessed.

For years Cardinal O'Connell, who ruled with absolute command over the minds and lives of the Boston Irish, had intrigued Pascalina. She had never met the legendary O'Connell, whose power over the Church in America was then so great that he would not come to Rome. Though he was never officially called to the Vatican in all the years of Pius XI's reign, the prelate previously had always found some excuse to make periodic visits to the Eternal City. The Vatican now felt it was wise—because of the Roosevelt-Coughlin feud—to seek audience with the towering and resonant O'Connell. The Pope had advised Pacelli that he'd better confer with the prelate and let him know that the papacy was entirely behind him over Coughlin.

Whenever the nun had heard the Boston cardinal's name mentioned by any of the Vatican hierarchy, it was as if the talk centered about another pope, a greater and more powerful Church ruler than Rome could remember. Though O'Connell's domain was a single American diocese, this thundering, autocratic cardinal archibishop was a Church law unto himself. In the eyes of many, O'Connell considerably dwarfed Pius XI as a man and as an influence, and to many he seemed a threat to Christ Himself.

At first Pascalina could not reconcile what it was about O'Connell's strange, sometimes un-Christlike way that stirred such fascination. Everything she had heard about the aging cardinal archbishop was so unlike Pacelli, the only man for whom she felt love and great respect. In many ways O'Connell denigrated the very elements that so attracted her to Pacelli. She knew that the Boston cardinal was widely disliked among liberals, mainly because of his hard coercion of Catholics. O'Connell's way was to whip the minds of the Boston Irish into a fanatical belief in Christ; to instill obsessive fear of Almighty God and the specter of hell.

Pacelli's manner was quite the opposite. His was the diplomat's technique of gently steering Catholics into love for Jesus, and he had turned the hearts of millions with his suave way.

The two cardinals were as physically different as they were temperamentally apart. Pacelli was frail and gave the appearance of an extremely devout figure. O'Connell stood huge and tough, Pascalina's idea of a two-fisted Irish labor leader of the era, always ready to stand ground against man or institution.

There was, however, one common denominator, other than the wearing of the red hat, that connected the two prelates and drew in Pascalina. Strangely, both men had a sometimes crippling mother complex. The nun easily identified with their obsessions. She, too, was possessed by a weakness of her own, a passion to mother extraordinary men. Could that be the reason, she wondered, that she was so anxious to meet Cardinal O'Connell?

During the drive to Boston in a limousine arranged for by Duchess Brady, Pascalina sensed an unusual uneasiness on Pacelli's part. She felt that he had taken her along as moral support for his planned encounter with O'Connell. Bishop Spellman rode with them, and he, too, seemed fidgety. Cardinal O'Connell was Spellman's superior, and even though Spellman was very close to the Pope and Pacelli, his life under O'Connell had become exceedingly trying.

Cardinal O'Connell had never wanted Spellman to be auxiliary bishop of his diocese. But Pius XI had finally become fed up with the arrogant prelate and was determined to tweak the old man's nose by forcing Spellman upon him. The Pontiff had consecrated Spellman bishop of Boston in 1932, granting him the right of succession to the post of archbishop upon O'Connell's retirement or death. From that day on Spellman found himself "in the terrible middle" between the pope and the Boston cardinal.

Even though he had the robes and authority of bishop, Spellman admitted during the drive that he was being humiliated by O'Connell at the slightest pretense. The bishop pulled from his pocket a memo by the cardinal and nervously read it aloud.

"I trust it will not be wasted advice to suggest to you . . . not to allow yourself to get any false conception of your importance," the cardinal had advised the bishop. "One of your recent letters to me savored of arrogance, a quality which ill befits a subordinate."

Hours later, when Cardinal Archbishop O'Connell stood in the impressive archway of his palatial residence on Boston's fashionable Commonwealth Avenue, beaming an exuberant greeting upon Pacelli, Spellman, and herself, everything Pascalina had heard about the prelate suddenly seemed absurd. She was overwhelmed by the graciousness of O'Connell's manner and the charisma that flowed easily from this most unusual man.

Could this prelate possibly be the cardinal archbishop who had so bitterly contested the election of Pius XI at the conclave of 1922, she thought to herself? Years before, Pacelli had told her that O'Connell had boldly accused his predecessor, Cardinal Secretary of State Gasparri, of deliberately rigging the papal elections in favor of Achille Ratti, the present Pope.

"This is a great disappointment!" O'Connell had defiantly told Gasparri at the time, referring to Ratti's election as Pontiff.

Pius XI had never forgotten the unprecedented insult. O'Connell had remained just as bitter and had kept mostly aloof from the Vatican in the fourteen years that followed.

Ironically, Rome had once been O'Connell's place of great joy. In his early life he had spent six years in the Eternal City as rector of the North American College. But during the reign of Pius XI the animosity on both sides had steadily grown.

"Let malicious tongues wag!" O'Connell had once written Spellman in response to the Vatican's criticisms of the scandals within his Boston archdiocese. "What do they really matter," the prelate added, his rancor mounting against his Vatican critics. "Boston seems to be the butt of jealous maleficence from the incompetent and the jealous minded, who can only pull down, never build anything, not even build a Christian conscience."

Finally, after all the years of animosity, the papacy and O'Connell were drawn together in 1936 by a common enemy, Father Charles Coughlin, the radio priest.

In Pascalina's estimation O'Connell could not have been more indulgent toward Pacelli. The aged cardinal even went out of his way to flatter Spellman, and she felt O'Connell was being especially ingratiating toward her. The prelate had the reputation of treating nuns like so much chattel, yet he insisted upon sitting down at his grand piano to play a delightful minuet, which he claimed he himself had composed and was dedicating to her.

As if O'Connell's artistic flourishes weren't surprise enough, Pascalina actually felt the shock running through Pacelli when the Boston cardinal began reading aloud a screenplay he had written for Greta Garbo, his favorite actress.

Bishop Spellman sat nervously on the edge of his seat throughout the reading, appearing to be entirely engrossed as O'Connell rambled on, page after page. Knowing Spellman's character so well, Pascalina realized it was easy for the jolly bishop to chuckle at the least provocation. She was sure that O'Connell's peculiar behavior was tickling Spellman's funny bone. He looked like he was about to burst into laughter at any moment, and she could see how terrified he was for fear of no longer being able to control himself.

All idle chatter ended after dinner, though, when O'Connell's legendary and demanding pomposity took full command. They were in the library at the time, sipping brandy, and Pascalina's presence was explained by Pacelli as for the purpose of taking notes.

It was all very direct and quite brief. Pacelli had come to the

United States upon demand by Cardinal O'Connell and President Roosevelt to silence Father Coughlin. FDR had insisted for months prior to the election that the Vatican take firm action against the radio priest. But it was O'Connell, seeing his own power seriously challenged and his treasury less endowed, who had placed the greatest demands upon the papacy to dispense with Coughlin.

There was no doubt in Pascalina's mind, after listening to Pacelli's recital to the Boston cardinal of his secret talks with seventy-nine American bishops, why O'Connell had been so ingratiating that evening. Pacelli had done a splendid job of undercutting Coughlin among the entire Catholic hierarchy of the United States.

It was as if the board of a major corporation had met behind closed doors—the verdict was that clear. Upstart Coughlin, no matter the nature or substance of the issues, was out. The public was to be given a veiled excuse for the radio priest's exit, with Coughlin himself elected to do the explaining. As far as the press and public were concerned, Pacelli would steadfastly maintain that he had "a pleasant and blessed vacation in the United States."

As Archbishop Cardinal O'Connell walked Pacelli, Pascalina, and Spellman to their car, his loyal black Scottie barking away by his cane, the nun easily understood why O'Connell had become such a power. Once a desperately poor boy of Irish immigrant parents and now a multimillionaire, he was a complex man of nerve and gall, a doer and a survivor.

Known as "Gangplank Bill" by his detractors because he was so often seen boarding or departing pleasure craft to or from the Bahamas, the cardinal had his darker side. He had suffered three nervous breakdowns. His nephew, Monsignor J.P.E. O'Connell, whom the cardinal had made chancellor of the Boston archdiocese, was forced out of the Church in disgrace because of a sordid sex scandal. But worse still, a bizarre murder had been committed in the cardinal's own household by one of the male staff.

O'Connell had boldly exercised his immense power to suppress these shadowy happenings in the Boston media.

Because the encounter with the old prelate had been terribly strained at times, Pascalina afterward was grateful that Spellman had been along. She had never known anyone with a more adroit knack for easing the most unpleasant situations. If it had been just Pacelli and herself, she knew, they would have remained tense for hours.

They were scarcely settled in the limousine when Spellman put Pacelli and herself on an entirely different track. The bishop used all manner of lighthearted persuasion on Pacelli to make the hour's drive down to his hometown in Whitman. Spellman was practically pleading to show off the "quite elegant" residence that he had built for his family. Though he was now the famous auxiliary bishop of Boston, she realized he still had a very keen desire, like so many people who came from simple stock, to show the world that they had arrived. Coming from a humble life herself, she could see how important it was to Spellman for the cardinal secretary of state to visit his home. Ever since she had met Spellman, he had spoken proudly of his family's livelihood being derived solely from a small grocery store.

"Eminence, we go to Whitman," Pascalina urged Pacelli, wanting so much to please Spellman. "It will do us all good to relax," she added, gently patting Pacelli's hand.

The cardinal secretary of state was still in a dark mood, but she had seen him in far worse states of mind and knew exactly, after all those years, how to take command of any deteriorating situation.

"Driver," the nun said, leaning over the front seat, "take us to His Excellency's residence in Whitman."

Pacelli looked at Pascalina with a pretense of anger. But she glared defiantly back at him in an amusing mock reply.

"You are a hard woman!" the prelate said, gently tapping the back of her hand. All three broke into laughter, Spellman looking quite delighted.

As Pascalina had suspected all along, photographers from the Boston and Whitman papers, their cameras ready to click, were gathered as their limousine turned into the circular drive fronting Spellman's impressive mansion. Early in the trip from Boston she had become suspicious when the bishop, only moments after leaving Cardinal O'Connell's residence, asked to use the rest room at a gasoline station. She had watched him go inside the building and use the public phone. Knowing Spellman's cunning ways so well by then, she had guessed that he was alerting the press.

Pacelli, as much a publicity-seeker as Spellman, looked entirely relaxed amid all the snapping away. His smile remained broad just as long as none of the press asked searching questions about his visit to the United States.

When the photographers attempted to take the nun's picture, the cardinal secretary of state stopped them immediately. Abruptly raising his hand in objection, he shook his head in a show of irritation. No one dared after that. It was always simple for Pacelli, and for most of the hierarchy, to get the press to back down quickly and without any show of objection.

Spellman's surprisingly luxurious Italian-style villa thoroughly captivated Pacelli. Using his favorite phrase to describe his feelings upon seeing the house, the prelate shouted: *"Fantástico! Fantástico!"*

Pascalina had a different reaction. She wondered to herself how someone such as Spellman, who had been only a simple priest a few years before, could possibly afford such a fine mansion. Having lived in the Papal Palace for nearly six years, Pascalina by then was well acquainted with plush and splendor. Yet it still was a shock that a rather new bishop had a palatial residence that he personally owned. Spellman's had eleven bedrooms, but despite the excessive number of chambers she was more astounded by the bishop's two exceptional baths on the first floor.

The nun watched Spellman darting breathlessly about the place, showing Pacelli everything, pointing with obvious pride to the masterpieces of Christ and other holy figures that were hung throughout. In Pascalina's eyes he was the preening peacock. She simply had to prick the bishop's balloon, she thought, for it was her nun's nature to bring anyone, even a member of the papal hierarchy, down from what she called "the foolishness of the clouds."

At the precise moment when no one was watching, Pascalina led Bishop Spellman to the most imposing of the bathrooms on the first floor. She chose one that he himself had designed, a dazzling Hollywood-style affair done in Venetian black marble with lilac fixtures and ceiling-to-floor mirrors throughout.

Pointing to what she considered "a bizarre toilet," the nun, who had grown up using outhouses on her father's farm, demanded of the bishop: "What in Heaven's name is this all about?"

Perhaps for the first time in Spellman's profusely talkative life, the roly-poly bishop was entirely speechless. Pascalina shook a finger close to his nose and whispered, "Naughty, naughty, Bishop Spellman!"

As the embarrassed churchman turned all colors, the nun walked away shaking her head, pretending to be terribly ashamed of a bishop with a bathroom like that.

On the eve of their return to Rome the cardinal secretary of state was given a warm, family-style reception by the President of the

United States. Pascalina had hoped she would be invited to the small, private affair at Roosevelt's Hyde Park home, but she was entirely overlooked. Pacelli and Spellman, she was certain, had kept her a secret from the President.

It would have been far too political and irregular for Pacelli, as cardinal secretary of state, to have met with Roosevelt before the election. But with the President's landslide victory two days past, and with FDR having carried forty-six of the forty-eight states for a second-term mandate, the Holy See had everything to gain by joining in a public display of friendship for FDR and his New Deal.

The press was given no word of the cardinal secretary of state's private talk with the President. All Pacelli said of his meeting with Roosevelt was "I enjoyed lunching with a typical American family."

The prelate did reveal to Pascalina in confidence the details of his secret discussion. "White House recognition of the Vatican is assured," he said upon returning from his meeting with Roosevelt. "The President is grateful that the noisy priest will talk no more." Pacelli was gleeful.

Within days Father Coughlin took to the air to announce his complete withdrawal from public affairs. The radio priest, in answer to a skeptical press, denied that any pressure had been placed upon him by the Church.

But on November 5, 1954, nearly eighteen years later, Coughlin told the truth. In reply to a query from Father Gannon, the radio priest revealed for the first time that Pacelli had indeed silenced him. Coughlin also exposed the devious means by which he had been taken off the air.

"May I set down what I know relative to the incidents associated with me and the termination of my broadcast," Coughlin wrote in part.

> ... Cardinal Pacelli visited America and had conversations with our high government officials, which conversations could be regarded as a type of informal pact. ... Small as I was, it was necessary to silence my voice even though I must be smeared as an anti-Semite, as a pro-Nazi and a bad priest, when really all I was, outside of trying to be a Christian and an American, was an anti-Bolshevik, anti-Nazi and an anti-warmonger. ... Needless to say, the smear was effective, and I was eliminated by devious ways and means—all indirect yet more effective than were these ways and means direct.

At the time the priest wrote his letter to Father Gannon, Pacelli had been Pope Pius XII for fifteen years. Even so, Coughlin pointedly concluded with a blast at the Holy Father. "You are entirely free to print whatever I have written for I have no fears from any man living insofar as I have arrived at that point when it is better to serve the truth than it is to follow misdirected diplomats."

On November 7, 1936, amid the cheers of thousands, the cardinal secretary of state, along with his small group of aides, Pascalina included, sailed from New York for return to Rome.

In his farewell the prelate told America: "We thank the blessed people of the great land of the United States for the wonderful and most peaceful rest and vacation, and we will always remember you in our prayers."

Back again in Rome, Pascalina found herself more confused, more at a crossroads, than ever. The trip to America had certainly not provided the opportunity she had hoped for a heart-to-heart talk and understanding with Pacelli. To the contrary, the anything but forthright manner with which Father Coughlin had been deceptively sealed off by Pacelli did not do credit, in her estimation, to the character of the Holy See. It was not that she necessarily agreed with Coughlin's political values, but she most certainly was not in accord with the Church's failure to act with principle.

A woman already at middle age, Pascalina found herself asking many of the introspective questions she supposed any sane person of her years might seek answers to were they in her position. Many years before, at a tender age, Pascalina had given her life, her most priceless possession, to the Church for only one reason: She had every faith and confidence in the teachings of Christ.

Now, day after day during her hours of prayerful meditation, she agonized over the right and wrong of closing her eyes any longer to the Vatican's expedient, self-serving tactics. The Coughlin incident, though minor in her estimation to far more grave violations of truth and integrity by the Vatican, seemed the catalyst for her increasingly serious soul-searching.

If duplicity, even harrowing lies, had been used against Father Coughlin, she now believed that any assault on morality and ethics by the Vatican was quite conceivable. This was hardly out of character in a nun who saw everything in terms of black and white, while the politically motivated hierarchy dealt in shades of gray.

Italy's war on Ethiopia fit that conception. For years Mussolini had been preparing the world for his empire-building. He had boasted time and again to millions of followers from his famous Rome balcony that Ethiopia was to be his first "annexation."

The Vatican had a great deal to gain in the fascist take-over of the North African nation. Though the Holy See historically professed its neutrality with warring states, and traditionally condemned military force, the Vatican now suddenly found an exception in what it called a "just war." Ethiopia, also known at the time as Abyssinia, had been largely Catholic from the fourth century through the eighth century, when it broke away from the Holy Roman Catholic Church and followed the beliefs of the Coptic Church (the Egyptian Christian Church), considered to be heretical by the Vatican. With the country under fascist rule, the Holy See would be free to proselytize the conquered people. Mussolini's power as Italy's conquering hero had been greatly enhanced, a decided advantage for the Church. Il Duce's fascist regime was more securely entrenched, and there was far less likelihood of the Italian nation turning to atheistic communism or reverting to the anticlerical governments that had plagued the papacy in the past. Then, too, Ethiopia had a large slave population, which Il Duce pledged to free, a humanitarian stand that further served the papacy's reasoning.

The virtually defenseless Ethiopians had been terrified at the prospect of war and had begged the League of Nations to stop Mussolini's expansionist plans. The world body answered Ethiopia with lip service.

The Holy See had been in a strong psychological position to avert war. Since Italy was solidly Catholic and the fascists had a pact with the Vatican, it seemed reasonable that had the papacy spoken out, Mussolini, fearing the brunt of world opinion, would have backed down.

But even as the war clouds darkened, the Vatican chose to walk a careful political tightrope, claiming at the time that the Holy See must remain neutral to maintain credibility in the eyes of the world. On the surface the Pope struggled to appease both sides by playing the papacy's cards close to his chest. He finally faced the boiling issue only two months before the outbreak of war, when little choice remained for him but to bow to the pressures of world leaders.

"Clouds darken the sky over Italy and Abyssinia," the Pontiff had stated on July 28, 1935.

> No one should deceive himself that they may not contain dire events. We hope and believe always in the peace of Christ and His realm, and we have complete confidence that nothing can happen which is not consistent with Truth, Justice and Love. One thing, however, appears certain to Us—namely that if the need for expansion is a fact, we must also take into consideration the right of defense, which also has its limits, and a moderation which must be observed if the defense is to remain guiltless.

Pius XI's noncommittal words, meaningless to the Ethiopians, were taken as solace by Il Duce. Great Britain publicly attacked the Holy Father's halfhearted position. "The Pope appears to be so timid as to give the impression that he supports Mussolini," Sir Samuel Hoare, the British foreign minister, said afterward in his official statement. Still, the British took no military action.

To Pascalina, who now had intimate awareness of the Vatican's sleight of hand, it was apparent that the papacy had self-serving motives in its failure to stand against Mussolini in his seizure of Ethiopia. Though she was petrified at the thought of doubting the integrity of her own Church, the evidence against the Holy See seemed more than circumstantial.

In her study of the behind-the-scenes shuffling, it became clear that the Vatican had secretly backed Mussolini in the fascist conquest of Ethiopia. The papacy had gone so far as to have used the war to further its own gain. In snatching the brass ring of opportunity, the Holy See had become a major stockholder in Italy's largest munitions plants and some of its allied war industries. During the six-year period since receiving the $92.1 million through the Lateran Treaty, the Vatican's shrewd treasurer, Bernardino Nogara, had pyramided the funds into a vast reserve now estimated at hundreds of millions of dollars. The ambitious Holy See, having grown more temporal and capitalistic than spiritual, had turned the tables on the fascist government. The Church now held large interests in many of Italy's most important industries: banking, automotive, chemicals, and insurance. Its hold on the nation's utilities was even greater, with substantial interests in Italgas, major supplier of gas to thirty-six cities, and in Società Finanziaria Telefonica, Italy's main telephone company.

Ironically, Mussolini had been forced to come to the papacy for significant financing of his unholy war with Ethiopia. Even though Christ was the Prince of Peace, the Vatican, seeing war as profitable business, had seized the opportunity and made huge loans to the fascist government.

On the day of Mussolini's invasion of Ethiopia, October 3, 1935, bishops and priests of the Church had been on hand, sprinkling holy water on the fascist troops as they left Italy's shores. The Holy See had gone so far as to bless the guns and tanks and war planes of the aggressor state.

Waving a fascist flag, the archbishop of Siena had taken position before the military, and in a loud voice praised the Black Shirts to the highest. In his prayers the archbishop predicted that fate was on Mussolini's side. "Italy, our great Duce, and the soldiers are about to win victory for truth and righteousness!" he declared. Another prelate, the bishop of San Miniato, then stepped forward to shout: "For the victory of Italy, the Italian clergy are ready to melt down the gold of the churches and the bronze of the bells."

In a cruel conflict that lasted barely nine months, the fascists swept through Ethiopia, spraying village after village in eight separate attacks with poison gas. About 250 tons of the deadly gas were used by the fascists between December 30, 1935 and mid-March 1936. Some 50,000 defenseless citizens were killed or injured. Said Ildefonso Cardinal Schuster, archbishop of Milan and close friend of Pius XI: "On the plains of Ethiopia, the Italian standard carries forward in triumph the Cross of Christ, smashes the chains of slavery, and opens the way for the missionaries of the Gospel." Cardinal Schuster then referred to Mussolini as "he who has given Italy to God and God to Italy."

To commemorate the fascist victory, the Pope had sent the archbishop of Rhodes to Ethiopia's capital, Addis Ababa, as his official apostolic visitor to celebrate a Pontifical Mass. The prelate offered the prayers of the Holy See for "all the heroic soldiers of the Italian army, which the world admires but which Heaven has no need to marvel at, since they are God's ally."

Pascalina's years of subtle rationalizing and her growing doubts of the Holy See had a cumulative effect at this time, her most vulnerable age. She was at the change of life, a most difficult period for her to be wrestling with confusions of truth and morality. Then, too, the fact that she was in religious life did not lessen for a moment her distress at the onslaught of middle age, with its threat to her physical beauty. Her life with the cardinal secretary of state was no help; her frayed nerves were on edge enough without learning of Pacelli's strong say in the very transgressions she found so painfully crushing.

"Christ is the Prince of Peace!" the nun shouted angrily at the prelate, not caring at the time how out of line she might appear. "Has the Holy See forgotten Jesus for the profits of war?"

Pacelli stood speechless before Pascalina, horrified by her all too pointed words.

In the eyes of the world Pacelli was the so-called Vice-Pope and apparently heir to the throne of Saint Peter, but the nun was dressing him down just as if she were an angry judge condemning a heartless criminal.

Pascalina ran from him and closed herself away in her room; the tears were welling up, and her whole body was shaking violently.

"I had shut my eyes to too many things for too long," she recalled with much sadness many years later. "I felt a slow, subtle erosion had been taking control of my mind and soul."

Serving for so many years alongside the cardinal secretary of state in the Vatican's secretariat, witnessing firsthand the routine, matter-of-fact duplicity of international diplomacy, had robbed the nun of some of Christ's most precious values.

While Pacelli and others of the hierarchy resorted to expediency in certain matters of truth and honor, Pascalina thrashed about in her soul, blaming herself for standing idly by without taking action against overt evil.

Her years in the Vatican, she believed, had considerably lessened her resistance to abrasions upon her character. Pascalina's confessor had warned her repeatedly of the Vatican's constant chipping away at her solid integrity. She thought of this "whittling away of con-science" as "the seduction of me," and blamed herself mostly for not facing up to the fading of her ideals "until it was almost too late."

Finally, Pascalina realized that her answer would come only in communication with Jesus—through her daily hour of sacred medi-tation with Him. At first, during those painful, anxious moments of silent reflection—an avowed obligation of her religious order—she felt the torment mount within her soul. Then Christ's words came in clear warning. She seemed to hear Almighty God telling her that though she had never taken part in any major wrong or sin, she had done nothing remarkable to combat the evils of the hierarchy. Despite all her years of soul-searching and troubled conscience, despite her position of influence at the elbow of enormous religious power—the mother figure who held the ear of the one man who practically ran the Holy Roman Catholic Church now that the reigning Pontiff was clearly dying—she had too long restrained her voice and instincts.

Pascalina knew then that she had to come to grips at once with the slow, insidious course of her life and take a firm stand. If she failed to act, she would be destroyed by the very crimes and sins that she had sworn with holy vows to fight against.

But within a week of Pascalina's outburst, before she had seized the gauntlet that Christ would cast her way, Pacelli himself took action. For several days the prelate had avoided speaking to her, nor would he even look her way. Whenever he was required to pass her desk, he kept his eyes buried in papers to avert her attention. She knew that he was deeply troubled, but she could not decide whether he was angry at her or terribly troubled by his own conscience.

At week's end the cardinal secretary of state dropped his bombshell. Pascalina had just seated herself at her desk when suddenly he poked his head out of his office and asked her to come inside. When she entered, he closed the door behind them for complete privacy.

"I have decided to resign," Pacelli said, his shocking, sobering words tumbling out before she had chance to say a word of greeting. His determined expression, the haggard, sallow look upon his face—everything about his manner—convinced her that the prelate had fully made up his mind. "My conscience troubles me deeply," Pacelli went on in a low, choked voice, his eyes as serious as his tone. "Your words have caused me to reexamine my conscience, particularly in the matter of Father Coughlin and Holy Mother Church's position in Ethiopia."

"Eminence, should you not first speak with His Holiness?" she nervously blurted out. She was in such a confused state that she hardly realized what she was doing as she reached out and took both his hands in hers. In warm, motherly fashion she pleaded, "Perhaps you can convince the Holy Father to correct some injustices and prevent others from happening?" Her mind was beginning to clear. Perhaps, after all, Pacelli was more principled than expedient, she reasoned. Once he had been her ideal priest and perfect example of human love and compassion. If success had made him less of a good cleric, she now felt it was political influence that had tarnished him. His sincere repentance told her there was plenty of character left in him with which to rebuild a better papacy.

"I have spoken to His Holiness," Pacelli replied, looking even more hopeless. "Pius is not about to change. He forced me to get down on my knees before him and swear never again to defy his authority." The cardinal secretary of state, now almost in tears, turned abruptly and went to the window; he could not bear her to see the full extent of his shame.

"But, Eminence, you always seemed to have such influence over His Holiness," she exclaimed with surprise, feeling more confused than ever.

"That is because I always manage to say what His Holiness wants to hear," Pacelli confessed. Disinclined by temperament to delegate authority and a respecter of no one's feelings, Pius XI discouraged independence and initiative in his subordinates. Sir Charles Wingfield, the British minister to the Vatican, once remarked of the strange relationship between Pius and Pacelli: "His own secretary of state is said to be often unwilling to make representations which would likely annoy him."

"Pius is an old man," Pascalina persisted. "How long has he left to live?" Her instincts convinced her that Pacelli must remain in office for the good of Holy Mother Church. She felt certain now that her hold upon him would keep him in line. But at the moment, Pacelli was not listening.

She pleaded with him to take no drastic action for a few days, at least until enough time had passed to make certain that he was positive of the enormity of his decision. The nun kept up her insistence until finally Pacelli agreed.

Her prayers and perseverance appeared to prevail, for as the days passed she saw Pacelli's resolve start to slacken. The Pope suffered a slight heart attack, and this sudden crisis in the papacy buttressed her argument.

"Eminence, I prayed to Jesus today that He would make you the next Holy Father," Pascalina confessed as she placed a sumptuous slice of blueberry pie before him at dinner. The dessert was one of the prelate's favorites, as it had been her father's. She was hoping that Pacelli would relent as easily as Papa Lehnert had when she insisted that he bathe in the barn those many years before.

"Dear Sister Pascalina," Pacelli began, looking up at the nun, a delighted smile lighting his face, "what do you think I should do?"

It was all over then. She wanted to throw her arms about him, but her sacred vows said "No!" Though she reluctantly guarded her conduct, her words were spoken demurely: "Eminence, I would like you to do what our dear Lord asks, that you remain as cardinal secretary of state and serve Him with all your love and integrity."

As the threat of war loomed in early 1939, the nun moved with ever-increasing authority and mystery within the Church's high world of international politics. Still garbed in the prosaic, bulky robes of a simple sister, she was a woman of influence, though without title or portfolio, in a male chauvinistic sphere.

A major crisis in the papacy, which Pascalina years later described as "the will of God," had set the time in history for the nun—at age forty-five—to take a meaningful stand with the cardinal secretary of state.

On February 10, 1939, the eve of the tenth anniversary of the Lateran Treaty and the day set for celebration of the sixtieth year of Pius XI's priesthood, Pacelli was abruptly shaken from sleep and rushed to the Pontiff's quarters. The Holy Father had suffered a severe heart attack during the night. Pacelli was just able to kneel at the old man's bedside and take an almost lifeless hand in his when the Pope died.

Pacelli, as camerlengo, was now in full command of the Holy Roman Catholic Church. The time finally was at hand, Pascalina realized, to take Pacelli in charge, a self-imposed responsibility from which the nun would never budge.

VII

No one, not even Pascalina, could understand the defeating emotions that overcame Pacelli now that he faced the immediate prospect of becoming pope. It was altogether heartrending for her to watch Christ's deputy, this popular and revered leader of the Church who almost assuredly would become Holy Father to nearly a half billion Catholics, fall apart at this last moment. He was behaving like an actor trembling before his supreme role.

"Miserere mei!" Pacelli tragically repeated over and over to her after summoning her quite unexpectedly to his private quarters in the Papal Palace. She had found him alone, his face contorted with emotion as he paced the floor, wringing his hands pathetically. "Have pity on me!"

For quite some time there had been little doubt among the high inner circle of the papacy that Pacelli would become the new pontiff. Pius XI had repeatedly told the hierarchy in recent years that Pacelli had all the best qualifications to succeed as Holy Father. As a manipulator of statesmen and nations, the trained, astute diplomat towered above all other candidates for the throne of Saint Peter.

Yet, even though Pacelli had the superb advantage of being cardinal secretary of state and, as camerlengo, was in command of the pending conclave to elect a new pope, his first priority in Pascalina's eyes must be to pull himself together. The critical decision still remained for the Sacred College of Cardinals to do the official choosing.

She had every reason to be apprehensive. She knew all too well that if the hierarchy, as disposed as the majority was toward Pacelli, even suspected the prelate's vacillation and unraveling display, they'd turn from him in an instant.

Years of experience had taught her that no expression of sympathy or cajoling on her part would bring Pacelli out of his acute despair. His black moods had to run their course.

On the other hand the nun, always ready to grasp at opportunity, wasted no time.

"You do all the brooding you like, Eminence," Pascalina said impatiently, without the slightest show of compassion. "There is no time to waste. I go to prepare the papal quarters for your presence."

She knew that Church tradition required days of exhausting responsibility and detail between the death of a pope and the naming of a successor. Pacelli was too emotionally immobilized to move alone, without her. Fortunately she had enough inspiration and intensity to make whatever major decisions and moves that she, in her own wisdom and experience, considered essential.

With no authority whatsoever from Pacelli or from any of the hierarchy, Pascalina swept into the dead Pope's quarters and brushed out everyone and everything. She moved just as deliberately as did yet another unsympathetic regime nearly twenty years later, when she herself would be abruptly stripped of authority and ousted from the Papal Palace.

Pascalina assumed that Jesus would want no one at Peter's throne but Pacelli, even in spite of the prelate's array of human flaws. She had the added confidence that her own strength of character and staunch belief in the teachings of Christ would both enlighten and buttress the future pope.

Whatever Pacelli's reservations, they seemed secondary to Pascalina. What remained important to the nun was the potent effectiveness of her bolstering spirit upon his faltering uncertainty.

"Jesus is always with you and I will never desert you," she reassured him that night when he could not sleep.

No woman in history had ever been inside the heavily guarded, closed-off Vatican arena during a papal conclave. Since the earliest days of Christianity the conclave was a place of male glory where only high Church powers were allowed in to vote. Now the voting was restricted solely to cardinals.

Yet, knowing Pacelli's sad, weakened state, she defied Vatican tradition and told him at breakfast after his sleepless night: "I go with you to the conclave and remain at your side throughout the election." She spoke with determined confidence.

Even though Pacelli was camerlengo, with full authority to admit whomever he and his fellow cardinals chose as aides, he looked aghast at her brazen insistence on violating the sacred sanctum.

"No!" he retorted in commanding voice. The idea of him, the cardinal secretary of state, or any prelate, bringing a woman to the strictly male and private papal election seemed entirely out of the question to him.

"Yes! I go there," Pascalina insisted, equally determined. "Tell me if Jesus Christ ever excluded any woman from His household. I have seen what certain Vatican ways have done to you as a good priest. I beg you, Eminence, please consider my way for a change." She paused. When she again spoke, her voice was soft, tender. "Eminence, I have prayed to Jesus for the inspiration to help make you a good, strong pope."

For the first time, after nearly a quarter of a century of being together, the future pope's arms went about the nun. He clung to her, like an errant boy against his mother's breast, seeking forgiveness and courage. There were tears of joy in their eyes at that warm, touching moment.

"Dear God, please help us!" she whispered.

On the afternoon of Wednesday, March 1, 1939, nineteen days after the death of Pius XI, the papal conclave began with Rome's usual show of great ceremonial solemnity.

By noon the area about Saint Peter's Square, including the Papal Palace, the Sistine Chapel, and the Hall of Saint Damaso, was entirely sealed off from the world.

Most of the princes of the Sacred College of Cardinals had already gathered. Pacelli, as *Chef de l'Église* (acting Chief of the Church), somberly greeted each prelate in the impressive marbled assembly Hall of Saint Damaso. Some came alone to him, others in groups.

The full body of the Sacred College consisted of sixty-two cardinals at the time. Most were old men, mainly Italians, although a significant number were from the United States and other foreign nations that had large Catholic populations.

Pascalina, laden with Pacelli's special needs and medicines, arrived amid all the confusion of the settling-in. There had been no "right" moment for the nun to make her entrance. Her timing was of little importance anyway, since sooner or later the entire hierarchy would be aware of her presence. Besides, she was the type who preferred to "get the embarrassment over and done with early."

Numbers of prelates were standing about in groups, holding informal conferences, as the nun entered.

She had never before seen men look so horrified and speechless at her presence.

"I felt like such a strange, undesired curiosity," she said laughingly as she reflected over the long years. "For an instant, I wanted to run back to the palace and hide."

Though normally she was a nun of extreme discretion, her dramatic entrance was a deliberate attempt to make it clear to all how close she was to Pacelli. If she had sneaked in, their scandal-conscious minds would have imagined all manner of immoral goings-on, Pascalina had concluded. The old-fashioned cardinals just had to accept reality, she told herself. Pacelli was not in the best health—his spirit called for strong bolstering, and his body required her close care. No matter what the mighty hierarchy might think, Pascalina's far greater, overriding concern was the prelate's critical need of her at this crucial time.

Not for a moment did she allow her embarrassment to show. With head high and face set stern she made her way through the astonished prelates. Her look was straight ahead, and her face imperceptibly flushed. "Nuns have a way of discreetly avoiding eye contact," she said long afterward, more than a little facetiously.

As scores of red hats turned to follow her direction, she went straight to Pacelli's conclave quarters, a simple cell—one for each cardinal—set up temporarily in one of the halls of the Papal Palace.

Appearances mattered little to her at the time. Pascalina had what she considered "an important function to carry out." As Pacelli's protectress, she had spared none of her own reputation. It was not so important to her that the cardinals might denigrate her among themselves; what was important was Pacelli's need of her.

"I have always felt that none of us is so strong that we can live every part of life without someone being there to strengthen our backbone at the right moment," she said. "I had come to realize by then that even a great pope has his human moments, his times of weakness."

Pascalina was too astute not to have considered all of the possible ramifications of the potentially embarrassing scandal. There was no doubt in her mind that being alongside Pacelli under such circumstances was straining blatancy and rashness to the hilt. But even after assessing all the risks, she had decided to go ahead with what could have been an exceedingly explosive situation.

"Eminence was an ailing man and too distraught at the moment to act decisively," she reflected. "I felt it was my responsibility to protect him, and, in the doing, serve the Holy See. At the time, Eminence was sixty-three and I was forty-five. Both of us too old to be ridiculous. If the Sacred College of Cardinals was so lacking in understanding and compassion as to misjudge the situation, it mattered little to me what conclusions they arrived at. In my heart, there was only one paramount consideration. As long as Jesus knew everything was right, that was all that counted."

The nun's calculated risk in defying the age-old chauvinistic tradition of the papal conclave was not as great as might have appeared. With Europe on the threshold of World War II, the Princes of the Church felt at the time that the Vatican sorely needed Pacelli's vast diplomatic ability and experience to steer a safe course for the Holy See. Pascalina had no doubt that the temporal-minded cardinals, who chuckled so easily at the implications of any man-woman relationship, nevertheless would not allow gossip, no matter how eyebrow-raising, to stand in the way of the Church's vested interests. She was convinced that the prelates, though shocked by her presence, would raise no official objections, and she proved to be right.

Sleeping arrangements had always been a major problem during Rome's conclaves, and the papal election of 1939 was hardly an exception. Makeshift apartments, one each for the sixty-two cardinals, had been rushed into construction immediately upon Pius XI's death. Situated on three floors of the Papal Palace, the quarters were extremely simple, both in arrangement and in their sparse furnishings.

Each apartment had three rooms with two or more cots, a table per room, and a few chairs. A crucifix was hung with such prominence in each of the quarters that, upon entering, the dying figure of Christ caught the eye before anything else.

Most cardinals were so accustomed to the plush, good life that they did not take easily to the stark simplicity. As so many disappointed prelates had done during earlier conclaves, many showed their contempt by referring to the humble quarters as "cells."

Pacelli's quarters, labeled Cell No. 13, were no different than any of the others. Many of the cardinals went about in utter frustration, complaining of the sequestered routine and privations. Pascalina remained entirely undaunted as she arranged all of Pacelli's needs. She cared only that her special priest be as comfortable as she could possibly make him.

The nun sincerely hoped that the other cardinals were as well served as Pacelli. Their aides were males, either priests or laymen, and all long known to be trustworthy and subservient. Like herself, these assistants were sworn to secrecy and were not entitled to vote.

As Pacelli continued on that first afternoon with the minor formalities attendant to gracious welcoming, some of the hierarchy who had arrived early went to sleep. They excused themselves by claiming they were taking advantage of Rome's traditional habit of napping in midafternoon. Others prayed. Numbers made the rounds of old friends, some to see if any colleague had been given better accommodations.

Pascalina kept to herself inside Pacelli's cell. For about an hour she prayed and meditated, on her knees, before a small statue of Jesus, Pacelli's favorite.

By late afternoon the cardinals were all in robes of purple, the hierarchy's mourning garb for the late Pius XI. Pascalina watched as they assembled and marched in solemn procession to the Sistine Chapel. Many were holding firmly to their red hats against blasts of early March wind as they crossed the walled-off courtyard. With the noble Swiss Guard in ceremonial splendor at their flank and rear, Pacelli led the way. They were chanting, *Veni Creator Spiritus.*

One by one each cardinal came by seniority to the main altar of the Sistine. There, prelate after prelate sank to his knees, made the sign of the cross, and swore his solemn oath. Pledge upon pledge was made to Almighty God that each and every vote for the future pope would be cast "freely and deliberately, uninfluenced by political advantage, or any worldly consideration."

At nightfall Pacelli, as acting Chief of the Church, ordered a search of the entire conclave area for any possible hidden intruders. He barred from the secret proceedings everyone without proper cre-

Sister Pascalina of the Teaching Sisters of the Holy Cross (circa 1935).

Eugenio Pacelli *(left),* ‌
age twelve, takes a brea‌
with other students durin‌
a countryside excursion ‌
Italy in 1888. (UNITE‌
PRESS INTERNATIONAL)

Archbishop Eugenio Pacelli, papal nuncio to Bavaria, distributes food and
clothing to starving civilians and veterans in Munich at end of World
War I. (UNITED PRESS INTERNATIONAL)

Eugenio Cardinal Pacelli at his desk in the Vatican during the early years
of his tenure as Vatican secretary of state (circa 1932).
(UNITED PRESS INTERNATIONAL)

enito Mussolini signs the historical Lateran
reaty in 1929. (UNITED PRESS INTERNATIONAL)

Archbishop Eugenio Pacelli, Vatican diplomat, with Italian Premier
Benito Mussolini and other fascist
leaders in formal pose following
the signing of the Lateran Treaty
in the Vatican in 1929. (SOURCE
UNKNOWN)

Eugenio Cardinal Pacelli, now Vatican Secretary of State, presides
over the signing of the Concordat
between Germany and the Vatican in 1933. (ULLSTEIN)

Archbishop Cesare Orsenigo, papal nuncio to Germany, talks
with Adolf Hitler at a formal reception in Berlin
in January 1936.

Archbishop Cesare Orsenigo, Pope Pius XII's personal emissary, at diplomatic reception for Adolf Hitler and Joachim von Ribbentrop in Berlin prior to World War II. (PAUL POPPER PHOTO)

Joseph P. Kennedy (*left*) and Marvin McIntyre (*right*), FDR's presidential secretary, officially welcome Eugenio Cardinal Pacelli to President Roosevelt's home in Hyde Park in November 1936. Bishop Spellman is seen in the background. (UNITED PRESS INTERNATIONAL)

Mrs. Nicholas F. Brady, a papal duchess, kisses the Secretary of State's ring as she bids farewell to her prominent guest, Cardinal Pacelli. Spellman is at his right. (UNITED PRESS INTERNATIONAL)

Father Charles E. Coughlin addresses a political rally in Cleveland with the zeal that inflamed his followers and, privately, enraged the Vatican (May 1936). (UNITED PRESS INTERNATIONAL)

President Franklin D. Roosevelt during a tour of New York's five boroughs in 1940 is accompanied by Archbishop Francis J. Spellman, whom FDR called "my favorite bishop." The pair are shown chatting in the presidential limousine en route to Fordham University. (UNITED PRESS INTERNATIONAL)

rank Costello descends the steps of the Fed-
ral Courthouse in New York in 1951 after
ompleting sworn testimony before the Senate
rime Investigating Committee. Cardinal
pellman made a wartime deal with Costello
t President Roosevelt's request. (UNITED
RESS INTERNATIONAL)

Charles "Lucky" Luciano in Rome,
1951, eager to return to the United
States from his Italian exile. (UNITED
PRESS INTERNATIONAL)

Count Galeazzo Ciano, Italy's fascist foreign minister and Mussolini's son- in-law,
with Eugenio Cardinal Pacelli and other Church dignitaries. They assembled at
the Sistine Chapel in February 1939 to pay final homage to the deceased
Pope Pius XI. (UNITED PRESS INTERNATIONAL)

His arms outstretched in dramatic appeal, Pope Pius XII addresses a huge crowd in the streets of Rome after the second bombing of the city by Allied planes (August 1943). (ACME PHOTO)

Mother Pascalina at dedication ceremonies on July 19, 1967, of a monument honoring the late Pope Pius XII for his heroism in braving enemy fire to bless the wounded during the Allied bombing of Rome on the same date twenty-four years before. (*Il Messagero* PHOTO)

Above: Ernesto Cardinal Ruffini, Archbishop of Palermo, is greeted upon his arrival in New York by Cardinal Spellman in 1956. Despite Pascalina's warnings to Spellman of Ruffini's Mafia conections, Spellman voted to elect the Sicilian prelate Pope upon Pius XII's death in 1958. (UNITED PRESS INTERNATIONAL)

Right: Ernesto Cardinal Ruffini, Archbishop of Palermo, leaves polling booth in Sicily during 1953 elections. Pascalina learned that Mafia bosses bowed to Ruffini, who became known to some as "the king of the two Sicilies—the religious and the political." (UNITED PRESS INTERNATIONAL)

William Cardinal O'Connell of Boston
strolls the gardens of his residence with his
Auxiliary Bishop, Spellman, after word was
received of Spellman's appointment as
Archbishop of New York. Though O'Connell put on a public face at the time, his animosity toward Spellman was long-standing.
(UNITED PRESS INTERNATIONAL)

Bishop Fulton J. Sheen bids farewell to
Francis Cardinal Spellman at Idlewild Airport in 1952 as the latter embarks on an
overseas trip. Despite their public smiles,
there was much hostility between the prelates. (UNITED PRESS INTERNATIONAL)

Archbishop Richard J. Cushing is warmly
greeted in the Vatican by Pope Pius XII
during the Boston prelate's visit to the Eternal City in 1950. (UNITED PRESS INTERNATIONAL)

From the balcony of Saint Peter's Basilica, Pope Pius XII delivers his 1952 Easter address before an estimated three hundred thousand people thronging Saint Peter's Square. (UNITED PRESS INTERNATIONAL)

Pascalina's nemesis, Eugene Cardinal Tisserant, Dean of the Sacred College of Cardinals, at his desk in the Vatican (circa 1958). (UNITED PRESS INTERNATIONAL)

Tisserant is the first cardinal to arrive at Castel Gandolfo following the news of Pius's imminent death (October 1958). (UNITED PRESS INTERNATIONAL)

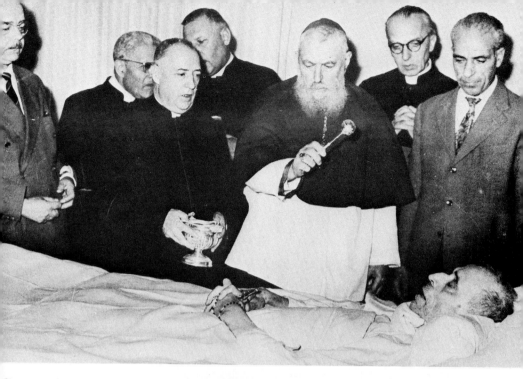

Eugene Cardinal Tisserant, Dean of the Sacred College of Cardinals, administers blessing to the deceased Pope Pius XII in papal villa at Castel Gandolfo. Dr. Galeazzi-Lisi *(extreme left),* the pontiff's physician, offers silent prayer. (UNITED PRESS INTERNATIONAL)

Sister Pascalina leaves Saint Peter's Basilica following funeral mass for Pius XII in October 1958. (UNITED PRESS INTERNATIONAL)

Sister Pascalina, "one [of] the most rarely pho[to]graphed women in t[he] world," according to UP[I] is shown *(second fr[om] right)* in the choir loft [of] Saint Peter's Basilica [in] 1956. (UNITED PRESS [IN]TERNATIONAL)

La Popessa in her papal car on a rare occasion when she failed to draw the curtains that shielded her from onlookers. Pope Pius XII insisted that the nun's trips about Rome be conducted in the utmost secrecy. Date unknown. (WIDE WORLD PHOTO)

Mother Pascalina and Marchesa Elisabetta Rossignani, sister of Pope Pius XII, attend dedication services of a statue honoring the memory of the late pontiff in Saint Peter's Basilica on December 3, 1964. (PAUL POPPER PHOTO)

Mother Pascalina arrives by plane in Rome in June 1963 to attend funeral services for Pope John XXIII. (*Il Messagero* PHOTO)

Sister Pascalina's favorite photograph of Pope Pius XII.
(PRIVATE COLLECTION)

dentials, even the highest Vatican officials who were not members of the Sacred College of Cardinals.

At 7:17 P.M., Pacelli himself locked all doors on the inside, and Prince Ludovico Chigi Albani, Marshal of the Conclave, simultaneously locked them on the outside. All telephones were disconnected at that precise moment.

From that point on, everyone within the conclave was shut away and would not be allowed contact with the outside world until after the election. Secrecy was so tight that all windows of the Papal Palace itself had been whitewashed from within or covered with canvas to close out prying eyes.

"A feeling of indescribable strangeness swept over me which I had never felt before," Pascalina said at being closed away within the exclusively male sanctuary.

In keeping with Church tradition the eve of the election was more social than ceremonial. Dinner was served in the refectory, but Pascalina ate by herself at the rear of Pacelli's cell. The small, bland meal was prepared by the Sisters of Saint Vincent de Paul in the palace's kitchen, well outside the official conclave area. Each serving was passed on trays to the sequestered quarters through small, well-guarded openings in the refectory's wall.

After brandy and coffee it was customary for everyone, Pascalina included, to retire. The old cardinals were sleepy and wanted to be well rested for the big day ahead.

Pascalina remembers the day of the papal election as "a mixture of ceremony and balloting and a great deal of confusion."

The entire body of hierarchy arose before dawn. From her cot at the rear of Pacelli's cell she heard the noisy scurrying about of the old cardinals. The walls were so thin, even the slightest sound was clearly audible.

She couldn't help but smile to herself at hearing their complaints. Many were still impatiently grumbling about their strange new surroundings. Some muttered more angrily about the inconveniences. A few were frustrated about being unable to sleep. With the excitement of being there and worry over Pacelli, she, too, hadn't been able to doze, let alone sleep.

The day began officially with Pacelli saying a special Mass in the Pauline Chapel to honor the Holy Ghost. Pascalina, as the only woman in this great and full assemblage of cardinals, was deeply touched. The immense significance of the opening ceremony, and the historic impact of her presence there, struck her all at once.

"The magnificence of actually being present, at the conclave's sacred prayer for a new pope, was a moment superior to any I had ever before beheld," she said.

Yet she wanted none of the awkward spotlight, and seated herself inconspicuously at the rear of the chapel. Still, she felt the embarrassment of their hard stares. It was especially difficult on her when she later made her way down the center aisle to receive Holy Communion. As the nun approached the altar the first rays of the new day's sun came through the magnificent stained-glass windows and settled upon her black robes.

"I cannot explain how strange I felt with all eyes on me," she said. "Then the sun placed me all the more in the embarrassing spotlight. But when Eminence passed the Sacred Host beyond my lips, peace and comfort came over me. I was greatly strengthened."

At midmorning the cardinals assembled in the Sistine Chapel, the conclave's election headquarters. As each prelate filed in he went quietly and directly to his own special throne. There were lines of these canopied ceremonial chairs, trimmed with velvet and gold fringe, set along the walls of the Sistine. The cardinals looked quite regal to Pascalina as they prepared themselves for the voting. Each had before him all of the necessary balloting equipment: a desk, a paper ballot, a pen, sealing wax, a candle, and matches.

It was easy for Pascalina to be hidden from sight in the Sistine. She positioned herself in a far corner, yet she could keep her eyes trained on Pacelli. The nun had every intention of making herself instantly available at all times to attend to whatever of his needs that might arise.

Even at some distance she heard the faint scratching of the many plumed pens. Cardinal after cardinal was writing his choice for pope on a simple ballot that bore the Latin words "I choose as Sovereign Pontiff The Most Reverend Lord Cardinal ——"

The election of pope was Pacelli's almost from the start. On the first ballot he received thirty-five votes, only seven short of the necessary two thirds for victory.

In a matter of minutes after the votes were counted, black smoke billowed above the Sistine. The impatient throng in Saint Peter's

Square moaned in disappointment at the conclave's traditional signal that no pope had yet been chosen.*

Victory for Pacelli came on the second ballot. Pascalina expected him to react as she did, to burst forth with joy. But instead he took a most shocking, almost unbelievable stand. To the utter astonishment of the entire assemblage, Pacelli turned down the election. Since Peter there had been two hundred and sixty pontiffs, but the cardinals present could recall only one instance when anyone flatly refused the honor of being pope after being elected to head the Holy Roman Catholic Church. This occurred during the conclave of 1922 when Camillo Cardinal Laurenti turned down his election and Achille Cardinal Ratti subsequently became Pius XI.

Pascalina was completely dumbfounded.

"I ask that another ballot be cast," Pacelli called out from his throne. "I ask that each Eminence search his heart and vote for someone other than me!"

Without further word Pacelli descended and walked from the hall, leaving the full assemblage of cardinals standing in silence and shock.

The nun was devastated, more for his state of mind than for his rash act.

He appeared so strained that she feared the worst.

Rushing after him, she found Pacelli in the secluded Square of Saint Damaso. He was in deep thought, his legs weary beneath him.

Pascalina understood and sympathized with all the misery and dread the new Pope was going through. Though neither spoke, she could see how plagued he was by inner doubts and insecurities. He had foreseen for some time the probability of his election as Holy Father, but only now did Pacelli fully face the reality of his frightening predicament.

With the major powers at the brink of war, and the Holy See caught between as a result, Pacelli was completely overwhelmed. Indeed, the thought of all the agonizing decisions he'd be called upon to make as Holy Father was tearing him apart.

In his anxiety Pacelli stumbled and fell heavily on the marble steps. It happened so fast, she couldn't reach out to him in time. The

---

*The Holy See's primitive use of smoke signals to announce results of papal elections is almost as old as the Church itself. In sending up white smoke, ballots are mixed with wood shavings and wax, then burned by two of the cardinals in a small black iron stove at the rear of the chapel. Wet shavings were used to render the smoke black.

Swiss Guards, some distance away, rushed forward and helped the prelate to his feet.

"Dear Jesus, help him!" Pascalina implored in nervous whisper.

"Miserere mei!" he cried, again this plea of "Have pity on me!" that she had been hearing so often from his lips since Pius XI had died. There was great anguish upon his face, and in his voice, as he continued speaking to her in low, worried tone. "I am not worthy! Something within me cries out in despair. I do not hear the voice of Our Dear Lord—as I had expected at this most important moment— saying to me, 'Eugenio, you have the moral strength, the physical stamina to be Christ's Vicar on Earth.'"

Pacelli was badly shaken and he limped as he walked, so the nun placed his arm about her shoulder, praying that she would be enough of a crutch.

"Dear Eminence, it is not for you to decide," she whispered into his ear. "Jesus has spoken and has chosen you, Eugenio Pacelli, to be the Holy Father." She suggested that they go to the Papal Chapel and pray for strength and guidance. He nodded his assent, looking obviously relieved at the thought of having more time away from the milling, chattering hierarchy. Yet, even as they made their way slowly into the Papal Palace, he said nothing in reply.

At the altar they went to their knees before a statue of Christ, and together they murmured the Lord's Prayer. When they came to the words "Thy will be done . . ." he paused to ponder deeply their full meaning. After a long moment she felt him brighten slightly, and her spirits rose, even more with his tender, reassuring squeeze of her arm. But that was all the indication Pacelli showed of any change of heart. They blessed themselves and went in silence back to the Sistine Chapel.

He strode with her at his arm through the gathering of prelates, still without word or any meaningful expression of his intentions. The cardinals, more astonished now than before, stopped at once their worried chatter and kept silent as Pacelli took his position upon his throne.

The hierarchy had agreed among themselves to accede to Pacelli's wishes and cast one more ballot. Pascalina feared that perhaps they'd elect another candidate, now that they had seen him react in such unorthodox manner.

But she was entirely wrong. This time the vote was unanimous.

At that joyful moment—the most exciting of her entire life—

thoughts of his birth on March 2, 1876, sixty-three years ago to the day, flashed through the nun's mind. His adoring sister, Elisabetta, had told her years before a seemingly unbelievable story of his baptism just two days after his birth. Even then the infant was in no festive mood at another religious ceremony, his christening. Elisabetta said everyone was horrified—especially the clergy—when "he howled vigorously as his priestly great uncle, Monsignor Giuseppe Pacelli, pronounced him Eugenio Maria Giuseppe Giovanni." But another priest, Monsignor Jacobacci, interpreted the child's strong will as a good sign. Taking the infant with the tiny wisp of black hair into his arms, he held Eugenio aloft for all the guests to see. Said the old monsignor prophetically, "Sixty-three years from today the people of Saint Peter's and all Rome will loudly praise this child."

Now, upon his election as Holy Father, Pacelli once again was acting difficult and causing as much embarrassment to those around him as the day Monsignor Jacobacci made his startling prediction. He still gave no outward indication that he would accept. The tense silence of the moment indicated that the hierarchy itself also feared the worst.

Cardinal Caccia-Dominioni, deacon of the conclave, approached Pacelli. In a firm tone, Dominioni asked: *"Accipisne electionem?"*

Pacelli did not reply for several moments. She could see that his mind was continuing to deliberate the many concerns about his own value and the serious issues to be faced by the Church.

Pascalina was trembling, greatly overcome by an all-consuming fear she had never before known.

The cardinals were becoming increasingly impatient, many appearing on the verge of anger or disgust.

Finally, Pacelli spoke.

"Accepio," he said in broken voice, his words spoken in such a soft whisper, he was hardly audible.

A great cheer resounded throughout. The cardinals pushed and shoved through their own ranks in their drive to kiss the feet of the new Holy Father. Pacelli was now the two-hundred sixty-first pope, the first in centuries to be of Roman birth.

In spite of Pacelli's delaying performances it was still the shortest papal election in memory.

"What name will you bear?" the dean of cardinals asked. Ever since the first pope had changed his name from Simon to Peter, it had been traditional for a new pontiff to follow the same practice.

"I will be called Pius because of my grateful memory of Pius XI," Pacelli replied.

There was a stampede of cardinals to the rear of the chapel, to send up white smoke to tell the whole world of Pacelli's election.

One prelate was so jubilant, he snatched Pascalina by the hand. "Come, Sister, this moment is too wonderful to miss!" he shouted as he pulled the nun forward through the onrush of purple-frocked old men.

In minutes the first faint feather of white smoke rose from atop the Sistine, and some sixty thousand people jamming Saint Peter's Square broke into delirious exhilaration.

The thunderous applause and the roar of the crowd continued on and on, even as Pascalina went to the sacristy to prepare the new Pope's robes for his grand entrance on the papal balcony.

When Pacelli himself entered the sacristy, she saw an entirely different look in his eyes. There was an inner strength coming from him that she had never before seen; a strength that she had been ardently praying for.

He took both of her hands in his. "Thank you, Sister, for all your courage, and your strength, and all your devotion," he said tenderly.

She stood there with tears upon her cheeks as he left to change into the robes of a pope.

When he later reappeared, Pacelli was in a white cassock and rochet, wearing as well a red stole and mantle. He was the altogether perfect image in her eyes of what the Holy Father should look like.

At precisely 6:00 P.M., Cardinal Dominioni appeared in the floodlights on the papal balcony outside Saint Peter's. Below stood the sprawling mass of eager worshipers.

A sudden hush fell over the crowd, and all of the sixty thousand people went silently to their knees.

"I bring you glad tidings," the cardinal announced in Latin. "We have a Pope! He is Eugenio Pacelli, and he will be known as Pius XII!"

Pascalina was on her knees too. She was peering from a window inside the palace as the Holy Father, in full regal robes, came upon the balcony.

"Pacelli! Pacelli! Pacelli! Pacelli! Pacelli!" the people shouted, chanting his name over and over again in utter euphoria.

Tears of supreme happiness poured down her face as Pius XII took his rightful authority from God. With upraised arm the Pope imparted Christ's blessings upon the multitude.

"Urbi et Orbi," His Holiness began in prayer. Afterward, the Pope broke into the most spontaneous and joyful smile she had ever seen. In her eyes the Pontiff now looked as regal and commanding as if he owned the world. Eugenio Pacelli was Vicar of Christ, Bishop of Rome, Successor of the Prince of Apostles, Supreme Pontiff of the Universal Church, Patriarch of the West, Primate of Italy, Archbishop and Metropolitan of the Province of Rome, Sovereign of the State of the City of the Vatican, Servant of the Servants of God.

Yet, an hour after leaving Saint Peter's balcony, Pascalina found the Holy Father in his quarters in the Papal Palace, "sobbing as if heartbroken." Barrett McGurn, in his book *A Reporter Looks at the Vatican,* wrote of the Pope's breakdown: "Whether the cause of the tears was fear, a sense of inadequacy, mere exhaustion, or all of them, is unknown."

Later that night the full body of the Sacred College of Cardinals gathered one more time in the Sistine Chapel. Beneath the famous crucifix of Christ each prelate came on his knees to Pius XII—then fully recovered and serene—to swear loyalty and obedience. Apparently none at the time could possibly realize that in kneeling to Pius XII, they one day would be bowing to Pascalina as well.

The conclave was about to close when the nun's image and reputation were suddenly threatened. A member of the press caught her slipping out a side door. The reporter was so astounded at seeing a nun where no woman had ever been allowed, he went directly to the Vatican's press office for explanation.

The press relations representatives were as startled by the news as the journalist himself. At first they maintained a "No comment" position. But after several days of pressing the issue the reporter was given this explanation:

> Special authorization of the Congregation of Cardinals permitted Mother Pascalina to remain there so that Pacelli should lack nothing of his customary diet, or of the medicines necessary to his well-being. It was generally felt that Pacelli would suffer were he deprived of his own particular way of living, which was the more necessary to him since he had just relinquished his duties as secretary of state to assume the onerous task of camerlengo.

It was evident that Pascalina would have to remain all the more hidden now that Pacelli was Pope. But she was well conditioned by then for the secret life. All her years with Pacelli had given her the mind and the will to accept her role with ease and grace and without complaint.

"This mystery woman of the Vatican seldom left the Papal apartment, and then mainly on charitable errands," Church historian Corrado Pallenberg wrote of Pascalina:

> [The nun] rigorously supervised everything, from major decisions to minute details. She kept the Pope's papers in order, his desk supplied with writing paper, his fountain pen filled, and she changed the Pope's cuffs, which he so often soiled with ink while writing.
>
> He [Pius] took to dictating to Pascalina not only official papers, but also the daily entries in his private diary. . . . This became a regular practice . . . and so Pascalina was able to share the Pope's innermost thoughts. His trust in her was complete, and with good reason, for she never once, not even inadvertently, betrayed his confidence. Because of her exceptional and delicate position, Pascalina became absolutely inaccessible to most people. Many who actually lived in the Vatican never saw her.

Lost as the Pontiff so often was in thought and prayer, Pallenberg speculated that "Pius XII probably no longer even noticed her presence, as everything she did was done so quietly, swiftly and without fuss."

He described Pascalina as "short-tempered, despotic, frightfully outspoken; she ruled the Papal household with an iron hand. . . . The other three German nuns who served in Pius XII's household were all from her same order of the Holy Cross of Menzingen [and] were terrified of her. But she could also be kind in her gruff sort of way."

While historian Pallenberg saw Pascalina in one light, there were those few among the hierarchy who looked upon the nun in a more sympathetic and understanding way.

Richard Cardinal Cushing reflected with candor and authority upon the nun's place within Pius XII's pontificate, a position without precedent in the history of the Roman papacy.*

"It was an extremely unsettling time for Sister Pascalina, wise and

---

*Cushing was appointed archbishop of Boston by Pius XII following the death in 1944 of William Cardinal O'Connell.

strong as she was," Cardinal Cushing said. He had been close to the nun and Pacelli, and spoke of Pascalina's role at the start of Pius XII's reign.

"Here was a woman of peasant birth who was suddenly projected into a place of great religious and political power at a time in history when the world was coming apart," the prelate added. "All the 'isms,' capitalism, communism, Nazism, and fascism, were snarling at each other."

Indeed, Hitler had brought Europe to the brink of war. Amid the universal outcry for sanity the Holy See—with a new Holy Father— appeared the one remaining hope in a divided world. Pacelli—as secretary of state—had been revered as a masterly diplomat and now, as Pope, was expected to wave a brave banner for peace. For nearly a decade as Pius XI's foreign minister, and for fifteen years before that as the Church's most promising prelate, he had shown leadership and rare courage. But few besides Pascalina knew the extent to which Pacelli's strength had come from his predecessor. Now Pacelli himself held the reins and was looked to as the infallible Holy Father.

Even as the world prayed with blind hope, the new shepherd of Catholicism kept his head in the clouds, portraying a mystical, medieval conception of the papacy. To Pius XII, Church grandeur and ceremony transcended for the moment all practical immediacy. Determined that his investiture be the mightiest spectacle of religious pageantry in Rome's modern history, the Pontiff busied himself eighteen hours a day with what Pascalina considered "pretentious plans" for his coronation. In the ten days between his election as pope and the papal coronation, the nun had her first real taste of his love of pomp and circumstance.

Pacelli saw his great dream fulfilled on March 12. Some seventy thousand spectators, many from various parts of the world, stood cheering him in Saint Peter's Square. In a dramatic break with modern custom he had insisted that his be the first outdoor papal coronation in nearly a century. Dressed in white ermine with a jewel-studded crown upon his head, he stood tall and proud, high atop a mammoth pavilion specially constructed for the occasion. And with the world set to explode, the new Pontiff spoke in platitudes offering ceremony rather than solution.

Pascalina could not reconcile Pacelli's utter humility during the conclave with his complete turnabout during the coronation. To her, Pacelli's investiture was "a shocking display of pomposity," and their first time alone after the ostentatious ceremony, she had not one but several pointed questions to put squarely before the Holy Father.

"Holiness, forgive my bewilderment, but I fail to understand your extreme changes of heart," she began in low key, deliberately appearing somewhat detached so as not to ruffle him unnecessarily. They were in his private quarters, and she helped him remove his ermine cape, then hung it carefully in a closet.

The penetrating dark eyes of the reed-thin, sensitive Pontiff followed her closely. He bore a look of sympathetic understanding. "At the conclave I was confronted with the realization that I—merely an ordinary man—was to be placed in an extraordinary position as Christ's Vicar on Earth," he explained in a patient tone. "This thought humbled me greatly and gave me good reason to search one final time into my mind and soul to determine if I was worthy. But the coronation was quite another matter. The pomp and adulation were not for me, but for the honor and glory of Almighty God. I am only a symbol to remind the faithful to adore Him."

Though Pius's explanation somewhat relieved her doubts of him, she was far more concerned about his complete failure to take any stand whatsoever on the rapidly deteriorating world situation. How strong a pope he planned to be in international affairs had become the pressing issue in the nun's mind.

"What do you plan to do about Hitler?" she impulsively demanded, her eyes showing serious concern. Suddenly her fears and worries overshadowed her usually calm voice and poised manner. "As Holy Father, you have the influence to speak out effectively against him."

Pius did not react with the fiery response that she expected; her inferences of his do-nothingism apparently did not strike a sensitive nerve. Rather, he appeared serenely confident, and, ignoring her intense emotions, he invited her to seat herself before him. Taking the nun's hand in his, a tender smile upon his lips, he answered in a controlled, pleasant tone.

"Sister Pascalina, I know that you speak with an honest heart— with concern and love for people everywhere and for my welfare most of all," he said. He seemed to her as kind and filled with love as the shy altar boy whom she had liked so well as a child at Saint Sebastian's Church in Ebersberg. Her intense frustrations began to moderate with Pacelli's reasoned approach.

"The world, unmindful of broader values, all too often seeks simplistic solutions to many complex problems," he continued. "When a mere man becomes the Holy Father, he cannot allow emotion or impulse to sway his decisions. The Holy Father must constantly ask of himself many questions. His Holiness cannot afford to act rashly, but must seek solution on the side of what is best in the long run for the greater good of humanity as a whole."

"Certainly you, Holiness, are not inferring that a despot like Hitler, in the long run, serves the greater good of mankind," she broke in, once again trying to repress her own emotions.

"By no means, Sister Pascalina," Pius calmly replied. "In the case of Hitler, it would be all too easy for the Holy Father to follow what might seem rational or obvious or inevitable to the world. If the Holy Father were to think only in a temporal manner that would be the political and popular move to make. But there are many millions of the Catholic faithful whose minds have been captured by Hitler— and these blinded souls would be lost to Holy Mother Church were our actions to be overt or extreme. If these souls are to be saved, the Holy Father must act with discretion. Of course, Hitlerism must be destroyed, but our method must be subtle. We must be deliberate, yet we must remain temperate." The Pope looked pleadingly at the nun. "Pray for me, Sister," he added, squeezing her hand. "It is not easy being Holy Father."

As he spoke she saw another side of Pius's not often penetrated character—a practical and skeptical and newly revised mind. Apparently reading her thoughts, he continued with an even more frank appraisal of the papacy's position. "It is inevitable, for all the reasons I have expressed, that the Holy Father shall invite, at any and all times, a ceaseless crossfire of criticism and attack, even hate. From this sad and hopeless position, Church and papacy can never expect to escape. We must forever endure the onerous weight of criticism."

His message appeared clear to her; as Holy Father he was prepared to moderate and mediate but no longer to stand up and fight.

A sudden and dramatic change came over the Pope's face. He arose with a fixed, unseeing glance; at once he became a gaunt, expressionless, and lonely figure, and retreating to an adjoining room, he closed the door behind him.

Where now, she asked herself, was the courageous, defiant Pacelli who had stood so valiantly against the plundering Reds who, with guns blazing, had stormed their nunciature in Munich those many years before?

It remained for the nun to become as backbone to the Pope's mind and strength. There was no self-seeking power or grandeur in her motives; rather she saw herself now mainly as buttress—and still protectress—to the Supreme Pontiff. Anticipating the untiring demands of the papacy that lay ahead, the endless hours of deliberations, the frustrating responsibilities, she secretly pledged her fullest support. Her self-appointed task was to fuel the Pope's fortitude, inspire and console him, support his every worthwhile endeavor—yet be his ever faithful and caring guardian. To do all this with tact and success, she would need to fathom the deepest of the Pope's thoughts and moods, his feelings and motives.

Her best way, she determined, was to be her own true self.

Pacelli's first official act as Pius XII was to court Hitler. Despite his elaborate explanation to her of the papacy's need to walk its own chosen path, Pascalina was infuriated by "the condescending message" that the Holy Father first wrote the German Führer. From the mid-1930s, Nazi repression of Catholicism in Germany had grown increasingly relentless. Numbers of priests and nuns had been brought to trial upon all sorts of trumped up excuses, and many had been given stiff sentences. In her eyes Pacelli's move defied all reason.

Hitler himself had publicly denounced the Church and the Catholic clergy. Speaking of clerics in general, Hitler said:

> While always talking about love and humanity, they are in fact interested in only one thing, power—power over men's souls, and hence over their lives. The Catholic Church is like a scheming woman who at first contrives to give her husband the impression that she is helpless and guileless, only to take over power, finally holding it so securely that the man has to dance to any tune she plays.

Certainly Pacelli's predecessor, Pius XI, in his final days had shown no love of Hitler and the Nazis. In his Christmas message of December 25, 1938, only a month and a half before his death, the old Pope leveled one of the Church's fiercest attacks against any nation.

"Let us call things by their true name," Pius XI had said.

> I tell you, in Germany today a full religious persecution is in progress. A persecution which does not shrink from using every weapon: lies, threats, false information, and in the last resort phys-

ical force. . . . A lying campaign is being carried on in Germany against the Catholic hierarchy, the Catholic religion, and God's Holy Church. . . . The protest we make before the whole civilized world cannot be clearer or more unequivocal.

Now, with the old Pope gone, Pacelli seemed lost in vacillation and compromise.

Alden Hatch, one of Pacelli's authorized biographers, compared the two popes, claiming they were strikingly different in almost every way. Pius XI was as militant as Pius XII appeared divided and yielding. Of Pius XI, Hatch said, "[He had] a hard will. He was like a dormant volcano, slow to erupt, but capable of violent bursts of energy."

Despite all that Hitler had done to insult and weaken the Church, and even though Pius XI had written a deathbed encyclical calling upon the world to rid itself of Nazism, Pacelli and his circle of hierarchy were of a more conciliatory mind toward Nazi Germany. They took a complete about-face stand to the deceased Pope's unyielding position. In fact, they were actually bending to the Nazi Führer, as Pacelli had naively done in helping to subsidize Hitler's rise with Church funds twenty years before.

The new Pope's militant predecessor in his dying days had so aggressively stirred tensions with Nazi Germany that Pacelli felt it incumbent to offer Hitler an olive branch. The German prelates were effusive in their encouragement and support when the Holy Father announced a new track of papal appeasement toward Hitler. "The world will see that we have tried everything to live in peace with Nazi Germany," Pius XII told his ardent clerical supporters.

Though Pascalina had no authority to speak her mind officially, she was ready to burst with anger during the session with the German membership of the Sacred College of Cardinals that Pacelli had called to thrash out a compromise with Hitler. The extremes to which the Pontiff and his clerical backers went to placate the Führer were altogether appalling to her. Their conciliatory remarks were recorded in the minutes of Pius XII's first official act.

Holy Father: In 1878 Leo XIII at the beginning of his Pontificate sent a message of peace to Germany. In my modest person, I should like to do something of the same sort. [Here he read the draft of the letter to Hitler in Latin.] Is that all right? Does it need altering? Or amplifying? I should be most grateful for Your Eminences' advice.

Cardinal Bertram: I don't see there's anything to add.

Cardinal Faulhaber: No definite wish can be expressed in a letter of this kind. Only a blessing. But there's one point. Must it be in Latin? The Führer's very touchy about non-German languages. He won't want to call in the theologians to explain it.

Cardinal Schulte: As far as its contents are concerned, excellent.

Holy Father: It can be sent in German. If it's treated as a purely protocolar affair, the implication about the bad state of affairs for the Church may be missed. And we are concerned above all with what is best for the Church in Germany. For me that is the most important question. Perhaps it could be done in both Latin and German.

Cardinal Faulhaber: Better to send it in German.

So it was finally decided to send the message in German as well. Then the following problem arose:

Holy Father: Do we address him as "Illustrious" or "Most Illustrious"?

Cardinal Schulte: Most Illustrious! That's really going too far. He hasn't earned that.

Cardinal Innitzer: Should you use the plural in addressing him?

Other Cardinals: That is normal usage.

Cardinal Innitzer: I mean in the salutation. Do you address him as Sie, or Du?

Cardinal Bertram: A Third Reich regulation dispenses with titles. I should say Sie.

Holy Father: In Italian you now say Tu or Voi. Personally, I say Lei. But I suppose it's different in Germany, now.

Cardinal Bertram: You haven't referred to him as Dilecte Fili [Beloved Son]. Quite right! He wouldn't appreciate that. [Joking] He'd like the Holy Father to cry "Heil! Heil!"

Cardinal Innitzer: In the school the priests have to say "Heil Hitler!"—and "Jesus Christ—Thy Kingdom come!"—that's the link between Earth and Heaven.

It was agreed that the usual form of greeting, Dilecte Fili (Beloved Son), would hardly be appropriate in Hitler's case. The final text read:

> To the Illustrious Herr Adolf Hitler, Führer and Chancellor of the German Reich! Here at the beginning of Our Pontificate We wish to assure you that We remain devoted to the spiritual welfare of the German people entrusted to your leadership (Obsorge). For them We implore God the Almighty to grant them that true felicity which springs from religion. We recall with great pleasure the many years We spent in Germany as Apostolic Nuncio, when We did all in Our power to establish harmonious relations between Church and State. Now that the responsibilities of Our pastoral function have increased Our opportunities, how much more ardently do We pray to reach that goal. May the prosperity of the German people and their progress in every domain come, with God's help, to fruition!
>
> Given this day, 6th March, 1939, in Rome at Saint Peter's in the first year of Our Pontificate.

To Pascalina, sitting as a note-taker in the official session, the setting seemed entirely bizarre. She felt herself in a strange, disbelieving daze, listening to "frightfully condescending conversation being carried to pathetic extremes," she recalled long afterward, her face sad and remorseful. "It was like watching a Shakespearean tragedy. There was the Pope and his council of cardinals on their knees to Hitler."

What Pascalina had so long admired in Pacelli as an able secretary of state and astute diplomat, she now saw as only part of what was altogether essential in "the character of a Pope of leadership and strength."

It was absolute to her that "a Pontiff of Christ not only preach the word of God, but practice his teachings and be a moral force irrespective of all costs and sacrifice."

The conflicts between spiritual and temporal values, she was convinced, posed the dilemma that Pacelli the diplomat, and Pacelli the Pope, had to resolve.

Throughout her lifetime Pascalina has remained silent in her opinions of Pacelli's early pontifical appeasement of Hitler, yet sorrow still reflects in her eyes at that moment of papal humiliation. Even after more than forty years the disappointment remains, Pacelli's poor judgment obviously unforgiven.

Sitting as she did at the advent of Pius XII's reign, secure at the throne of religious power, Pascalina was taking on a new perspective. Within the nun there was forming a new dimension of understanding toward the shortcomings and failings of organized religion. She saw in a new light the Holy See's questionable collaborations with foreign leaders.

Her life until then had been mostly formative in its concepts. Hers was a plodding evolution beyond the simple values: faith, morals, ethics, prayers, privations.

Now she was seeing the papacy on a giant screen. She viewed the Pope, as spiritual leader of hundreds of millions of Catholics around the world, holding the crucial flame of public opinion in his mystical chalice. Just why Pacelli could not fully grasp the enormity of his power as Holy Father, she even now failed to comprehend fully. A German herself, she felt instinctively confident that Hitler, even as tyrannical as he was, would move with far greater caution against the upraised hand of a formidable pope.

If she were to be backbone and decision maker to this vacillating, compromising pontiff, she would have to move slowly and with great subtlety, for those were the ways of the Church. In hopes of bolstering the Pope's anything but awesome spirit, Pascalina began her supportive process with her own self-inspired diplomacy, yet still with surprising directness.

"The Holy See today stands alone as a viable instrument of peace," Pascalina gently reminded the Pontiff. The Pope and the nun were alone, the council of cardinals having just retired after the drafting of their ill-fated letter. "Hitler is making a mockery of the Catholic Church," she added. "The Holy See can prevail against Nazism only if the Holy Father speaks with strength and without fear of consequences."

She was reasonably certain that Pacelli continued to revere the memory of Pius XI. Banking on her instincts, she struck for sentimental advantage by reaching out to Pacelli's heart.

"Holiness, you will recall that Pius XI, on the eve of his death, condemned Hitler and the Nazis," she said. Pascalina somehow saw the moment as a time when she could strike common sense into Pacelli. "As you know, my good and loving friend Pius XI's encyclical of denunciation was in complete contradiction of everything that was decided today."

But what Pascalina did not take into consideration was that the old Pope was dead. The sharp, almost contemptuous way the Holy Father looked at her for one brief instant made clear just how insolent she appeared to him at that moment.

"Keep to your place as a woman and a nun!" he shouted. "And let the dead rest in peace!"

Never before had Pacelli spoken so sharply to her. Certainly never so bitterly. Now that Pacelli was the Holy Father himself, had her beloved priest and friend risen so high in his own mind that there was no longer need for her opinions? No place for all she had been—and could be—to him?

Pascalina felt her full German fury rise within her. Even though he was Holy Father, the woman—the human being inside her trembling body—wanted to shout all the words that were at the tip of her tongue: "You have no right talking to me that way! Not after nearly twenty-two years of devotion and dedication to help make you what you are! I know that popes and cardinals think of nuns as simple servants. Yet I am a person, and I want to be treated like the decent human being that I am!"

But the words never came. Her hard life on the farm, the years of rigid drilling that she had received from severe Mother Superior and the other tough old nuns at the convent—her vow of obedience too— had their effect on her; Pascalina felt far greater loyalty and service to Jesus Christ than to Eugenio Pacelli. Had not God Himself given her the inspiration to serve as the mistress of Pius's mind and soul? If she was successfully to carry out her mission, her common sense and strong will told her to act with control of spirit and clarity of mind.

Though crushed by his words, Pascalina kept her fire to herself; only the bitter cold of her eyes and the firm, set manner of her jaw and lips gave any indication of what was going on in her mind. She turned abruptly and walked out; the nun had learned to win her victories after he had cooled down.

And calm down he did. Later that night as the nun was about to retire, the Pope came knocking timidly at her door. She hesitated before answering; then as she was about to unfasten the latch, she heard him say, in a rather meek tone, "Sister Pascalina, I have remembered you in my prayers this evening. Now have a good night's sleep." It was his way of apologizing, and he returned to his own room.

What continued to trouble her, as the weeks passed, was the Pontiff's totally unexpected disregard of Pius XI's hard-line policy toward Hitler. Had Pacelli been truly devoted to the old Pope, she wondered? Or, like any human, had Pacelli shown loyalty and affection to Pius XI only because he was Pope and his superior at the time?

She recalled Pacelli telling her that he had been severely humiliated by Pius XI's verbal trouncings on many occasions. Could His Holiness be living with a grudge against the previous Holy Father? Pacelli had been forced to remain on his knees before the old Pope for as long as an hour at a time—even while he was secretary of state and second in command of the papacy.

The deceased Pope's "authoritarian and almost insolent" attitude toward Pacelli was substantiated by Count Galeazzo Ciano, Italy's foreign minister. Ciano was Mussolini's son-in-law and an intimate of numbers of the Vatican's hierarchy.

"Everybody is terrified of him [Pius XI]," Ciano wrote in his diary of August 26, 1938. "He treats everybody with arrogance, even the most illustrious Cardinals." Quoting Francesco Cardinal Borgongini-Duca, Pacelli's aide at the time, Ciano wrote: "When Cardinal Pacelli ... goes to report, he has to write down all his instructions at the Pope's dictation, like any little secretary."

Pascalina saw in Pacelli's flash of anger toward her a far more vulnerable side than she had previously suspected. Despite all the pain that any negative thoughts of Pacelli brought to her mind and soul, she now could confirm the truth in what Ciano had written about him on March 18, that the Pope "intends to follow a more conciliatory policy than Pius XI [toward Germany]." Earlier, on the day of Pacelli's election as Holy Father, Ciano had also written in his diary of the Vatican-Nazi connection:

I received the report of the election to the Papacy of Cardinal Pacelli. It did not surprise me. I recall the conference I had with him on the tenth of February. He was very conciliatory, and it seems also that in the meantime he has improved relations with Germany. In fact, Pignatti [Count Bonifacio Pignatti, Italian ambassador to the Holy See] said only yesterday that he [Pacelli] is the Cardinal preferred by the Germans. At the dinner table I had already said to Edda [Ciano's wife and Mussolini's daughter] and to my collaborators, "The Pope will be elected today. It is going to be Pacelli, who will take the name of Pius XII."

In the six months between Pacelli's election and the outbreak of World War II, the Holy See's appeasement of Nazi Germany left little doubt in Pascalina's mind of the Pope's misguided sentiments.

Knowing that Pacelli was a passionate Germanophile, she wondered if all the years he had spent in Germany and his love of the German people had colored the Pope's vision. He had worked so hard as papal nuncio to Germany and had built a great concordat for the Church with that predominantly Protestant nation. Was he afraid to face the reality that the treaty would be entirely meaningless if all ties with Germany were broken? Then, too, the German hierarchy apparently had taken a strong hold on him.

So successful was their Teutonic influence that the Pope was convinced of the benefits derived by the Church from the Nazi persecutions of its clergy and nuns. In describing Hitler's atrocities upon Catholics—the laity and the frocked—Joseph Cardinal Schulte, archbishop of Cologne, told Pacelli and others of the German hierarchy: "The general interest in Church affairs is more lively than before [the persecutions]."

Pascalina was even more stunned when the Holy Father shrugged his shoulders nonchalantly and replied: "Such is the effect of persecution."

"The churches are full to overflowing," Cardinal Schulte continued.

"The same in Austria," Theodor Cardinal Innitzer, archbishop of Vienna, added.

"Well then, we must not lose courage," Pius XII remarked without expression.

Though the Pontiff subsequently called for peace on several occasions, his words were as bland as his spirit. "We have not yet abandoned hope that the governments will realize their responsibilities to preserve their peoples from so grave a disaster, the terrible responsibility of an appeal to force," he said on August 19, only a week and a half before the outbreak of World War II. Never at any time, before or after, did he publicly denounce the aggressors, Hitler and Mussolini, by name.

Pascalina took the call when François Charles-Roux, France's ambassador to the Vatican, told the Pontiff that Germany was about to march on Catholic Poland. The nun, risking further wrath, begged the Pope to condemn Hitler publicly before it was too late. She reminded him that "moral guilt is incurred by omission" and that "silence has its limits."

This time His Holiness appeared to listen with a sympathetic ear. But when he spoke out hours later, the Pope's words were no more effective than his now most infamous cliché: "Nothing is lost by peace; everything may be lost by war."

It was becoming increasingly apparent that the minority of cardinals who failed to vote for Pacelli during the conclave's first ballot were not so wrong when they said of him: "He is a man of peace and what the world needs now is a war pope."

Later that night Pius returned to his desk, "pondering, writing, and hoping." Pascalina, sharing his despair and tension, came to him so that they might say their late-night rosaries together.

Both were on their knees in prayer when word was received that Nazi troops were crossing the Polish border. World War II had begun.

"Pius sat rigid for a long time, too stunned to think," Alden Hatch, Pacelli's biographer, reported. "Then he fled to his little chapel and, weeping like a child, flung himself to his knees and poured out his grief to his Father."

Pascalina came to his side later that night, seeking him out only after the Pope had gathered himself and would not be embarrassed by her presence.

"How unwise you must think I am at times," he said in a low whisper. The nun did not reply, yet her heart and soul broke with sorrow, as much for the world as for her misguided Pacelli.

"His Holiness looked so old and pitifully tragic at that moment," Pascalina recalled four decades later, her voice laden with sadness.

VIII

From the day Pacelli became pope, Pascalina leveled as much criticism and attack within the palace's kitchen as she did upon the papacy's executive suite.

"These bananas are rotten!" she exclaimed in a loud, harsh tone as she took charge of the servants in the kitchen the very day that Pacelli took command of the Holy See. Her nose was in the air and her face was contorted in disgust as she fingered the decaying fruit on a counter by the sink. The servants, a group of old nuns, stood clustered together, looking terribly frightened as the arrogant figure in black darted about their domain, her robes rustling with her fury.

"But, Sister Pascalina, His Holiness Pius XI always liked his bananas mellow," one of the saddened nuns timidly remarked, cocking her head sideways at Pascalina. Bent over and shrunken by age, and with a pathetic plea on her shriveled face, the sister was making every attempt to avert a confrontation.

"I don't care how Pius XI wanted his bananas!" Pascalina retorted, her patience strained to the breaking point. "Pius XII is now Pope, and I don't want His Holiness eating garbage!" She was scrutinizing the clutter that was stacked everywhere—particularly in the pantry and scullery—leaving no doubt that their domain would now be run strictly according to her own perfectionist way. "If you nuns cannot run this kitchen right—if you cannot see that this place is kept clean and that good food is brought here—I will do all the cleaning and do all the grocery buying myself!" Her voice had reached a strident pitch. She turned sharply about, her anger overflowing as she walked with determined stride from the room, shutting the large, heavy door forcefully behind her.

Within minutes she was in the palace's rear courtyard—out of breath from anger and impatience—ordering the Swiss Guard to see that the papal limousine was brought around immediately.

"Take me to the fruit market!" she commanded the driver as the immense black vehicle pulled up in front of her. "I have a million responsibilities to take care of today, so make it fast!" she shouted as she herself pulled open the door, leaving the Swiss Guards aghast at her independence and impatience.

Seeing the fire in her eyes, chauffeur Angelo Stoppa tore through Rome's streets as startled pedestrians quickly scattered from their path. In Piazza Navona the papal limousine pulled up in such a screeching stop only inches from a throng of milling shoppers that some of the frightened and angry people began screaming and hurling insults.

"You horrible slut!" one woman shouted angrily as the nun emerged; the stranger's violence seethed from her eyes and showed in the clenched fist that she waved close to Pascalina's face. "You ride around in the Pope's big car and come here to buy cheap food," the woman continued, screaming her sarcasms.

"Do not let her stay here!" another woman cried out. "The Pope and his cardinals have no pity on us. We poor people of Rome starve while they in their fancy robes live in palaces in splendor with all their gold! Now this nun—this creature who acts for the Pope himself—comes to take our food!"

The crowd was moving forward in a slow, menacing wave toward Pascalina.

"The clergy makes fools of the poor!" a man shouted. "The clergy makes the words of Christ sound empty! The clergy crucifies the Christ you say you love, rich nun!"

"Go back and hide your face in the Pope's big palace, you foul woman!" still another voice was heard above the raging crowd.

Never at any time in her life had Pascalina backed down from any threat. As a child, she had stood her ground time and again against a militant father—defying him by going off to the convent even when it meant losing her family for all time. Later, when the Reds stormed the Munich nunciature, she had remained valiantly alongside Pacelli. Now, although terrified, she was not about to show fear either.

Despite her rising panic Pascalina could still understand the emotions that impelled these enraged people. Having herself come from poverty, it was not hard for the nun to relate to the frustrations of embittered peasants who felt betrayed.

Her indignation at their sad plight moderated her fright and gave her the fighting spirit that she needed to hold her ground. Scrambling quickly to the running board of the papal limousine, she stood high enough above everyone so that they could clearly hear her words.

"You have every right to feel angry!" Pascalina called out in a firm, loud voice. "But do not blame the new Pope, Pius XII, for the mistakes of the past. Pius XII is a good and holy man! A compassionate man! He understands the needs of the poor. To show you how much Pius XII loves you, I ask all people here to pick out and take home whatever you want at the food markets today. Then send the bills to the Holy Father. My name is Pascalina. Put my name on the bills and I will make sure that you receive your money."

The mood of the crowd eased perceptibly, and a smile flashed across the nun's face. "God bless you! God bless everyone!" she joyfully called out. Her rapidly increasing courage dispelled all fear within her. As she took further heart her words began to overflow with exuberance. "Now, I want all of you to show the new Holy Father that you, too, are as good and kind as he!" she shouted. "I want you to pick out the best bananas—the best fruit here—and bring it to me as a gift for His Holiness!" Her natural charisma was taking command, and the throng, eager to fulfill her wish, scattered anxiously about. Men and women and children then carefully selected the choicest fruit of all kinds. Then, like repentant youngsters approaching Mother Superior, they came humbly to Pascalina with their arms filled, their eyes pleading for forgiveness in the form of a smile from the stalwart nun.

That night, after the servant nuns had retired and Pius himself was finishing up his long and arduous first day as pope, Pascalina asked the Pontiff to follow her to the kitchen.

"Holiness, see all the wonderful fruit and vegetables the good people of Rome have sent you!" she exclaimed as she playfully held handful after handful of the colorful produce before him. At no time had she made reference to the traumatic scene earlier that day, which had precipitated the outpouring of generosity.

But Pius was too aware of Pascalina's manner and motives after all their years together—too aware as well of the thinking of Rome's anticlerical peasants—to be taken in by her coy remarks.

"What surprises have you in mind, Sister Pascalina?" he asked, a knowing half smile upon his lips.

"Your Holiness!" she replied, attempting to appear shocked and hurt by his words. "You make it sound as if I had a calculating mind!"

"Being a Roman by birth and having lived in Rome much of my life, should I believe now that someone waved a wand over the heads of Rome's peasants and turned them to love the papacy?" the Pontiff retorted. "On the other hand, that maker of magic could be a nun called Sister Pascalina, who chooses to give away the Vatican treasury to buy the love of those peasants," he quickly added with a wry look. She understood then that the Holy Father knew everything that had occurred in the marketplace that afternoon. Without doubt the chauffeur had spoken to someone, and that someone had then run directly to the Pope with the whole story. She was furious with Stoppa, the driver, but she was too shrewd to show the Pope how much she was bothered.

The Holy Father placed a gentle arm about her shoulder, and in an understanding voice he said, "Sister, you did right this afternoon. It was a good gesture and a wise one, from every point of view. I am thankful to Almighty God that you were not harmed, and that the good peasant people of Rome think more kindly of the new Holy Father. But in case you think as they do—that the Holy See has limitless funds to give away—I want you to see for yourself that everywhere throughout the universality of Holy Mother Church our fortunes are not so bright."

As she had led him in anticipation to the kitchen, he asked her to return with him to the papacy's inner sanctum. But his surprise was not a welcome one. Speaking in a tone of alarm, Pacelli told her in confidence that his predecessor, Pius XI, had kept many of the papacy's major problems to himself. Now, in going through confidential correspondence, the new Pope had discovered earlier that day that the New York archdiocese—second only to the Vatican itself in influence and power—was more than $28 million in debt. Equally alarming, the Church's treasury in New York—America's most prestigious diocese—was worsening at an alarming rate as each day passed.

The new Pope blamed the staggering deficit on one man, Patrick Cardinal Hayes, who for eighteen years had been New York's archbishop. Known universally as the "Cardinal of Charity," he was a spiritual and kindly old prelate who never had the heart to turn away anyone in need. Hayes had died six months before, but not until he had given the needy over the years most of his diocese's liquid assets almost down to its last dollar.

"Bishop Spellman once told me that for years during the Depression in the United States, he had witnessed lines of people outside Cardinal Hayes's residence in New York, waiting to get inside the diocesan house where the cardinal himself would hand out large sums of money to everyone who asked his aid," Pacelli told Pascalina.

"Well, isn't that a function of Holy Mother Church, to aid the poor and indigent when they are in need?" she asked, pointedly indicating her approval of the old cardinal's actions.

"True enough," the Holy Father replied sincerely. "But at the time, the New York archdiocese was hardly able to survive. By being overly generous, Eminence Hayes completely depleted the diocesan treasury, and eventually the diocese was unable to pay its just bills. Now, there are those to whom the Church owes $28 million. Robbing Peter to pay Paul hardly seems fair and just. To be charitable is Christlike, but prudence also has its virtues."

After Hayes's death New York Catholics had clamored for the Holy See to appoint another of his kind and generous type; such a personage they saw in Bishop Stephen J. Donahue, the deceased cardinal's beloved auxiliary and protégé.

But Pacelli's predecessor had been too shrewd to allow another "easy mark," as some of the Vatican hierarchy termed Donahue, to continue Hayes's "free handout policies." Pius XI had seen Donahue as, like Hayes, "a shepherd of Christ in the pulpit," which was quite fine for the Holy See's image but not for its ledger.

Then, too, the old Pope had a favorite of his own for the post of archbishop of New York—Archbishop John T. McNicholas of Cincinnati, whose generosity to the papacy exceeded most Catholic churchmen's. Pius XI had actually selected McNicholas, but while the official papers lay on the Pontiff's desk for signing, he suffered a heart attack and died.

The press throughout the world had run articles and pictures of McNicholas as the papacy's choice to head America's most influential diocese, but now the new Holy Father had misgivings.

"Bishop Spellman has told me that President Roosevelt does not like Excellency McNicholas," Pacelli continued, his mood becoming grave. "According to Spellman, McNicholas has irked Roosevelt by coming out publicly against the first peacetime draft of American boys for military service. He has been preaching against Roosevelt's 'peace propaganda,' which he feels could lead America into war, and he has even urged Catholics to form 'a mighty league of conscientious noncombatants.'"

She thought to herself how appeasing all this sounded, but did not dare venture her strong opinions to the Holy Father: "Must Holy Mother Church always placate all these politicians?" she asked herself. "First it was Mussolini! Then Hitler! Now Roosevelt! Who next? Politicians are all alike! Show them weakness and they answer with terror!"

"Bishop Spellman has splendid instinct," Pius continued. "You will recall how brilliantly His Excellency conducted all matters when we were in the United States three years ago. His advice concerning our relationships with the American cardinals and bishops—and with the press, too—under those most trying circumstances, was commendable. Bishop Spellman is President Roosevelt's favorite holy personage. That is simply because His Excellency has the mind and tact to appreciate the delicacies required in conversing with a man like the President. Bishop Spellman quite wisely never forgets that Holy Mother Church always requires good friends in high places."

"Holiness, since you have already set your mind against Excellency McNicholas, why not appoint Bishop Spellman?" she finally broke in, stating the question with her customary frankness. "But appoint him on his merit, not merely to appease Roosevelt! There are sounder reasons for Excellency Spellman to be given charge of the New York archdiocese." She had known Spellman for a decade and had grown to appreciate his talents. His training as auxiliary bishop of Boston under the most difficult and exacting Cardinal O'Connell had placed Spellman in excellent stead for the demanding post. "Holiness, he is loyal to you," she reminded the Pope. "He is shrewd and knows how to persuade people to donate large sums of money and valuable gifts. Bishop Spellman was the best American money-raiser the Vatican ever had."

Though the Vatican hierarchy had long been aware of Pascalina's closeness to Pacelli, it would have thoroughly shocked the old prelates were they to know that the new Pope was discussing his most important and pressing decisions with the nun. Worse still, it would have seemed abominable to them had they realized that Pius XII was seeking direction from a woman in the selection of one of their rank to head the choicest of Catholic dioceses.

From Pius XII's point of view, he had the utmost confidence in Pascalina's intellect and always would give serious consideration to her ideas and suggestions. Occasionally he disagreed with the nun, most particularly with her ideas toward Hitler. Until the very outbreak of World War II, Pacelli had been convinced in his own mind that his policy of appeasement toward the Nazis better served the Church's interests than the militant stand the nun proposed.

Though Pascalina argued strongly for Spellman's appointment—discussing with Pacelli the night he became pope all the sound reasons that seemed to make the Boston bishop the wisest choice—Pius still gave no indication of what his final decision would be. She knew that Pacelli, like herself, had great affection for their old and dear friend. But she also realized that the Pontiff hadn't gotten to his high throne without carefully weighing all of the issues in any situation. Then, too, he often vacillated so greatly, she could never be certain of what he would do or say next.

As the days passed, rumors began to spread concerning Pius XII's failure to proceed officially with his predecessor's promise to Archbishop McNicholas. Speculation grew that the Pope was seeking a way out of McNicholas's appointment to give his "pet" Spellman the honored post.

"I knew how trying those days had become for both Bishop Spellman and Archbishop McNicholas," Pascalina later recalled with sympathy. "I wanted to remind His Holiness that tensions could be considerably relieved if he took action, but I knew it was not my place to say anything. Pius XII was the type of person with whom I could freely speak my mind—provided that he first brought up the subject. On a matter as important as the selection of an archbishop—especially of a diocese as significant as New York—any interference by me after that first night's discussion would have precipitated his stern rebuke."

Finally, with his nerves unable to withstand uncertainty any longer, Spellman phoned the nun from Miami. "The bishop said he was taking a few days off to rest himself in the sun," she said later, adding that Spellman confided to her that the "'strain is beginning to tell on me.' Though I knew he was hinting for some word, he told me that he had no hopes or desires for the appointment."

"I am of two minds," Spellman said to Pascalina. "I'm willing to go to New York. But I don't want to go where I'm not wanted. The New York clergy prefer one of their own native sons. I'm considered an outsider and not popular with them. I'd prefer to remain in Boston and perhaps succeed Cardinal O'Connell at some future time."

Spellman was a bit more explicit in a letter to his family, written the same day he phoned the nun. "I am feeling well, but the magnitude of all the happenings produces such a conflict that I am overcome with joy, apprehension, and I don't know how many other things."

The Pope finally broke the news of Spellman's appointment to Pascalina a week after his coronation. They were alone in the papal chapel and about to say their nightly rosary together when he casually let drop the anxious message. "My decision is made," he whispered in a bland tone of voice as they knelt before a statue of Jesus. "You have convinced me, Sister Pascalina." Seeing her expression instantly light up, he smiled at her in a knowing manner, then added a teasing postscript. "Your friend is in!" He blessed himself and began their prayers. Though Pius said nothing further, his message was clear enough for the nun to draw her own conclusions.

Pascalina understood all that was necessary about Vatican protocol, and—for the time being—would breathe no word to anyone of what the Pope had told her. Even if Spellman himself were to call again, she'd act innocent of all knowledge.

From that point on it remained for Archbishop Amleto Cicognani, the Vatican's apostolic delegate in Washington, to serve as the Pope's intermediary in arranging the appointment. But it wasn't until April 12 that Spellman received the big news from Cicognani. An airmail special delivery letter from the apostolic delegate stated:

> I have the honor to inform Your Excellency that the Holy Father has in mind to name you Archbishop of New York. . . . Before the appointment is made, however, an expression is desired of your willingness to accept it. . . . If Your Excellency will wire me "Letter of April eleventh received and suggestion approved," I shall understand it to indicate your acceptance. . . . This communication is sent under the strictest secrecy and must remain entirely confidential until the information it contains is published in Rome.

Everything remained confidential, as Rome ordered, until April 23, when Archbishop Cicognani again contacted Spellman—this time by phone—telling the bishop that the announcement would be made by the Vatican the following day. "I feel that a bombshell is going to explode," Spellman wrote in his diary that day. He immediately dispatched a note to Roosevelt. "I wish you to be the first one to know that the Holy Father has appointed me Archbishop of New York," Spellman wrote the President.

Pius XII made it official with his formal announcement, which stated in part: "His Excellency, Francis J. Spellman, Auxiliary Bishop of the Diocese of Boston, has been appointed by His Holiness to the high honor of Archbishop of the Diocese of New York."

Archbishop McNicholas, who had been told by the dead Pope, Pius XI, less than three months earlier that he was to be archbishop of New York, was left high and dry, without a single word of explanation from the Vatican as to why he had been shunted aside.

Many within Rome's hierarchy were enraged, suspecting Pascalina of using extraordinary influence on Pius XII in the naming of Spellman. The angry cardinals and bishops were particularly concerned over their obvious loss of prestige and power in not being consulted. How a pope of the Holy Roman Catholic Church could be so greatly influenced by a nun on such a vital issue became the paramount concern of the Sacred College of Cardinals.

The fierce competition among the Catholic clergy for ecclesiastical appointments is described by the Reverend D. P. Noonan, an associate of the late Archbishop Fulton J. Sheen's, in his biography of the television preacher. Father Noonan writes: "The thirst for power among priests, monsignors, bishops and cardinals [goes] totally unchecked, simply because there [is] no one to check it. . . . Ambition is the ecclesiastical lust!"

Boston's crotchety archbishop, William Cardinal O'Connell, who had taunted Spellman from the day he became a priest, expressed a jocose view of how so many of the Catholic clergy felt at the time of the rotund archbishop's appointment. Said the venerable O'Connell in referring to the Vatican's elevation of his unpopular former clerk: "That's what happens to a bookkeeper when you teach him how to read."

Almost from the moment Spellman became archbishop, Pascalina began to see marked changes in her longtime friend. Though an

ocean had separated them much of the time in the seven years since
he had left Rome in 1932 to become auxiliary bishop of Boston, she
had kept abreast of her friend's changing ways. Both had maintained
their close personal contact by mail and transatlantic phone, and he
would travel to the Vatican quite regularly, sometimes as often as
once a year. He was now fifty—thirteen years younger than Pius—
and clearly stronger in character than the unsure and apologetic
priest she had met almost a decade before. Spellman was much more
a man of the world by the time he became archbishop than was Pius
himself. The years seemed to have given Spellman stature, while time
appeared to have robbed Pacelli of much of his stalwart character
and to have drawn him slowly inward and introspective.

Spellman no longer needed to rely mainly on Pacelli. He had
arrived, and what was of immense added importance to his influence
and authority, he had Roosevelt as his other powerful mentor. His
carefully timed little subtleties—his name-dropping—indicated to
her how much Spellman played upon his ties to the White House,
perhaps as greatly, she thought, as he used his direct line to the
papacy.

Pascalina was aware that Spellman had been using his charm on
Pius since the beginning. She was sure that the Pope, too, knew what
was happening. Yet Spellman always managed his maneuverings
with such taste and discretion that Pius never seemed to mind.
"Indeed, Holiness was usually somewhat amused, even fascinated, by
the charming American," she reflected.

The nun was also acutely aware that FDR, himself an extreme
opportunist, had come to regard the prelate in much the same fashion
as did the Pope. In recognizing all of the prelate's Church trappings,
the White House saw his immense value and sought to trade upon
his influence.

"The new archbishop would quite humanly forget himself at
times," she later remarked, "and, while in the presence of those he
knew, such as myself, he would flaunt his rather unique position of
influence between the two important heads of state—His Holiness
and the American President." To Pascalina, it appeared that Spellman—now that he ran the New York archdiocese—was flexing his
muscles "in the rather childlike fashion my young brothers did when
Papa gave them some added responsibilities on the farm."

Shortly after taking over his new post, Spellman phoned the nun from New York with an order that she immediately go through the Curia's files for pictures of the Pope and himself posing together, which he wanted for the press. Speaking in a most authoritative voice, the archbishop coldly told Pascalina: "I shall expect you to have copies made today and sent to me by overnight mail!" He hung up with a curt "Thank you."

"He certainly didn't sound like the jolly Father Spellman I had known and loved in the past," she remarked later, laughing merrily at thoughts of the incident. "I sent His Excellency mail that night, but it contained none of the photographs he had requested," she added, thoroughly enjoying her recollections. "Instead, I enclosed a copy of his class essay, which he had written as a young student at Fordham University. I had found his essay in the files years before when I was his assistant in the Curia's press office. It had given me a chuckle then, but it wasn't until His Excellency became archbishop that I realized what fun I'd have in returning it to him."

The paper read in part: "The love of myself, though seemingly self-ish, is nevertheless a strong one. My pleasure at present is the gratification of my ambition to amount to something worthwhile. . . . Should I therefore allow anything to interfere with, or thwart, my ambition? With God's help, no."

In her covering note to Spellman she wrote: "Your Excellency, sorry, but the photographs will take a little time to find. Meanwhile, thought that you would enjoy a bit of nostalgia. Your ambitions seem to fit as much these days as when you first wrote of them way back then." In a postscript the nun added, tongue in cheek: "The mails are so slow. Your 'thank you' note for my intercession in your behalf has yet to arrive."

Though Pascalina, in keeping with her Mother Superior nature, felt it was her responsibility to "bring Excellency Spellman down to earth whenever he showed his brash, self-important side," both she and Pius XII nevertheless remained "thankful to Almighty God that His Excellency was the Holy Father's choice."

Upon becoming archbishop, Spellman immediately went to work to clear up not only the New York archdiocese's financial plight but that of the Church throughout the United States. Unknown to Catholics and even to many within the hierarchy in the United States, near chaos characterized the Holy See's financial affairs in America.

Long-overdue debts had accumulated to almost $200 million nationally, in addition to the $28 million owed by the New York archdiocese.

Spellman named as his financial adviser his longtime friend John A. Coleman, one of Wall Street's ablest and most influential brokers. From then on the Holy See in America was into big business in a big way.

In their successful drive to turn the heavily debt-ridden New York archdiocese into the richest in the world, the ambitious pair began by playing upon Spellman's "amazing capacity for getting things done by the give-and-take of favors through powerful people." Day after day they staged luncheons and dinners with bankers, industrialists, Wall Street traders, corporate executives, labor leaders, real estate brokers, financial editors—anyone of influence in any field.

Titles in the Knights of Malta, the Holy See's most prestigious organization of laymen, were offered as bait to the wealthy and powerful who sought personal gilding in exchange for funds and favors. The title of knight became so eagerly sought after by Catholic laymen that it was not uncommon for an aspiring applicant to give Spellman from $50,000 to $100,000 for the honor. Some Catholics were known to have paid the New York archbishop as much as $200,000 to be named a knight.

Spellman became so greatly indebted to Coleman and trusted him so implicitly that he eventually appointed the financier to the top post of the Knights of Malta. From then on Coleman was known as "The Pope of Wall Street."

The archbishop took Knights of Malta funds and sums from another of the Church's secretive male organizations, the Knights of Columbus, to use as seed money for investments. The New York archdiocese also established its own bank, the Archdiocesan Reciprocal Loan Fund, to borrow and lend money. Soon the high-pressure team of Spellman and Coleman began making deal after deal—huge multimillion-dollar transactions—principally with the Catholic establishment's elite in big business, industry, and commerce.

In one deal alone during Spellman's reign $30 million was invested through Coleman in the purchase of stock in National Steel, Lockheed, Boeing Aircraft, Curtiss-Wright, and Douglas Aircraft. Large Church investments also were made in other leading U.S. corporations, including Goodyear, Firestone, General Foods, Procter & Gamble, Standard Oil, Westinghouse, and Colgate-Palmolive.

A considerable interest in the Lambert Pharmaceutical Company, manufacturer of Listerine Antiseptic, was bequeathed to Spellman by the firm's founder and later sold by the archbishop for $25 million.

Spellman was rarely one to let personal feelings or ethics stand in the way of opportunity. He heatedly denounced from the pulpit certain motion pictures that he considered unfit and immoral. *Forever Amber* and *Baby Doll,* both made by Paramount, were loudly condemned by him. Spellman nevertheless viewed Paramount, despite its Church-censored movies, as a particularly wise investment. Just how heavily the Holy See invested in the motion picture company in later years has never become known, since the stock was traded through disguised channels.

Almost all Church investments have been made through dummy corporations, or in the names of those commissioned to act as straws. The negative image of a religious organization being into big business in a big way has been the chief consideration for its coverture.

Spellman even drew upon his personal hobbies in considering investments. An avid baseball fan and even a fairly good player himself while in high school and college, he thirsted for the glamour of owning a part of the New York Yankees. Though the team was not for sale at the time, Spellman—using Knights of Columbus funds—settled for the purchase of the Yankee Stadium grounds and the surrounding parking lots.

Always the pragmatist, morality stood second to money on Spellman's list of priorities. His attacks were frequent on show business people for what he considered the entertainment industry's "loose morals," yet that did not stop the archbishop from building a close relationship of his own with Broadway showgirl Mabel Gilman Corey. When Corey became widowed from her wealthy steel-magnate husband, William E. Corey, Spellman persuaded the former dancing beauty to turn over to him her entire $5 million inheritance.

In a handwritten letter to the Chase Manhattan Bank, Corey directed the transfer of all her wealth to Spellman's New York archdiocese. She wrote:

GENTLEMEN:

I desire to transfer my bank balances and all securities and property belonging to me, of which you are custodian, to the Archdiocese of New York. Will you please deliver to His Eminence,

Francis Cardinal Spellman, or his representative, a current statement of my assets and give your cooperation in promptly effecting
the transfer of title.

Very truly yours,

MABEL GILMAN COREY

Another show business personality—the famed Major Edward
Bowes, who made millions in the 1930s and 1940s introducing future
stars on his hit *Amateur Hour* radio show—willed $3 million of his
$4.5 million estate to Spellman.

Even the Mafia bent to kiss Spellman's ring. New York mobster
Frank Costello, who along with Lucky Luciano dictated the U.S.
underworld's illicit drug and prostitution operations, was particularly
taken by Spellman's Church authority and charm. Through Spellman's connection with Costello the magnificent bronze doors of New
York's Saint Patrick's Cathedral were presented as a gift to the
Church.

Though Spellman was by far the greatest business head the
Church has ever had in America, he was not the first U.S. churchman to connect the Holy See with commercial ventures. Perhaps the
biggest undertaking in earlier years was its important role in the
establishment of the Bank of America. Though this was long before
Spellman's time, it remained for the coming of the Spellman era for
the Holy See to reap the profits of its early investment, a mere
$150,000 for which the Church received 51 percent of the bank's
stock. During the Spellman years the bank built its assets to over $25
billion.

According to Father Richard A. Ginder, a well-respected writer
and priest specializing in Catholic financial affairs, the Holy See's
influence in America's financial life grew to staggering proportions
during the Spellman years. Writing in the Catholic publication "Our
Sunday Visitor" in 1960, Father Ginder described the wealth of the
Holy See in the early 1960s in these terms: "The Church is the biggest corporation in the United States . . . and our roster of dues-pay-
ing members is second only to the tax rolls of the United States
Government."

At one point in Spellman's career *Fortune* magazine reported that
the revenues of the New York archdiocese alone exceeded $150 mil-
lion annually, and his parochial schools were worth another $22 mil-

lion. But it was Spellman's financial wizardry that proved to be the archbishop's greatest asset.

In one deal alone the archbishop got New York's City Hall to pay him $8.8 million for land and some old buildings valued at a fraction of the amount. The site and its structures, located in upper Manhattan, belonged to Manhattanville College, owned by the New York archdiocese. Spellman then quickly turned around and bought 250 acres of far more preferable property in the rich estate area of Purchase, New York, which he picked up for a mere $400,000. There the prelate built a new and ultramodern Manhattanville College, largely with the millions from his deal with New York's City Hall.

Without doubt the Holy See's interests in gambling—particularly bingo—also contributed considerably to its wealth. Legalized in New York State on January 1, 1959, nearly nine years prior to Spellman's death on December 2, 1967, Catholic organizations in New York realized nearly $90 million from bingo operations alone in the decade ending in 1969.

The additional advantage to the Church remained in its unique nonprofit designation, which enabled the Holy See to earn its fortunes without payment of taxes.

A staunch believer that "money makes money," Spellman spent huge sums as fast as the funds came in. He frequently invested as much as $90 million a year in construction. The money went into the building of 130 Catholic schools, 37 churches, and 5 large hospitals, along with numbers of other institutions.

Within just a few years Spellman had created a cash surplus for his archdiocese of about $182 million. As time went on he was to rule a real estate empire for the Church in New York that has been estimated in the billions of dollars.

"Is it any wonder that some of the hierarchy in Rome were so envious of Eminence Spellman?" Pascalina recalled with a wry smile. "Eminence Tisserant, who was least appreciative of all the good work being done in the New York archdiocese, would refer to Eminence Spellman as 'Cardinal Moneybags.'"

On one occasion Tisserant's derision almost got the nun in trouble. She told the Holy Father that a special friend was arriving the next day with a sackful of money. Pius at first was only half listening, but before all of her words were out, he abruptly looked up from his desk, and in a tone of great interest he asked: "Who is this special and generous friend?"

"Cardinal Moneybags," she blurted out without realizing what she was saying. The Pope's look of amazement caused her insides to quake with embarrassment, and she felt the hot flush on her face swiftly rise to her temples. She was sure that the Holy Father was incensed with her, but Pius's face quickly relaxed. With no sign whatsoever now of what he was thinking, he said in calm voice: "When referring to Excellency Spellman, you mustn't call him 'cardinal' while he's still only archbishop." Pascalina thought she saw a faint smile on the Pope's lips as he nonchalantly returned to his paperwork.

The next day the nun felt even more regretful of her words when Spellman himself arrived, acting his old jolly self again. He first planted a warm kiss on her cheek, then, while beaming a broad smile, he handed her a big black satchel stacked with American currency and checks. "This is for His Holiness!" he exclaimed in his old effervescent manner. Spellman bent close to her ear, and like an errant youth—the picture she so often had of him in her mind—he whispered: "There's a million dollars inside!"

"And how much is there for me?" she asked jokingly.

The archbishop reached into his pocket and pulled out a quarter. Handing her the coin, he retorted playfully, "It's all I have left." He broke into laughter, and she laughed heartily too. It was wonderful seeing Spellman again as his "old and lovable self."

Loyal Spellman never failed Rome in his generosity. Throughout his reign as head of the New York archdiocese he dutifully remembered Pius every year with his customary $1 million donation.

Nor did Spellman fail Roosevelt. Early in World War II the U.S. President put the clever archbishop's special talents to important use in behalf of the nation. FDR's problem was a very real one, with serious consequences for the Allies. In the three months after Pearl Harbor, Nazi sabotage had been wreaking havoc with U.S. and other Allied troop and supply ships off the Northeast coast. Hitler's German-American Bund, comprising large numbers of German-American Nazi sympathizers, was largely responsible for the destruction of vessel after vessel critical to the war effort. Twenty-one ships were torpedoed in January, another twenty-seven in February, and fifty in March, causing what was described by historian Rodney Campbell as a naval disaster approaching that of Pearl Harbor. The most humiliating and devastating of the attacks by the Bund was upon the huge French luxury liner the S.S. *Normandie,* which the German sympathizers on February 9, 1942 set aflame and capsized at its Manhattan berth. The *Normandie*—said to be able easily to outrun the fastest U-boat—was being converted at the time into a major troop carrier, capable of transporting an entire division overseas.

Spellman was called to the White House for an emergency meeting with the President. FDR confided his utter frustration to the archbishop, who by then had become military vicar of the U.S. armed forces. Spellman was told that the Germans "are winning the battle of the Atlantic." In spite of America's great resources, control of the Eastern Seaboard was in the hands of the German-American Bund and Nazi submarines, the archbishop was told. Not only did the Germans have accurate information long in advance of sailing dates of the carriers and cargo ships, but a deadly cordon of U-boats lurked off the U.S. coast. The Nazis, according to the President, were sinking U.S. and British ships almost at will.

Roosevelt was convinced that only the Mafia, with its control of the docks along the East Coast waterfront, could stop the sabotage. FDR's thinking was that Mafia leaders, who sprang from Catholic heritage, could be inspired by a prelate of the Holy See to take countermeasures for the sake of their country. The President was sure that Spellman, because of his manipulative power and devoted patriotism, was the prelate of choice for the job.

Spellman was stunned for the moment by the President's startling request, but the priest was too experienced to display his feelings. The idea of a prominent leader of the Holy Roman Catholic Church approaching a crime boss of the underworld for a favor, even one in behalf of the United States government, seemed unthinkable at the time to the archbishop.

Yet Spellman felt certain that the President was all too aware that Frank Costello, the underworld's "prime minister" and a member of the Mafia's national council, was a regular churchgoer. Costello was occasionally seen praying at Saint Patrick's Cathedral, Spellman's own church, and the archbishop was known to have at least a speaking relationship with the mobster.

"I shall first have to confer with the Holy Father for permission," Spellman told Roosevelt. The archbishop was secretly praying that the Pope would say no; that would still leave Spellman in a good position with the President.

Noting Spellman's hesitation, FDR chewed on his cigarette holder during a moment of serious thought; then, pulling it from his lips in a gay gesture and with head smugly cocked and a roguish smile, he said: "There is no substitute for victory, my dear Bishop. Tell the Holy Father for me what my good friend Winston [Churchill] so wisely said in defining wartime morality. 'If by some strange stroke of fate the devil came out in opposition to Adolf Hitler, I should feel constrained, at least, to make a favorable reference to the devil in the House of Commons.'"

Pascalina had never seen Spellman so distraught as the day he arrived in the Vatican in late March 1942. He paced her office in circles and was wringing his hands as the words tumbled out nervously. "The President wants me to seek a deal with the underworld for the United States government," the archbishop told her in confidence. "How am I to present such a horrible idea to the Holy Father? And how can I afford to turn down Roosevelt?"

The archbishop had always seemed so in control of himself that the nun was more surprised by his emotional undoing than by his words. "Nothing that any politician says or seeks surprises me any longer," she replied matter-of-factly, trying to avoid answering his question directly.

"Would you please broach the subject with the Holy Father before I speak with him?" he asked in near-pleading manner. "I will then be guided by your advice."

Pascalina hesitated, then agreed reluctantly. "I did not think it fair to be placed in the center of such a controversial matter," she said later. "I went along with His Excellency's request only because of the respect and friendship I had for him."

But she got no further with the Pope than if Spellman had tried himself. The Holy Father was too experienced in diplomacy to personally turn a deaf ear to a president so powerful as Roosevelt. The United States, with its huge Catholic population and vast wealth and resources, had been steadily opening its arms to the Vatican, and Pius was as anxious as FDR to keep their relationship rosy.

She found Pius equally anxious to avoid facing Spellman directly on the issue—to the archbishop's own relief. "Mother Pascalina, you are such a splendid diplomat in such matters," the Holy Father said smoothly when they were alone in his office. "Whisper in our American friend's ear that he has no need to bring up such talk with me. It would be far more pleasant if His Excellency and I confined our private audience tomorrow to a brief prayer." The Pope smiled and tapped a loving touch on the nun's shoulder. As he opened the door to let her out, Pius added softly, "I have full confidence in Archbishop Spellman's discretion. The decision is his."

And so began what the United States government code-named "Operation Underworld." Spellman, as military vicar of the U.S. armed forces, was advised to meet with Lt. Commander Charles R. Haffenden for his instructions. As commander of the Third Naval District, Haffenden was responsible for the safety of all U.S. troopships and cargo vessels along the Eastern Seaboard.

The naval officer instructed the archbishop to contact Mafia boss Frank Costello and talk with him at a clandestine rendezvous.

The unlikely pair met in a lower Manhattan tenement house. When Spellman arrived, Costello rushed forward to greet him. The mobster knelt and kissed the archbishop's ring.

"We all have a patriotic duty to perform for our country in time of war," Spellman told Costello.

The gangster professed his patriotism and assured the archbishop of his good intentions.

"I am both honored and overjoyed to be of service to my church and to my country," Costello replied.

Weeks later Spellman again met with the President. This time, the prelate exuded great confidence. Costello's promises had already produced results. The swiftness of the Mafia attack was startling even to the President. Word had gone out from Lucky Luciano, with whom Costello had conferred, ordering the immediate halt of all sabotage of U.S. troopships and cargo vessels. Luciano, boss of bosses of the U.S. underworld, though serving thirty to fifty years behind bars in New York State's prison at Dannemora, had the power to do what the U.S. government had consistently been unable to accomplish.

Even as the President and Spellman met, Mafia lieutenants and soldiers in charge of the docks were countering the Nazi saboteurs all along the Eastern coastal ports. Within weeks the entire waterfront was quiet.

The U.S. government rewarded Luciano handsomely for his efforts. After he had served only a fifth of his fifty-year term, the federal government pressured the state of New York to release the gangster. In 1946, a year after the war in Europe ended, Luciano was set free and deported to Naples.

Luciano's release would have been effected earlier but for a dilemma in Washington. The White House feared public reaction at turning the mobster loose and allowing him to remain in the country. Yet Luciano could not be returned to his native land while Mussolini remained alive. Il Duce had fought the Mafia for years and would not permit any compromise. It was only after the fascist dictator was assassinated in 1945 that the U.S. government moved to free Luciano.

Pascalina was later asked if Pius XII's papacy had collaborated with the White House in helping Luciano obtain sanctuary in Italy. The nun refused to comment.

If the Church did participate, it would be difficult to explain its actions in lending a helping hand to a hardened criminal, especially one under sentence of up to fifty years for heading a prostitution ring. Then there was Luciano's crime record after arriving back in Italy, where, following months of boring idleness, Luciano was back in the rackets. This time the Mafia's boss of bosses was directing a narcotics syndicate, illegally transporting drugs from Sicily to the United States.

Luciano died of a heart attack on January 28, 1962, at the Naples airport. He had gone there to meet a film producer interested in doing his life story. His death at sixty-five, Italian police said, occurred just as they were about to arrest him for running a huge international drug ring that had smuggled $150 million worth of heroin into the United States during the previous ten-year period.

"It was a blessing when he [Luciano] passed away," Pascalina recalled. "I remember saying a prayer to Jesus for the repose of his soul."

When Spellman himself died in 1967, the Church in the United States, which he had found debt-ridden twenty-eight years before, had assets exceeding $80 billion.

The Holy See also reached the peak of its spiritual influence in America during Spellman's twenty-eight-year reign. Church membership in the United States showed an impressive rise. From about 21 million in 1939, the Catholic population grew to over 45 million at the time of Spellman's death.

Never before in the new world was the faith of Catholics in their Church more apparent or less challenged than during Spellman's golden age of Catholicism. The communicants were prompted by his autocratic regime to think in terms of the absolutes of right and wrong. They were fired as well by preachings of self-denial with no room for compromise. In the United States, at least, it was an unequaled period of both "blind faith" and remarkable generosity toward the Holy See.

In the early days of Pius XII's reign, when Spellman's appointment as archbishop of New York was so bitterly attacked by the Church hierarchy, blame and condemnation were heaped upon Pascalina for pressuring in his behalf. But even though Spellman proved himself in exemplary fashion, doing better than the papacy dared dream, not once did anyone within the Vatican or elsewhere throughout the Church acknowledge that but for the nun's intercession for her friend, the Church in America might well have remained where Spellman found it—in dire straits.

IX

One afternoon in late May 1940—nearly nine months after the start of World War II—Cardinal Tisserant, the bearded French prelate with the cynical mind and biting tongue, walked straight past Pascalina's desk without glancing her way and went directly into the Pope's empty office, planting himself squarely in the Holy Father's chair. Pius was off in his own private quarters after having reluctantly yielded to the nun's insistence that he briefly rest himself from his eighteen-hour days and worries over the war.

Incensed at seeing her archenemy Tisserant—to whom politics meant everything—assume so much self-importance, Pascalina rushed in behind him. "Eminence!" she shouted. "Remove yourself at once from the Holy Father's place!" The tiny nun's eyes were ablaze with anger, and her clenched fists trembled as she stood defiantly before the enormous prelate, who was already puffing away on a huge cigar, his feet propped up on the Pope's desk. "And put out that cigar this instant!" she demanded, looking as if she were about to snatch it from his mouth.

Tisserant, a powerful leader of the Sacred College of Cardinals, looked shocked at her rage. Though the prelate himself was a tough fighter—his sharp words known to have divided the Vatican's hierarchy into allies or enemies virtually as a matter of course—he halfheartedly yielded to the nun. Stamping out the cigar and slowly raising himself to his feet, Tisserant muttered a sarcasm about the Pope that further fed Pascalina's wrath. "The papal conclave made a mistake!" he said with a snarl of contempt. "What the Holy See needs is a wartime pope, not a diplomat!" Time and again the nun had heard him slander the Holy Father with these pointed innuendos.

"Quite the contrary!" she retorted. "What His Holiness needs is loyalty among his hierarchy. Pius certainly does not need cardinals who take the side of their nation before the welfare of the Holy See!" Pascalina added, pointedly referring to Tisserant's French background.

Finally, Pascalina now had her own full-blown confrontation with Cardinal Tisserant. She had been secretly hoping for years to face down the galling prelate whom she knew held Pius in disrespect. The cardinal freely admitted that he looked down on the Pope, mainly because of Pius's weak position in the war.

Tisserant's stand was one that the strictly neutral Pope refused to take, a stand far beyond what Pius and Pascalina felt was in the best interests of the Holy See. The cardinal called for all-out support of the Allies by the Holy See and Church denunciation of the Nazis and fascists.

The female in Pascalina had wished that Pius would roar back at the chronically critical and outspoken French prelate. But the Pope had his own way of handling delicate and difficult matters. Whenever Tisserant had become too overbearing, Pius had simply ended the discussion by abruptly breaking in and completely changing the subject.

In her defense now of the Pope, Pascalina wanted to show Tisserant that she would stand by Pius to the very end. She wanted Tisserant to know how very strong the bond between her and the Pontiff really was.

"You know very well, Eminence, the Holy See must maintain neutrality in war!" she said, still speaking in a defiant tone.

"Neutrality . . . perhaps." Tisserant—the only non-Italian cardinal in the Vatican's Curia—snapped back. "But how can the Holy Father remain silent when we keep hearing reports day after day of the persecutions of our own clergy and the killings of the Jews?"

He paused, his eyes blazing with scorn.

Pascalina, who lived within the papal apartment, had Pius's ear around the clock, an arrangement that was more than Tisserant could bear. She was well aware of his ill feelings and had become all the more aggressive, largely because he had complained to Pius time and again about her.

"The woman thwarts all of our opinions and decisions," the cardinal had once said to the Holy Father, referring to matters between the Pope and the Sacred College of Cardinals. Though Pius usually listened to the loud and demanding prelate in stone-faced silence, Pascalina had never backed down to the hierarchy, nor had she ever failed to reply heatedly to their implied insults. She had spent her formative years in a household of contentious men, lashing out at their weaker instincts and shortcomings,* and she saw little reason now to back down from the Sacred College of Cardinals—a group of men, after all, for whom she held no overriding respect.

"You, woman, have a great deal of influence with His Holiness," Tisserant said with contempt upon resuming his tirade. "Tell Pius to stand up as Jesus Christ would stand up! Otherwise, you are as much at fault as the Pope himself!"

Tisserant had made his point, and he abruptly walked out. Pascalina stood speechless, looking dumbfoundedly after him. The confrontation had proven somewhat of a surprise to her, because when she searched beneath her anger, for the first time the nun found herself in agreement with Tisserant.

Pascalina had met her match in the brilliant, portly "Il Francése," who, though in his mid-fifties, was still as much a partisan militarist battling for France as he was an able and ardent Vatican churchman. On the French army's general staff during World War I, he had distinguished himself as an outstanding intelligence officer. He spoke thirteen languages: French, English, Italian, German, Russian, Persian, Greek, Latin, Hebrew, Arabic, Syrian, Amharic, and Assyrian. The latter five Semitic tongues he had fluently mastered.

Despite his stormy temperament and impetuous, often profane aggressiveness, the crudely outspoken Tisserant was still thought of in the Vatican as one of the finest minds in the Church. Sometimes for his own pure enjoyment the cardinal teased and baited his adversaries, a perverse trait that Pascalina likened to "a cat playing with a mouse." But most of the time the cardinal's arguments were so

---

*Her older brothers had learned early enough not to tangle with the young Josefine. On her eleventh birthday she was bathing her pet Schnauzer—a gift from Mama—when three of her brothers sneaked up from behind and tossed a small snake into the washbasin. The gray puppy began jumping about so wildly that Josefine was soaked with suds. She looked angrier than they had ever seen her, but she said nothing. The next night, however, when her brothers were cleaning up for their regular Saturday night on the town, Josefine walked in on them unexpectedly. As the boys were soaping themselves all over, she casually tossed three garter snakes—one for each of the pranksters—into their half-filled barrel.

impassioned that he would incur the resentments—even the wrath—
of those with whom he disagreed.

At the start of World War II, Tisserant's respect for Pius had
taken on a particularly sour note. The lasting animosity had become
evident when the Pope refused to release the cardinal from his post
as head of the Vatican Library, a request of Tisserant's so that he
could return to France for service in the war. Despite his advanced
age the prelate had seen his military skills as indispensable to his
native government, and complained bitterly to fellow cardinals: "I
am in a state of utmost uselessness being nailed down here in the
Vatican and, therefore, I have insisted to the Holy Father that he
assign me to France."

Though his animosities toward the unyielding Pope intensified
throughout Pius's lifetime, the wily, unbridled Frenchman also boldly
challenged Pacelli's successor, Angelo Cardinal Roncalli. Even on
the day Roncalli became Pope John XXIII in 1958, following the
death of Pius, Tisserant still showed his brash arrogance. When Roncalli appeared for the first time in the ermine cape of a new pope,
Tisserant abruptly took the Holy Father by the arm and, pulling him
to one side, whispered sternly into the Pontiff's ear, "Holiness, you
are wearing the wrong kind of shoes!"

Without as much as bothering to look down at his feet, Pope John
characteristically threw his arms in the air, and while shaking his
head nonchalantly the rotund old Pontiff replied: "Surely, Eminenza
Tisserant, we have more important things to think of than shoes."

Amid the storm over his controversial wartime stand, Pius's
instincts as a diplomat cautioned him to steer the Church along its
historical path of strict neutrality. Still, he was painfully aware that
many considered his silence pro-German and anti-Semitic. Some of
the Pope's harshest critics—particularly Tisserant—were his own
papal advisers.

Historically every pope has had his "senate," the Sacred College
of Cardinals, to contend with in setting papal policy. In Pius's case
there was Pascalina as well, a tough-minded middle-aged nun.
Though Pascalina virtually worshiped Pius and remained by far the
best friend that the lonely, melancholy Pontiff ever had, she—among
all his critics—was ultimately to prove his greatest source of anguish
with respect to Adolf Hitler. She always made sure that her advice

was gently administered in the strictest privacy—unlike Tisserant, who went to extremes in his character assault upon Pius, exercising a deliberate meanness that played a large part in the Pope's loss of face. Even as the Holy Father took careful measure of Hitler, Mussolini, Roosevelt, Churchill, and each of the other wartime leaders, weighing the truths and falsehoods pouring from both sides, Tisserant lashed out with increasing fury against Pius's policies.

"Our rulers do not want to understand the real nature of the conflict and insist on supposing that this is a war like wars in the past," Tisserant stated in one of a series of caustic and bellicose attacks upon the Pope during the early stages of World War II.

Then, on June 11, 1940—the day after Italy entered the war—he wrote his compatriot Emmanuel Cardinal Suhard, archbishop of Paris:

> Germany and Italy will set about destroying the inhabitants in the occupied areas as has been done in Poland. . . . The Fascist and Hitlerite ideology has transformed the consciences of the young . . . all those under 35 are ready to commit any crime granted they can attain the goal set by their leaders. . . . I'm afraid that history may be obliged in time to come to blame the Holy See for a policy accommodated to its own advantage and little more. And that is extremely sad . . . above all when one has lived under Pius XI.

Even New York's Archbishop Spellman, for whom Pascalina and the Pope had done so much, expressed strong feelings against Pius's silence. In a letter to Vatican Secretary of State Luigi Cardinal Maglione, Spellman surprisingly minced no words in his criticism of the Pontiff:

"The prestige of the Pope has declined sharply in America owing to the Pope's unclear pronouncements," Spellman wrote. "On account of pro-Axis statements by the Italian bishops, American Catholics no longer have the same confidence in the Pope's impartiality, because he is behaving first and foremost as an Italian, who probably sympathizes with Mussolini's imperial ambitions."

Spellman's letter was considered so offensive by the Vatican secretary of state that it was never shown to Pius.

Pascalina came across the correspondence months after it was written, and was appalled. Yet she knew that Spellman was too politically wise to have reached such extreme conclusions idly.

In the nun's view the war seemed to be closing in on Pius. After all the ominous signs, she felt compelled to force the Pope into taking some form of positive action.

It was the night of June 10, 1940, and Pius was working late in his office. Pascalina came in and told him that he looked tired and depressed.

"Indeed, I am exhausted from worry," Pius acknowledged, removing his glasses and rubbing his eyes. Deep black circles made his gaunt, emaciated face look older than ever to her. "Word has reached me that Mussolini has declared war on France and Britain," he said in a grave tone. Il Duce, considering war a glorious venture and overcome with humiliation at having to stand idly by as Hitler alone made history, had joined with the Nazis and moved his men and machines against Great Britain and France. The Vatican was now a target, isolated within the war zone.

Pascalina was understandably as stunned as Pius. "Holiness, I am convinced now that the Vatican itself will be bombed," she said, looking terribly concerned.

Pius nodded in despair. He spoke on about other worsening problems that troubled him greatly. The Pontiff was upset by reports that increasing numbers of Catholics, including some of his own hierarchy, were condemning him for showing so little sympathy toward the persecuted Jews of Germany.

"This Holy Father may go down in history as being anti-Semitic," the Pope told the nun, his voice as sad and discouraged as his expression. "The Holy See must aid the Jewish people to the best of our ability. But everything we do must be done with much caution. Otherwise the Church and the Jews themselves will suffer great retaliation." The Pope's gaze now was far away, and there were tears in his eyes. "Better that the world think of Pius XII as being anti-Semitic than for the Holy See to wear its valor and virtue on its sleeve so that the Nazis can claim more victims."

But was the Pontiff being entirely honest with the nun and himself? Had not the papacy's hands been tied to some degree by Hitler because of mistakes of the past? Embarrassing mistakes largely of Pacelli's own mind that were his undoing now?

Years before, while nuncio to Germany and later as Vatican secretary of state, Pacelli had forged a partnership of sorts between the Holy See and Nazi Germany. The Church had looked upon Pacelli's work as the framing of a pact not too unlike its Lateran Treaty with fascist Italy.

The concordat—as the Holy See preferred to call the pact—was signed by Pius XI and Hitler in 1933. It ordered the Holy See's clergy to swear oaths of fealty to Hitler and the Third Reich. It further ordered that prayers were to be said publicly for the Führer and Germany by Catholic bishops and priests. The Church, in effect, pledged never to oppose Hitler's dictatorship.

For its part the Third Reich had promised to respect and safeguard the Holy See's churches and all of its property, including monasteries, convents, seminaries, rectories, and parochial schools. There would be no outside interference, Hitler swore, or encroachment on the Church's rights and property.

Pacelli had believed at the time that there was much self-serving logic in the Vatican's reasons for coming to terms with Europe's spreading dictatorships. There were 45 million Catholics under Hitler, and Italy's population, 96 percent Catholic, was fascist-dominated. For years the Nazis and the fascists were the Holy See's best defenses against communism, a movement long bent upon the total destruction of the Catholic Church and the seizure of all its property and wealth. Most of Europe had been struggling in financial failure and was politically impotent, the very elements that played into the hands of the Reds. Prior to World War II, Pacelli had felt that without Hitler and Mussolini the continent would surely fall into communist hands. He had been convinced at the time that were Italy to turn Red, the Vatican, and everything it owned, would easily and quickly belong to the Bolsheviks.

To protect itself, the Church had concordats in modern times with as many as thirty-five different nations but never looked upon any of these pacts as a violation of its neutrality. A double standard was apparent, for, as in the case of the Vatican's pact with Hitler, how could the Church remain neutral in the truest sense when it had sworn fealty to Hitler and the Third Reich?

Pascalina had maintained for years that there was incongruity in such Church-state pacts and consistently warned Pacelli against the likely ramifications. In her mind the concordat with Germany was never more than a naive pact of brotherly love and support by the Vatican for the Nazis. But Pacelli had refused to listen to the nun.

Despite Pascalina's hatred of Hitler and the Nazis, there was irony in her feelings, for her sentiments were solidly with the Führer when it came to a choice between Nazism and communism. As Hitler's armies crossed the Russian frontier in June 1941, the nun showed as much jubilation as the Pope. They both joined in joyful prayers. Even in defiance of world opinion, Pius and Pascalina said novenas for the Nazis and asked God to intercede for their total victory in Russia.

Their joy was purely in what they considered the best interests of the Holy See. They believed that of the Church's two main political enemies, Nazism and communism, the Reds were the more dangerous, simply because Hitler was not out overtly to destroy Catholicism, as were the communists. Cardinal Secretary of State Maglione, in explaining the papacy's position to Myron C. Taylor, Roosevelt's personal envoy to the Vatican, said the Pope hoped that communism would be defeated by the Nazis. In its war against the Reds, a weakened Germany would then be at the mercy of the Western powers.

But to conclude that Pascalina was pro-German because of her anticommunist stand would be a misconception. If anything, her leanings were far greater on the side of the Allies. Throughout the early part of the war, the nun persisted whenever the opportunity arose to urge Pius to speak out in condemnation of Hitler.

In the late summer of 1942—nearly a decade after the Vatican-Nazi pact and almost three years into World War II—the Pope finally looked tragically to Pascalina for a solution to his most terrible problem. She had never believed in living in the past but quickly seized the present and future for opportunity.

"Holiness, the world believes little of the truth of the Nazi atrocities," she said one night after dinner in late August. She was eager to spark his imagination and hopeful of some positive action on his part. "It remains for you, as Holy Father, to speak out. The people will then be convinced, and they will rise up in righteous indignation."

But Pius remained impassive. "Roosevelt and the British have already spoken out against these alleged war crimes," he replied discouragingly. "Their words have done practically no good."

"That is because people do not accept such stories coming from the Allied leaders with vested interests," the nun persisted. "The

Allies issued so much false propaganda during World War I that people are naturally skeptical."

"But even our own clergy in Germany have no real evidence, just hearsay, that these alleged exterminations are taking place," Pius said.

"Could it be that the clergy, like most people, refuse to believe that such a holocaust could be perpetrated by civilized men?" she asked.

"You feel that Roosevelt is telling the truth; that the American President can be trusted?" Pius asked, sounding quite skeptical.

"I feel that no politician can be fully trusted," Pascalina replied matter-of-factly. "Holiness, may I suggest that you speak with the President, perhaps through Archbishop Spellman. Demand the truth! If full assurance is given by President Roosevelt that these atrocities are taking place, perhaps Your Holiness should then prepare an encyclical denouncing these horrible war crimes. If you, as Holy Father, were to reveal the mass extermination of Jews, people all over the world would believe you. Every decent human being on earth would rise up. The sheer force of right over terrible evil would prevail, and the Nazi philosophy would be crumbled in its own disgrace."

The Pope was deeply moved by Pascalina's words. It was thus agreed that he would contact Archbishop Spellman to obtain absolute assurance from Roosevelt that the Nazi atrocities were indeed taking place and were not the imagination of Allied propaganda.

As Pius and Pascalina talked that night, the humidity became so oppressive within the ancient palace that she proposed they seek some relief by strolling the paths of the secluded papal gardens. "Holiness, perhaps the air will help us formulate constructive plans," she suggested.

Outside, they talked further about the risks of aiding the Jews and the possibility of Hitler's and Mussolini's propaganda being turned against the Holy See.

Both Pascalina and Pius were realists, and they made a cool estimate of the grim probabilities resulting from any overt act against the Axis. Diplomat that he was, Pius XII understood the fierce national pride of the Germans and the Italians: World War II had become a battle unto death. Were the papacy publicly to attack Hitler or Mussolini now, there was little doubt that the Axis forces would move upon the Vatican and take over the Roman Church.

The Allies, the United States in particular, were urging the Pope to move the papacy to a neutral nation, preferably somewhere within the Western Hemisphere. Archbishop Spellman had visited with the Pope, at the request of President Roosevelt, specifically to argue for the transfer of the papacy from within the Axis' grasp.

But Pius steadfastly refused. "I told His Excellency [Spellman] that the Holy See would not become a propaganda machine for either side, the Allies or the Axis," the Pope advised Pascalina.

"But the people themselves must not be persecuted because of their leaders," Pascalina said. "There must be an answer, and the Holy See is that answer in large measure."

But the Pope refused to budge. By then he was barely listening because of utter exhaustion, and they went back into the Papal Palace, she now as despairing as Pius himself. The Holy Father's stubbornness seemed to her impossible to overcome.

Yet the next day Pius was his usual energetic self again. She heard him phoning Spellman in New York, asking the archbishop to speak directly with Roosevelt to verify the authenticity of the Nazi atrocities.

Later that week Spellman called back. "Your Holiness, President Roosevelt has given me every assurance that the vicious Nazi war crimes are entirely true," the archbishop told Pius. "Thousands of Jews are being gassed to death in concentration camps and other thousands are being burned alive in ovens."

As the Pope hung up Pascalina could see how upset he was. In his fury Pius told her to phone Diego von Bergen, German ambassador to the Vatican, and arrange for the Nazi to come to the Papal Palace.

Von Bergen's arrival several days later was met with a severe tongue-lashing by the Pope and a bitter denunciation of Nazism. "If the Germans win, it will mean the greatest period of persecution that Christianity has ever known," Pius told von Bergen.

The Nazi official remained silent and stone-faced throughout the Pope's tirade. Though obviously seething within, von Bergen held to a politely aloof manner. His words, when finally spoken, were coldly menacing. "I shall report your feelings, my dear Holy Father, to the Führer. Do not be too surprised if relations between the Third Reich and the Papacy are broken off."

The Pope did not flinch. Calmly, yet in a severe tone, he replied: "In such event, there could be but one outcome—the downfall of the state."

A standoff between the Vatican and the German government followed for the time being. Other than his dressing down of the Nazi war leader, the Pope continued to remain silent on the atrocities.

With the strain of war taking a severe toll on the Pope, Pascalina was all the more convinced that her first and foremost responsibility remained Pius's welfare—no easy task, even for one as totally dedicated as she. "He's such a baby!" she'd whisper to herself time and again, forever shaking her head in exasperation behind his back.

Pius's breakfast toast always had to be just a bit golden, or there'd be a tantrum. And he was forever forgetting where he last placed his glasses. "Mother Pascalina, come at once and find my glasses!" he'd roar.

Once when she was in deep concentration with Monsignor Giovanni Montini (later to become Pope Paul VI), poring over a forthcoming papal encyclical, Pius demanded that his personal needs take immediate precedence over Church business. "Mother Pascalina, come here this minute!" he bellowed.

She rushed breathlessly to his side. Pius looked up impatiently and shook his electric shaver at her. "You haven't cleaned this gadget in days!" he snapped.

But Pascalina was no easy mark, even for the Holy Father. "Shame on you, Holiness!" she retorted in mock anger. "You should do a little penance today by cleaning it yourself."

The nun laughed as she took the instrument from the Pope. And he laughed along with her. It was one of the few times during the war that Pascalina saw Pius laugh. She knew it was his little way of getting her attention; he so often needed her presence, and she so loved to be needed by him.

The Nazis took command of Rome on September 8, 1943, and though Hitler's troops surrounded the Vatican, Pascalina was even more persistent that the Pope speak out against the Führer's inhumanities. The nun and the Pontiff were strolling the rose-scented papal gardens, an almost nightly practice of theirs during the war years.

"Holiness, if you cannot bring yourself to denounce Hitler," she advised the Pontiff in an understanding tone, "then the least the papacy can do is lend its full support to the Jewish people whom the Nazis are persecuting."

She stopped where the pathways intersected and plucked one of the large red flowers, a favorite of Pius's, and handed it to the Holy Father, a warm, loving smile upon her face.

As the Pope savored the flower's pleasant fragrance, she saw how deeply his thoughts ran. Obviously, Pius was pondering all of the risks implicit in her appeal—dangers to the Holy See that were far greater now than ever before. The German secret police and the fascist police, too, had imposed strict surveillance upon Vatican City. The nun and the Pope knew all that was involved in secreting Jews across border lines that separated the Vatican from Nazi-occupied Italy.

Yet Pascalina saw sympathy take form in the Holy Father's eyes. She had struck a responsive chord—and she grasped her chance with an outpouring of her impassioned feelings.

"Holiness, we can provide sanctuary within the Vatican for thousands of Jews escaping Nazi Germany," she pleaded, sounding like a little girl who was looking to her father for the impossible.

"Dear Sister Pascalina, Our Holy Savior speaks through your mind and heart," Pius said with tender understanding. "You have moved the Holy Father at last!" The Pontiff raised his right hand and placed his blessing upon her brow.

Whether it was Pascalina or the Pope himself whose idea it was that night to form the Pontifical Relief Committee remains unclear. But this relief effort in behalf of the Jews would become what has since been regarded as probably the greatest Christian aid program in the history of Catholicism.

With the Nazis in command of Rome, the Pope had to seek German cooperation for the committee to function. But since Jews were to be aided, extreme tact—even duplicity—on the Holy Father's part was entirely essential. Vatican Secretary of State Luigi Cardinal Maglione was dispatched to pay a personal call upon German Field Marshal Albert Kesselring, the occupying general, inviting him to meet with the Pope in the Papal Palace. Cardinal Tisserant was asked by Pius to be an observer, and Pascalina was to be there as recording secretary.

Kesselring appeared surprisingly cooperative and promised the Pope to respect the Holy See's independence and integrity. The Vatican would be off limits, and the Nazis would not violate the Holy See's churches, basilicas, convents, or colleges. The field marshal further promised to protect Castel Gandolfo, the papal summer residence, even though the retreat was seventeen miles outside the Vatican and deep within the war zone.

The field marshal told the Pope that in return for Nazi cooperation, the Führer had asked that His Holiness release to the world a statement that the German troops were behaving "correctly." Pius agreed to the request, and the following day *L'Osservatore Romano* announced that the Nazis were respecting Vatican territory and all of its religious structures.

During the meeting the Pope of course made no mention whatsoever of the papacy's plans to help Jews. In the further attempt to deceive the Nazis into allowing Jews free access to the Vatican, Pascalina had previously proposed to Pius the sly idea of having identity cards issued to enable bearers to enter and leave the Vatican at will. The Pope suggested the idea to Kesselring, and the Nazi general went along with the plan. The field marshal agreed to allow the papacy to print the cards bearing only the Pontiff's stamped signature.

Believing everything was set, Pascalina could not have been more delighted. But she hadn't counted on the Pope having far greater problems with his own hierarchy than anything they had previously imagined would come from Kesselring.

The outburst by the Sacred College of Cardinals was heard when the Pope quite naturally placed Pascalina in charge of the Pontifical Relief Committee. Had she not done a splendid job during the aftermath of World War I for the people of war-torn Munich?

The august body of cardinals, however, looked upon Pascalina's appointment from an entirely different point of view. A woman, even though a nun, sitting at the head of a committee of prelates! To the Sacred College of Cardinals, the egotistical Tisserant in particular, the idea was inconceivable and intolerable.

"No!" Cardinal Tisserant shouted in defiance of his Pontiff. "Has His Holiness gone mad?" he asked his colleagues.

Pius was astounded by the rebellion within the Sacred College, yet his vacillating nature caused him to procrastinate once again. He couldn't say no to Pascalina, and neither could he say yes to the papal hierarchy.

Pascalina was enraged and felt the time had come for her to take matters entirely into her own hands. Without bothering to give a second thought to the possible consequences, she began to process innumerable pleas for help from Jews within Nazi-occupied lands. Her work was started in the dimly lit, vaulted cellar beneath the Papal Palace.

When Cardinal Tisserant surprised her late one night, an angry, demanding look upon his face, she was so tired and angry herself that she pointed to a dead rat in a corner of the cellar.

"If you don't leave me alone, I'll throw it at you!" she yelled.

Astounded, the old prelate turned on his heel and was quickly gone.

In the weeks ahead the nun risked everything for the Jews. Turning her important responsibilities to Machiavellian advantage, she falsely issued hundreds of papal identity cards. These were secreted to Jews in occupied territories so they could pass as Christian through Nazi lines for safety in the Vatican.

It wasn't too difficult to conceal the forged cards among the many thousands of valid ones issued as a matter of course to all Christians entering and leaving the Vatican. The Nazis were quite aware of the forgeries and pressured the Pope to tighten up on their issue. Pius promised to do so, but his stalling tactics were so effective that they caused no more of a problem than to exasperate the German high command. The increasingly angry Nazis got the impression that he really did not care, but there was little recourse left them. Had it not been for world opinion, undoubtedly the German high command would have moved drastically against the Pope.

On many occasions Pascalina and Pius spent anxious moments peering from the windows of the papal apartment as Jewish refugees flashed their false identity cards to Nazi border police to gain safe passage into the Vatican. Throughout the remainder of the war thousands of Jews crossed the painted line between occupied Rome and the Vatican for shelter in churches, basilicas, and other papal buildings. At least 15,000 alone were housed at Castel Gandolfo.

Food, clothing, medicine, and cash were provided the refugees by the Holy See. The food kitchens alone cost the Vatican about $7,000 a day. To finance the undercover program the Pope obtained disguised donations from Catholics throughout the world, and all persons attending papal audiences were asked to bring food, with the result that thousands of tons of provisions were secured in that manner.

Ironically, Pascalina was never happier than during that clandestine period, never more in her element. The pathos, the gratitude, pouring from the faces of the orphaned Jews, who for so long had been terrified by Hitler, gave her a richness of feeling she had never before known.

Day after day she was seen darting about, taking care of a thousand and one Papal Relief responsibilities. The nun appeared to supervise everything, and personally tended to many of the details herself.

Each of the thousands of refugees had to be assigned to rooms and everyone fed on a daily basis. Huge amounts of food had to be ordered several times a week and the papal kitchens kept running around the clock. Then, too, many had to be clothed. The bed linens alone that had to be changed every day were enough of a full-time job.

On numerous occasions the Nazis became suspicious that Jews might be among those harbored within the Vatican. Time and again they sent special agents to check on the refugees within the Papal Palace. But never once were they able to outwit the Bavarian nun who so well understood the German mind.

Pascalina succeeded largely because she turned her charm on the German ambassador to the Holy See, Baron Ernst von Weizsäcker, whom she knew to be secretly anti-Nazi. The nun had met von Weizsäcker on July 5, 1943, when he was received in private audience by the Pope. She immediately sensed his true friendship to the Holy See, and her confidence was fully justified.

"Observing the German ambassador's devotion to Jesus, I suggested to His Holiness that he invite von Weizsäcker to join the Holy Father in private prayers in the papal chapel," Pascalina later said. "Pius agreed, and several times thereafter the three of us said the rosary together. Though no mention was ever made by His Holiness to the ambassador that the institutions of Rome were packed with Jews, our good friend 'the Baron,' I am sure, was aware of everything," Pascalina said, brightening at memories of their triumph. She knew that had he chosen to do so, von Weizsäcker had the power to act against them, for he had served as under secretary to German Foreign Minister Joachim von Ribbentrop, Hitler's close friend.

The nun's instincts were right on target. Sure enough, the ambassador successfully prevailed upon the German high command in Italy to stay clear of the Vatican's railway service in and out of Italy. Through this vital, uninterrupted channel food and supplies poured into the Vatican. With the Nazi high command looking the other way so much of the time, the Pope and the nun dispatched convoys of supply-laden trucks to Castel Gandolfo and other papal sanctuaries for the beleaguered Jews.

Even with her highly placed friend in court, Pascalina never for a moment let down her guard. At the slightest provocation she moved like a shadow in the night through scores of secret staircases that linked the thousands of rooms within the palace and other Vatican buildings, warning the Jews that Nazi agents were on the prowl.

By torchlight she led the most sought-after of the refugees through hidden tunnels within the palace's walls. She hid hundreds more Jews deep within the cellars of the palace. Oftentimes she had them transported out of the Vatican, in trucks disguised as food-delivery vehicles, and driven to safety in Spain and Switzerland.

The spiriting of refugees was the major task but not the only form of the Pope's and Pascalina's activism. At one point Rome's chief rabbi, Israel Zolli, sought an audience with Pius to speak of the special plight of Italian Jews within the Eternal City. The Nazis had demanded a ransom of one million lire and one hundred pounds of gold from the Jewish residents of Rome; otherwise their homes would be taken from them. The Jews had raised the required lire but could not acquire the gold. Could His Holiness help?

The Pope did not hesitate. Within twenty-four hours the ransom was paid. With the Holy Father's permission Pascalina undertook the responsibility of having numbers of priceless holy vessels melted down to provide the required gold.

Later in the war some fifty-five thousand Jews were spirited by the papacy out of Romania at the request of Grand Rabbi Isaac Herzog of Jerusalem. The rabbi had appealed to the Pope to use Pascalina's committee to channel the Jewish refugees through the Vatican.

In reaching Pius, Herzog had originally approached Monsignor Angelo Roncalli, the apostolic delegate to Turkey and Greece, who was stationed at the time in Istanbul. The amiable and well-liked Roncalli—who fifteen years later succeeded Pacelli and became Pope John XXIII—was known by much of world Jewry to be facile enough to charm all sides: the Allies, the Axis, and the papacy itself. The Jewish Agency of Palestine had received his help on several occasions in saving Jews in Bulgaria, Slovakia, and Hungary from Nazi persecution.

In first contacting Roncalli, Rabbi Herzog wrote:

> M. H. Barlas, delegate of the Jewish Agency in Turkey, has brought to my knowledge the very valuable assistance you always give him in his efforts to come to the help of our unfortunate brothers and sisters who are in the Hitlerian hell, when it is a question of countries where the spiritual influence of the Catholic Church is strong enough. I well know that His Holiness the Pope is opposed from the depths of his noble soul to all persecution and especially to the persecution, unheard of in its ferocity and without parallel in the history of the human race, which the Nazis inflict unremittingly on the Jewish people, to whom the civilized world owes so much from the spiritual point of view. I take this opportunity to express to your Eminence my sincere thanks as well as my deep appreciation of your very kindly attitude to Israel and of the invaluable help given by the Catholic Church to the Jewish people in its affliction. Would you please convey these sentiments, which come from Sion, to His Holiness the Pope along with the assurance that the people of Israel know how to value his assistance and his attitude.

After the war Grand Rabbi Herzog came in person to Pius to "officially thank the Holy Father and the Holy See for manifold acts of charity on behalf of the Jews."

Though many attacks have been leveled against Pius XII for his failure to speak against Nazi atrocities, papal war relief provided to Jewish refugees by Pius and Pascalina has been acknowledged and applauded many times over the years by prominent Jewish leaders. Maurice Edelman, president of the Anglo-Jewish Association, visited with Pius and Pascalina after the war to thank both personally for all they had done for the Jews. Papal intervention, Edelman said, "was responsible during the war for saving the lives of tens of thousands of Jews."

Bernard Wall, a leading Jewish writer, also praised Pius and Pascalina for their charitable work in behalf of the Jews. In his *Report on the Vatican,* Wall said, "the papacy helped young Polish Jews escape to the United States with Vatican credentials."

The American Jewish Welfare Board wrote Pius in July 1944 to extend its warm appreciation for the protection given Jews during the German occupation of Italy.

By war's end nearly 200,000 refugees, both Jewish and others, had been sheltered and fed by the Vatican, and another 400,000 Jews were saved from certain death by the Holy See.

In gratitude for all that Pius and Pascalina had done for Jews, the World Jewish Congress expressed its heartfelt praise and further donated twenty million lire to Vatican charities.

Pinchas E. Lapide, the Israeli consul in Italy, effusive in his praise of papal war relief, declared: "The Catholic Church saved more Jewish lives during the war than all other churches, religious institutions and rescue organizations put together. Its record stands in startling contrast to the achievements of the International Red Cross and the Western Democracies."

Pascalina rarely left the Vatican throughout the war. When the nun did journey into Rome, it usually would be on an errand of charity. Pius would make sure that his loyal and beloved counselor and companion was well protected. She was driven in a small car, always with blinds fully drawn so that as few people as possible would catch sight of her.

Usually these short visits were in behalf not only of Jews but of the Roman aristocracy as well. The fascists had toppled many aristocrats from power and stripped them of their wealth. Too proud to ask for help, these newly impoverished Romans were visited unexpectedly by Pascalina. Using her utmost tact, she would persuade each to accept the Pope's financial assistance "as an act of the love of God."

Nor were Rome's poor ever forgotten by the nun. Week after week throughout the war she went about in her little private car, handing out small sums of money to those she found begging in the streets.

With the Nazis in command of Rome, Pius feared the possibility of imminent attack by the Allies—despite Roosevelt's assurances to the contrary.

In May 1943, three months before the Nazi occupation of the Eternal City, His Holiness had written the President, expressing confidence that innocent people would "be spared as far as possible further pain and devastation, and their many treasured shrines . . . from irreparable ruin." In his answer dated June 16, 1943—at the very time when the Allied decision to bomb Rome was being made in Washington—Roosevelt wrote Pius:

Attacks against Italy are limited, to the extent humanly possible, to military objectives. We have not and will not make warfare on civilians or against nonmilitary objectives. In the event it should be found necessary for Allied planes to operate over Rome, our aviators are thoroughly informed as to the location of the Vatican and have been specifically instructed to prevent bombs from falling within the Vatican City.

Though Roosevelt's letter was comforting to Pius, his years of experience in the diplomatic service had taught him how easily changing events affect the minds of statesmen.

"With the Germans surrounding Rome, we must have absolute guarantees from President Roosevelt that Rome will be declared an open city!" Pascalina overheard Pius tell Archbishop Spellman on the overseas phone. The Pope insisted that the New York archbishop meet with FDR as soon as possible to remind him once more that the Eternal City, the world seat of the Holy Roman Catholic Church with all of its historical and artistic treasures, must be kept entirely immune from the war.

Rome, though, as the capital of Italy and the center of the Catholic world, was already figuring prominently in most of the war plans of both the Allies and the Nazis. On the part of the Germans, Rome's sacred character was regarded as an asset, and although the city was not too important in a military sense, it figured importantly in psychological warfare. To the British, Rome was an unpopular symbol whose destruction would not be mourned. Back in the days of the blitz, Italian planes had appeared with the Nazis over London, and the British spirit of retaliation was strong. Antiquarian sentiment was rare in the rank and file, and the fact that Rome was so closely identified with papal history struck no responsive chord in the hearts of British leaders. To the Americans, on the other hand, it was, as General H. H. Arnold described the Vatican, "a hot potato." Catholics in the armed forces represented an impressive proportion of the nation's strength, while at home there were twenty-five million of their coreligionists who were for the most part loyal supporters of Roosevelt's policies.

Immediately after talking privately with the President in the White House, Spellman flew to Rome. He met with the Pope and found Pascalina at the Holy Father's side.

"The President gave me his solemn word that Rome will be declared an open city," Spellman said emphatically. "The President said that he had conferred with Prime Minister Churchill and that plans were made by the Allied nations to protect Rome and the Holy See from the ravages of warfare. There will be no bombing of Rome, nor attack upon Rome by the Allied Forces. Holiness, that is the solemn pledge of the President of the United States."

The Pope felt greatly relieved, as did the nun. Though neither trusted politicians, it seemed highly unlikely in Pius's mind, or in Pascalina's, that Roosevelt would dare perpetrate an outright lie to the Holy Father, even if expressed indirectly through Spellman.

The New York archbishop was barely airborne for return to America when Pius began writing his encyclical *Mystici Corporis*. The Pontiff, for the first time, went all-out in his condemnation of the Nazis and asked the prayers of everyone for an Allied victory.

He castigated what he termed "legalized murder" of the Jews, calling their slaughter "a violation of natural and Divine law."

Pascalina pleaded for the Pope to name Hitler in the encyclical as the "barbaric butcher behind the massive holocaust."

For days Pius weighed the ramifications of actually branding the Führer as "a killer of mankind." Finally he agreed to go along with Pascalina's suggestions.

The more Pius worked on the encyclical with Pascalina, the more deeply motivated he became. The nun took advantage of his intensifying emotions and urged that he himself read the encyclical over the Vatican radio. The Holy Father told Pascalina that he would ignore the risks and withhold nothing. He promised to call upon the people of the world to rise up against the horrors of Hitler's gas chambers and ovens at Auschwitz and Dachau.

But as the days passed leading up to the reading of the papal encyclical, Pius began to have mixed feelings. He instinctively felt "uncertain of the President's veracity," he said.

"My respect for the American President was destroyed when I learned that Roosevelt knew of the pending attack on Pearl Harbor five days before it happened," he continued. "The British were also aware beforehand of the Japanese plan. My heart bleeds for the persecuted, but the Holy See must remain above the scoundrels on both sides whose motives are purely selfish."

At the last moment the Pope made substantial deletions in his encyclical. Although he delivered an all-out attack on Germany for its persecutions, he made direct reference neither to Hitler nor the Nazis.

Pascalina's disappointment was obvious to the Pope, and he attempted an explanation.

"I have often considered excommunication [of Hitler], to castigate in the eyes of the entire world the fearful crime of genocide," Pius said. "But after much praying and many tears, I realize that my condemnation would not only fail to help the Jews, it might even worsen their situation. . . . No doubt a protest would have gained me the praise and respect of the civilized world, but it would have submitted the poor Jews to an even worse persecution."

If Pius was right in his analysis of Hitler, he was as accurate in his skepticism of Roosevelt. The Pope's early doubts of FDR were confirmed on the morning of July 19, 1943, when air raid sirens sounded a shrill alarm throughout the Vatican. Pascalina was with Pius in his office at the time. The Pope was conferring with several foreign dignitaries when the sharp blasts of antiaircraft guns resounded.

The nun and the Pope jumped to their feet and ran to the windows. The pale blue sky was dotted by balls of black smoke from exploding antiaircraft shells. As they watched in horror the papal windows were rattled by more blasts of heavy explosions. Pascalina saw a thick column of smoke and dust spiral slowly skyward. Other columns followed, forming a huge dark cloud over the Vatican.

She could see that Rome's great railway terminal had been struck by bombs from enemy aircraft. The diplomats, as startled as the Pope and the nun, excused themselves and abruptly departed. Pascalina and Pius, praying fervently, remained at the windows, together imploring Christ's intercession to save Rome.

More aircraft suddenly swooped through the thickening black smoke and spread across the summer sky. The nun could see the planes' markings as they streaked low over Saint Peter's. Allied aircraft were demolishing the city! She saw anger flaring in the Holy Father's eyes. The Pope had been deceived by Roosevelt. Pius moved decisively to his desk. He picked up the phone and called Monsignor Giovanni Montini, then unofficially under secretary of state.

"How much cash is there in the Vatican bank?" the Pope asked.

"About two million lire, Holiness," Montini replied.

"Draw it out immediately, and take the first car you find in Saint Damaso Courtyard," Pius ordered. "We will join you."

Pascalina and the Holy Father ran down the stairs of the Papal Palace, meeting Montini as he crossed the courtyard. Montini was carrying a huge black bag filled with cash. Pius pointed to a small car parked nearby and each jumped in, with Montini behind the wheel.

"Go as fast as you can!" Pius shouted. As they raced through the streets of Rome bombs rained from the low-flying Allied aircraft, exploding everywhere.

"Faster!" Pius shouted, but Montini scarcely needed prodding. They were moving with such speed, Pascalina felt they were almost flying across the winding Tiber and up the Corso Vittorio Emanuele.

Pius continued to pound the dashboard with his fist, his anger and emotion overwhelming him. "Faster! Faster!" the Pope repeated over and over again. Flames were streaking through the thickening smoke that lay ahead.

Their car crossed the plaza to the front of the railroad station. Smoke was billowing from inside the great structure, claiming the lives of scores of people.

Barricades had been set up by police and soldiers, and they could not proceed farther. Pascalina, Pius, and Montini jumped out of their car at the same time. People, desperately frightened, milled about wringing their hands and screaming in fear. When they saw the Pope, everyone began shouting for help. *"Il Papa! Il Papa!"* they cried out.

Pius was told that the ancient church of San Lorenzo had been partially demolished and that a bomb had fallen in the nearby cemetery of Campo Verano. The Pacelli family was buried there, and Pius would discover that the remains of his father and mother had been blown from their graves.

To their right, just beyond the enbankment, crackling flames were destroying scores of passenger and freight cars. Explosions sounded all about them. Pascalina saw buildings totter and watched as smoke poured from rows upon rows of houses. She heard the screams and moans of people pinned beneath the burning rubble. Bodies and parts of bodies were strewn about, and the wounded were lying everywhere.

Those who could still stand clustered around the Pope, clutching at his white cassock. Pascalina wanted desperately to help everyone, as did Pius and Montini, but women were clawing at each of them. In the panic they were powerless to move. Hundreds were weeping in common grief. The nun knelt alongside Pius and Montini, and their lips began moving in prayer.

When they finally were able to rise, they began ministering to the wounded. For hours they did everything possible to save as many of the injured as they could attend to. Pius and Montini gave the last rites of the Church to scores upon scores of the dying.

Later, when nothing remained to be done for the injured, the Pope told Pascalina and Montini to begin distributing the Vatican money to those in need. As Pius directed the operations a tearful mother shoved a small body into his arms. The Holy Father stood tenderly holding the dead child, all the while speaking words of consolation to the multitude of mourners.

Pascalina and Montini continued to hand out the money, giving freely until the sack was entirely empty. Long into the night they remained with the crowd, going from person to person, trying their utmost to be consoling.

It was almost dawn when they finally got back into their car to return to the Vatican. Pascalina, like Pius and Montini, was bleary-eyed from tears and exhaustion. The blood of the dead and the dying was encrusted on her habit and splattered upon their cassocks.

The air raid—with 521 Allied planes taking part—had killed hundreds of Rome's civilians.

Upon arrival at the Papal Palace, Pius took Pascalina by the arm, directing her to his office. It was already the start of a new day. Without any thought of sleep the Pope dictated a letter to President Roosevelt, which she took in shorthand. It seemed inconceivable to the nun that—despite all the horrors of warfare, which Pius himself had witnessed firsthand; despite all the death and destruction, which the U.S. President had pledged to the Pope would never happen to Rome or the Vatican—Pacelli would still have any faith in Roosevelt. In defiance of almost all comprehension, the Pope's weak nature prevailed as he pleaded once more with the American politician, using words that were bland and entirely guarded, that no further bombings of Rome and the Vatican would be made by the Allies.

"As Bishop of this sacred city, We have constantly tried to save Our beloved Rome from devastation," Pius wrote in part. "But this reasonable hope has, alas, been frustrated."

In Pascalina's view the British minister to the Vatican, Sir Francis D'Arcy Osborne, summed up the tragic situation in exact terms. "There is no doubt that the Pope is a victim of the President's notorious charm and political adroitness," Osborne commented.

Roosevelt apparently shrugged off the Pope's plea as being of little consequence, for on August 13, less than three weeks later, the U.S.

war machine and other Allied military forces were again attacking the Eternal City. Rome was once more raided from the air; this time the Allied bombers centered their destruction on the district of San Giovanni near the Pope's own church, Saint John Lateran.

At last Pius showed his anger; upon returning from the scene of the renewed destruction, his fury appeared worse than the nun had ever seen. But instead of attacking his enemies, the Pope vented his frustrations upon Pascalina and Tisserant. Pius ordered the nun and the cardinal to his office, and summarily dressed them down.

"As long as I remain the Holy Father, the Holy See will never again violate its rule of neutrality," the Pope said, his eyes burning into Pascalina and Tisserant. "The scoundrels on both sides in the present war have shown their dishonor. In the future, the Holy Father shall continue to listen to you both, as I have in the past, but I will remain firm within my own better judgment."

X

Clearly the war was having an intense emotional effect on Pascalina, at times strengthening her human commitment, while on other occasions demoralizing her faith in the Church and in nations for their cruel and amoral manipulations.

There were heartening moments resulting from her exhausting toil and the risk of aiding those in need—particularly the Jewish refugees—that built her courage and fortified her self-respect. "I was attaining as much inner reward out of helping helpless people as they appeared to receive from being given sanctuary," she reflected. "My work made me feel like a good person, strong and needed."

Yet she was often haunted by disappointment and disillusionment with those at the top in whom she once had placed great trust and confidence. The few who knew her well—principally the Pope and her priest-confessor—sensed the agony of her masked frustrations. Pius understood her hidden yearning for a renewed confidence in the fundamental idealism of her youth, but he did little to ease her pain.

Early in her childhood she had approached life and religion with rare and truly remarkable dedication. She had fashioned great dreams of her Church standing stalwart and compassionate—like a kindly, defiant giant—against all evil. Popes and cardinals and heads of state were all Godlike in her young fantasies, men who ruled with honest minds and kind hearts, and despised lies and hypocrisy as intensely as she did. During those long-ago times, as now, her caring and zeal in helping others had always been bright and boundless, as Christ asked. "The willingness to give a damn," as her priest-confessor once described her fervent feelings, always was at the center of Pascalina's thoughts. And still she remained courageous enough to show her fire to anyone who sinned or failed.

Now, at middle age, in a selfish world at war, her fundamental foundations—her hope and faith in the leaders of mankind—were very nearly unhinged. This nagging trauma had taken shape during the many years she was confidante to Pacelli the diplomat, and now it was full-blown with Pacelli as Pope. As her exposure to international politics had increased, so had her early beliefs and dreams centering upon the Vatican and other seats of world power gradually diminished, then entirely soured. If her mother, or anyone else who loved her, could see Pascalina's drawn face at that point in her life, they would read how sadly disappointing Pius XII and many within the hierarchy seemed to her so much of the time.

Her system of justice—more demanding now as she approached her fiftieth birthday—called for clear answers to the most pressing of imponderables: life's values. Over and over she asked herself how far the Holy Father and the hierarchy were prepared to go in their responsibilities—in their decisions and actions—to preserve human decency and integrity. So many of life's golden rules, so much of mankind's dignity, had gone horribly awry that she often felt angry and vengeful and afraid. Where among the institutions of the world, where among the people of power, could one find honest example? Who and what remained to trust? There seemed to be no certain answers in her mind.

With the ways of the world—the Vatican included—turning ever more self-seeking, Pascalina called out to Christ time and again for Divine guidance and help. She had held faithfully for years to her task as mistress of Pacelli's mind and soul, but not always did he listen. And since he was Pope and she only a nun, what wand remained for her to wave? "Dear Jesus, though I am merely a servant of a Church ruled by men, please give me the wisdom and opportunity to light the way for the Holy Father!" she pleaded on her knees. "The suffering people of the world continue to cry out to Holy Mother Church to help spare them from the tyrannies of Hitler and Mussolini. I beg of You, Blessed Jesus, to have His Holiness hear my words and heed my warnings!"

To Pascalina many of the world's problems—particularly the weakening of the human spirit—sprang from decadence in high places, its presence apparent to her even in the Vatican. Time and again since her arrival in the holy city more than a decade earlier, certain of the clergy had insulted her morality. Their utter disregard of what the nun thought of as "some of the most basic considerations of female respect and propriety" often left her seething for hours. She had been in the Vatican scarcely a week when she saw "an Italian cardinal pinch a lady's bottom." It happened in one of the Curia's offices, and she never was able to forget the experience, or to forgive the prelate.

Her disenchantment was all the more traumatic since she had grown up looking upon priests "in such idealistic awe," she recalled years later, at age eighty-seven. "They were the epitome to me of everything that was pure and perfect. Perhaps I sound like a prude in this day and age," the nun added, looking a bit awkward. "But there are standards of morality we must all hold to, especially if one is of the clergy, and most especially if he is of the hierarchy." To her "the cutting of corners, be they of a moral or ethical sense," was what she saw too much of everywhere, including the Vatican.

"My disgust was what gave me the mind and courage to stand up and face those of the Sacred College of Cardinals who were traitors to the teachings of Jesus Christ," Pascalina said. And no one was to prove more abrasive and sometimes crude in his manner of expressing himself than Cardinal Tisserant. Even some four decades later Pascalina could not forget the anger and exasperation Tisserant caused the Pope and herself on the night of July 25, 1943, when the prelate came storming into the papal apartment entirely unannounced and unexpected. The Pontiff and Pascalina were on their knees, saying the rosary together at the time.

"Great news, Holiness!" the French cardinal shouted, beads of perspiration apparent upon his face. "The guineas have come to their senses at last! The king has put that bastard Mussolini in chains!" Tisserant, in utter glee, was unable to control his emotions. He pounded the Pope's desk with his fists in exhilarated staccato style.

Pascalina was more astounded by Tisserant's language than by his news. Infuriated, she came to her feet and struck Tisserant across the face, the hardest slap she had ever given anyone in her life.

Pius was as stunned by Pascalina's actions as he was by Tisserant's news. The Pope and the nun had heard gossip that Tisserant was a "man of salty language," but never before had the cardinal taken such liberty in the Holy Father's presence.

The French prelate succumbed to rage. "This is what happens when you bring a woman into a man's world!" he roared at the Pope. "Well, let me tell you more, Holiness," he continued, coldly pointing a finger at the Pope, then at Pascalina. "Word has been received by the Sacred College that the other son of a bitch, Hitler, is about to retaliate for the taking of that fascist, Mussolini!" Tisserant paused and abruptly straightened himself to his full height. He pressed his bearded face close to the Holy Father's. "Hitler has ordered your capture, my dear Pope. Indeed, if you resist, the Nazis, those stinking slime holding Rome, have been ordered by *der Führer* to shoot you dead!"

Again Tisserant paused. Pius and Pascalina were aghast and sat in stunned silence as the cardinal's anger poured from his eyes. He said no more. No one spoke. After a long, agonizing moment Tisserant walked out, slamming the door behind him.

Despite Tisserant's warnings the Pope instituted no immediate precautions against Hitler's threats. Pascalina knew better, and took it upon herself to instruct the Swiss Guards to be on constant alert for any unexpected attack upon His Holiness.

Word had reached Hitler in early September 1943 that Pascalina was falsifying papal identity cards to allow Jewish refugees safe haven in the Vatican. As in any state, the Vatican was not immune from informers, and Pascalina always believed—but never could prove—that someone within the hierarchy with pro-Nazi leanings had betrayed her. The Führer was growing increasingly belligerent toward the Holy See for providing sanctuary to the Jews and diplomats of Allied nations.

"I'll go into the Vatican," Hitler threatened on September 9, 1943. "We'll grab it! Yes, the whole bunch in there! I couldn't care less! . . . We'll drag them out, the whole swinish pack of them. . . . We'll have no more attempts by the Church interfering in matters of state. . . . The time is coming when I'll settle my account with the Pope!"

With Hitler's threats against Pius ringing in her ears, Pascalina was unable to sleep for many nights during that summer of 1943.

The nun was cheered, however, when Rome was finally declared an open city, or at least what the Pope and she and all of the Vatican believed to be the case. An official proclamation by the Italian government came through on August 14, the very day after the Allies' second bombing of the city. Until then she and Pius had only the dubious personal assurances of leaders on both sides to rely upon.

Pascalina also heard whispers that Mussolini's time had come. King Victor Emmanuel had seen the handwriting and had moved speedily to remove the dictator. The king, after ordering Il Duce's arrest and imprisonment, immediately appointed Marshal Pietro Badoglio, an antifascist, to replace Mussolini as head of Italy's new government.

Badoglio came at once to the Pope with promises that the new Italian government would respect the Vatican's autonomy. But Pius and Pascalina had heard so many false pledges from both sides since the start of the war that they remained entirely skeptical.

If the nun and the Pope had any faith left in the words of Roosevelt, or Churchill, or Hitler, such faith was quickly dashed. In only a matter of weeks enemy aircraft were heard overhead. This time Vatican City itself was attacked. The Holy See's churches and basilicas, and even its clergy and civilians, were bombed and strafed from the air.

"We never found out which side it was, the Allies or the Axis, that sent the bombers," Pascalina recalled. "But we had our suspicions. Twice deceived in the past, how could we have further confidence in anybody?"

The noose was tightening on the papacy. The Pope and the nun became even more convinced of the serious consequences that lay ahead after Hitler, in a daring and skillful parachute attempt on September 12, snatched Mussolini from heavy guard at Campo Imperatore in Italy's Abruzzi mountains, and immediately installed him as head of a neofascist government with headquarters in northern Italy.

Imprisonment had driven Mussolini mad with rage. Il Duce needed no urging from Hitler in seeking revenge. Hitler saw violent emotion simmering in his broken war partner. The Führer steered his puppet's violence toward the Vatican, pointing Il Duce in the direction of the Jews being sheltered within the papacy's walls.

Soon bands of rampaging neofascists from Italy's northern provinces were streaming toward the Eternal City. The Black Shirts were bent upon killing the Jews and perhaps the Pope himself.

Pascalina pleaded with Pius to take immediate defensive action. Being as close as she was to the Holy Father, the nun knew that he was so battered by the horrors of war that he often seemed off in a daze. Pius was also too prone, in her estimation, "to leave everything in the hands of God."

"We must barricade the Jews in Saint Peter's!" Pascalina urged the Pontiff when the Nazis took over Rome.

The doors of Saint Peter's had never before been sealed during the daytime hours, but the Pope knew the time had come for unprecedented action.

"Go tell the Swiss Guards of my orders to seal the basilica!" Pius told Pascalina. "But first see that all Jews within the Vatican take sanctuary there."

"And you, Holiness?" the nun asked, her voice trembling. She was fearful that Hitler and the neofascists would carry out their threats against Pius. "Where will you remain?"

"The Holy Father shall stay here, in the palace!" Pius replied. The Pontiff's utter defiance was apparent in his blazing eyes. "Let us see if any man, Hitler and Mussolini included, dares to attack the Pope, the symbol of Jesus Christ on Earth!"

Pascalina felt proud of Pius's absolute courage. He had never failed Christ, or himself, in any moment of great confrontation.

"We were not intimidated then by pistols pointed at us," Pius said as they remembered the terror that had gripped Munich after World War I, "and we will be even less frightened this time."

"Holiness, with your permission, I will remain here with you!" the nun said.

"You do not have my permission!" the Pope replied sharply. "Go! Take sanctuary in the palace's cellars."

"No, Holiness!" Pascalina insisted, her words coming in a rush. "After the Jews are safely sealed in the basilica, I will return here. With or without your permission! My place always is at your side!"

The nun looked as determined as Pius had ever seen her. He knew how utterly useless it would be for him to argue.

The Pope shook his head slightly in sad surrender. "Hurry back, Mother Pascalina!" she heard him softly whisper. As he spoke the Pontiff went to his knees in prayer.

When he rose, Pius looked militant and ready for any attack. He picked up the phone and ordered the papal guards to arm themselves with rifles and machine guns.

The Pope stationed his armed guards all along the border—a broad white line painted across the pavement to separate the Vatican from Rome. Upon sight of the khaki-clad papal soldiers, the Nazi and fascist troops, also armed with rifles and machine guns, advanced for attack. But before a single shot was fired, German Field Marshal Albert Kesselring, sensing the uproar that undoubtedly would resound throughout the world if the Nazis seized the Vatican by military force, ordered his troops to hold their fire. The commanders on both sides conferred, and it was agreed that Vatican neutrality would be observed; neither the Nazis nor the papal soldiers were to cross the painted borders or fire upon each other.

The closest the Nazis or fascists came to carrying out their threats against the Vatican thereafter was a raid by a single plane during which, on the night of November 5, four bombs were dropped. One demolished a mosaic studio near the Vatican railway station. Blast and debris shattered windows of the high cupola of Saint Peter's. The remaining bombs fell in open spaces, smashing windows of the surrounding buildings and nearly wrecking the Vatican radio station.

With the enemy on both sides attacking the Vatican, Pius was under mounting pressure from the Catholic hierarchy throughout the world to abandon Rome and establish the papacy within a neutral nation.

In response, the Pope on February 9, 1944, summoned all cardinals stationed in Rome for an audience in the Sistine Chapel. Pius abandoned Church protocol and spoke to them in the simple white cassock of his everyday work garb. The Pontiff reminded the hierarchy that early in the war he had ordered all Catholic bishops to remain at their stations. Now that the war had come to the Vatican, however, with both the Allies and the Axis powers in open attack upon the papacy, the Holy See's position had become extremely grave. Pius insisted upon absolving all of the prelates from their oaths of fealty; oaths that each had sworn to uphold five years before in the same chapel.

"We release you from any obligation to follow our fate," he told the Catholic hierarchy. "Each one of you is free to do what you think best." Still, Pius made it abundantly clear that he himself had no intention of abandoning his post as bishop of Rome. "If anything should happen to the Holy Father," the Pontiff said, "if the Holy Father is imprisoned or killed, you must gather together wherever you can and elect a new pope."

White-faced and with tears streaming from their eyes, each of the cardinals refused the Pontiff's command. As they had five years before, they again went to their knees and kissed the Holy Father's feet, each prelate once more pledging his undying faith and loyalty.

Cardinal Tisserant, genuinely moved, was among the first to demonstrate his fealty.

Pascalina, watching from the rear of the chapel, was on her knees in prayer and tears.

The following day the Allies again broke their pledge to the papacy. For the third time the Vatican's sacred shrines were attacked. Bombs rained heavily against the Holy See from American planes. This time the attacking aircraft struck the Pope's summer residence at Castel Gandolfo, where some fifteen thousand refugees were being sheltered. More than five hundred persons, many of them Jews, were killed in the U.S. aerial bombardment. Castel Gandolfo, into whose modernization Pius, while secretary of state in the early 1930s, had poured millions of Vatican dollars, was almost demolished.

Then five days later—on February 15—the Allies once again resumed their senseless saturation bombings of sacred shrines. American planes, under the command of General Bernard Freyberg, dropped a total of 576 tons of explosives on the abbey of Monte Cassino, reducing the historic landmark to rubble and killing an undisclosed number of peasants who had taken refuge there.

On March 1, the eve of the fifth anniversary of Pius's election as Pope, Nazi aircraft struck the Vatican. Pius was about to seat himself at a special, private dinner that Pascalina herself prepared in honor of his anniversary, when both heard the roar of a low-flying plane. Six explosions resounded throughout the palace, shaking its ancient walls. One of the bombs struck so close that she saw fragments fall in the Court of Saint Damaso as it exploded only a few feet from the outer walls of the papal apartment.

Eleven days later, on March 12, the fifth anniversary of Pius's coronation, the Holy Father made his first appearance in public since Rome's occupation by the Nazis. Speaking to a vast crowd of three hundred thousand, which flowed from Saint Peter's Square back across the Tiber, the Pontiff blasted both the Allies and the Axis powers for breaking their pledges to him and attacking the Holy See.

"How can we believe that anyone would dare to turn Rome, this noble city which belongs to all times and all places, into a field of battle and thus perpetrate an act as inglorious militarily as it is abominable in the eyes of God?" the Pope asked.

The tides of battle by then had turned sharply against Germany and Italy. In less than three months, on June 4, the Allies marched into Rome and the Nazis fled in retreat.

Pascalina, whose prayers from the start were for the Allies (except on the occasion of Hitler's attack on the communists), "felt enormous relief."

"I had sympathized with His Holiness throughout in maintaining the Holy See's historic position of neutrality in warfare," she said. "But in my daily prayers to Jesus, I begged Our Lord that Hitler and Mussolini be defeated. I told His Holiness of my prayers and hope early in the war. Every day thereafter the Holy Father prayed along with me for the same intentions."

In mid-July, some six weeks after Allied forces had liberated Rome, Pascalina had a strange caller. Mussolini sent his mistress, Clara Petacci, as his secret emissary. The woman came in disguise during the night, hoping to strike a deal for the crumbling dictator.

Signora Petacci asked Pascalina to intervene with the Pope in behalf of Il Duce. Mussolini remained in command of the neofascists who were fighting alongside the Nazis in northern Italy. But Petacci said he was ready to sell out the Führer if the Pope would act as his intermediary with the Allies.

Pius was incensed with Pascalina when she later told him of her meeting with Petacci.

"You spoke alone with that woman, without my knowledge and permission?" the Pope shouted angrily. "Petacci is Mussolini's mistress! They have been living together for years in mortal sin!"

"Holiness, how do you know the truth of such scandal?" the nun asked softly. She had learned of late not to lose her temper when the Pope lost his.

"Ask anyone in the Vatican. Ask those among the hierarchy!" Pius retorted impatiently.

"And what do you suppose they whisper about us, Holiness?" she queried. "I have been living under your roof since I was a young girl. We know that in God's eyes, our lives are pure. Yet who, even among the Sacred College of Cardinals, believes the truth about us? Why, then, Holiness, are you so quick to judge others?"

The Pope was at a complete loss for reply.

The nun took Pius's hand and raised it to her lips. "Holiness, let us hope and pray that we are not the only decent people alive," she said quietly. "Even though you are Pope and I a nun, we are not the best of humans, nor the worst either."

Pius appeared chastened, but he was obviously still confused. "Why did this woman come to you?" he asked.

"Signora Petacci came with a message from Mussolini himself," Pascalina replied. "Il Duce is seeking your intervention in the war. He is hoping for some sort of Italian political solution."

"Does Hitler know of this?" Pius asked.

"No, he does not," the nun said. "Signora Petacci assured me that Mussolini has had little conversation of late with Hitler. Il Duce is now totally disenchanted with the Führer. He has called Hitler's attack on Russia 'megalomaniacal.' According to Petacci, Mussolini considers himself little more than a prisoner of the Germans. He realizes that his own star is waning. Il Duce is in his sixties and she tells me that he is a very depressed man."

"I will not see Mussolini!" Pius said firmly. "Nor will I talk with him!"

"Mussolini is repentant," Pascalina reminded the Holy Father. "He was baptized a Catholic. Though he became an atheist, you, as Holy Father, cannot refuse to help bring him back to Almighty God."

"Mussolini is a wily devil!" the Pope retorted. "Whenever he is down for the moment, he will conceive of any trick to regain power. The Holy Father will not serve as Il Duce's pawn!"

"But will you aid him some way?" she asked quietly, almost imploring the Pope's help.

For a long moment Pius was in deep thought. He then told Pascalina: "Tell this Petacci woman to have Mussolini contact the archbishop of Milan with his plan for peace. If there is merit in the peace proposal, I will carry forth from there on. That, my dear Mother Pascalina, is the most I will do for Mussolini, or for any of those other architects of war, be they Hitler, Stalin, Roosevelt, or Churchill."

At Pascalina's suggestion Clara Petacci advised Mussolini to present his peace proposition to the archbishop of Milan. Il Duce sent his son, Vittorio, with a plan aimed at opening negotiations with the Allies.

The archbishop was sufficiently impressed, and he forwarded the proposal to the Vatican. Since the nun was in on the scheme from the start, Pius suggested that she consider the plan carefully before he would even give it a moment of his time.

What Mussolini was essentially seeking was sanctuary somewhere in the West for himself, his wife and children, and his mistress, Clara. If it were to be granted, the dictator, disgraced and tired of war, was prepared for what was tantamount to unconditional surrender.

"Mussolini is prepared to give up," Pascalina advised Pius. "Holiness, I suggest you forward the proposal to Allied headquarters. It will help greatly to shorten the war and save many lives."

After studying Mussolini's proposal the Pope agreed reluctantly with the nun's idea. Pius sent the papers along to General Dwight D. Eisenhower, commanding general of the Allied forces. He included a covering letter, written in his own hand, urging the Allies to accept Il Duce's offer.

In a matter of days Eisenhower wrote the Pope a curt reply, summarily rejecting the entire proposal.

"His Holiness felt General Eisenhower was telling the Holy See to mind its own business," Pascalina recalled. "While the General's letter was polite, it was cold. Eisenhower implied that the Allies had Hitler and Mussolini in their iron grasp and they were not going to show any mercy."

Pascalina reported the Allies' rejection at once to Clara Petacci. It required much effort on the nun's part to reach the woman by phone at Mussolini's hideout in Milan.

That was the last contact Pascalina had with Petacci until late April 1945, when correspondence from her arrived at the Vatican.

"I am following my destiny," Petacci wrote Pascalina in her note of April 25. "I don't know what will become of me, but I cannot question my fate."

By the time the letter was received, Pascalina was well aware of what had happened to Petacci. Mussolini had told her to leave Milan with him in a ten-car caravan the same day she wrote the nun. Il Duce was to make a final stand with his remaining neofascist army somewhere in the north of Italy.

The dictator had also instructed his wife and children to remain behind in Milan. He left his family several documents, including letters to Churchill, which he hoped would provide safe passage for them to a neutral country.

"If they try to stop you or harm you," Il Duce instructed his wife, "ask to be handed over to the English."

At dawn on April 26, Mussolini and Petacci, riding in an Alfa Romeo with Spanish license plates, started up the winding west shore of Lake Como. They drove through heavy drizzle for more than twenty-five miles, then stopped at a hotel to await the arrival of some three thousand fascist troops.

After pacing the floor in vain for more than twenty-four hours, Mussolini ordered his caravan to continue north without the additional troops. It was his final command. As Il Duce and his companions approached Dongo, bands of Italian antifascists attacked without warning. Their caravan was surrounded, and all were quickly captured.

Numbers of extremists, wild with exhilaration from their great coup, demanded Mussolini's immediate execution. Some were also screaming for Petacci's life. Others, cooler-headed, wanted Il Duce and his mistress turned over to the Allies.

The fate of Mussolini and Petacci was resolved on April 28 when a three-man execution squad quite unexpectedly took matters into their own hands. The terrorists mercilessly gunned them both down.

The bodies of Mussolini and Petacci were taken back to Milan, then strung up by their feet in the Piazza Loreto. For days they remained hanging, their heads dangling to the ground. "A lesson for all who would persecute the human race to see and learn by," Cardinal Tisserant remarked to Pascalina as he pointed in glee to photos of their hangings in a Rome newspaper.

Two nights later Hitler committed suicide. In a week, on May 7, 1945, World War II in Europe was over.

Though the free world was delirious with joy, Pascalina brooded over the scars that the ravages of warfare had left upon the Holy See, most particularly upon the Pope himself. Both his physical and mental health had deteriorated. Though Pius had always showed a hopeful face to the world, the nun had often found him brooding alone in his private quarters. He had eaten less and less, and slept poorly. A man over six feet tall, the Holy Father was an emaciated one hundred and thirty pounds.

Looking back, the nun, at eighty-seven, paused and her eyes grew misty with the sorrow that still remains. As Pius XII's closest confidante, she had learned through him of the atrocities that both sides—Allies and Axis—kept well hidden from the world.

"Almost every day, throughout all the years of the war, the Holy Father, as the spiritual head of more than 350 million Catholics, was the recipient of confidential information. Often it was some horrible news or devastating statistic," she said, choked with emotion. "I will never forget when His Holiness was told that in Poland alone, 2,647 priests were taken to concentration camps and either gassed to death, or shot. As horrible as that news was, there were times when the revelations were exceedingly more terrifying."

The nun again paused and turned her sad gaze off into the distance, obviously trying to piece together—after thirty-six years—her perspective now on Pius's policies during World War II and in the aftermath. When she resumed, she spoke first of the Pope's reactions to the deaths of Mussolini and Hitler.

"When His Holiness was told of their demise, he said nothing, holding to the Catholic teaching that one does not speak unkindly of the deceased. But I could tell from the grim expression on his face that he could never bring himself to forgive them for their crimes and sins. Yet, he went to the Papal Chapel on both occasions and said silent prayers for the repose of the souls of Mussolini and Hitler. I joined him in those prayers.

"Relations between His Holiness and President Roosevelt became distinctly cooler after the bombardment of Rome in 1943," she added. "He never really trusted any of the world leaders after that. To Pius, the Allies' plan for a Grand Alliance after World War II that included communist Russia was a sellout of the free nations of Europe, Poland, and others. Think now how right His Holiness was!" She shook her head sadly.

"People ask, 'Why did Pius XII remain silent?' " Pascalina continued, her tone indicating how protective she still remains of Pacelli and his image. "It is easy enough for anyone to ask such a question. But when the lives of millions of people were at stake, the Holy Father was obliged to use discretion. At one point, Hitler threatened to exterminate many thousands of additional priests and others of the clergy if His Holiness were to speak out in condemnation. Perhaps when one considers that terrible price upon human lives, one might understand the reasons for Pius's silence."

Pascalina rose abruptly. "I would like to show you a respected historian's view of who was the more honorable—the Allies or the papacy—when it came to helping Jews and others during World War II." At that point she excused herself and left the room. A few minutes later the nun returned with John Toland's biography of Adolf Hitler. Opening to a passage on pages 760 and 761, she read aloud Toland's report:

> The Church, under the Pope's guidance, had already saved the lives of more Jews than all other churches, religious institutions and rescue organizations combined, and was presently hiding thousands of Jews in monasteries, convents and Vatican City itself. The record of the Allies was far more shameful. The British and Americans, despite lofty pronouncements, had not only avoided taking any meaningful action but gave sanctuary to few persecuted Jews. The Moscow Declaration of that year—signed by Roosevelt, Churchill and Stalin—methodically listed Hitler's victims as Polish, Italian, French, Dutch, Belgian, Norwegian, Soviet and Cretan. The curious omission of Jews (a policy emulated by the U.S. Office of War Information) was protested vehemently but uselessly by the World Jewish Congress. By the simple expedient of converting the Jews of Poland into Poles, and so on, the Final Solution was lost in the Big Three's general classification of Nazi terrorism.

Pascalina closed the book. Her stare, filled with repressed anger, heightened the cold silence of the long moment; enough indication of the terrible hurt that she had felt all those years.

"How unfair that His Holiness was forced to suffer so much of the blame," she finally said amid the tears. "The self-righteous Allies—particularly Roosevelt, who would accept nothing short of unconditional surrender, even though it meant prolonging the Holocaust—were devious enough to shift responsibility. The Allies blamed Pius for his so-called 'silence' to escape the world's criticism for their disgraceful hypocrisy."

XI

World War II ended with the formal surrender of the Japanese on September 2, 1945. Eight days before, Pascalina had turned fifty-one. The Pope was then nearly seventy, and at times as much a mystery to the nun as when she had first met him twenty-eight years earlier.

The world had no sooner settled down amid its hopes and prayers for a lasting peace, than Pascalina detected ominous new clouds gathering on the Vatican's own horizons in the form of rumored crimes and scandals within the Holy See. If true, the allegations could be devastating to Catholicism, all the more so were they to become public.

It was claimed that the Church in Sicily had fallen into corruption, the accusations made in an anonymous letter that was slipped under the nun's office door late one night. The unsigned correspondence said further that Catholic priests and monks were agents of the underworld. Confessionals were allegedly being used by the clergy as spy centers to gather information on persons opposed to the Mafia. The clerics were charged with making notes of what they heard for underworld figures.

The Sicilian peasantry, living in pathological fear of the Mafia, would never have dared to talk had they not trusted their priests. The people chose to obey the Mafia's code of *omertà* and suffered in silence rather than face the terrible wrath of organized crime. Whole communities bowed their heads in pathetic resignation, their ignorance and poverty fueling the Mafia's crimes. In one place alone, the town of Mazzarino, the Mafia's reign of terror was hurled at everyone who spoke in the confessional of their hatred of the underworld. Catholic men and their wives and children became the horrified victims of the hooded Franciscan friars, or witnesses to their brutal crimes. Mazzarino was under seige by brown-robed clerics who had taken vows of poverty, chastity, and obedience in the Order of Saint Francis, one of the most respected religious bodies within the Holy Roman Catholic Church. Their leaders were Padre Carmelo, Friar Agrippino, Friar Vittorio, and Friar Venanzio. There was murder by hanging or beheading, there was attempted murder, there were sexual assaults and orgies, there was extortion. There seemed no end to the crimes.

"I am afraid!" were trembling words heard whispered everywhere by the cowering peasants. The people grew all the more terrified with the awful realization that their trusted priests had turned upon them and had squealed their secrets to captains and soldiers of the Mafia. Though they had taken vows of poverty, the bearded Franciscans were shrewd businessmen, too, buying and selling property and pocketing the sky-high profits. They were even into loan sharking, lending money at exorbitant rates of interest.

Even some of the kindliest of friars carried guns and cooperated with the worst criminals. One group of priests eventually confessed that they themselves committed all sorts of crimes. "The Mafia exists," Friar Vittorio said as he stood accused. "We had to come to terms [with the Mafia] to avoid the worst in the village." Another priest, Friar Agrippino, declared, "If we don't obey, they'll kill us."

It was not surprising that Pascalina was first among the upper echelon of the papacy to be alerted to these crimes. Since she was confidante to the Pope and his closest friend, it was well known in the Vatican that anyone hoping to reach Pius's mind or heart would find the *virgo potens* (powerful virgin), as she became known, the best pathway. Letters by the hundreds addressed to the Holy Father, many in care of the nun, poured into her office each week. At his request she screened scores of them, until her eyes were blurred and red.

She would also listen for hours almost every day to lines of people, nonclergy as well as priests, bishops, and even cardinals, hearing their "endless ideas, speculations, and grievances." Once she became so exasperated that she complained to the Holy Father: "It seems that everyone has a complaint, or secret information, or plan that supposedly offers better ways of doing everything!"

Pascalina said nothing to the Pope about the letter of clerical indictment, nor hinted of its charges. She felt that he had enough on his mind, and she did not want to trouble him with what might well be baseless speculation.

As time passed the tales of the Sicilian crimes were more frequently heard by her and came from a number of reliable sources. Still, she continued to cup her ears whenever anyone as much as touched upon what she termed "baseless scandal." She even refused to be moved by a young priest who came to her with substantially the same charges, telling him that it all sounded like "such preposterous nonsense." The nun was sure that prejudiced persons, out to destroy the Church, had "concocted the stories in their entirety" from the start, and now "unfortunately even those who love the Holy See believed the ridiculous claims."

"Except for Jews, there were many non-Catholics in those days who would manufacture any sort of wild charge to discredit Holy Mother Church," she later recalled. "I've never known a Jewish person who attacked the Holy See in vile manner. It is not in the Jewish character to behave that way. But, unfortunately, there were those who still clung to the sad memories of pre-Reformation days. It was persons of such bitter mind whom I first blamed for the atrocious attacks on the Church in Sicily."

After several months Pascalina grew so troubled by the increasing frequency of the attacks upon the character of the Sicilian clergy that she finally decided to reveal everything to the Holy Father. Fearing the shock and drain it would have upon him, and not wanting to spoil his Christmas holidays, she waited until early January 1947.

Yet the Pope was not as moved as she had expected. After hearing her out, he remained as unconvinced as she herself originally had been. "Mother Pascalina!" he said as he shook his head in amazed disbelief, "how could one as brilliant as you be so easily taken in?" He paused and stared at her, pretending to be ashamed of her naiveté. "Do you really believe that our dear, devoted clergy would take to sin and crime?" he asked.

It was obvious to her that Pius could not conceive that any of his priests were capable of such wrongdoing. Nor would he permit himself to dwell for a moment on such horror. He arose, his deliberate sign that the subject must end. "I am tired," he said with emphasis. "I am going to get some rest." He turned and coldly walked out, leaving her with mixed feelings of astonishment and depression.

"I kept asking myself, 'Did you do the right thing by telling him?' " she said years later. "For the moment, I was convinced that I had made a big mistake."

But several days later Pascalina had a change of mind, and she came to realize the wisdom of confiding in the Holy Father. This was confirmed when His Eminence, Ernesto Cardinal Ruffini, the highest ranking churchman in Sicily, arrived for a private audience with the Pope. Apparently, during the intervening days, Pius had had second thoughts and summoned Ruffini for a talk. For years the archbishop of Palermo had been held in rather low esteem within the Vatican, some clerics even disparagingly referring to him as "the king of the two Sicilies, the religious and the political."

Now the Pope was about to conduct his own private investigation. He made his intentions clear to Pascalina by his severe tone and actions, especially when he himself pointedly closed the door in her face once Ruffini was seated within the papal inner sanctum. She could not remember when Pius had previously excluded her, except during deliberations that would prove too delicate for her ears, in his estimation, or when something was taking place that he knew she would not tolerate.

Until that day Ruffini had always been shown favored status by the Pope, but for what reason, Pascalina was unaware. The previous year, when Francis Cardinal Spellman was in Rome to receive his red hat, she had hoped he might shed some light on Pius's unusual affinity toward the Sicilian archbishop.

"Holiness is more considerate of Archbishop Ruffini than of any within the Sacred College of Cardinals," she had said in wonderment to the American prelate. "Even Eminence Tisserant, whom we know is destined to become Dean of the Sacred College, does not receive Holiness's respect to the degree shown Ruffini."

But Spellman, like Pius, had refused to touch even slightly upon anything connected with the Church in Sicily.

Later she had learned, with some shock, that Cardinal Archbishop Ruffini was an intimate of Don Calogero Vizzini, the mayor of Villalba, Sicily. Vizzini was said to run the Sicilian Mafia and was spoken of as "the most powerful man throughout the Italian province."

It was not altogether strange, in her mind, for the Church to have at least a nodding acquaintanceship with the Mafia. The two shared certain common beliefs, as viewed by Norman Lewis, a respected journalist who spent many years investigating Sicily's secret crime organization. In his book *The Honored Society,* Lewis points to the Mafia in feudal Sicily as having an "iron morality of its own." Accordingly, says Lewis,

> The Capo-Mafia considers himself a lawgiver concerned with the welfare of his people, and prides himself on watching over the advancement of deserving juniors in the organization with the assiduousness of the master of novices of a religious order. In his own eyes, he never steals from the community, but he can see no objection to exploiting his power over men to enrich himself.

Pascalina, as sophisticated and experienced as she was in the political intricacies of the Holy See, understood the advantages to the Mafia in allying itself with the Church, if only as a matter of expediency. But what were the benefits for the papacy in such an alliance, if one did indeed exist? This was what troubled her most.

Since neither the Pope nor Spellman would discuss the Mafia matter with her, the nun, strangely enough, had looked to Cardinal Tisserant for enlightenment. The French prelate may have appeared loud and crude to her, but she appreciated his outspoken honesty.

"Ruffini is a powerful man in Sicily," Tisserant once told Pascalina without hesitation. "Even Vizzini, who runs the Mafia there, bows to him. Vizzini not only kisses the ring of the archbishop of Palermo, but he kisses his ass as well," Tisserant said, and roared with laughter. "Pius is afraid to take action. Afraid that any stand the papacy might take would lead to widespread governmental investigations and prosecutions. With our clergy involved, the publicity alone could wreck the Church. Besides, Ruffini is too powerful for Pius to tackle."

Tisserant again burst into laughter. He apparently saw the link between the Church and the Mafia in Sicily as a tragicomedy to be enjoyed thoroughly. "How do you suppose Pius's hypocritical papacy can wiggle out of this dilemma, dear Mother Pascalina?" he asked, his leering face only a hair's breadth from hers.

The nun knew there was more to the cardinal's words than mere banter. Tisserant, whatever his shortcomings, would never imply wrongdoing without basis of fact. Yet nowhere in her mind could she conceive that Pius would condone the commission of sin or crime by the Catholic clergy in Sicily. She was equally convinced that the Holy Father himself was innocent of any misdoing.

When Cardinal Ruffini emerged from his command audience with the Pope, she asked Pius if the Sicilian situation had been discussed. "It is none of your business!" he angrily retorted. "Tend to your own affairs and whatever work remains to be done!"

Understanding him as well as she did, Pascalina knew that Pius was not as angry as he appeared. It was obvious to her that he found himself in a corner for the moment, and was squirming. She knew too that it was wise for her to retreat for the time being, and she did.

But as the days passed she became increasingly insistent that Pius explain his reasons for evading her questions. Though she always waited until he was in the right mood, he remained as noncommittal as ever. Her fears increased every time he adamantly refused to discuss the matter.

The Pope's mistake, in her mind, was in taking the same track he had followed during World War II in his failed stand on the Nazi atrocities. Pius's silence had hurt him severely in the eyes of world Jewry. Failure now to act boldly in handling the Church-Mafia connection could destroy the credibility of the Holy See. To her way of thinking, the Pope could not go on wrestling with his confusions and evade forever the mounting corruption and crimes on the island off Italy's boot. He had to act decisively, she was convinced, and cut all existing ties between Holy Mother Church and the Sicilian underworld.

She became even more certain of how right she was after her encounter with a terrified citizen of Mazzarino, Sicily, who had come to the Vatican pleading for his life.

"He was Signore Angelo Cannada, a fragile little person, nearly eighty years old," Pascalina recalled. "His life, like that of many other people of Mazzarino, had been threatened by Franciscan priests and monks who demanded huge amounts of extortion money. Signore Cannada was the only victim who refused to pay, and stood up to the Franciscans."

The old man begged to talk with the Holy Father and lay proof before His Holiness of the ongoing crimes by the Catholic clergy. But despite Pascalina's pleas Pius's doors remained closed. She was so disappointed and upset by the Pope's coldness that she took matters into her own hands. She asked the old man to return, and she heard him out fully.

At the time, it mattered little to Pascalina that she'd have an angry Pope shouting at her afterward. She was learning, through the pathetic-looking Cannada, who spoke explicitly of crimes by the Franciscans, of the powerful grip the underworld had upon the Church in Sicily.

"When one understands the full philosophy of the Roman hierarchy, it is not surprising that the nun, despite her long and intimate place at the very top of Pius's papacy, could have remained unaware of certain goings-on," observed Father James Rohan, a Jesuit historian.

The Franciscans had been among the holiest and most dedicated of religious orders within the Holy Roman Catholic Church. Founded in 1209 by Christ's great and loyal follower, Saint Francis of Assisi, the Franciscans were so well regarded by the Holy See through the centuries that several of their members were made popes.

Large-scale corruption and crime did not seep into the order until the turn of the twentieth century. In 1901, for reasons that remain unclear, bands of Capuchin* Franciscan friars of Mazzarino began roaming the rural Sicilian countryside, waylaying and robbing travelers and the local peasantry. Terror tactics thereafter grew steadily within the order in Mazzarino and became a part of everyday life. Priests blackmailed peasants and extorted money and goods. Women were brought to the monastery at night, dressed in Franciscan habits to disguise their identities. The Franciscans' ancient monastery in Mazzarino became the scene of debauchery, orgies, and pornographic activities.

Perversion was only part of the evils. Cannada told Pascalina of a pitched battle he had once witnessed between the peasants of Santo Stefano and monks of a local monastery. He spoke of seeing a priest behead his own abbot on a refectory table.

"Only as recently as 1945, the bishop of Agrigento was shot and nearly killed by a monk who was also a Mafioso," the old man related. "The Franciscan monastery in Mazzarino, at this very time, shelters bands of robbers who share the proceeds of their crimes with monks and priests living there."

Cannada begged Pascalina to ask the Holy Father to send a commission of Vatican clergy to Sicily for a full investigation.

The nun told Pius everything the old man had said, and the Pope thought the whole story so incredible that he refused to take action.

Four days after Cannada's return to Mazzarino, a band of masked

*Known officially within the Church as the Order of Friars Minor Capuchin, they are one of three autonomous branches of Franciscans.

men called at his home, just as he lay down from his long and disappointing trip to the Vatican. Holding rifles at his head, the men dragged the terrified Sicilian from the house to his vineyard, where they shot him.

Pascalina was infuriated by the news of Cannada's murder, and she told the Pope exactly how upset she was.

"Holiness, how can you justify your place as Holy Father when people cry out for help, and you do nothing?" she cried. "When are you going to rid yourself of your appeasement mentality and stand strong and brave for what is right?"

She expected him to become angry and defend his failure to act. But he remained calm, saying only in a somewhat placating tone, "Mother Pascalina, you are right. You are always right." Pius knew that mere words weren't enough at this juncture to convince the nun of his sorrow or immediate intentions. What she took as his insensitive manner only incensed her all the more. Were it not for her vow of obedience, she would have lashed out with fierce anger, even though he was the Holy Father.

Fortunately she held her tongue. She was later to learn that Pius had already set machinery in motion to rid the Church of crime and corruption in Sicily. Cardinal Ruffini had been called back to Rome by the Pontiff for a dressing down and an order to end at once the Mafia connection in Sicily.

The next day, when the archbishop of Palermo was seated for the closed-door confrontation, Pascalina was present at the Holy Father's elbow, upon instruction by Pius.

"Eminence Ruffini, I have been given a sad account of the alleged behavior of the Franciscans who are serving in Sicily," the Pope began in a quiet voice. Pascalina sensed the control he was exercising in containing his anger. "Is there truth to these rumors?"

The Sicilian prelate looked aghast at the Pope's candor. "Holiness, the Franciscans are the most numerous of all the orders of Holy Mother Church. Their followers throughout the world are said to number between four million and five million Catholics," Ruffini replied, his tone one of injured pride.

It was plain to Pascalina that the cardinal was trying to influence Pius's thinking by pointing to the Franciscans' numerical strength and the weight they carried internationally.

"I am fully aware that there are many good and holy priests and monks among the Franciscans," the Pope retorted, an obvious bite in his words. "I believe the Franciscan order is as fine as anyone will find anywhere. It is the behavior of some of our sons serving in Sicily that concerns me."

Pius abruptly came to his feet and glared down at Ruffini. "What do we know of the murder of that old man, Cannada?" he demanded in a tone seething with anger.

The cardinal looked horrified. "I do not know what you are talking about, Holiness!" Ruffini replied, trembling. The nun was uncertain as to whether or not the prelate was telling the truth. It appeared to her that the Pope was equally unsure.

"If you are unaware of what is transpiring in your own diocese, Eminence Ruffini, then it becomes the responsibility of the Holy Father to find out for himself!" Pius shouted.

Turning then to Pascalina, the Pope spoke in a calmer tone. "I understand the funeral of the old man, Cannada, takes place tomorrow. Mother, you are to attend as my observer. I trust your eyes, your ears, and your words," he said with pointed emphasis. "I shall also send along a representative of the Holy Father to show the Franciscans of my sincere sorrow for Cannada. My observer will appear as a symbol to all Sicilians of the Holy See's deep displeasure at the manner of the old man's death."

The Pontiff turned back to Ruffini. "Eminence, you may leave now," Pius said, his manner still severe. "The Holy Father suggests that you go directly to the chapel for meditation. Afterward, return to your province and tell the Franciscan priests and monks serving in your diocese that they too should meditate. There will be many questions to be answered by everyone in the near future!" The Pope raised a pointed finger at the cardinal. "If there are further crimes in your diocese and any of our clergy are accused, I will hold you, Ruffini, personally responsible!"

Pascalina had never been more proud and overjoyed as she was at that moment by Pius's strong and honorable stand. She felt humbled and ashamed, too, of her own earlier lack of faith in his character.

The instant Ruffini closed the door behind him, she rushed into the Pope's arms, tears of joy filling her eyes. Pius bent and kissed the nun on the forehead. It was the first time that his lips had touched her skin with such intense fervor.

"Holiness, I am so very proud of you!" she said, looking fondly upward into his eyes.

"I should have acted sooner in this instance," the Pope said sadly, the sorrow of Cannada's murder evident upon his face.

"Only a great Pontiff has the strength to admit his mistakes," she responded tenderly.

"A true Pontiff of Christ rectifies his past mistakes," Pius added, releasing her. "He does so by taking affirmative action in the future."

She felt sure then that the Holy Father meant to do everything possible to clear the horrible state of Church affairs in Sicily.

Upon Pascalina's arrival in Sicily she found much of the province still living in the eighteenth century. Violent death was commonplace. The homicide rate in Palermo, the seat of Cardinal Ruffini's power, had reached the highest in the world with as many as fifty murders in fifty days. The Italian province, a Mediterranean island of 9,925 square miles, had become the international center for heroin traffic, regular shipments pouring in from the Middle East for processing and shipment to foreign countries, principally the United States.

Many of the Franciscans were indeed as sinister as the nun had feared. "It was grotesque!" she said, recalling with anguish the crimes she discovered. "A Franciscan priest, Padre Carmelo, came to Signore Cannada's widow after the funeral and demanded three million lire. He was acting in complicity with Mafia extortionists. The priest told the widow to sell her property in order to raise the money. If she refused, the same tragic fate her husband had suffered, he warned, would be met by her son. I begged the woman not to comply," Pascalina added. "But she was too terrified to listen. Like most peasants in Sicily, she ended up giving the Franciscan priest everything she owned."

The nun was so angered by the actions of the Franciscans that she stayed on in Sicily, with the Pope's approval, to gather all the evidence she could find. She spoke with numbers of sources, mainly Sicilian peasants, whose lives had been made intolerable because of the Church-Mafia connection. She learned of the sufferings imposed by the Franciscans from the family members of the victims of murder and debauchery and extortion.

With Pius's approval Pascalina presented her evidence to the newly appointed chief of police of Mazzarino, which had become the center of the Franciscans' operations. The police official, Maresciallo

Di Stefano, had been checked out by the Vatican and found to be honest and dedicated.

"I explained to Signore Di Stefano that the Church's holy vows were receiving scant attention from Franciscan priests and monks in his town," Pascalina said. "I told the police chief that His Holiness implored his help in bringing the criminals to justice."

"But why doesn't the Holy Father himself act?" Di Stefano asked. "All the Pope need do is strip these clergy of their vestments and excommunicate them."

"The Holy Father wants justice to be rightfully served," she replied. "Arrest these clergy! See that they receive a fair trial! If the priests and monks are convicted, Pius will mete out punishment. They will be defrocked and excommunicated. You have my word! You have the word of the Pope himself!"

It would be years before the police chief had enough evidence to bring the Franciscans to trial. No one, in the meantime, had dared come forward to serve as a witness at the pending proceedings. All who had spoken up were terrorized afterward by the Sicilian Mafia.

Di Stefano had seen enough to be certain of the crimes. "The Franciscans were clever operators," he said.

> They were the shrewdest of businessmen, and many carried loaded guns, some even had submachine guns for protection. Their interests ranged from loan sharking to pornography. Their personal wealth was enormous. Even though they had taken vows of poverty, most of the priests and monks had millions of lire stashed in various banks throughout Italy.

As the investigations increased and evidence against the Franciscans mounted, the Pope grew fearful that their crimes and scandals would shatter the faith of Catholics and bring terrible disgrace upon Holy Mother Church.

Yet he urged Pascalina to continue her collaboration with the Sicilian police in helping to bring the criminals to justice. Pius's unrealistic hope was that everything could be quietly accomplished with no leaks to the outside world.

"The press must never be allowed to publish these diabolical acts by the Franciscans!" the Pope insisted to the nun. "The faithful everywhere would be horrified. Their faith in Holy Mother Church would be greatly threatened. Our dear Lord must not suffer the loss of souls because of the devils among us."

But Pius was to learn that there was no way effectively to silence the world press if the Franciscans were brought to trial. The papacy had been spoiled over the years by Vatican correspondents and other religious writers who took their direction from Church higher-ups, publishing nothing that might anger Rome.

It was quite another story, however, when it came to sensational court testimony. Not only would such news be in the public domain, but the papacy feared an onslaught of visceral attacks by anti-Catholic journalists who'd like nothing better than to discredit Catholicism. Pius and Pascalina were all too aware of this significant sector of the press that remained alert to "humiliate Holy Mother Church and drag down the House of God."

After weighing all the potential dangers, Pius apparently thought the Holy See would be better served by a complete about-face on his part. The Pope considerably toned down his righteous stand and turned the full force of Vatican influence toward delaying prosecution of the Franciscans.

"In the remaining years of Pius's papacy, Mother Pascalina did everything she possibly could to have the Holy Father uphold the papacy's pledge to support the Sicilian authorities in their investigations of the Franciscans," Archbishop Richard J. Cushing noted at the time.

> But her hands were tied in many ways. Even though Pascalina was very close to the Pope for most of her life, she was still looked upon as a mere nun at times, even by Pius himself. On any issue as explosive as the Franciscan crimes in Sicily, Church clergy maintain an inbred, prejudiced mentality which is entirely convinced that the male mind is right in the final analysis, and must never yield to female pressure. Pius was certainly a pope with that kind of intellect.

Cushing further blamed Cardinal Spellman as being largely responsible for putting the brakes on the prosecution of the Franciscans. The prelates had known each other for many years. As young priests, they were roommates at the rectory of the Holy Cross Cathedral in Boston. Upon the death of Cardinal O'Connell in 1944, Spellman used his influence with Pius XII to have Cushing named O'Connell's successor as archbishop of Boston. A falling-out between the pair occurred shortly afterward when Cushing, a towering, rough-spoken Boston Irishman who once worked as a laborer building streetcar rails, refused to knuckle under to Spellman's seniority and authority.

"Spellman saw the Catholic mind, especially in the United States, as exceedingly fragile in matters of faith," Cushing explained.

> He dealt largely with the upper crust, those we used to call 'lace curtain Catholics'; rich executives who lived up in the clouds, and, like so many Catholic women, had as much touch with reality as a Persian cat. Spellman's fear was that if most Catholics thought their priests did anything worse than forget to say the rosary every hour on the hour, they'd drop dead of shock.

It wasn't until four years after Pius died in 1958, and when John XXIII reigned as pope, that the Franciscans were brought to trial in Sicily. Even under the beloved and holy John, the power of the papacy was clearly at work. Though a number of the priests and monks were charged with a variety of serious crimes, including murder, attempted murder, and extortion, all were found innocent. The world press, with few exceptions, entirely ignored the sensational trials. When news did appear, the Franciscans attempted to be made out as scapegoats and innocent victims of persecution.

"John had a far more effective way of dealing with the news media than Pius," Cushing explained. "In many ways, John was the shrewder of the two. His humble, rather beguiling manner won people over far more effectively than Pius's cold and direct authoritarian words.

"Misguided liberals, especially those of the news media, hated Pius for his silence on the Nazis' persecutions of the Jews," Cushing continued.

> They looked upon Pius as a devil, while they were quick to make John a saint, often simply because he seemed just the opposite to Pius. They were wrong in both instances. Neither pope was as good nor as bad as he was painted. In many ways, they differed only slightly, except in style. But the liberal news media could not see this. I can't say that Pope John muzzled the media, because I have no such evidence. But it was certainly strange that such sensational crimes by the clergy were so ignored.

At no time did Pascalina lose sight of the continuing crimes by clergy of her own faith. In 1963, a year after the Franciscans were exonerated, her prayers were finally answered. Each of the previously indicted priests and monks was hauled back into court on appeal by the prosecution. Their earlier verdicts were overturned. This time they were found guilty of all charges, and each was sentenced to serve thirteen years in prison.

When asked to comment on the shocking crimes and the conviction of his priests, Father Sebastiano, the provincial of the Capuchin order in Sicily, took a calm, philosophical view. "Even among us, somebody sometimes makes mistakes," he said.

Throughout the years Pascalina kept trying to fathom the seemingly imponderable mysteries of Pius's mind; particularly why he had made such a complete about-face during the Church-Mafia connection. "At times, Holiness would be fully dedicated to a cause, as he first was in his desire to end crime by the clergy in Sicily," she recalled. "Frequently, he would then procrastinate; he would dwell upon the harm that might result from some bold stand on his part. Sadly, he would often alter his whole course of action." As she reflected on the long-gone past, Pascalina paused to weigh her own thoughts. "Pius was a holy man," she resumed with a nod of positive assurance, "but unfortunately, like so many of us, he, too, was misguided on occasion."

XII

In the postwar period of vast world changes—the nuclear age, exploration of outer space, the "iron curtain" separating East and West—the papacy itself underwent its own major transformations and traumatic upheavals. The Vatican was so divided that a state of hostility, unparalleled in modern times and well hidden from outsiders, existed between the Pope and the Sacred College of Cardinals. Though many ecclesiastical and temporal issues separated the present Pontiff and his hierarchy, policy differences in the Vatican's high echelons were always part of Church history. In the reign of Pius XII, however, it was the Pope's totalitarian rule and the nun at his side that remained central to their war of words.

With Pascalina's influence upon Pacelli steadily increasing, the hard liners among the hierarchy—particularly Cardinal Tisserant, the most powerful of the prelates—leveled unprecedented criticism against the Holy Father for giving the woman such extraordinary authority.

Many of the cardinals had come to believe that they had made a terrible mistake in electing Pacelli pope. In the decade since the conclave the autocratic and remote Pontiff had forged a militant dictatorship and deliberately remained aloof from his papal senate. With their voices seldom, if ever, listened to by a pope wanting little or nothing to do with them, the prelates felt insulted and so frustrated at times that they often boiled over among themselves.

Particularly aggravating to the humiliated hierarchy was the knowledge that Pius XII's hard rule—which often collided head-on with their influence and special interests—was largely of Pascalina's design. The nun was increasingly resented—even hated—by some of the cardinals for a number of reasons, not the least being that she was a woman with enormous authority over the Holy See, which for almost two thousand years had been run strictly by men. They hated her all the more because she was severe and refused to bend to their red hats and purple robes, and had the Pope to back her up.

She herself dismissed all talk of her extreme dominance over the Holy Father as being "simply preposterous." Anyone as much as implying that she held grip on Pius's psyche was "ignorant of the truth," she said, or was "envious of my place with His Holiness." Or even "trying to be malicious," the last a pointed reference to Cardinal Tisserant and others of the hierarchy within the Sacred College of Cardinals, more and more of whom would come to seek her downfall.

But the nun's actions contradicted her interpretation of her critics' comments. If Pius's reign was looked upon as totalitarian in substance and style, there was much of Pascalina's German hand in its clever molding. She was regarded as largely responsible for the Pope's excessive one-man authority and nepotism.

"In every successful organization, there can be only one leader, and that leader must be wise and courageous, and be feared by those under him," the nun said years later when expressing her views of how the Holy See was run by Pius XII to the exclusion of the Sacred College of Cardinals.

When it came to downgrading the hierarchy's authority, the Holy Father almost always followed Pascalina's advice. On those rare occasions when he hesitated to keep the cardinals in check, she brought the Pope back in line, using her subtle diplomacy to best advantage.

Her hold upon Pius—even when he was set to act contrary to her thinking—had been especially evident following the death in 1944 of Luigi Cardinal Maglione, the Vatican secretary of state. The Pope had mentioned to her after the burial that he had several cardinals in mind to succeed Maglione, any one of whom he felt was qualified.

Shaking her head sympathetically, Pascalina interrupted Pius with gentle words of advice as he was about to rattle off their names. "Holiness, you spend so much time convincing others far less astute than yourself to do your bidding," she said. "Why not simply be your own secretary of state?"

The nun prevailed. Then, after the Pope had considerably

increased his own authority by taking on the Vatican's number two post himself, she had a further unprecedented plan. "Holiness, your nephews, Prince Carlo [Pacelli] and Prince Giulio [Pacelli], are so devoted to you," she said. "Though they are not of the clergy, they are, nevertheless, brilliant and experienced. Would they not serve you better as advisers than so many of these cardinals, men who are often lazy, and without too much common sense? Many cardinals resent your authority, and they are scornful of me because I will no longer let anyone take advantage of your great compassion."

Pascalina successfully built an iron curtain around the Pope, shielding him from those she considered "unnecessary wasters of the Holy Father's valuable time." Her excuse was that the Pontiff, having consolidated the Holy See's two highest offices of pope and secretary of state into one superauthority, was "giving so much of himself, he had to be spared."

Some she banished entirely from ever seeing the Pope, such as Giacomo Cardinal Lercaro, archbishop of Bologna. To the serious-minded nun Lercaro appeared more like a comical character than a cardinal. "I could easily picture Eminence Lercaro as an ice cream vendor pushing a cart through Rome's streets, but I had great difficulty imagining him officiating as a prelate," Pascalina recalled. The nun had reason for her thinking, since Lercaro was often seen walking Bologna's streets wearing the strangest of hats instead of the cardinals' red biretta. The friendly, fun-loving prelate hoped to identify with his parishioners by donning the headwear of whomever he conversed with—a fireman's helmet, a railway engineer's cap, even a pizza maker's huge balloon-like attire—anything out of the ordinary that drew attention. "The Holy Father—always dignified and proper—would have been horrified and have taken it out on me afterward if I allowed a cardinal, or anyone among the clergy who made a farce of sacred attire, to waste his valuable time," the nun remarked.

The Sacred College of Cardinals, Tisserant in particular, she deliberately froze out almost entirely. Though the prelate kept after Pascalina several times a week for an audience with Pius, she always had a handy excuse ready to put him off. As time went by the nun would make the dean of cardinals wait as long as two months to see the Pope.

Outsiders who had no direct connection with the Vatican often had an easier time getting through Pascalina to meet with the Holy

Father than did many of the Church hierarchy. Those of the world of entertainment were especially favored. She had a distinct weakness for motion picture stars, especially Hollywood's male idols, and most particularly Clark Gable.

When Gable was in Rome as an American military officer during the war, Pascalina kept Bishop Angelo Roncalli waiting nearly two hours on one occasion to accommodate the star of *Gone With the Wind*.

Even had she foreseen that Roncalli would one day succeed Pius as Pope John XXIII, "I still would have given Signore Gable priority," she reminisced. "Bishop Roncalli had enough of His Holiness's ear, while Signore Gable's time was limited in Rome."

She smiled as she added a postscript to her memories. "Besides, the actor was a favorite of His Holiness's. And I, too, was a devoted fan."

Pius himself favored the tenor and style of his autocratic reign. The Pontiff, withdrawn and monastic of nature, had a mystical, almost medieval conception of the greatness of the papacy. Then, too, the war's devastations and his own advancing years—Pius was now in his early seventies—had made him even more of an introvert. Because his hope was to be worshiped rather than feared, some thought the Pope silently approved the nun's sharing of the blame.

Pascalina was especially sensitive to the dramatic changes in the Pontiff's character. In earlier years, while secretary of state, Pius remained the cool and suave diplomat. But with each passing year as Holy Father of the Universal Church, the arrogant and authoritarian manner that lurked just beneath the surface bobbed up with ever-increasing frequency. It greatly worried the nun that the Pope "just didn't seem to care as much as he should about his holy image in the eyes of his subordinates."

Though most of the time the Pope earnestly sought to be loved and respected, no one was spared the wrath of his sudden outbursts, not even Pascalina, who was the handiest target of his abruptly changing moods. At times the Pope showed such hatred of those who failed him, some thought he was incapable of genuine love. For the Holy Father, symbol on earth of the Prince of Peace, to be so volatile and even "vocally cruel" at times toward his inferiors, was astounding to a great many.

Pascalina bore the brunt of the Pope's aloofness toward his papal senate. Though his treatment of the Sacred College of Cardinals was usually one of formal courtesy, Pius often confided in the nun his secret contempt for many of the Vatican's hierarchy.

"Holiness was such a hard, efficient, and precise worker himself, he could not accept slackness, delays, or the mistakes of others," Pascalina said, remembering how all too often she had been forced to sit in silence as Pius dressed down any subordinate who offended him. "When he found someone in the wrong, no matter of what position within the Holy See, Holiness let the offender have a piece of his mind without any mincing of words."

Bishop Angelo Roncalli (later to become Pope John XXIII) received a papal rebuke shortly after the Pope had made the old prelate nuncio to France. The Holy Father, an inveterate user of the phone, wanted his officials to be immediately available whenever he called. It was exasperating to Pius that the easygoing, people-loving Roncalli was always moving about, and the Pope never seemed able to reach him. But when he finally did, Pascalina heard the Pope shout into the phone: "From now on, Bishop Roncalli, you are not to leave the nunciature without my permission! You understand?" With that, Pius slammed down the receiver. The Pope's severe tone, his piercing black eyes and tightly pursed lips, made Pascalina think how much he then resembled Mother Superior, back in her convent-training days, when the head nun had become infuriated by one of the disobedient novices.

Another Vatican official, Monsignor Giovanni Montini (one day to become Pope Paul VI), seemed always to spark Pius's wrath. "I pitied him so in those days," Pascalina recalled. "Monsignor Montini was a thin little person and always had such a frightened look on his face whenever His Holiness had him report to the papal office. On one occasion Monsignor Montini brought the Holy Father a telegram that had been addressed to someone else. Holiness was infuriated at being so idly interrupted. I thought the Pope was about to shout at the monsignor. But ignoring poor Montini, he shouted at me instead. 'Mother Pascalina, teach this monsignor how to read,' the Holy Father called out in a harsh voice. 'Take him into the next room and begin by having him recite the alphabet.'"

Monsignor Domenico Tardini, whom Pope John XXIII would appoint Vatican secretary of state following Pius's death in 1958, could rarely please Pacelli. Pascalina believed that the Pope actually looked for the slightest reason to put down Tardini. Once, when Tardini mispronounced the name of the French town of Rodez, Pius abruptly corrected him. Yet, as Tardini read on from his manuscript and the town's name came up time and again, he kept pronouncing it the wrong way.

"I watched the Holy Father become increasingly exasperated," Pascalina said. "Still, he did not rebuke the monsignor, as I had expected, knowing His Holiness's perfectionist nature so well. The next day, however, after poring through dictionaries—an almost daily practice that His Holiness so much enjoyed—he called Monsignor Tardini back to his office. Pointing to the dictionaries' correct pronunciation, His Holiness said, 'Monsignor, I told you yesterday how the name of Rodez should be pronounced. Now study this! And when you have learned to pronounce Rodez, I want you to stand before me and repeat the town's name until I am sure you can say it correctly.'

"Many thought I was the cause of those terribly embarrassing incidents," she related many years later. "To the contrary, I often had no knowledge of what precipitated Holiness's outbursts. It was most difficult for me to be put in such an adverse position."

It was also especially trying on the nun's nerves when Pius would suddenly seize the phone to vent his frustrations. He'd attack anyone who struck a wrong nerve. Time and again she tried desperately to restrain the Pope's unbridled impulsiveness.

Often she'd grab the phone from him, but Pius would wrestle it back. He'd make his call, no matter what she would say.

"*Qui pàrla Pacelli* [Pacelli speaking]," the Pontiff would say in an icy tone. He'd then proceed to tell the offender in great detail how he had transgressed. Finally, without giving his horrified victim any chance to explain, he'd abruptly hang up.

The only recourse anyone had was to request an audience with the Pope. But the result was usually futile. Even though Pius was an outspoken advocate of brotherly love, rarely were pleas for mercy ever heeded.

Pius probably had fewer friends among the Vatican's Italian hierarchy than most popes, and for good reason. Those of the clergy he chose to serve as his advisers were practically all foreigners to Rome. The Holy Father's blatant partiality toward clerics who stemmed from German blood was obvious. Some Italian churchmen even considered Pius's prejudice an insult.

Both his confessor, Father Augustin Bea, and his private secretary, Father Robert Leiber, were German Jesuits. A third of Teutonic origin, Father Hendrich, helped draft Pius's speeches. Monsignor Ludwig Kass, former head of the German Center party, was brought to Rome by Pius to serve as administrator of Saint Peter's, a post traditionally held by Italian prelates.

It was generally believed in the Vatican that Pascalina's heavy-handedness was behind the Pope's choices, since she herself was also of German heritage.

But even the German cardinals whom Pius favored were isolated from his official brain trust, those who were the real movers and shakers of his papacy. Only men who bore the nun's exacting stamp of approval were let in on top-level decisions and policy-making. The tightly knit circle comprised the Pope himself, Pascalina, Papal Count Enrico Galeazzi, the Vatican's architect who was also Spellman's longtime friend and mentor, and the Pontiff's three nephews: Prince Carlo, Prince Giulio, and Prince Marcantonio Pacelli.

Cardinal Spellman, whom Pascalina kept informed of all of the papacy's secret inner workings by transatlantic phone and cable, remained the only prelate the Pope and the nun considered worthy of inclusion.

By failing to surround himself exclusively with Italian prelates, Pius felt more of the hierarchy's smoldering hostility. Italians of the Sacred College of Cardinals complained that they were being trampled upon. And though their reasons for resentment were steadily intensifying, Pius closed his eyes and ears.

Though Pascalina herself kept the hierarchy at a distance, the nun was secretly concerned about the Pontiff's high-handedness toward the prelates. Knowing full well that Cardinal Tisserant, whose influence grew steadily, was fiery and volatile enough to cause all sorts of problems, she pleaded with Pius to stop antagonizing the prelate and others of the already alienated hierarchy.

But the Pope would not budge from his characteristic ways. He continued to prepare everything in great secrecy, then sprang his important decisions and undertakings upon the Vatican hierarchy entirely without warning.

The prelates, having historical responsibility for ecclesiastical policies, were usually furious with Pius's faits accomplis. All too often the Pope's decisions were in direct conflict with their own initiatives and ambitions.

Perhaps the Vatican's most stabilizing force at the time was Alfredo Cardinal Ottaviani, the well-respected functional head of the

Curia. With Pius as both pope and secretary of state, the influential Ottaviani's authority was more psychological than official. There was hardly one among the hierarchy who did not approach the scholarly cardinal, who had been around for years, with a complaint about Pius.

"I spend weeks preparing a plan to improve Vatican relations with France," Monsignor Tardini, pro–secretary of state, angrily protested to Ottaviani, "but the only word His Holiness hears is the one I mispronounce."

The formidable Ottaviani, who had spent so much of his adult life in the Curia, merely shrugged and repeated what he had been saying over and over to so many of his colleagues. "We are old soldiers, my dear compatriot, who must serve the Church blindly." Tardini, like most others, shook his head in utter frustration. But before allowing the monsignor to turn away in anger, Ottaviani placed an arm about his old friend's shoulder and remarked with a wry wink: "Popes pass, but the Curia lives on."

Ottaviani had Church history to call upon as example. Pius XII's cult of personality—his belief that one man, though he hold the dual power of pope and secretary of state, can short-circuit the Curia— was extremely shortsighted. Though the Curia, including the College of Cardinals, was highly critical of Pius XII, and on the constant verge of outright rebellion, its standstill was far more effective. The wheels of the Vatican—Church decisions and actions—were slowed to a snail's pace.

Though Pius so often condemned the Curia to Pascalina as being "backward," the clergy weren't blind, as the Pope learned after they deliberately stalemated the Vatican into chaotic inaction. Pius's insult that he didn't need "collaborators" but would "go it alone" was the last straw in the head-on collision between the Pontiff and the hierarchy.

The cardinals, quite humanly, had to place blame somewhere, so they targeted Pascalina as their scapegoat.

"The woman is the main cause of this terrible impasse!" Cardinal Tisserant complained again and again to Cardinal Ottaviani. The Curia's leader became so tired of hearing the charges reiterated by Tisserant that he finally lost his temper and roared back at his long-time contemporary: "Eminence, what do you propose that we of the Holy See do—hang the nun by the neck on the altar of Saint Peter's?"

Many of the more conscientious cardinals did not easily accept Ottaviani's placating words but lived in fear of further, so often surprising, papal announcements. Their greatest shock had come when the Pontiff announced the establishment of a Vatican bank as a camouflaged instrument to profiteer from the world conflict.

Pius XII's papacy had seen World War II from the start as big business, and early on had decided to move in on the enormous profits. Pascalina had been as much a part of the plans to enrich the Holy See through the hostilities as the Pope himself. As Pacelli's right arm for so many years, the nun maintained a sharp, objective mind behind her genteel features.

"If the Church is to remain a potent force in spreading the word of Almighty God," she told a skeptical cardinal, "it must continually seek new means to increase its financial influence."

The cardinal, like so many of his colleagues, was highly critical of the Pope's move in setting up the bank. Even though Pius took Pascalina's suggestion and named the bank the *Instituto per le Opere di Religione* (Institute for Religious Works), and claimed its purpose was to "keep and administer the capital intended for religious congregations," most cardinals failed to believe anything of the sort.

The hierarchy flatly refused to accept the nun's explanation that "everything is in strict accord with the canons of the Church." She was acting on Pius's instructions to reveal nothing of the bank's secret operations.

From its day of opening in early 1942, Pius's bank had become the cover for a worldwide smuggling operation, with numbers of the Pope's most trusted clergy as agents and couriers. These prelates and priests, whom the Vatican called *uomini di fiducia* ("men of trust"), had been recruited and trained by the papacy's tight inner circle to spirit vast sums of money and securities across foreign frontiers. In almost all instances the heads of foreign governments closed their eyes to the papacy's vast international covert operations, and passed word along to customs officials to look the other way.

The Church's historic neutrality in warfare was not altogether altruistic. It proved as convenient an excuse for the papacy in building its greater financial might as it did in maintaining the goodwill of Catholics on both sides of the war.

Neutrality also allowed for the exchange of favors and funds by the Holy See to either side, and for subtle, undercover deals depending upon how the winds of warfare were shifting. When the tide of battle began turning against Hitler and the Nazis were bogged down at the outskirts of Moscow, Pius, for the first time, had doubts that the Germans were going to win the war.

"The mounting impetus of the American initiative will soon affect the balance of power," Pius had predicted to Pascalina as early as the winter of 1941–42. "Hitler has met his Waterloo in Russia, and American armaments, men, and industrial might soon will be forcefully felt everywhere."

The Pope's great fear at the time was the communist threat to the entire continent. Pius had visions of the Reds sweeping through Europe and setting up atheistic dictatorships in Germany, France, and Italy. The Vatican would be quickly brought to its knees, he had felt certain, and stripped of its wealth and historic possessions.

The Vatican bank had seemed the best means of shifting the Holy See's vast treasury to whatever nation offered the papacy the most promise and security in the forthcoming postwar era.

Pius was looking to Pascalina for ideas, for he had trained her to think as he did in business and finance, and now he considered her essential to his own wizardry.

It was she who suggested that Spellman be the main conduit of Vatican funds to be taken in and out of countries around the world.

"Holiness, as you are aware, Archbishop Spellman has done a remarkable job of putting the Holy See's financial house in order in the United States," Pascalina reminded the Pope. "It may be advisable to consider him as your chief courier in the transfer of major funds and securities to foreign nations. As military vicar of the American armed forces, His Excellency travels regularly to numerous nations."

The nun was using Pius's own brand of delicate diplomacy in guardedly suggesting that he take advantage of Spellman's built-in immunity from suspicion. The archbishop's Roman collar and worldwide influence were blessings, she felt, that no covert operation could afford to overlook.

The Pope was as enthusiastic as Pascalina was at the prospects. Without hesitation Pius ordered papal protocol into immediate action for Spellman's early arrival in Rome.

When whispers of the Holy Father's "unprecedented and daring stratagem" reached Cardinal Tisserant, the French prelate prepared pointed and sarcastic dialogue for his assault on the plot. The New York archbishop was his main target.

"Greetings, Excellency Spellman!" Tisserant buoyantly exclaimed when the "Pope's pet" appeared in the Vatican. The cardinal spoke in his most exacting English, showing only a trace of accent. "How is our chief undercover agent doing these days?"

Tisserant had timed his grand entrance at the precise moment, obviously for the greatest dramatic effect. With the Pope off for his regular afternoon nap, the Frenchman found the American archbishop alone with Pascalina in her office outside Pius's suite. The cardinal appeared delighted with himself in successfully embarrassing a colleague of the hierarchy. He was particularly overjoyed to ridicule Spellman, for whom he seldom made any attempt to disguise his dislike.

The nun was infuriated at seeing her old friend so humiliated. If Spellman was inclined "to turn the other cheek," she wasn't about to let Tisserant bask in self-satisfaction.

"Since when does a Frenchman use a microscope when it comes to the manner of making money?" she sharply retorted.

"Touché, Mother Pascalina!" Tisserant shot back. "Now I can see why the Holy Father has you around. Your wit is as brilliant as your sparkling beauty. If only your personality equaled your other fine gifts, even I could then appreciate your value!"

The nun had studied the cardinal closely over the years, and she felt instinctively that this was not the time for counterattack but merely a bit of verbal play.

"If Eminence Tisserant was being difficult," she later explained, "it was probably because he felt left out of important decisions."

Pius and Spellman agreed with Pascalina that Tisserant's cleverness and connections could be decided assets in the international operations of the Vatican bank. What part, if any, Tisserant later played has not been disclosed.

But Spellman's role was significant and remarkably successful, as seen by the papacy. Using to a fare-thee-well his titles as archbishop of New York and military vicar of the U.S. armed forces, the prelate became "as slick and skilled in transporting vast amounts in cash and securities as the most celebrated and daring of international smugglers," according to his biographer, Father Robert I. Gannon.

During Spellman's extensive military travels to nations around the world, the New York archbishop transported a variety of wealth—bank notes, stocks, bonds, gold, and silver—that was said to be in the many millions of dollars. He was never in fear of detection, or in danger. Safely ensconced in his important clerical garb and with all the credentials necessary from FDR, the so-called American Pope, with his cherubic smile, hadn't the slightest concern of being searched. And he never was.

And neither were the hundreds of other Catholic clergy of all ranks who served the papacy as agents for its international banking operations. Throughout World War II, and even afterward, priests and those of the hierarchy transported in and out of the Vatican the equivalent of hundreds of millions of American dollars in various forms of currency and other securities.

With the great powers on both sides of the war as its silent partners, there were no governmental restrictions on the papacy as to how its wealth was transported or invested. The Church's trained eye was constantly on the watch for the most promising investments. Little consideration was given during Pius's reign to the integrity of the ventures or to the policies of the nations—democracies or dictatorships—in which the investments were made.

Having financially backed Mussolini's invasion of Ethiopia and Generalissimo Francisco Franco's take-over of Spain, the papacy by then was an old and experienced hand at supporting totalitarian governments. If the Nazi war machine was able to fatten the Vatican's coffers considerably, the Holy See's conscience was eased by rationalization. Earned profits, Pius told Pascalina, "would spread the good work of Holy Mother Church."

The papacy felt it was as fair with its fortunes in dealing with the nations at war as it was in its adherence to neutrality. When the Pope saw the tides of battle turning against the Axis, the Vatican swiftly began making huge investments in U.S. war plants. Supporting both sides financially in the war was explained by the Pope as a form of neutrality. But the question remained in many minds of how the Church of the Prince of Peace could defend its integrity while underwriting the materials of warfare.

It had long been the great dream of both Pacelli and Pascalina to make the papacy the center of world charity. Certainly, to have been as lavish in its housing and feeding of tens of thousands of Jews during the war, the papacy's expenditures had run into many millions of dollars. Then there were additional massive outlays for Europe's other war-ravaged masses—refugees and displaced persons—during the postwar era, which cost tens of millions more than the Vatican could afford. If the Church were to rely solely on its domestic holdings and charitable donations, and if the Holy See were to continue to feed, clothe, and provide medical supplies to millions in Finland, Norway, Greece, France, Belgium, Holland, Ethiopia, Malaya, and other countries, the Vatican had constantly to replenish its revenues, by whatever profitable means.

No longer was Pascalina's conscience seriously troubled over the Vatican's methods of making money, despite the fact that some fifteen years before, when the Holy See had received the $92.1 million through the Lateran Treaty with fascist Italy, she had greatly mistrusted Bernardino Nogara, the papacy's financial wizard. That misapprehension had long since been settled.

Within days after Pius had been crowned Pope, Pascalina had urged the Holy Father to investigate Nogara. For years the financier's unprecedented position—solely in charge of all of the Vatican's funds—had caused rumors to spread that unlawful transactions were being made. Pascalina and Pacelli had thought it strange that the entrepreneurial layman operated out of a small and secretive office down the hall from Pius XI's apartment in the Papal Palace. It also had seemed unorthodox to them that despite all of the millions of Church dollars that flowed through Nogara's hands, the important financier had only two people—a bookkeeper and a male secretary—to help him out. They wondered why the banker had not selected as aides members of the clergy, but chose instead laymen like himself.

But neither Pascalina nor Pacelli was in any position to challenge Nogara's operation. Under the dictatorial Pius XI even Pacelli himself—as influential as he appeared to the world as Vatican secretary of state—had no influence whatsoever over the Vatican treasury.

Some within the Vatican hierarchy had occasionally challenged Nogara's policies during Pius XI's reign, but they always acted with cautious words. The papacy itself and most of its clergy took the financier's word for everything, even though all types of unorthodox investments were made by the shrewd layman. Church money was poured by Nogara into one country after another: Germany, France, Yugoslavia, Albania, Italy, Britain, Canada, the United States, and a variety of nations in South America.

Thanks to Nogara the Holy See at one point was said to own up to 20 percent of all shares traded on the Italian stock exchange. The Church's financial holdings in the United States became even greater than, and as diversified as, those in Europe. With its huge investments in Riviera casinos as well as in Perrier mineral water and the Miller breweries, the papacy had appeared to draw no distinction. Only the bottom line seemed to count with Nogara.

Most of the cardinals and other high Vatican dignitaries had shown little reluctance in taking advantage of the papacy's newfound prosperity. Plush apartments and big black limousines had become a way of life for almost all of the prelates. Even though their shiny new limos were red flags to Rome's impoverished Catholics and a dead giveaway with number plates bearing the initials SCV (for *Stato Città Vaticano,* or Vatican City State), the Church's high and mighty had remained coldly indifferent. It appeared to matter little that cynics translated the cars' letters to mean *"Se Cristo Vedesse!"* ("If Christ could only see this!")

Disgusted by the hierarchy's brazen display of affluence, Pascalina had waited for years to put Nogara to serious test. When Pacelli became the new Holy Father, she urged him to settle, one way or another, the persistent rumors that the financier had personally made off with at least half of the Church's wealth.

"Holiness, some of your own relatives are experienced in matters of high finance and should be appointed by you to a committee to look into Nogara's operations," Pascalina had advised Pius XII at the time.

But after the most scrutinizing investigation, Nogara was given a completely clean bill of health. Not only had the long-maligned Nogara, who was then almost seventy, done an honest and first-rate money-management job, but he had brought into the Vatican many millions of additional dollars throughout the severe worldwide depression of the 1930s. It was largely the fortune earned by Nogara, himself a Jew, that made possible Pius's and Pascalina's Papal Relief Committee that did so much to aid Hitler's persecuted Jews.

How could she any longer question Nogara's methods or success when so much good had resulted for so many of the world's neediest?

Though time and again Pius credited Pascalina as the master craftsman behind the Vatican's bank and its scale of operations, she denied his praise, telling him repeatedly that the advice received by her from Pacelli himself and Nogara made all of the difference. The nun and the financier—for their help in building the Vatican bank— were remembered in special Masses said by His Holiness.

The papacy showed its gratitude to Spellman, particularly for his covert smuggling operations, by awarding the New York archbishop its high blessing—a red hat. At Pius's first consistory, held in February 1946, Spellman was made a cardinal and automatically elevated to the Sacred College. The Pope had waited to honor his favorite churchman until Spellman's old nemesis, William Cardinal O'Connell of Boston, had passed away. O'Connell had died in 1944, maintaining till the end resentments against his one-time underling that had run on for years. The spiteful prelate had plagued Rome not to give Spellman a red hat as long as he, O'Connell, remained alive.

Pius XII's special, favored treatment of Spellman did not sit well with too many of Rome's hierarchy, but most were entirely infuriated when the new Holy Father, at the same consistory, raised fourteen other non-Italians to the rank of cardinal and thus reversed the traditional balance of power within the Holy See. Only twenty-eight Italian cardinals remained in the Sacred College, while the new majority (forty-two) were from foreign countries.

"Holiness, the Italians are now a minority," Pascalina said. "Have you considered the consequences in reversing tradition?"

"Indeed, I have!" the Pope replied with a knowing smile. "It means that I, as Holy Father, could have a foreign successor." Pius had delivered his most blatant insult and severest blow to the Italian majority of the Sacred College of Cardinals.

The nun was almost certain that Pius had Spellman in mind as his successor, and had opened the door for such a possibility. But she feared the Pontiff had failed to consider an even greater possibility, the election of another foreigner, French Cardinal Tisserant.

"It then occurred to me why Eminence Tisserant had remained so calm throughout the consistory," she recalled. "Indeed, he appeared to be quite genuinely delighted, an attitude he had never before shown since Holiness became the Holy Father."

XIII

Pascalina began to detect subtle, troubling changes in the Pope's physical health during the winter of 1949–50. Generally, his mind appeared as sharp and active as ever, yet at times his thoughts would wander. Pius was as alarmed as she, and both were deeply concerned that those around them, particularly the hierarchy, might take some unprecedented action not against Pius himself, but quite possibly against Pascalina.

Pius still remained one of the most powerful of modern-day pontiffs, and the likelihood of the College of Cardinals suggesting he step down, now that he was in his seventies and ill much of the time, was never a question. But the Vatican's bitterness toward the nun, whom they contemptuously disparaged as "the German general," was at fever pitch. Her possible banishment through pressure from the hierarchy was no longer spoken of in mere whispers.

Strangely enough, Pascalina herself recognized that her predicament was largely of her own making. One high Vatican churchman after another had been alienated by Pascalina's desperate desire to shield her beloved Pontiff from too close scrutiny and pressure.

Indeed, the long-smoldering battle between the nun and the hierarchy came to a near explosion one afternoon in the fall of 1949 when the Sacred College of Cardinals asked for an accounting of the papacy's funds. Tisserant had been elected—along with Monsignor Domenico Tardini, the Vatican's pro–secretary of state—to ask Pius for a complete financial statement, secret information that no pope was ever known to have given anyone, even the highest-ranking cardinals. The huge, bearded French cardinal came pounding into her office puffing on a cigar, followed by Tardini. In a loud, coarse voice the cardinal said without preamble, "Woman, give us the balance sheet! The Sacred College demands the information!"

Pascalina had heard rumors that the hierarchy was planning to ask the Pope for an accounting. But she hadn't dreamed that a matter of such vital importance to the Holy See would be handled so brashly.

Though taken completely by surprise, she still held her ground firmly, answering Tisserant's demands with an icy, defiant stare. Her complete silence and brazen look infuriated the cardinal. "Either you give us the report, woman, or we'll get it from the Pope himself!" he shouted, his rage rising as he pounded her desk with his fist. "It's not the Pope we don't trust. It's you!"

Pascalina, although now as infuriated as Tisserant, held her composure. Showing not the slightest concern, she coldly reached for the phone. "Send the Swiss Guards immediately!" she ordered, speaking with a calm yet commanding voice into the receiver.

In a flash the helmeted papal soldiers were in the doorway.

"Remove these intruders at once!" she demanded, pointing to Cardinal Tisserant and Monsignor Tardini. She had pulled herself to full height at her desk and was now every bit the German general her deriders often called her behind her back. The Swiss Guards were as astounded and speechless as the prelates.

"We will leave of our own accord," Tisserant said quietly, his eyes blazing in cold anger. The prelate's look defied any soldier to lay a hand on him. "Woman, may God have mercy on you from now on!" she heard him say as they marched off.

Pascalina remained standing—though she was shaking terribly inside—until all were gone.

Certainly neither Pius nor she released a financial statement to anyone, including the Sacred College of Cardinals. "We held to papal tradition," she said later. "One responsibility of the Holy Father is to make certain that sufficient resources are always on hand to perpetuate the charities and the religious work of the Holy See for the welfare of all Catholics. To divide His Holiness's supreme authority with any source would open the doors to the likely dissipation of the great holy and charitable work of Holy Mother Church."

But Tisserant accepted none of the nun's words or actions. Months later when Archbishop Richard J. Cushing of Boston was visiting with Tisserant, the French cardinal was still smoldering over Pascalina's bold stand.

"It was bad enough in the early days when the woman still took her orders from Pius," Cardinal Tisserant said bitterly while recalling the incident to Cushing. "But now she wields such power that many of the hierarchy have come to deride her as 'La Popessa.'"

By then the nun aptly fitted the title. She had learned of a major scandal involving the Knights of Malta, the Holy See's influential laymen's organization, and was determined that the Pope clean house of the cardinals and others who were running the secret society and turning it into an international money-making racket. Pius was slow to move against the Knights of Malta because several of the Holy See's leading prelates were involved, including Nicola Cardinal Canali, one of the most powerful members of the Sacred College, Bishop Angelo Roncalli (later to become Pope John XXIII), and their own close friend Cardinal Spellman.

"You know what a sensation in the press an investigation would cause," the Pope told Pascalina when she urged him to look into the alleged corruption.

"But, Holiness, you—as Holy Father—cannot sanction a cover-up of scandal," the nun replied. Both she and the Pontiff were aware of the battle being waged by Cardinal Spellman and Cardinal Canali for control of the immensely lucrative Knights of Malta. They were also cognizant of Bishop Roncalli's naiveté in innocently getting himself into the center of the erupting scandal.

Pascalina had become suspicious of the society's illicit practices upon learning that Americans were contributing to Cardinal Spellman as much as $200,000 each for the title of knight. The contributors had been told by the New York archbishop that the money was to be sent to the Vatican for religious and charitable purposes. But Spellman sent Rome only $1,000 from each donation and kept the rest for use as he alone dictated.

In Paris a further dark cloud hung over the French branch of the Knights of Malta. Bishop Roncalli had appointed Baron Marsaudon, a close friend and thirty-third-degree Freemason, as head of the strictly Catholic organization.* The baron's appointment was made at a time when Church law strictly forbade all Catholics from becoming Freemasons or participating in Freemasonry. To defy this canon of Catholicism meant excommunication from the Holy Roman Catholic Church.

---

*The thirty-third degree is the highest rank conferred upon members of the international secret fraternity.

Cardinal Canali—keeping close watch on the brewing scandals and the enormous financial stakes that were involved—wanted Rome to take over the Knights of Malta's entire international operations and place him in charge.

With much reluctance the Pope finally gave in to Pascalina's persistent nagging for an investigation, but he clearly let her know how little enthusiasm he had for the plan. "Cardinals have the privilege of being above suspicion," he told her in a curt tone. "Mother Pascalina, you must learn to have more respect for the purple," he added, referring bluntly to her repeated criticisms of the purple-robed cardinals.

The nun, though hurt, was all the more dismayed the next day when Pius advised her that he was placing Cardinal Tisserant in charge of the tribunal to investigate the charges and render the final verdict.

"Holiness, you are making a terrible mistake!" the nun replied anxiously, shattered by the Holy Father's decision. She completely overlooked the Pope's admonishment of the previous day, explaining, "Eminence Tisserant will do nothing constructive but will use the trial to his own advantage!"

"Tisserant is a Frenchman, and the French branch of the society is involved," the Pope angrily retorted, incensed that she would dare express such defiance.

"What a ridiculous excuse," the nun thought to herself, but said nothing further. She bowed curtly, and walked out.

Much of the year was spent by Tisserant and four other cardinals conducting what Pascalina called a "kangaroo court." One of the trial judges was Cardinal Canali, a close friend of Tisserant's whom the French prelate had handpicked. The outcome had been predicted by Pascalina from the start.

"The purple is above suspicion!" Tisserant—in proud and boastful stance—told the Pope of the verdict in the nun's presence.

Pascalina was outraged. She wanted so much to say, "The purple is in mourning for the sins of its wearers, cardinals like yourself, Tisserant!" But once more she kept her tongue. "Only because I was in the Holy Father's presence," she later emphasized.

Her defeat by the cardinals made Pascalina all the more determined to heighten her barricade of the Pope. From then on only a handful of the papal inner circle, those few who had won the nun's confidence and respect, were allowed to cross the papal threshold on a regular basis. She put few, if any, restrictions on Pius's three nephews, Carlo, Giulio, and Marcantonio Pacelli, and the Vatican's governor general, Enrico Galeazzi. Not one of the four was a member of the hierarchy, or even a priest. But all had earned Pascalina's confidence in handling the papacy's vast financial holdings, since Bernardino Nogara—the Vatican's old and venerable treasurer, whom she had grown to trust and respect—was around only part time. As treasury experts, Pius's relatives pleased the semiretired Nogara and served the Holy Father loyally and brilliantly, trading stock in many of the world's major corporations and sitting on boards of directors.

Cardinal Spellman remained the only member of the Church hierarchy to receive her blessing for ready access to the papal inner sanctum. Conversely, even Pius's sister, Elisabetta, who had been his closest friend throughout childhood, had to find the nun in just the right mood to be granted a papal audience.

Pascalina objected to Elisabetta solely because the old woman had a habit of hiding a bottle of rare wine in her heavy skirts for the Holy Father, and began pouring glassfuls as soon as she was alone with her brother.

"Elisabetta, don't you dare give Holiness another drink!" Pascalina shouted in mock anger as she barged in on the rollicking pair one evening in late 1949. "It's wonderful hearing you two reminisce about the past, but must you both toast every milestone in your lives? Holiness is not a well man, Elisabetta," the nun gently admonished.

"For heaven's sakes, Pascalina," Elisabetta retorted, looking perturbed. "Eugenio is no longer a baby! And you are not quite that old to be sounding like such a fuddy-duddy. Now leave us alone and stop listening at the door!" Though pretending to be very disturbed, Elisabetta thoroughly enjoyed her unique position. As Pacelli's beloved sister, she could get away with pointed remarks that Pascalina would never overlook if said by anyone else. Yet if Elisabetta came too often to visit her brother, she, too, would find the nun closing the door in her face.

The one regular visitor that Pascalina was most anxious to keep entirely out of the papal apartment was the Pope's physician, Dr. Riccardo Galeazzi-Lisi—even though His Holiness and the doctor were longtime friends and Pius had unquestioned faith in Galeazzi-Lisi's capabilities as a physician.

But in instances of such touchy personal matters as the choice of who was to be his general physician, Pius almost always won out. He usually proved "grouchy enough" to get his own way, Pascalina recalled long afterward. Her memories of those past incidents brought a twinkle of merriment to her eyes. She admitted to having never understood "Holiness's naiveté" in believing that Galeazzi-Lisi—whose medical skills lay only in fitting eyeglasses—had the training and competence to treat all forms of illness.

Of course, Pascalina had her reasons for isolating Pius from much of the political pressures of the Vatican and insisting that he surround himself with more expert medical attention.

"Holiness had worked hard all of his life," she explained. "His pontificate had been a period of unremitting struggle and worry. He had been torn throughout by anxiety for the safety of the world. Holiness would spend as much as eighteen hours a day writing and giving audiences. In the course of a year he sometimes addressed hundreds of thousands, even millions, of the faithful. I worried constantly that so frail and ascetic a man could possibly survive the worry and work he imposed upon himself."

When Pius came down with a severe cold in late December 1949, Pascalina feared it might lead to pneumonia—since he had had so many attacks of the dread disease during his lifetime. The time had finally come for the nun to speak her mind about Galeazzi-Lisi.

"Holiness, that alleged doctor hasn't the ability to treat even your pet birds," she complained, shaking her head in disgust as she spoon-fed the bedridden Holy Father an elixir Galeazzi-Lisi had prescribed.

"You see everything wrong in every one of the few friends I have left," the Holy Father impatiently retorted, making a pained face at the bitter taste of the medicine. "You're jealous of everyone who is close to me."

"That's utterly preposterous!" she exclaimed, placing her hands on her hips and looking terribly offended. "I'm trying my best to look after your health, and you accuse me of selfish motives!" In her exasperation she felt like adding, "Well, if you have such faith in the old doctor and his magic potions, take his ridiculous liquid yourself." But she held her tongue and simply placed the bottle and a spoon calmly on the table by his bed and went about tidying up his room—all the while looking painfully hurt.

The Holy Father, feeling guilty that he had offended his good friend, kept gazing her way, hoping that she'd look back and show a smile of forgiveness. But she didn't. When the nun finished, she said quite stiffly, "Holiness, your room is in order now. Call me when you need further care and I will be pleased to phone your doctor. Perhaps the next time he'll try to cure you by dancing about the bed." With that, she bowed dutifully, then walked haughtily from the room.

Pius barely recovered in time for the commencement of Holy Year on January 1, 1950—one of the Catholic Church's most sacred events, which reigning popes have held periodically since 1300. Throughout the entire twelve months of Holy Year, also known as the "Year of the Jubilee," Catholics are called upon by the Holy Father to take part in special devotions and prayers to repay their debts to Jesus Christ and to do penance for their sins.

Pius XII took advantage of the historical event to announce a great new Church dogma, the first in eighty years. On November 1, 1950, the Pontiff officially proclaimed the Assumption of the Blessed Virgin Mary, an affirmation that caused so much worldwide controversy among persons of all religions, his own Catholics included, that the Pope's infallibility and credibility were both seriously threatened.

Pius claimed the body of the Mother of God had not disintegrated like those of ordinary mortals but was raised directly into heaven in full form, as had been the body of her Son. The Pope, whose rulings are considered by the Church as infallible in matters of dogma, told Catholics that this basic article of faith was now "absolute doctrine of Holy Mother Church."

Pius's papacy then followed with what some considered an even more contentious announcement. The world was told that the Blessed Virgin Mary had appeared before the Pope while he was strolling in the papal gardens. The vision of the Madonna was said to have occurred on the same day Pius announced his dogma. The Holy Father claimed that Mary had even appeared twice previously on the days preceding the official Church confirmation of her Assumption.

Catholics and skeptics alike were still further surprised by Pius's revelation that he had personally witnessed the sun rotating out of orbit as the Virgin Mary appeared. He described the sun as spiraling downward to the horizon and then, like fireworks, swinging rapidly back to its original position.

According to Dr. Galeazzi-Lisi, "Pius was profoundly moved, and interpreted his visions as a sign of Divine approval for the proclamation of dogma he was about to make."

Even some of the more conservative among the Roman hierarchy were as astounded by the Pope's revelation as were the Church's bitterest critics. But to avoid the open controversy that certainly would have led to ridicule, Vatican comments were limited to hushed criticisms and irritated grumblings.

Those who hated Pascalina placed most blame upon her. "That woman is fanatical on some matters of faith," Valerio Cardinal Valeri, an officer of the Curia, angrily charged. "She puts almost as much belief in Mary as some Catholics place in Christ. She's behind most of this."

But the nun had her own ready defense. "The Assumption of the Blessed Virgin Mary has been a long-held belief of popes and prelates since the earliest days of Holy Mother Church," Pascalina said. "In creating a new dogma, Holiness was confirming more than fifteen hundred years of Catholic belief that the Holy Mother of God was taken up, body and soul, to be with Jesus in heaven."

But disbelievers, anxious to press an issue that might more fully embarrass the Holy See, struck away at the Pope's infallibility. It was even suggested that Pius had used the supreme power of his papal office to grant glory to the Madonna that belonged strictly to Christ. Some even snidely suggested he was already senile.

Again Pascalina answered. "There is an extraordinary misconception as to the infallibility of the Pope," she said. "According to the tenets of Holy Mother Church, the Holy Father can be as mistaken as anyone in most matters, and it is no sin to disagree with him. It is only when the Supreme Pontiff solemnly speaks ex cathedra on faith and morals that he is held to be infallible. Holiness, a master of theology himself, had instructed his ecclesiastical scholars to examine all the evidence in every minute way, and to interpret the evidence for him. In proclaiming the dogma of Assumption, Holiness was officially confirming a belief long held by officials of Holy Mother Church."

As for her own belief in Pius's visions of the Blessed Virgin Mary, Pascalina answered: "I believe with all my heart and soul in the power of our Holy Mother. If she chose to appear before Holiness, I am sure she did."

All of the bickering and tension within Pius's papacy had become very wearing on Pascalina. She was in her mid-fifties, and there were times when she'd lay awake all night, unable to sleep, wondering if she had done the right thing in having left convent life as a young girl to serve Eugenio Pacelli.

"I had my moments of severe anguish when the papacy's entire weight seemed upon my shoulders," she later remarked. Now, as in the past, when the Pope had a problem—ecclesiastical or temporal—she would help him find a solution. When he was worried, she brought up his spirits. If he was ill, she nursed him and sat by his bed. Her eyes were his when he couldn't find something—a misplaced pen or a hard-to-find passage. She was not only his brain trust and domestic, she was his doctor and nurse, mother, sister, and dearest friend.

Now that the Pope was almost seventy-five and showing many of the more serious signs of advanced age, the nun found herself heavily burdened with the papacy's awesome responsibilities.

Pascalina would have preferred that her life turn out differently. She had most wanted to serve Christ, and, to her, the holiness and comfort of the convent had seemed ideal. Surely the politicking and jealousies and the many tempests within the Vatican were enough to sway the most devout. But the nun's answer to herself always remained the same. "I felt I had chosen the right course for me," she said. "A true servant of Our Savior must first consider all the strength and beauty and light that flows from the good and noble within the clergy; those priests and prelates who most surely predominate in the service of Almighty God."

In her lonely hours of anguish the nun had her rosary beads and a faith in Jesus Christ that carried her calmly through the long, dark nights and prepared her emotions for the day ahead. "I placed everything in the hands of Our Savior," she would say. "Before I ever made a decision, or took a stand, I asked myself, 'How would dear Jesus and the Blessed Mother decide and act?' When I was convinced of the right course, I acted without fear. Though I was never more than a nun, I would not allow anyone, even though he be priest or prelate, to dishonor Our Lord. When I spoke my mind for what was ethical and honorable, I became hated for it. There was great sadness in my heart, for no one wants to be disliked. Yet at no time were there regrets on my part. Only the mistakes of Holiness himself brought tears to my eyes, for, in my mind, he remained a great and holy man, no matter what his human errors."

Though the divisions between the Pope and the Vatican widened quickly from the Holy Year on, the hierarchy nevertheless had to consider the advantages of the explosive publicity Pius had generated. More than four million Catholics and others of all creeds had passed through the Vatican during the religious spectacular of 1950. Untold millions in foreign currency were received in large and small donations to swell the Church's treasury well beyond its record heights.

When rumors began to spread concerning the hierarchy's coolness toward the Holy Father for his virtual disregard of them, both sides showed two faces, one privately, the other in public. In deference to the dignity of the Holy See, the portrayal to the world by Pius and the men of the red hat was one of all love, and piety, and close affinity.

"One would never think that Pius XII and those of the Sacred College ever held anything but love for each other in their hearts," Archbishop Cushing commented at the time.

The animosity between the Pope and his hierarchy reached its peak in 1953, when the temper of the Sacred College of Cardinals threatened to boil over publicly upon Pius's announcement that he intended to appoint new cardinals from a number of foreign countries. Pascalina was as anxious as the Holy Father to see the Sacred College become internationalized, but she had her reservations. "Holiness, you realize all the pressure from the Romans that will descend upon your head," the nun sympathetically reminded the Pontiff prior to the consistory. "But you are right. If Holy Mother Church is to thrive throughout the world, we know that people everywhere must have representation."

"Dear Mother Pascalina, I am not overly concerned about the Italian membership," the Pope replied in a placid manner. "I am the Holy Father of all Catholics everywhere, and furthermore, I am an old man now. What can anyone do, particularly when I am behaving in the best interests of the Holy See?" The Pontiff paused and a smile came upon his lips. He then added: "What is there to fear when I have a good friend and warrior like you to do battle for me?"

The Pontiff called together his second consistory on January 15, 1953, and named twenty-four new cardinals. With twenty-seven nations then represented, the once solidly Italian majority in the Sacred College was further reduced to slightly more than one-third of the full complement of seventy. Rome's native-born hierarchy was naturally infuriated by Pius's deliberate slap. It had been serious enough, in their view, when Pius broke the Italians' monopoly hold on the Sacred College during the 1946 consistory. Now the Italians found themselves a pitifully weakened minority.

Pius named cardinals from China, India, Australia, and Armenia, and thirteen from North and South America alone. "We want the largest possible number of peoples and backgrounds to be represented so that the Sacred College of Cardinals may be a living image of the Church's universality," the Holy Father declared when announcing his historic appointments.

The communist nations of Poland, Yugoslavia, and Hungary— viewing Pius's internationalization of the Sacred College as a major threat to their atheistic governments—prevented their prelates from attending the consistory. Stefan Cardinal Wyszynski, primate of Poland, and Alojzije Cardinal Stepinac, primate of Yugoslavia, were awarded their red hats in absentia. Wyszynski was subsequently interned and Stepinac was held under house arrest. A third, Jozsef Cardinal Mindszenty, primate of Hungary whom Pius had made a prince in 1946, had been sentenced to life imprisonment after becoming a cardinal.

Pius's direct slap to those of his own nationality appeared all the more alarming to the Italian cardinals because it seemed obvious that he had deliberately slammed the papacy's door in their faces.

Monsignor Domenico Tardini, the Vatican's pro–secretary of state, looked upon the Pope's move as a direct insult to himself. Tardini was not too much younger than Pius and had served the Holy Father devotedly for years, despite all of the pressures and criticisms the Pontiff had heaped upon him. Not only did Tardini think that he deserved to be made a cardinal, but many of his associates had led him to believe that he'd be among those chosen. When the monsignor learned that he had been passed over, he became irate. Storming into Pascalina's office the day after the consistory, Tardini—sounding as much like Cardinal Tisserant as the old Frenchman himself—bellowed: "You're to blame!" He pointed an accusing finger directly at the nun and added: "I'm going to write a book about the politics of Pius XII's reign!" Then, as if he had been taking lessons from Tisserant on how to make his point effective, Tardini abruptly stormed out. The monsignor actually did write his book after Pius died.*

---

*Tardini's *White Book,* published in 1960, was a critique of Pacelli's life during his reign as Pius XII.

Monsignor Giovanni Montini, who even in the early 1950s already had his eye on the papal office, reacted quite differently in his disappointment at not being elevated to the cardinalate. Montini, like Tardini, was a Vatican pro–secretary of state and had long served as loyally and diligently. But the quiet and reserved Montini would never react vocally. "He merely sulked for weeks afterward," Pascalina recalled. "I don't believe he even said 'hello' to me for a long while."

Perhaps the most grateful of the newly appointed cardinals was Angelo Roncalli, the former Vatican nuncio to France and now bishop of Venice, who was one of the few Italians elevated by Pius to the Sacred College. The affable Roncalli unexpectedly dropped by Pascalina's office with gifts of gratitude for the Pope and the nun—a pet goldfinch for Pius and a pair of hand-carved rosary beads for her.

She was overjoyed by the new cardinal's thoughtfulness but felt guilty and embarrassed because Roncalli—of all the prelates—was the one who most often had felt the brunt of her impatience.

"But, Eminence, I had nothing to do with your appointment," she protested in all innocence.

"You are so wrong, Mother Pascalina!" the future Pope John XXIII replied with a knowing smile and a bow. "Your failure to oppose me was what turned the trick."

The old Italian membership of the Sacred College of Cardinals generally was so outraged by Pius's consistory that they turned to blaming themselves for ever having allowed the Pontiff to achieve so much power. The fact that Pius was also secretary of state appeared to anger them as much as their losing control of the Sacred College.

Yet he had gotten away with the dual role, and now they were more certain than ever that the Holy Father was setting the stage for a non-Italian to become his successor.

"The cardinals believed that Pius was systematically depriving them of all authority," Archbishop Cushing said. "He was the kind of pope who was accustomed to doing everything possible by himself. He also realized that over half of the Italians in the Sacred College of Cardinals were either so old or in such ill health that they could not carry out their duties with the type of efficiency Pius demanded."

Two major factors apparently prevented some of the very old and more irate Italian cardinals from speaking their minds to an increasingly prodding press. One consideration was Cardinal Tisserant, who was then dean of the Sacred College and known to have an eye on becoming pope himself. Tisserant's chances increased with each new non-Italian cardinal appointed to the college. No one among the hierarchy cared to bicker with the erudite foreigner who—though no supporter of Pius—"had nothing but praise for the internationalization of the cardinalate."

A second consideration—perhaps the one that mostly held the old prelates from stating their grievances to an eager news media—was Pius's visibly failing health. The hierarchy finally concluded among themselves that it would not be wise to challenge the politics of a dying pontiff, beloved by millions throughout the world. This became all the more apparent to the Italians after Pius's consistory was so widely acclaimed for its emphasis on the universality of the Church.

Pascalina appeared not nearly as concerned about the Italian issue as she was about discovering how close to the end Pius seemed to be. Early in 1954 the Pope suffered a severe and sustained attack of hiccups, which, together with other internal disorders, weakened him considerably. For a man nearly six feet tall, Pius was then down to a mere hundred and five pounds.

"From then on Holiness was very sick," Pascalina recalled. "But his ardent spirit kept him working at a tremendous pace. Nothing was too unimportant or too exhausting for him to undertake."

Rarely did the Pope or the nun indulge themselves in lighthearted moments. But this was not unusual for either, since both were prodigious workers and seemed to get whatever pleasure and comfort they needed in keeping constantly busy. Whenever anyone questioned Pascalina's habits by asking when she found time for fun and relaxation, her answer was always the same. "I could never imagine myself being anything but a nun, buried in work and prayer."

On those rare occasions when she scanned the society columns or entertainment pages, she'd often smile and think how utterly lost she would have felt in those circles. She was not critical of women like the Duchess of Windsor or of stars such as Greta Garbo or Ava Gardner, but she never wanted to be like any of them.

Still, there remained something of the teasing coquette in the nun, a buried trait she'd allow to be seen only during the most special moments. Pascalina thought she might have overplayed her hand on one such occasion. The Holy Father had finished saying Mass one summer morning in 1954, and was returning to his office when she crept up quietly behind him. Pulling Pius to one side, the nun whispered that she was about to turn sixty.

"Holiness looked shocked at my forwardness," she later recalled. Stone-faced, he turned and walked off. She was sure that he was irritated with her for "being silly enough to bring up such a trite matter." For hours afterward she condemned herself. "I felt that I should have known better," she said. "All his life, Holiness was so attached to religion and work that any thought of sentimentality appeared as a waste of time to him."

But Pius was not as insensitive as Pascalina had imagined. On the night of August 25, the nun's sixtieth birthday, the Holy Father called her to his study. "Happy Birthday, Mother Pascalina!" he shouted as she entered, his voice filled with as much enthusiasm as she had ever heard from this ailing old man. Looking as gleeful as a young boy, he pointed to a table by his desk. There he had placed a small white cake with a tiny figure of a nun in black robes. The Pope had already lit the candles.

She was stunned, then quickly burst into delighted laughter. "But, Holiness, there are only sixteen candles, and I am sixty!"

His eyes growing misty, the Holy Father moved toward the nun and lovingly took both her hands in his. "Mother Pascalina, you will always be sixteen to me!" he said tenderly. He bent and kissed her on the forehead.

They had come to the papal villa at Castel Gandolfo, where they planned to stay until fall. Pascalina had begged him to go there earlier in the year, hoping the restful setting would coax him back to health. But Pius was too dedicated and restless to take time off. With the fast pace he continued to keep, she felt they might just as well have remained back in the Vatican.

Pius wrote twelve speeches that summer on a wide variety of subjects, and he seemed ready and anxious to do at least twelve more. Pascalina complained to the Pope's confessor that the Holy Father had written and delivered a total of twenty-two addresses since his illness the past winter, and was "ruining his health."

Upon hearing of her complaints about his habits, the Pontiff became furious and denounced the nun for what he called "nagging behavior." "If you do not stop telling me, the Holy Father, what I am to do, I will send you back to the Stella Maris retreat house!" Pius shouted at her in anger.

She was entering his suite at the time with a tray of fruit and coffee that she had prepared as his midafternoon snack. His totally unexpected attack so startled her that she stopped in her tracks and, as her anger flared, placed the tray heavily onto the floor.

"I will leave in the morning!" she retorted, her eyes flashing. "It will be a long time before you find another nun who is as good to you!"

The Pope knew by her deliberate refusal to address him as "Holiness" how upset she was.

Though she waited around long enough for Pius to make some sort of apology, he failed to show even the slightest sign of repentance. Finally she turned and fled his quarters, so infuriated the tears wouldn't come.

But within the hour, Pius ordered Pascalina to return. As a nun who had taken a vow of obedience, she had no recourse other than to go back to him at once.

"Mother Pascalina, I am sorry!" the Holy Father said as she entered, his expression and tone now as sad as his state of health.

At no time in her life had the nun been able to stay angry with her beloved Pacelli. Her heart was racing with joy as she immediately sank to her knees and kissed his Fisherman's Ring.

"Mother Pascalina, you know I cannot go on without you," the old Pope said. There was a break in his voice as he guided her to a chair beside him. "But it is wise that you soon consider leaving the Vatican. We both know that I am not going to live much longer. It would be better for you to be away from Rome when the end comes."

She tried to break in, but he motioned her to remain silent.

"You must allow me to find you a peaceful haven," he continued. "A place where you can spend your remaining days after I am no longer the Holy Father."

"Holiness, I cannot find it in my heart to leave you," she begged. "No matter what the future holds, I shall always remain at your side."

Without replying, he slowly rose and went to the window, giving the impression that he wanted to gaze out over Rome. But she knew that he was trying to hide his tears.

"You have been such a good and loyal friend," she heard him say in a near whisper. "And yet you have received so little in return." The Holy Father turned and faced the nun, his countenance drawn and sad. "Mother Pascalina, you may remain as long as you desire. But I want you to think of yourself for a change."

The summer was long and hot, and Pascalina prevailed upon Pius to remain at Castel Gandolfo well into the fall. But instead of showing progress, the Pope's condition grew steadily worse. The violent hiccuping returned, and he could not eat regularly. When he did take nourishment, his stomach was unable to retain much of anything.

On November 27 they returned to the Vatican. During the drive back to Rome the nun was in the rear seat of the papal limousine with the Pontiff's feeble head propped against her shoulder.

For days he lay breathing shallowly on his narrow bed in the Papal Palace. She was constantly at his side, holding his hand, feeding him, whispering prayers along with him. His thin skin was so white and drawn that it appeared translucent through her tears.

Now and then he would smile up at her and pat the back of her hand. She would remain long after he slipped into sleep, just in case he awakened and needed something, or to dab at his brow. Several nights she found him too ill for her to leave, and so she sat in a rocker close by, occasionally to nod off and come awake.

A battery of eighteen consulting physicians was on standby duty around the clock, each of them in despair for Pius's life. They spoke to Pascalina of peritonitis, or failing kidneys. Some advised an operation, while others said surgery was impossible.

By December 1 all hope seemed gone. Pius was too weak to lift a hand, and his heartbeat could barely be detected.

Crowds began to gather in Saint Peter's Square to pray, and television camera crews started setting up equipment. His death was only hours off, she was told by the doctors.

Every hour Pascalina retreated to the Papal Chapel, where Pius for years had said Mass every morning. "Dear Jesus, be merciful to Holiness," she implored. "He is a good man. Forgive him for whatever he may have done wrong, for Eugenio Pacelli never sinned intentionally."

When she returned to his bedside, there was an obvious change in Pius's condition. Though he still remained weak, his mind was suddenly crystal clear. "Mother Pascalina, I want to be left alone tonight," he said. "No doctors, no one, not even you! I am expecting a vision."

The nun protested. "Holiness, you are too ill to be left alone!" she pleaded.

The Pope struggled to raise himself. "Mother, do as I say!" he commanded. Pascalina, in tears, backed slowly from the room.

Pius was alone when he awoke during the early hours of December 2. He felt weaker than ever, and believing that the end was approaching, he began his favorite prayer, *Anima Christi* (Soul of Christ). When he reached the words *"in hora mortis meae voca me"* ("in the hour of my death call Thou me"), the Pope said later that he saw Jesus Christ standing at his bedside.

"O bone Jesu!" the Pope cried out in exultation. *"O bone Jesu! Voca me; iube me venire ad Te!"* ("Oh, good Jesus! Oh, good Jesus! Call Thou me; order me to come to Thee!")

But the Savior had not come to summon the Pope into Heaven, as Pius later explained. Instead, Christ had appeared, according to the Pontiff, to give comfort to the Holy Father. "And after a little while, he went away."

A few hours later Pius was well and out of bed. Pascalina was first to enter his room, and he greeted the astounded nun with a hearty "Good morning, Mother Pascalina! I am happy to see you!" Then, in a tone of extreme exuberance, he added, "This morning I saw Our Lord . . . silent in all His eloquent majesty!"

The Pope told the nun of the events leading up to the vision. He claimed that on the previous day he had heard "a very clear voice announce quite distinctly that he would have a vision."

A squadron of physicians entered while Pius was talking, and they were as astonished as Pascalina. In his subsequent report Dr. Galeazzi-Lisi stressed Pius's state of health at the time.

"The entire story was told by the Holy Father with remarkable presence and clarity of mind," the physician wrote. "It should also be pointed out that precisely on that same morning of December 2 the Holy father, having briefly described what had happened, turned to current business and, among other things, made his final revision of his speech to the Catholic lawyers, the text of which was read to their convention on the following day."

It was the first time in nearly two thousand years that any pope— other than Peter, who founded the Church—claimed to have seen Christ.

Within two weeks the Pope was writing his Christmas message and planning to deliver it himself over the Vatican radio. Critics would say it was one of Pius's finest addresses.

But it wasn't until after the New Year that Pascalina felt certain the Pope was well on the road to recovery. She knew that he was his old self again when he began bellowing at her. "Mother Pascalina, come here at once!" she heard him shout from his office. "I don't know what I've done with my eyeglasses!"

She was horrified, however, when Pius then insisted that he was going to tell the world of his vision of Christ.

"I want everyone to hear of the miracle that Our Dear Savior has performed in order to increase their faith in Almighty God," the Pope said. But Pascalina held to another view. From the moment he had first mentioned the revelation, she had suggested to him that "nobody should hear of this. The doctors are under Hippocratic oath and will not say anything if you so order them," she had added.

Now, using painfully cautious diplomacy, she again reminded the Pope that he had been very ill at the time and about to receive Extreme Unction, the last rites of the Church.

"Holiness, people are such skeptics," she cautioned. "The critics of Holy Mother Church will howl with ridicule. They will point to your age and illness and—"

"Some will say that I am senile," the Pope broke in. "But for each one who doubts, thousands will believe. For that is what belief in Almighty God is all about. One must have faith to believe." He paused; then, taking her hand in his, he continued. "Mother Pascalina, you did not doubt the visions of our Holy Mother. Why do you doubt now?"

"You were not on the threshold of death at that time," she replied. She tried to sound as sympathetic and understanding as possible.

"How, then, can you explain my miraculous recovery from almost certain death?" the Holy Father asked. "Especially when Our Dear Savior told me that my time had not yet come?" Again he paused, and when the Pope spoke once more, his words were cautiously guarded to prevent insult. He hurt her deeply nevertheless. "Mother Pascalina, where is your faith in Almighty God?"

Pius was still not well enough for the nun to press the argument. "Holiness, forgive me if I have offended you," she said gently. "We shall not speak further of this matter, at this time. Later, perhaps, but for now, you must get your rest." She pulled the blanket over his arms, smiled lovingly at him, then left so that he could sleep.

Within the hour Pascalina was on the transatlantic phone with Cardinal Spellman in New York. Urging him to keep everything she was about to say in the strictest confidence, the nun spoke of the vision Pius had had of Christ. She confided the Pope's desire to proclaim the vision to the world, and suggested that Spellman come to Rome at once.

"Eminence, I am afraid of the consequences," she said. The cardinal appeared as concerned as Pascalina, and he assured her that he would be on the earliest possible flight to Rome. It was agreed between them that no word should leak out to any source, including the Sacred College of Cardinals, at least until after they had privately conferred.

By the time Pascalina and Spellman met in secrecy, Pius had already broken his silence.

Various accounts have appeared from reliable sources, both inside and outside the Vatican, as to the manner in which news of the vision reached the world. Among the first to break the story was Corrado Pallenberg, Rome correspondent for *The London Evening News* and the London *Daily Express*. A respected reporter of Vatican affairs for many years, Pallenberg wrote the following account in his book *Inside the Vatican.*

> The second Papal vision took place during his [Pius's] serious illness of 1954. One day his condition became so alarming that the Pope's Sacrist, the Dutch Monsignor C. Van Lierde, was called to give him Extreme Unction. But the Pope sent him away.
>
> The night before, or rather toward dawn, Christ had appeared by his bed and told him that his time had not yet come. This vision was described by the Pope himself to a group of Jesuits of the "For A Better World" movement, and they in turn made it public by giving the story to the Milan magazine "Oggi."
>
> I had also heard about it the day before "Oggi" appeared and, after having satisfied myself about its authenticity, sent it to The London Daily Express which printed it on the same day as "Oggi."

When the story came out in Milan and in London there was a bit of a rumpus. The Vatican press office was bombarded by requests for a confirmation but as they knew nothing about it, as so often happens where the Pope is concerned, they first issued an imprudent denial and then barricaded themselves behind the usual "No Comment."

"Oggi," however, incensed by the denial, protested to the State Secretariat and threatened to reveal the source of their information and to prove that the Pope himself had read, corrected and approved the article before it was printed. Finally, the Vatican press office was compelled to issue an official confirmation of the story.

A second version is contained in the book *Crown of Glory,* an official biography of Pius XII. The co-authors, Alden Hatch and Seamus Walshe, present this account:

When the vision of Eugenio Pacelli was made public nearly a year later, on November 18, 1955, there was a howl of disbelief. This was due in part to the manner of the presentation. The first account of this was written by Luigi Cavicchioli for the Italian picture magazine "Oggi." It created a world furor. Vatican telephones rang all day. The small staff was swamped by calls from the news media of the whole world. All of them got the same answer: "No Comment."

Since the Vatican never deigns to reply to any statement made about the Pope, this was the equivalent of a denial. For two days poor Cavicchioli was the most discredited reporter in the world.

Pius had not intended that the news should be made public in his lifetime. With his usual common sense he envisioned the controversy it would arouse. However, the Pope had confided the story of his vision to a few intimate friends—what human being could help it? One of these must have talked to Cavicchioli; for the "Oggi" story was substantially correct. And Pius could not conscientiously allow a newspaperman, however indiscreet, to suffer for telling the truth. On November 21, 1955, he ordered the Vatican press director, Luciano Casmiri, to confirm the truth of Cavicchioli's story.

Just as Pius had foreseen, the announcement produced a storm of skeptical comment. Though he was braced for it, the Holy

Father was deeply hurt by this reaction. Fortunately it was not universal. Far more people accepted it as simple truth. At his next public audience the crowd emotionally cried, "Viva il santo Papa!"

In its issue of December 4, 1955, "L'Osservatore Domenica," the Sunday counterpart of the Vatican paper, "L'Osservatore Romano," published the official story of the vision. It was probably written or authenticated by Pius himself.

Throughout the period of "No comment" and the Vatican's embarrassing affirmations, the mood of the Sacred College of Cardinals was explosive. In the view of some of the more skeptical prelates, Pius had chosen to bring the Deity into shameful controversy. Yet, if the hierarchy spoke out, or took any part whatsoever in the debate, they would be fanning the flames of what some considered "sensationalism." It finally was agreed that the only wise move was for the Sacred College of Cardinals to stay above the entire matter.

The breaking point came when someone leaked word that Pascalina had known all along about Pius's planned announcement of the vision, and that she had not told the Sacred College but instead had run to Spellman in far-off America. This was the final blow needed by Cardinal Tisserant and a few of his closer associates. The prelates waited until Pius was off addressing some special-interest group, and then they came marching in on the nun.

"Woman, are these stories true?" Tisserant demanded of her. She had often seen him upset, but never quite this infuriated. The nervous perspiration on his brow was dripping heavily into his thick beard. Several other cardinals, each staring icily, flanked him.

Pascalina knew she was outnumbered and outmaneuvered, and under such unfair circumstances she was not about to engage in any debate. She arose from her desk, and unwaveringly she returned each of their glares with a more frigid one of her own.

"Eminences, if you have any complaints, speak with the Holy Father!" she said, her words calm yet defiant.

Tisserant became even more livid, apparently because of her placid defiance. "Woman, your days are numbered!" he raged.

But she stood her ground. Perhaps the nun's silence and the tapping of her fingers on her desk brought each of the other prelates back to their parochial school days and memory of a Mother Superior ruling with frightening authority. After a long, painful silence each of the cardinals, without saying a word, turned and walked out.

Only Tisserant remained, but when she continued to glare back at him, he, too, left, shaking his head angrily.

Pascalina was almost as irate with Pius as she had been with Tisserant and the others of the hierarchy. When the Pope returned, she minced no words in telling him the trouble he had caused her. "Holiness, I had warned you not to speak of the vision," she snapped. "Yet you went ahead without saying a word to me. Now look at what this embarrassment has caused! If you wanted to let the world know of the vision, why didn't you make a formal announcement yourself?" Her voice almost broke with emotion. "Why didn't you dignify the vision the right way?"

Pius looked shocked. He demanded to know what had brought on "such an explosion of temper," and she told him.

Without saying a word, Pius picked up his phone and dialed Tisserant's number. "Pacelli speaking," the Pope said in his coldest, most severe voice. "You are to come to my office now, Tisserant! You are to bring the others with you!" The Pontiff hung up before the cardinal had a chance to reply.

Within minutes the prelates were at the Pope's feet, kissing his Fisherman's Ring.

"Arise!" Pius commanded. When they came to their feet, the Pope spoke his further dictum. Pointing to the nun standing off to one side, he ordered each cardinal to apologize. "Tell good Mother Pascalina of your repentance!" he commanded in an angry tone.

The cardinals faced the nun. Each bowed, then spoke words of apology.

Pascalina knew then that she was safe from further attacks, for the time being.

XIV

"Quotidie morior!" ("Every day I die a little!") became Pius's frequent lament when he and Pascalina were alone. Yet, throughout his declining years, publicly he bore the stamp of the patrician, clinging with dignity to the regality of his Supreme Pontificate.

To his subordinates Pius presented still a third picture, that of the instigator of a stormy internal papacy with a record of only sporadic brilliance. His temper was impervious, his disdain overbearing, his rudeness vicious. Few popes had made more enemies within the Vatican hierarchy.

As early as 1955 intellectuals within the Vatican were already calling Pius's melancholy reign "a disaster for the Church." In the view of many high churchmen—aptly described by biographer Paul Johnson—Pius's papacy seemed to have "lost any semblance of intellectual virility, any sense of pastoral mission, any desire to come to grips with the problems of the real world." Pope and Church, it was said, were "settling into childish, devotional dotage." Even as the world generally perceived the Holy See during Pius's papacy to be at its golden best, Cardinal Tisserant was claiming, "The Church appears to be dying with him."

Tisserant's condemnations were echoed by equally scathing attacks of others within the papal hierarchy. Pro–Secretary of State Domenico Tardini, for one, spoke of the Holy Father as "a weak Pope." Tardini condemned Pius for his "lack of trust in others" and his "incapability of working with the hierarchy." In granting audiences the Pope continued to give priority to almost everyone except his own cardinals and others of the hierarchy. The Holy Father's failures, Tardini added, were largely due to his "inability to open his spirit and confide with the clergy."

Cardinals and bishops throughout the world, responsible for vast congregations and faced with problems of great urgency, found that they could not obtain access to the Pope when they visited Rome, and were forced to make their own separate deals with Curia officials.

The hierarchy considered Pius's actions a direct slap. Historically, popes down through the centuries held what the Holy See calls *"di tabella"* audiences to allow the high functionaries of the Church to meet with the Holy Father on fixed days at fixed hours. Cardinals and heads of congregations and Catholic orders administering the machinery of the Church cherish their traditional right to be received by the Pope. Pius dispensed with these audiences in 1954, using illness as an excuse, and never again resumed them.

On one occasion the Pontiff, with Pascalina as his willing buffer, deliberately canceled an audience with Cardinal Tisserant at the last moment. Purposely to infuriate the French prelate, the nun told him to his face that Clare Boothe Luce and Gary Cooper were passing through Rome unexpectedly, and that she had to allocate the time allotted to Tisserant to accommodate the congresswoman and the actor at their "spur of the moment requests."

One cardinal, after waiting in vain for several months to be received by Pius, finally gave up in utter disgust. "Let's all dress up as football players," he said sarcastically at a meeting of fellow prelates. "Then we'll certainly be received right away."

Pro–Secretary of State Tardini became so frustrated by Pius's insensitivity toward the hierarchy that he wrote in his personal journal that Pius gave "his confidence to only a very few intimates, and of necessity this confidence has been extremely broad, and not always deserved." In this instance, Pascalina knew that the cleric was hitting specifically at her. While it mattered little to the nun what Tardini and others of the hierarchy thought of her, she was torn greatly by their blasts against Pius.

If the Pope was becoming too old and indifferent toward the realities of the immediate world around him, she loved him enough to want his papacy spared the growing ignominy. Yet her anger toward the hierarchy was tempered by experience and a sense of fair play. In her careful appraisal of the papacy's dilemma, she could not sincerely heap all blame on Pius's detractors. The Pope's "fortress mentality," his devotion to solitude and seclusion, were at least as much at fault.

At the start of his reign she had encouraged his insular style, believing then that with her as adviser and protectress, Pacelli had the mind and experience to carry the full weight of the papacy. But now the Pope's detached behavior and eccentricities seemed, at times, beyond control.

Approaching eighty, Pius lived much of his life in mystical meanders. It was becoming exceedingly difficult to keep him in touch with all of the Vatican politicking. She feared that unless something were done, a lifetime of attainment would be compromised. Urged on by a devotion that approached fanaticism, Pascalina had all but resolved herself to one last, brazen course in his defense when Pius's sudden and unexpected threat to resign the papacy forced her into action.

The Pope lived with the fear of becoming bedridden, and now there was more than mere hint from him that he might retire. While in the papal office tidying up Pius's desk one winter morning in early 1955, she came across notes that indicated his resignation was imminent. The Pope had made two lists—one that supported the idea and a second that enumerated reasons for remaining as Supreme Pontiff, at least for the time being.

Pascalina was so astounded that she rushed into Pius's study with his notes clutched in her trembling hands.

"Holiness!" she exclaimed, half out of breath, her abrupt, emotional entrance causing the Pope to look up rather startled from reading his breviary. "You cannot be seriously contemplating resignation?" she asked impatiently. In Pascalina's view there was nobody qualified to replace Pacelli on the throne of Saint Peter. Nor could any successor be trusted to carry on the strictly doctrinaire ecclesiastical policies of Pius XII.

"Mother Pascalina," the Holy Father replied calmly as he arose to comfort her. "The time has long been at hand for Pacelli—tired old man that I have become—to consider stepping down," he said in a bland, matter-of-fact manner, drawing her by the arm to a seat alongside him. Pius looked sadly resigned to what he considered the inevitable for any pontiff of his advanced age. "I remain at my post only because the doctors have assured me that I shall be as strong as I was before," he added in a solemn voice.

The implication was clear. Pacelli was not of the mentality to allow the Holy See to come apart while he languished in bed. If he had another setback, he indeed might resign on the spot.

Knowing how erratic his health was, the nun stressed the Pope's need to spare himself. "Holiness, your strength must be conserved for ecclesiastical affairs!" she said sternly. "Too much energy is lost on temporal matters." Her argument was set to protect the Holy Father from the exhausting day-by-day routine of Vatican pressures that so often proved time-consuming and fruitless.

Pascalina saw how thoughtfully Pius was weighing her advice, and she sensed the moment of decision was at hand.

"Holiness, you must be relieved of many of your temporal duties," she said. Her words were sounding as she wanted them to sound, like those of an authoritarian nun. "Holiness, I will help you. I will take charge of your temporal responsibilities." Even though she had given so much of herself to him and the Church, she knew that no Pope would allow any woman, not even a nun, officially to take on the duties and responsibilities of a pontiff. There seemed no other way but for her to act as "unofficial vizier," if this tired and frail old man were to live out his papacy.

The sun's morning rays filtered through the stained-glass windows of the richly paneled study as Pius arose to pace the room, pondering in silence Pascalina's sobering words. Never before in the long history of Christ's Church had a Supreme Pontiff been faced with so serious a dilemma—a woman proposing to act in behalf of a pope.

In the end, the Pontiff did not bless her with official authorization, but neither did he shake his head, nor speak words of denial. Relying on her sense of his mentality, Pascalina took his silence as a signal to move ahead.

There was, however, one important consideration neither gave thought to at the time, perhaps because of the urgency of their predicament. Both failed to acknowledge that Pascalina had become Pius's superior in a number of ways. "She had greatly benefited over the years through the training and experience she had received from this successful world diplomat and leader of men," Archbishop Cushing once said of the nun. The student had outgrown the teacher.

She had come to power as a practical, strong-willed, and hard-nosed pragmatist who despised procrastination as religiously as the Pope had zeal for indecision. Now Pascalina was scarcely back at her desk when the future of Pius's papacy was being reshaped in her mind. She alone would decide who would be allowed in to see the Pope, what papers Pius would sign, what order of business, temporal or spiritual, would receive papal priority.

To prevent any question that her directives were to be rigidly respected, she summoned officers of the palace guard to come at once to her.

"The Holy Father requires that the palace guard stand duty directly outside these quarters!" she commanded. "You are to admit no one to the papal apartment, regardless of position, without my specific order! That includes all cardinals and other prelates! And the palace guard is to remain on duty at all times, twenty-four hours a day, with no exceptions!"

Pius soon felt more vigorous than he had in years. He had more time for prayer and spiritual meditation, and to do what he enjoyed most, address large audiences. In 1955 he delivered more than sixty major speeches, and received some 380,000 people.

It was apparent to the Pope's relatives and few close friends that in his happy state "Pius felt thrice blessed with his able nun in charge." The "iron curtain" she had placed around their world shielded them from all the rancor in the Vatican that her unofficial appointment as vizier had caused. At the start of her stewardship, at least, the nun and the Pope remained blissfully above all verbal attack.

Eventually, though, word trickled to her ears that one of the Pope's most trusted aides had been spreading talk that her system was "tyrannical and humiliating to the hierarchy." She had her suspicions of who was initiating the undercurrent of criticisms and complaints. But it upset her even more upon learning that she was being increasingly ridiculed throughout the Vatican with marked derision as "La Popessa."

Soon afterward the first of the Vatican's high officials felt her lash. The nun suspected the gossiper to be Monsignor Giovanni Montini, the other pro–secretary of state. Her dislike of Montini was nothing new. It sprang from his coldness toward her when both served as lowly office workers in the Curia a quarter of a century before. Despite all the intervening years she never forgot Montini's jealous abuses when she received choice assignments over him.

Though Pascalina disliked Tisserant and Tardini for their caustic criticisms of Pius, she hated Montini for what she considered his "two-faced hypocrisy." Admittedly, Montini had worked hard for the Pope during the past sixteen years of Pius's reign. But she knew that the pro–secretary resented not being named a cardinal at the 1953 consistory and was eagerly hoping to succeed Pius as the next pope.

Pascalina considered Montini a liberal, and were he to become Pontiff, she feared that he would quickly tear away at Pius's conservative policies and lead the Church in ways Pius would never have approved.

On occasion the Pope had privately downgraded Montini to her, complaining that his deputy was "too progressive in his social and political outlook to be considered a reliable successor."

"Holiness furthermore felt that Monsignor Montini did not possess the stature to be Holy Father," she once told Cardinal Spellman. The nun made it clear to the prelate that the Pontiff barely tolerated Montini's sidewalk services, which he conducted for peasants and others in the streets of Italy. The monsignor went about carrying his own portable altar and Mass kit in a large briefcase. Though his followers labeled him "Jesus Christ's Chairman of the Board," Pius considered Montini's public oratory as "theatrics" that harmed rather than advanced the Holy See's image.

Spellman, a staunch archconservative like the Pope and the nun, appeared to be as much opposed to Montini as she was. When she informed the American prelate during his trip to Rome in 1954 that Pius might appease Montini by making him Vatican secretary of state, Spellman was stunned. He joined Pascalina in opposing the appointment and in pressuring Pius to oust the left-leaning Montini from the secretariat.

"Holiness, Montini must not be in a position to command votes at the next conclave," Spellman quickly advised the Pope at the time. Seeing that he was making little progress, the American then tread on Pius's sympathies. Spellman suggested to the Holy Father that if Montini became pope, Pascalina would be quickly banished.

Within a week of Spellman's talk with the Pontiff, Montini was removed as pro–secretary of state and exiled to Milan. The transfer was announced by the papacy as a promotion. Montini was made archbishop of the large Italian industrial city, the Pope's press office said, mainly because he would be "more valuable combating communism among Milanese workers." Historically, Milan was the traditional end of the line for all prelates who dreamed of ascending to the throne of Saint Peter.

The monsignor's banishment was characteristic of the Vatican. Before dawn on a cold, drizzling morning in early January 1955, Giovanni Montini—with tears in his eyes and carrying a single suitcase—climbed into a friend's battered old truck, laden with ninety cases of the aging monsignor's books, and drove off. Having fallen from the Vatican's high echelon, none among the clergy, not even those alongside whom he had worked for many years, bothered to wave good-bye. Eight years later, however, Montini's return to Rome was met with resounding triumph as he was carried in splendor for his coronation as Pope Paul VI.

In the midst of all the politicking and pressures, all the correspondence and phone calls, Pascalina still kept charge of the Pope's personal life. When he was tired, she would soothe him. When it was cold or damp, she worried about what he was wearing. When he felt even slightly ill, she immediately called a doctor. She was not only his vizier and protectress, she was everything to him.

Pascalina had her own eccentricities and strange likes and dislikes of people. Politicians were rarely among her favorites, and once in a position to show her set feelings, she did so with obvious displays of vengeance. The war had turned her against the leaders on both sides, certainly Hitler and Mussolini but also Roosevelt and Churchill, her memory of the latter being "so tarnished by their machinations" as to severely weaken her respect for them.

Whenever she received a call or message from any political source, she bristled instinctively. "In almost every instance, I knew they were out to use the Holy Father, usually for their own personal gain," she confided long afterward.

Pius was her direct opposite when it came to politicians. He still thoroughly enjoyed his private audiences with many heads of state, the exceptions being Roosevelt, Hitler, and Mussolini, whom Pius had turned against and labeled "the architects of war," each of whom had been dead for many years. On occasion Pascalina, too, had to admit that there were a few politicians whom she herself enjoyed. Those fortunate enough to be on her favored list were ushered into the Pope weeks, even months, sooner than higher statesmen whom she may have disliked. Premier Jawaharlal Nehru of India and

Prime Minister John Costello of Ireland had no difficulty whatsoever in seeing the Holy Father. King Mutara III of Ruanda-Urundi was always welcome in her eyes and received her most gracious smile. She had never forgotten Pius's first audience with the nearly-seven-foot African monarch. In his white plumed headdress set with pearls, the king was in tears of joy as he departed. "This is the most moving day of my life," he told Pascalina, warmly clasping her hand. She was the kind of sentimentalist who cherished such moments, but perhaps because she was a nun she would hardly admit her feelings, even to herself.

John Foster Dulles, President Eisenhower's secretary of state, was another favorite of hers, perhaps because his son had converted to Catholicism and become a Jesuit. Even so, Dulles found the nun "ruthless in her duty" during his audiences with the Pope.

On one occasion Dulles, to her thinking, had overstayed his visit with the Pope. Pascalina allowed Dulles an extra five minutes, then burst in on them when she still heard no signs of his departure.

"Heiliger Vater, Sie müssen essen!" ("Holy Father, you must eat!"), she said in a commanding voice. Her arms were folded and her feet planted firmly apart. "I was trying to look as much like a drill sergeant as I knew how," she recalled with a laugh many years later.

Dulles appeared quite perturbed, but the Pope remained cool and smiling. *"Ganz recht, Mutter Pascalina, ich lasse die suppe nicht kalt werden"* ("You are quite right, Mother Pascalina, I shan't let the soup get cold"), Pius replied.

The secretary of state, a student of German, understood the conversation and expected the nun to leave before making his own departure. But Pascalina stood her ground and showed no sign of moving out of the room.

Pius, looking a bit ill at ease, stood up, and with a forced smile he said, "Mr. Secretary, there is no power on earth that could make our good Mother Pascalina move when the soup is on the table."

When the nun was difficult or rude, it was because she thought first of Pius and what was best for him. She was passive as well, often sitting patiently with him for hours, helping him write addresses on a wide range of subjects. He found her ideas "inspiring and brilliant," and her knowledge "so broad her brain seemed to encompass just about everything." What she didn't know, she obtained from careful research; often she'd pore over books and manuscripts well into the early-morning hours.

Pope and nun wrote fact-filled addresses for him to deliver on every sort of subject. At times they'd argue with such intensity over some small detail that members of the palace guard, stationed directly outside, looked appalled at each other. Yet in a matter of minutes they'd hear bursts of laughter from Pascalina and Pius, each sounding as gleeful over the results of their work as young children opening gifts on Christmas morning.

"I felt that I was becoming well-versed on just about every subject," she reminisced with a smile. The topics they chose for Pius to address seemed to cover just about everything. They wrote of "Business and the Common Good," "Sports and the Christian Life," "Human Relations in Industry," "Books, Publishers, and the Public," "Literary Narcotics," "Toward Outer Space." Surprisingly, they seemed to have touched little on pure religion.

She did write an encyclical with him entitled *"Miranda prorsus,"* which dealt with the effect upon morals of the movies, television, and radio broadcasting.

Their co-authorship of a medical paper termed "Heart Disease and the Whole Man," was considered such an extraordinary review of the scientific literature that the noted American heart specialist Dr. Paul Dudley White praised it as "one of the best papers on coronary heart disease I have ever heard."

Though the nun felt obliged to keep the aged and ailing Pope from making mistakes, he, too, found it necessary on occasion to protect the hard-pressed and often exhausted Pascalina from letting her heart rule her head. She was in a particularly vulnerable state of mind one afternoon in the spring of 1957 when her close friend Cardinal Spellman phoned from New York with an urgent request. The prelate asked her to intercede at once with the Holy Father in his behalf in an ongoing feud with his auxiliary bishop, Fulton J. Sheen, the famous and colorful television preacher.

"Sheen owes me a million dollars and refuses to pay up!" Spellman exclaimed on the transatlantic phone line. Pascalina could easily tell by his tone how greatly disturbed the cardinal archbishop was. "Ask His Holiness to order Sheen to pay me the money," Spellman added.

When Pascalina told the Pope of Spellman's unusual petition, the

Holy Father shook his head impatiently, making it very clear that he had no intention of involving the papacy in an argument between two of his most celebrated prelates.

"Bishop Sheen is head of the Society for the Propagation of the Faith in the United States," Pius broke in, referring to the Holy See's important worldwide charitable organization. Then, calling attention to Sheen's tremendous popularity, the Pope added, "I am told that millions watch His Excellency every week on television, and that he is even more popular than Milton Berle, whoever Milton Berle is."

Despite the Pope's adamant stand Pascalina still persisted in Spellman's defense. "But, Holiness, you cannot overlook all that Eminence Spellman has done for the Holy See," she insisted. The nun referred to the financial colossus that the cardinal had made of the New York archdiocese and the millions of additional dollars he had earned or raised for the Vatican.

But the intellectual and articulate Sheen had done a great deal too for the Church, Pius reminded her, adding that it was Spellman himself who had plucked Sheen from his obscure post on the faculty of the Catholic University in Washington and set his fellow Irishman on the path to glory. Pius tried to downplay the feud between the prelates, claiming that it was merely "a trace of jealousy that separated these two shepherds of Holy Mother Church," which soon would blow over .

Spellman had long been the fair-haired prince of the Catholic upper crust in the United States and now was being eclipsed by the more charismatic and handsomer Sheen. The bishop had also proven himself to be a successful organizer and Church money-raiser— although he had not won the title of "Santa Claus of the American Church," as had the cardinal archbishop.

"The Holy Father must remain above any dissension between these two good shepherds," Pius told her straight out. His almost gruff manner indicated that she was to say no more on the subject. But they were at a stage in their lives when the nun no longer was easily put off by the Pope.

"Holiness, we cannot turn a deaf ear to Eminence Spellman," she insisted.

Pius was so annoyed with her that he shook his head in exasperation. "Perhaps old Tisserant isn't so wrong after all!" he mumbled in a decidedly vexed voice.

Pascalina was astounded that the Pope would make such a derogatory reference, pointedly aimed at her. "You're agreeing with Eminence Tisserant's prejudice against women?" she asked, looking aghast and hurt at the same time. When the Pope failed to answer, she abruptly turned and stalked out, refusing to make her customary bow to His Holiness.

Pascalina understood the Holy Father well enough to know that if she kept her distance from him long enough, he would eventually seek her out with an olive branch. And sure enough, before Pius retired that night, he was at her door, looking contrite. "Have your way, Mother Pascalina," the Pope said, sounding dejected and resigned. "Invite each of your misguided shepherds to Rome so that the Holy Father may speak in person with them."

Within days Cardinal Spellman and Bishop Sheen were in Pascalina's office for a face-to-face questioning by the Pope. Both prelates sat stiffly at far corners of the room, each refusing to speak or look the other's way.

"It was terribly embarrassing and awkward for me," she said afterward. "I was so relieved when Holiness finally opened the door and invited them inside the papal office. I was hoping that I would not be included, but I was."

No sooner had the cardinal and the bishop bent and kissed the Pope's ring, than Spellman—acting more righteous than she had ever seen him—came directly to the point.

"The bishop has broken his word and will not pay his debt to me!" the cardinal charged, pointing a finger squarely at Sheen, who sat off to one side, appearing to be entirely unconcerned.

"Holiness, there is no debt to repay," Sheen calmly replied.

The argument centered about large quantities of surplus supplies—principally food, clothing, and medicine—that Sheen, as head of the Society for the Propagation of the Faith, had obtained through Spellman from the United States government for distribution to impoverished people around the world. Spellman claimed that he had paid millions for the supplies, but Sheen maintained otherwise. And he refused to pay Spellman.

Pascalina thought the cardinal would explode when the bishop told the Pope, "His Eminence received all the surplus supplies free of charge."

"That's a lie!" Spellman retorted angrily, his moon-shaped face turning scarlet.

Sheen slowly rose. "Your Holiness, may I suggest that a call be placed to the White House?" he asked, appearing composed and entirely sure of himself. "Eisenhower can verify everything."

Spellman became all the more enraged. "Holiness, is not the word of the cardinal archbishop of New York to be trusted?" he demanded as his eyes bored into Sheen's.

Entirely ignoring Spellman's words, Pius calmly turned to Pascalina and asked that a call be placed at once to Washington. The nun was astounded by Pius's part in the dramatics, but immediately took steps to follow through. In a matter of minutes—as Spellman nervously paced the papal office and Sheen stood quietly examining a masterpiece depicting Christ above the Pope's desk—the President was on the line.

After a brief exchange of pleasantries between Pope and President, Pius—speaking in his most eloquent diplomatic tone—asked Eisenhower: "Mr. President, what do We of Holy Mother Church owe your great and kind government for all the wonderful surplus merchandise that the Holy See has been receiving for the poor of the world?"

"Your Holiness!" Eisenhower replied. "Hasn't Cardinal Spellman told you? These surplus goods were donated free of charge to His Eminence!"

Spellman was caught. But Pius was far too astute a diplomat to see his longtime friend humbled, particularly before another prelate of lesser rank. Then, too, the Pope knew that Spellman and Sheen both shared living and working quarters in the same diocesan house on Madison Avenue. He simply had to reconcile the famous and powerful prelates to prevent any word of their bittter feud from becoming public.

No sooner had the Pontiff put down the receiver than he stretched out his arms in warm entreaty, and with a generous smile he said buoyantly: "You are my most precious shepherds!" He gathered both Spellman and Sheen close to him, and as they all embraced Pius added in the most paternal tone: "To err is human, but to forgive is Divine!" The Pope raised his right hand and pronounced the papal blessing upon all. "Go in peace, dear shepherds!" he concluded with a smile still upon his face.

But once the cardinal and the bishop were apart from the Holy Father and back in Pascalina's office, Spellman was more enraged than ever.

"I will get even with you!" the cardinal shouted angrily at the bishop. "It may take six months or ten years, but everyone will know what you are like!"

Sheen remained characteristically unruffled. "Jealousy is the tribute mediocrity pays to genius!" the bishop arrogantly retorted, looking squarely at Spellman with his penetrating, deeply set dark eyes. Casting a salute and a smile at Pascalina, Sheen walked out.

Spellman got his revenge. Not long after, Sheen was out of Spellman's diocesan house. No longer was the bishop heir apparent of the New York diocese. His television series failed to be renewed despite its increasing popularity, and Sheen himself was transferred to a small diocese in Upstate New York, which Spellman and other prelates referred to as an "ecclesiastical Siberia." It is generally believed among many of the Catholic clergy that Spellman eventually prevailed upon Pius to use his influence to strip Sheen of his temporal trappings.

Pascalina apologized to Pius for having interfered in the first place against the Pope's better judgment. "I knew what Holiness had been thinking and saying to himself all along—'Pascalina should have minded her own business'—though he never uttered a word of reprimand to me," she said. "When I told the Holy Father how sorry I was, Holiness replied, 'After all your magnificent contributions all these years, how could I have the heart to criticize one small error?' Still, I prayed to Almighty God that I would be granted greater objectivity in the future to act more wisely."

Despite the confidence-shattering incident Pascalina still kept her faith in Spellman. "His Eminence was a very human person," she recalled, assessing her friend's qualities. "Eminence made his share of mistakes and sinned, as we all do, but for whatever he did wrong in his lifetime, Cardinal Spellman made up for it in so many great ways—most particularly through his many outstanding charitable contributions to those in need."

She remembers the cardinal as a fierce and lasting enemy to those who attacked him, but still a prelate of exceptional compassion. "I was deeply touched upon learning that one of Eminence Spellman's first acts after becoming archbishop of New York was to visit Bishop Bonaventure Broderick, a holy and kindly prelate who had been sent into exile many years before by an earlier pope. Bishop Broderick had been appointed by Pius X to be in charge of the papacy's Peter's Pence fund-raising campaign in the United States. But many of those in the hierarchy in America—particularly James Cardinal Gibbons, archbishop of Baltimore—resented the bishop's efforts and created false charges against him. The Holy Father who reigned at the time unfortunately believed the stories. Bishop Broderick was removed from all his authority and put out on his own with only a $100 stipend. Forced to earn a living outside the Church, he could find no work other than as a gas station attendant. From then on none of the ecclesiastics dared to have anything to do with the bishop.

"Eminence Spellman, as soon as he had the authority of archbishop, sought out Bishop Broderick," Pascalina continued. "He found the old man living in near poverty and virtual isolation. The cardinal brought the old bishop back to New York to live with him in the diocesan house and appointed him chaplain of Frances Schervier Hospital. Several years later, just before the old man died, Cardinal Spellman received a touching letter of gratitude from the bishop, in which was written: 'May God bless you always, dear Eminence Spellman, for having the courage of no other clergyman to stand by a poor soul to whom all others were afraid to even speak.' I saw tears in the cardinal archbishop's eyes as he folded the letter and placed it in his pocket."

At age eighty, the Pope's increasingly eccentric behavior was taking a heavy toll on Pascalina's nerves and her time. He acted ever more like an absolute monarch of the ancient regime, and his style of government was described by Celso Cardinal Constantini, chancellor of the Holy Roman Church, as "Byzantine and weird."

The public was beginning to be told of the widening chasm between the papal apartment, where all power ultimately resided, and the Curia, which the Pope snubbed. Guiselle Dalla Torre, who once edited the official Vatican newspaper, *L'Osservatore Romano,* criticized Pius in writing for "separating himself from direct contact with life." Others saw the Pope as a "commander increasingly divorced from reality."

Pascalina could scarcely disagree with the Pope's critics as Pius's behavior became more and more extreme. Though she remained in charge of many of his duties and responsibilities, she could do nothing but wince when the Pope commanded senior officials of the Vatican to address him on their knees. It was equally embarrassing for her when she was obliged to watch Pius force prelates to walk backward when leaving his presence. There was little to be gained for

Pope or prelates in their audiences, and she could not understand why Pius insisted that they come to him, or why he humiliated them.

Perhaps even more startling to her was to see reporters from *L'Osservatore Romano* commanded to kneel at Pius's feet, sometimes for an hour or longer, while he dictated lengthy articles on a variety of subjects.

Almost every day she had to plead with the Pope to take his afternoon walk in the papal gardens. He cherished his solitude so much that he ordered the gardens closed to the public. It was her responsibility to make sure that even the gardeners themselves disappeared from sight when the Holy Father strolled the tree-lined paths saying his breviary.

Except for his nephews, who remained regular callers, Pius now saw his family only once a year, usually for two or three hours on Christmas afternoon. He ate all his meals alone, except when he'd invite Pascalina to join him; this he would frequently do at the last moment.

Even in the final years of their lives together, Christmas remained the most important day in Pascalina's life. Pius would usually allow her to have her own small tree set up in some corner of the papal apartment. In the end he began grumbling about even that simple enjoyment of hers. The Pope made it clear to the nun that he preferred the traditional Nativity scene to the more Nordic Christmas tree. She kept her temper because she knew that at the last moment he would relent. And he did.

At this stage in her life Pascalina was feeling the brunt of her years. As with so many others her age, there were times when the aches and pains and the simple, everyday monotony of life dragged her down. She certainly was no longer the fortress of strength and spirit she had been throughout most of her years.

When she had to have surgery on her foot, Pius scarcely noticed. She shed tears, not because of the pain that lingered after the operation, but because he seemed not to care.

There were twinges of self-pity now and then for what she had missed. She had no close friends because of Pius, and she had given up her family for the Church. Now that the Holy Father was in decline, she seemed to think of her family with increasing frequency. What she disliked most about herself was the dark brooding that so often took charge of her mind. She had never been self-centered, but at sixty-three she couldn't shake the thought of what would become of her once Pius passed away.

The nun often prayed that Cardinal Spellman would become the next pope, not particularly for her sake, though she would certainly be secure with her old and dear friend as Holy Father. "Eminence Spellman is as good as the best of the cardinals," she'd say to herself. But she knew it was all wishful thinking on her part. Hers was still an era when only Italians stood a chance of becoming pope.

Pascalina missed her confessor, "the dear old priest" who'd been dead for years. It had been consoling for her to unburden herself to him. The cleric who now served as her confessor was a boy in her mind, and she couldn't bring herself to take long walks and have deep conversations with "someone so young."

She would look at Pius, and he would seem so much like a ghost to her now. "It's not the same anymore," she'd whisper to herself, a catch in her throat when she would think that way. "Nothing is the same." And she would wipe away a tear before the Pope could see her feeling sorrowful.

Pius took a long time to die. Throughout the four dark, draining years following his severe illness in 1954, Pascalina gave of herself without reservation. Her devotion lifted the shadows of his despair and placed a gleam where tears had clouded his sunken black eyes.

The early mornings were the hardest on her. When she entered the Pope's bedroom, she would often find him a pathetic, embarrassed figure, struggling to control himself. If he had a coughing attack, he'd be weak for several minutes and remain gasping for air. She would clean up after him without complaint. She always smiled for his sake when she found him in such states, and spoke encouraging words.

She laid out his most elegant vestments and helped him into them as he labored to dress himself. Much of the time she herself was exhausted and on the verge of collapse. But she never let him know. In the eyes of the world he had to wear a poised, confident facade, and her contrived liveliness never failed him. When Pius appeared at the altar of Saint Peter's before thousands of the faithful, he was the dignified, serene Pope to whom millions looked for strength and leadership. No one but Pascalina knew that she inspired the face the Holy Father wore in public, nor was it suspected how very close to death he was at the time.

With his health fluctuating like the weather, Pius spoke ever more seriously and often of stepping down. Sometimes she thought he was merely mouthing private words to her in moments of despondency. But when he showed real determination toward resigning by announcing to her his intention of informing the Sacred College of Cardinals, she was sure the Pope was on the verge of abdicating. Only her desperate pleadings prevented him from doing so.

At this juncture she wasn't fighting only for the old Pope, but more for the hallmark of his papacy. As a devout nun, she had come to accept death as a natural end of life and a new beginning. In her mind, Pius was now but a shadow of what he once was. She considered his death to be imminent, and she would handle it with serenity and grace.

"It was the mounting political drumbeat of the hierarchy that sounded fear throughout Pascalina," Archbishop Cushing would say. "She knew they were waiting anxiously to take control of Pius's throne and to besmirch his beliefs and standards."

Like Pius, Pascalina was exceedingly doctrinaire in her thinking regarding certain religious practices. She was as determined as Pius that the Holy See continue its medieval dominance and exercise control over almost every aspect of human existence. To her, the Pope held absolute authority, and whatever he commanded in the name of God should be followed without challenge.

"There will be a great falling away from Holy Mother Church if the bars of morality and ethics are let down," she predicted at the time.

In the early fall of 1958 Pius suffered a severe attack of hiccups that could not be controlled. Though a battery of physicians was summoned and all sorts of medical procedures were initiated, nothing seemed to relieve him. The toll on the Pope seemed even greater than the bout he had had four years earlier that nearly claimed his life.

Cardinal Spellman, at the time, was heading a pilgrimage from the United States that was en route to the Vatican. Upon Spellman's arrival in Naples he phoned Pascalina, and she urged him to come at once to Castel Gandolfo, where the Pope lay stricken.

"Holiness will not recover this time," she told Spellman in a grave voice on October 3, 1958, as they met alone in the library of the papal villa. "He's very weak." Her eyes were dry; she was too drained and worried for tears.

The nun and the cardinal loved the Pope, in their own ways, but they could not bring themselves to talk further at that moment of the fading away of his life. To them, Pius seemed better served by speaking of the future and what might be undertaken to protect what brilliance remained of his papacy.

Pascalina's resentment toward Rome's hierarchy was evident. How incredible it appeared to her that petty differences had created such animosity and division between the Pope and his house of cardinals. In her view it was mostly the hierarchy's fault for not overlooking the "eccentricities of an old man." She considered it "tragic for good men of God, influential leaders of the most powerful religion on earth, to have allowed such a disaster to happen." The teachings of Christ, the nun told Spellman, were being "subjugated by the politics of personal greed." The prelate could easily see how emotionally determined she was to prevent a catastrophe within the Church and to the legacy of her beloved Pontiff.

"They will choose someone his exact opposite, mainly to discredit Pius's papacy," Pascalina continued to the attentive Spellman. "Holiness is that much resented by some. As you are aware, Eminence, there are those who cry out for liberalization, but freedom without strong leadership will only lead to disaster for the Church. It is to be hoped that those who steer the Holy See will not find out too late."

They spoke of the likely candidates who might become the next Holy Father. She feared Tisserant's election, mainly because of his reprisals. But Spellman allayed her worries. "Even with the present internationalization of the Sacred College, Tisserant will never make it," Spellman confidently assured her. "He's made too many enemies."

Montini, the choice of the liberals who disparaged Pius, was more of a "dark horse" concern to the American cardinal. As for his own choice, Spellman hinted to the nun that he would cast his first ballot for another archconservative, Cardinal Ruffini, the archbishop of Palermo.

Pascalina was astonished. She knew that Spellman was aware of Ruffini's association with Mafia crime figures in Sicily. For the first time she wondered whether Spellman was much different from other prelates who were so disappointing to her.

As for her own speculations, the nun's greatest concern was, surprisingly, Angelo Cardinal Roncalli, the simple and passive seventy-seven-year-old patriarch of Venice. There were so many reasons that she could think of as to why this "poorest of dark horses" would be chosen by the cardinalate. Yet time and again, over the years, she had chased Roncalli from bothering the Holy Father with the same unconcern and ease that she had used in scattering chickens on her father's farm.

Pascalina had nothing against Roncalli. He was "a good soul," in her view, "a well-adjusted, agreeable old cardinal," but "an easy mark and on the threshold of eternity." She had little doubt but that the hierarchy would take quick advantage of the fat and usually smiling prelate and "twist him around their fingers." Certainly, Roncalli wasn't anyone to stand up in defense of Pius's papacy, she felt sure, for he had not shown that much liking for the Holy Father or for the style of his regime. Pius had kept a tight rein on Roncalli and allowed him no latitude in decision-making. Under the imperious Pope the cardinal was never his own man.

Spellman had downgraded Roncalli to her in the past, referring to him as a "harmless soul" with little more intelligence than a "simple banana man peddling his fruit." She noticed now that the cardinal no longer criticized the old bishop. She began to wonder if the election of Roncalli might be possible as a compromise between the Vatican's conservatives and liberals.

In the weeks ahead, when Roncalli became Pope John XXIII, the nun would think how prophetic she had been.

That evening while Spellman visited alone with Pius, Pascalina went to the Papal Chapel to meditate. In the midst of her grief and worry she needed the solid, steadying influence of prayer and communion with Jesus. It had been a long, tiring day and still there remained much more for her to do. She reminded herself to see Cardinal Spellman before he returned to his pilgrimage. And she wrote a note not to forget to feed the Holy Father's birds or to cover their many cages.

At midnight she slipped quietly into Pius's room while he was sleeping. She sat on her rocker by his bed, saying her rosary for him. If he were to awaken suddenly, she knew how comforted he would feel with her close by. There was nothing extreme in her exhausting herself. Most of her life she had given her best, her loyalty and love, her drive and imagination and wit and charm, to a man who expected everything, and gave her little in return.

To Pascalina, Pius was the Holy Father. All she wanted from him was his blessing smile, and an occasional pat on the back of her hand.

The end came finally on October 9 at 3:52 A.M., six days after Spellman's visit.

It is human to want to believe that great ladies are left in splendor or, at the very least, in much comfort. Pascalina was left with neither. She had never expected anything. Her vow of poverty, taken as a young girl, kept her penniless for life. For her it was enough that Pius had remembered her in his Masses and prayers.

Now that she was sixty-five, what was there left? The clouds that had been gathering through the years had darkened, and now surrounded her.

"Whenever a pope dies, it is an occasion for changes at court," she would say one day with resignation. "The dismissal of familiars and favorites, while quite disquieting, is usually rapid."

As for her immediate exile by the Church: "Loneliness is not simply a matter of being alone," she answered. "Loneliness is the feeling that nobody else truly cares what happens to you."

Epilogue

Her departure had been hurriedly arranged. No one from the Vatican was there to see her off. An old priest crossing Saint Peter's Square, who knew her only by sight, saw her struggle into a taxi with her two packed bags and cages of the dead Pope's birds. He said he felt ashamed that the Holy See did not see fit to be there to say goodbye to this woman who had given her life to the Church and had made such a lasting mark on Pius's papacy.

For a long time nobody seemed to know where she had gone, nor did anyone appear to care. Pius was now a memory buried beneath Saint Peter's, and those who inherited his legacy wanted her shunned and denied. In freezing her out, the hierarchy believed the bitter memories of Pius's rancorous papacy would fade with her isolation.

Her place of exile was a secluded convent in Switzerland, where the other nuns kept their distance from her.

For Pascalina the void was enormous. The nun and the Pope had filled each other's lives so completely that it was suddenly as if her entire world had stopped moving. Closed away from almost everybody and everything, she would have no one for whom to care or worry. She had planned her life around him, and his needs were always directed at her. "Mother Pascalina, come here at once!" the Pope had called at least a dozen times a day, especially in the last years. "I need this . . . I need that . . . I NEED YOU!"

All that was over now.

The first year was the hardest. "I did not sleep for three weeks after Holiness passed away," she said. "And I ate precious little."

For a long time words would not come, and she often felt ill. She had reached the breaking point, and she wanted to leave convent life, at least for a while. It would have given her recuperative bounce to return to her family's farm in Bavaria. Her parents were long dead, but some of her brothers remained. The Church would neither hear her petition nor allow her to leave.

She never lost interest in prayer or meditation, and even on her most despondent days she still sat straight in her chair, usually until ten or eleven at night, when those around noticed that she seemed to slip in spirit from them.

It was years before she surfaced from the monotony of her existence. Her uplifting inspiration finally came from Cardinal Spellman, the only cleric to visit her during her banishment. He was in his seventies and she in her late sixties as they sat holding hands in the Stella Maris retreat house in Switzerland.

"Stop pitying yourself, Mother Pascalina!" he finally broke in on her sad monologue of how badly everything had gone for the Church and herself since Pius's passing.

"You've always been the staunchest activist in support of the teachings of Christ. If you believe that the Holy See is failing these days to show proper example, what are you showing?" The nun knew that Spellman was trying his best to snap her out of her depression, and she appreciated the wisdom of his words.

Too long she had suffered the sorrows and pangs of lost love, Spellman counseled. If one so strong as she had withered and crumbled, what of other women, those of her advanced age and younger, when the men in their lives were taken from them? Who was there to understand and console?

"There are millions in the same predicament as you," the Cardinal said. "You are such a great force of strength for women everywhere to look to and call upon in their declining years. Gather together as many as you can. Build them a home. Give them new hope and new life."

Time and Spellman had prepared her, and soon afterward it became impossible for her to remain solitary. At last Pascalina had purpose again.

She planned to build a sanctuary for old and lonely women, but first she had to receive the blessing of the new Holy Father.

Though she was emerging from the shadows of her sadness, she feared that perhaps Pope John would not be too anxious to see her. The new Holy Father had made no contact with her while she remained in exile. But "he did not deny me an audience, or keep me waiting, as I had kept him during Pius's papacy," she later recalled.

As Roncalli himself had so often done during the reign of Pius XII, the nun walked in unexpectedly on the old Pontiff. She carried a shopping bag containing a large comforter that she had quilted for his bed while filling the long, empty hours. The anteroom outside the Pope's office was filled with people—some of them peasants—and practically everyone was standing since all the seats were taken.

"How different everything seems," she thought to herself, remembering the reverent tone of Pius's regime, when few were allowed to enter the papacy's solemn inner sanctum.

Suddenly, Pope John himself appeared in the doorway. Though he had no advance word of her coming, the Holy Father immediately picked her out from among his devoted followers. "Mother Pascalina!" he exclaimed, his face lighting up in surprise. "How nice of you to visit me!" he happily added, coming directly to her side. "And you've brought me a gift!" There was a generous smile upon his lips as he spoke. In an eager, playful mood the Pontiff snatched the bag from her, and with an arm about the nun's shoulder he led the way into his office.

Though relieved and pleased by John's warm and friendly welcome, Pascalina's lifetime of strict traditionalism made it difficult for her to accept public displays of such informality and effusion by a pope.

"I could not bring myself to call him 'Holiness,' for John had not the stature as Pope that Pius always held," Pascalina said. "I still thought of John as a cardinal, not as Holy Father, and I called him 'Eminence.'"

She had come to the Vatican for Pope John's approval and blessing of her plan, but despite her purpose, now that she had the ear of this old man she'd known so long, she began to unload.

It must have seemed impertinent to John, perhaps even hostile that this nun had arrived from exile to tell the Holy Father how wrong he and the Second Vatican Council were. To John, his task at hand was commendable. His papacy was dramatically modernizing the Church. Ecumenism, the liturgy, the role of the laity, were being brought to terms with the twentieth century. Religious liberty for all Catholics and a sense of brotherhood toward those of every religion were in the air of John's reign.

Pascalina saw severe trauma and danger for the Holy See in the revolt against the institutional structure of the Church. No matter how archaic Catholicism may have seemed to appear to its liberal critics, the nun stood for totalitarianism in religion.

"Opening the windows of the Church to the world"—as John had proclaimed—"will create an ecclesiastical tragedy," she bluntly told the new Pope. "People look to the Holy See for strong leadership," she added, sounding as if she were back admonishing Pius. "If you repudiate Rome's authoritarian heritage, if you deprive the human spirit of authoritarian direction, man's moral and ethical judgments will be overwhelmed. Sin and crime, then decadence, will too often seize control."

John was a kind and gentle priest, and all his life he had remained disinclined to argument. He would not embarrass any woman, least of all take on someone of Pascalina's reputation.

"Mother Pascalina, you are always thinking and brooding," the old Pope replied with a condescending smile. There was a good-natured twinkle in his eye. "A beautiful woman like you should stop worrying about the world. Think of yourself for once. Enjoy life. Let change take care of the future."

She bristled inwardly at being treated with such solicitude and chauvinism, but she kept her temper from flashing. John had a priest for an assistant, in the post she once held. This cleric had already entered the room, and he was assuming the stance she had so often taken when the time had come for the visitor to leave.

Pascalina had missed her opportunity to obtain the papacy's permission to build a home for elderly women. Her mission was lost for the duration of John's papacy, for that was the last time she saw the old Pope, or heard from him. He failed to respond to any of her future correspondence.

She waited for the next pope to come along. This time it was Archbishop Giovanni Montini, her cold and quarrelsome colleague at the Curia of more than thirty years, and now Pope Paul VI. It was somehow strange for the nun to think of the lowly office worker she had so often fought with as the Holy Father.

"In my young days he seemed like such a poke," Pascalina said with a laugh. "I used to love to torment him. If I saw that he was in a hurry, I'd deliberately rush ahead of him to the mimeograph machine. He'd be furious. The worst he ever dared to say to me was that he'd pray for the salvation of my wicked soul. I knew he meant what he said when he blessed himself afterward."

Pascalina was just past seventy when she contacted Pope Paul for an audience. She saw him scrutinizing her as she came in and knelt to kiss his ring. Her walk no longer had the grace she once displayed, but she still carried herself straight and with dignity. To her, he looked old and somewhat withered, and the sight of him made her suddenly conscious of her own years.

"I hope I don't look as ancient as you!" she quipped, the words tumbling out before she even realized what she was saying.

The Pope appeared appalled, but in a flash the muscles at his temples seemed to relax. "I see my prayers have not been answered," he retorted. "Pascalina, you are as wicked as ever!"

Paul laughed then, and she laughed. And the ice was broken.

Past animosities seemed unimportant to her now, almost trivial. More important was the question of whether or not Paul would forget and consider her mission with an untarnished mind. She spoke almost incessantly to him in the time allotted her, using the same brand of enthusiasm and energy she had lavished on Pius. She wanted her haven for sad, lost women, and she intended to get it. In the end, the Pope appeared to be won over.

"Mother Pascalina, you are a good nun," Paul said, gently touching her forehead with the Fisherman's Ring as she knelt for the papal blessing. Those were wonderful, rewarding words coming from the Holy Father. It was all that needed to be spoken between these two strange adversaries of the long-gone past; her instincts predicted a happy road ahead.

In time a magnificent tract of land on a great hill overlooking Rome was placed in Pascalina's name. The donor was said to be Count Enrico Galeazzi, the one-time governor general of the Vatican, old friend of Pius's and now Paul's trusted confidant. The nun's way was easily paved with the millions she needed to build her dream haven, the Casa Pastor Angelicus. Romanticist that she always was, Pascalina nestled her Casa within myriad stately trees and flowering shrubs. Soon women like herself, whose men were gone, were living in peace within her quiet refuge.

Neither Pascalina nor the Holy See would say how the financing came about, though much of the funding she herself raised. But all that is unimportant now. What remains is that her mission was accomplished. She cared mainly that the many women at the Casa held to their memories of the past and prayed to Jesus for the future.

It is unfortunate, she said, that her old friend and Paul's longtime foe, Cardinal Spellman, had not been as easily forgiven by the Pope. After Pius, Rome's power had swung bitterly and vengefully against the American prelate. Paul had not forgotten Spellman as the behind-the-scenes instigator responsible for his exile to Milan.

In the early years of Paul's reign, Spellman had infuriated the Pope more than ever. The cardinal, a hawk on Vietnam, had publicly sided with the United States position in the war. Spellman's stand was in direct defiance of the papacy's call for an end to the conflict.

Pope Paul's historic, precedent-setting trip to America, and his worldwide appeal for universal peace before the United Nations, appeared to have little effect on Spellman. Paul's dovish words seemed only to fire the cardinal's militarism all the more. Spellman afterward flew to Vietnam to encourage the U.S. armed forces toward even greater military action.

Perhaps it was Spellman's way of challenging Paul, Pascalina thought, unaware as she was of Paul's private showdown with Spellman while the Pope was in New York. A galaxy of unresolved problems shrouded Spellman's archdiocese, the richest in the United States. The proud and confident prelate now ruled a flourishing multibillion-dollar empire. Pius had roundly applauded Spellman for his achievements, but Paul looked upon the cardinal's successes quite differently. It was the questionable manner that the American prelate had used in rebuilding the once debt-ridden and nearly bankrupt New York diocese that worried the present Pope.

Spellman was so angry at the Pope's prying questions that he offered his resignation on the spot. The cardinal was over seventy-five at the time and about to celebrate his fiftieth anniversary as a priest. He was incensed by what he considered "ingratitude" after all he had done for the Holy See over the years.

Paul mulled over the resignation for a month, but before he decided to act, Spellman's remaining friends in Rome pressured the Pontiff to reject the offer.

In one of his rare appearances in the pulpit of Saint Patrick's Cathedral, Spellman spoke of his planned resignation and of Paul's refusal of it. "I accept this decision of His Holiness as God's will for me," he said.

Two years later, on December 2, 1967, Cardinal Spellman died. When news of her old friend's death reached Pascalina, she took it with calm resignation. "He is happier with Jesus," she said. "Cardinal Spellman's spirit had been broken."

In the rapidly changing world of the 1960s, Pascalina saw her Church torn between excessive change and excessive resistance to change. A time of social upheaval and public question was at hand, and violent convulsions were occurring throughout Catholicism.

As she had warned long before, the Holy See was already in deep trouble. Those after Pius, the hierarchy that attempted to bring the Church into the modern world, had destroyed most of the old Catholic culture. In the clerical revolt against authoritarianism, tens of thousands of clergy and nuns throughout the world were defecting. The seminaries were half empty, and one fourth of all priests requested Rome's permission to get married. Catholics by the millions were staying away from the Church. Only 50 percent of those who ordinarily went to Sunday Mass continued to attend. Surveys showed that nearly 90 percent of Catholic married couples were using Church-banned forms of contraception.

The Holy See's treasury suffered as severely. Donations to the Church were cut in half, and only 50 percent of those who once gave regularly to the Church continued to give. The papacy was stunned by the extent of Catholic mutiny at the grass roots. Eight out of every ten Catholics were disregarding Church laws governing birth control, divorce, and sex outside marriage.

Pascalina might well have sat back smugly and said, "I warned you." Instead she adopted a more philosophical explanation. "The well-disciplined, cohesive, mystical Church of Pius was severely compromised by those who followed him, and most especially by the Second Vatican Council," the nun said with great sadness.

She believed that Pius's papacy was "the centerpiece in a model of Church life," and, she added, "Pius spurned ecumenism and feared the increasing democratization of ecclesiastical decision-making. The vernacular Mass, the growing role of the laity in Church policies, and the rising debate over the Holy See's sexual ethics" she saw as "signs of decadence and profanation of Catholic heritage."

"Those who doubt Pius's beliefs," she reminded, "have only to look at the present record of the Church to see the disaster that has come about." She wiped away a tear as she spoke.

The days grow short. This book will see publication as Pascalina nears the age of eighty-nine, alive and well of mind and body, and still very much in charge at her Casa Pastor Angelicus. There, the women adore her thinking, and her smile and stamina, as she keeps herself and each of them working from five in the morning until after the late news at night.

"We have no time for 'down-in-the-mouth' ladies who sit around pitying themselves," she said, harkening back to Spellman's words. "We live by the teachings of Christ; that means good common sense and moderation in everything in life. With that philosophy, how can one not be happy?"

As for her greatest goal, "I pray that one day Pius will be canonized a saint," she replied. For years she has continued to work hard to see Pacelli proclaimed. In her mind Pius already is a saint. "Perhaps Holiness was stern and hard on occasion, but every great leader has to be," the nun said. "Holiness set the example for what is important in life. Catholics during Pius's papacy felt God's reward of peace in their hearts and souls. What greater gift can anyone ask?"

Pascalina has lost much in life, but her victories have been greater. When throughout the ages had a pope shared his throne with a woman? She was the mind and strength behind Pius's papacy, the most powerful woman in the Vatican, and undoubtedly the most important throughout the Holy See.

In history, she remains but a footnote. But if there is room for romantic thought in our changing world, Pascalina stands as an example to behold.

Notes on Sources

The gathering of information for what has evolved into this book extends over a period of thirty-five years in the accumulation of experience, contacts, and firsthand knowledge. This experience began in 1947, when, as a staff writer for the *Boston Sunday Advertiser,* I met Archbishop Richard J. Cushing of Boston, who was later to become a cardinal. I was assigned to write a weekly column with the prelate. Almost every Tuesday for four and a half years I interviewed the archbishop at his Archdiocesan House on Boston's Commonwealth Avenue.

Through our collaboration Cushing and I became intimate friends. The prelate opened the Church's archives to me and introduced me to the hierarchy's elite. A Catholic myself, I was further honored to be included in the circles of such respected churchmen as Francis Cardinal Spellman; Bishop Fulton J. Sheen; Reverend Robert I. Gannon, S.J., president of Fordham University; Right Reverend Daniel J. Donovan, executive director of the Archdiocesan Union of Holy Name Societies; Bishop John J. Wright (later to become dean of the American cardinals); and numerous others whose names could fill a page.

These associations and my role as a director of the Archdiocesan Union of Holy Name Societies, as well as being a Third Degree Knight of the Knights of Columbus, provided me with much inside knowledge of confidential Church affairs.

Historian Martin Gilbert, author of the official multivolume biography of Winston Churchill, has observed that a biographer must be both a detective and a dramatist. When writing about the impenetrable Church, I would add that one must also possess the trust and confidence of numerous intimate contacts among the clergy of all ranks.

In gathering the information for this book my associates and I conducted hundreds of hours of interviews with more than one hundred people who provided intimate firsthand knowledge.

Following the death of Cardinal Spellman, his brother, Martin H. Spellman, M.D., turned over to us the prelate's voluminous personal papers, diaries, records, and photographs.

We are particularly grateful to Mother Pascalina, who, despite her advanced age, patiently spent over thirty hours talking to me freely and frankly. She provided me with many valuable photographs, even though she knew that this would be an unauthorized biography over which she would have no editorial control.

Source material was also developed during more than six years of library research at The New York Public Library, the Boston Public Library, and the Biblioteca Nazionale in Rome.

Since the book's chronology extends over a period of nearly ninety years (commencing with the birth of Mother Pascalina), it is obvious that the dialogue does not always represent the exact words of the characters. The dialogue, however, does represent the best recollections of those whom we interviewed.

Our interviews, of course, were not a simple matter of question and answer. Rather, they entailed a meticulous process of queries coupled with the use of various notes, diaries, letters, news clippings, and other printed materials to aid our subjects in recalling specific moments to mind.

Thus, particularly with regard to reconstructing dialogue, we employed much the same technique as did author David McClintick in his book *Indecent Exposure*. As Mr. McClintick points out, it is dialogue that "captures the essence and spirit of the conversations that are reconstructed, as well as the personalities and styles of the characters, and that does so more accurately than paraphrase would." Besides, as he further states, "human beings do not speak in paraphrase."

Further Readings

Andrews, James F. *Pope Paul: Critical Appraisals*. New York: Bruce Publishing Co., 1970.

Anslinger, Harry J., and Oursler, Will. *The Murderers*. New York: Farrar, Straus, 1961.

Blanshard, Paul. *The Irish and Catholic Power: An Interpretation*. Westport, Conn.: Greenwood Press, 1972.

Bunting, James. *Bavaria*. New York: Hastings House, 1972.

Campbell, Rodney. *The Luciano Project: The Secret Wartime Collaboration of the Mafia and the U.S. Navy*. New York: McGraw-Hill, 1977.

Cavallari, Alberto. *The Changing Vatican*. New York: Doubleday, 1967.

Ciano, Count Galeazzo. *Ciano's Hidden Diary, 1937–1938*. New York: Dutton, 1953.

———. *The Ciano Diaries, 1939–1943*. New York: Doubleday, 1946.

Cogley, John. *Catholic America*. New York: Doubleday, 1974.

Dolci, Danilo. *Man Who Plays Alone*. New York: Pantheon, 1968.

———. *Waste*. London: MacGibbon & Kee, 1963.

———. *Report from Palermo*. New York: Orion Press, 1959.

Falconi, Carlo. *The Popes in the Twentieth Century*. Boston: Little, Brown, 1967.

———. *The Silence of Pius XII*. Bernard Wall, trans. Boston: Little, Brown, 1965.

Fitte, Roger Peyre. *Knights of Malta*. New York: Criterion Books, 1959.

Flamini, Roland. *Pope, Premier, President: The Cold War Summit Never Was*. New York: Macmillan, 1980.

Flynn, George L. *Roosevelt and Romanism: Catholics and American Diplomacy*. Westport, Conn.: Greenwood Press, 1976.

Friedlander, Saul. *Pius XIIth and the Third Reich*. New York: Octagon Books, 1980.

Gage, Nicholas. *Mafia, U.S.A.* New York: Playboy Press, 1972.

Galeazzi-Lisi, Riccardo. *Dans l'Ombre et dans la Lumière de Pie XII.* Paris, France: Flammarion Publishers, 1960.

Gannon, Robert I., S.J. *The Cardinal Spellman Story.* New York: Doubleday, 1962.

Gollin, James. *Worldly Goods.* New York: Random House, 1971.

Gorresio, Vittorio. *The New Mission of John XXIII.* New York: Funk & Wagnalls, 1970.

Gosch, Martin A., and Hammer, Richard. *The Last Testament of Lucky Luciano.* Boston: Little, Brown, 1974.

Greeley, Andrew M. *The American Catholic: A Social Portrait.* New York: Basic Books, 1977.

Guerry, Emile, Archbishop of Cambrai. *Popes and World Government.* Baltimore: Helicon Press, 1964.

Halecki, Oskar, and Murray, James F., Jr. *Eugenio Pacelli, Pope of Peace.* New York: Creative Age Press, 1951.

Hatch, Alden, and Walshe, Seamus. *Crown of Glory: The Life of Pope Pius XII.* New York: Hawthorn Books, 1957.

Holmes, J. Derek. *The Papacy in the Modern World, 1914–1918.* New York: Crossroad Publishing Co., 1981.

Johnson, Paul. *Pope John XXIII.* Boston: Little, Brown, 1974.

Katz, Leonard. *Uncle Frank: The Biography of Frank Costello.* New York: Drake, 1973.

Lash, Joseph P. *Eleanor and Franklin: The Story of Their Relationship Based on Eleanor Roosevelt's Private Papers.* New York: Norton, 1971.

Leckie, Robert. *American and Catholic.* New York: Doubleday, 1970.

Leuchtenburg, William E. *Franklin D. Roosevelt and the New Deal, 1931–1940.* New York: Harper & Row, 1963.

Lewis, Norman. *The Honored Society.* New York: Putnam, 1964.

Lewy, Guenter. *The Catholic Church and Nazi Germany.* New York: Holt, Rinehart and Winston, 1973.

LoBello, Nino. *Vatican, U.S.A.* New York: Trident Press, 1973.

————. *Vatican Empire.* New York: Simon & Schuster, 1970.

MacEoin, Gary. *What Happened at Rome.* New York: Holt, Rinehart and Winston, 1966.

Manhattan, Auro. *Catholic Imperialism and World Freedom.* New York: Arno, 1972.

————. *Catholic Power Today.* New York: Lyle Stuart, 1967.

————. *The Vatican Billions.* London, England: Paravision Books, 1972.

————. *The Vatican in World Politics.* New York: Horizon Press, 1972.

McGurn, Barrett. *A Reporter Looks at the Vatican.* New York: Coward-McCann, 1962.

Morgan, Thomas B. *The Listening Post.* New York: Putnam, 1944.

———. *A Reporter at the Papal Court.* New York: Putnam, 1937.

———. *Speaking of Cardinals.* New York: Arno, 1946.

Neauville, Jean. *The Vatican.* New York: Criterion Books, 1955.

Neville, Robert. *The World of the Vatican.* New York: Harper & Row, 1962.

Noonan, Reverend D. P. *The Passion of Fulton Sheen.* New York: Dodd, Mead, 1972.

Novak, Michael. *Open Church.* New York: Macmillan, 1962.

O'Brien, David J. *The Renewal of American Catholicism.* New York: Oxford University Press, 1972.

Pallenberg, Corrado. *Inside the Vatican.* New York: Hawthorn Books, 1960.

Pichon, Charles. *Vatican and Its Role in World Affairs.* Jean Misrahi, trans. Westport, Conn.: Greenwood Press, 1950.

Rhodes, Anthony. *The Vatican in the Age of the Dictators.* New York: Holt, Rinehart and Winston, 1973.

Ridley, Francis A. *The Papacy and Fascism: The Crisis of the 20th Century.* New York: AMS Press, 1973.

Rynne, Xavier. *Letters from Vatican City.* New York: Farrar, Straus, 1963.

Servadio, Gaia. *Mafioso.* New York: Stein & Day, 1976.

Tardini, Cardinal Dominico. *Pius XII–White Book.* Vatican, 1960.

Toland, John. *Adolf Hitler.* New York: Doubleday, 1976.

Wakin, Edward. *The De-Romanization of the American Catholic Church.* New York: Macmillan, 1966.

Wall, Bernard. *The Vatican Story.* New York: Harper & Row, 1956.

Walsh, Michael. *An Illustrated History of the Popes: St. Peter to John Paul II.* New York: St. Martin's Press, 1980.

Wayman, Dorothy G. *Cardinal O'Connell of Boston.* New York: Farrar, Straus, and Young, 1955.

Additional References— Periodicals and Newspapers

CHAPTERS 1-5

Pius XII's speech, Second World Congress of the International Road Federation, October 1955.
Life magazine, October 20, 1958, Vol. 45, No. 16, p. 21.
Newsweek, October 20, 1958, pp. 65–67.
Life magazine, December 13, 1954, p. 129.
World Events, 1925–1932, p. 484.
Architectural Digest, January–February 1977, p. 123.
United Nations World Magazine, December 1952.
The Wall Street Journal, September 14, 1960.
The New York Times Magazine, April 10, 1977, pp. 38–40.
Life magazine, January 21, 1946.

CHAPTERS 6-10

The New York Times, October 1, 1936, p. 1.
Private correspondence between Spellman and Roosevelt, 1918–1919, given to us by Dr. Martin H. Spellman.
The New York Times, October 2, 1936, p. 13.
Cardinal Spellman's handwritten letter dated September 29, 1936, from his private letters, diaries, and documents.
The New York Times Obituary, November 27, 1930.
Letter from Cardinal O'Connell to Bishop Spellman, September 25, 1936.
Cardinal O'Connell's handwritten letter to Spellman, June 26, 1936.
Letter from Rev. Charles A. Coughlin to Rev. Robert I. Gannon, May 5, 1954.
The New York Times, November 8, 1936.

Time magazine, November 3, 1958, p. 38.
The New York Times, September 5, 1938, p. 8.
The New York Times, December 3, 1967, p. 83.
The New York Times, December 5, 1967.
Handwritten letter of February 11, 1955, from Mabel Gilman Corey to Chase Manhattan Bank.
Oggi magazine, September 3, 1963.

CHAPTER 11–EPILOGUE

Newsweek, March 26, 1962, p. 30.
Time magazine, August 14, 1978, p. 36.
Brockton Daily Enterprise, December 4, 1967.
Life magazine, December 13, 1954, p. 133.
Time magazine, August 21, 1978.
New York Sunday News, January 23, 1977.
The New York Times Magazine, January 16, 1977.
Cardinal Spellman letter dated March 6, 1939, to Brother John Spellman.
Newsweek, May 24, 1954.
The New York Times, September 30, 1936.
The New York Times, August 31, 1917.
Letter from President Roosevelt to Archbishop Spellman, July 1944.
Letter of introduction of Spellman from Roosevelt to General Dwight D. Eisenhower, July 1944.
Letter from Archbishop Spellman to President Roosevelt, October 23, 1944.
Cardinal Spellman's notes regarding meeting between FDR and Spellman in the spring of 1945.
New York Post, September 24, 1957, magazine section, p. M-2.
Harper's Magazine, September 1965.
The Nation, November 22, 1971.
Joseph P. Kennedy correspondence to Enrico Galeazzi, June 18, 1948.
The Boston Daily Globe, February 20, 1946.
Cardinal Spellman's diaries from 1906–1918 and 1938–1945, regarding the war years.

Index